Another Side of Ethel Smyth

Ethel Smyth as a young woman

Another Side of Ethel Smyth

Letters to her Great-Niece,
Elizabeth Mary Williamson

Selected and edited by
Caroline E. M. Stone

Kennedy & Boyd

Kennedy & Boyd
an imprint of
Zeticula Ltd
Unit 13
196 Rose Street
Edinburgh
EH2 4AT
Scotland

http://www.kennedyandboyd.co.uk
admin@kennedyandboyd.co.uk

First published in 2018
First published in this edition 2021

Text Copyright © Caroline E. Stone 2018
Illustrations © Caroline E. Stone 2018
Cover design © Zeticula Ltd 2018, 2021

ISBN 978-1-84921-207-6

All rights reserved. No part of this publication may be reproduced, stored in a retrieval system, or transmitted in any form or by any means, electronic, mechanical, photocopying, recording or otherwise, without the prior permission of the publishers.

In memory of
Paul Lunde
who on his last weekend
5-7 August, 2016
read and advised on this work.

> Earl Bristol's Farewell.
>
> Grieve not, dear Love, although we often part.
> But know that Nature gently doth us sever
> Thereby to train us up with tender art
> To brook that day when we must part for ever.
>
> For Nature, doubting we should be surpris'd
> By that sad day whose dread doth chiefly fear us,
> Doth keep us daily school'd and exercis'd
> Lest that the fright thereof should overbear us.

Earl of Bristol's *Farewell* written out by Elizabeth Williamson for Caroline Stone c.1960

Ethel Smyth and Mary Hunter as young women

Contents

Illustrations	ix
Introduction	xi
The von Herzogenberg Family	*xxvi*
Henry B. Brewster (1850-1908)	*xxvi*
The Benson Family	*xxviii*
The Ponsonby Family	*xxxi*
Maurice Baring (1874-1945)	*xxxi*
Edith Somerville (1858-1949)	*xxxii*
John Singer Sargent (1856-1925)	*xxxv*
The Balfours	*xxxv*
1922	1
1923	3
1924	17
1925	29
1926	55
1927	61
1928	75
1929	81
1930	105
1931	135
1932	185
1933	217
1934	259
1935	281
1936	323
1938	331
1939	355
1940-1944	363
ES – Selected Bibliography	377
Index	379

Metropolitan Opera House

Lessee, - - - MAURICE GRAU OPERA CO.

GRAND OPERA
SEASON 1902-1903,
UNDER THE DIRECTION OF
MR. MAURICE GRAU.

WEDNESDAY EVENING, MARCH 11th, 1903,
at 7.45 o'clock.
DOUBLE BILL.
First Performance in America of

DER WALD
(THE FOREST.)
MUSIC-DRAMA IN ONE ACT
WITH A PROLOGUE AND AN EPILOGUE,
(IN GERMAN.)
MUSIC by ETHEL M. SMYTH.
Book by Ethel M. Smyth.

ROSCHEN	MME. GADSKI
IOLANTHE	MME. REUSS-BELCE
HEINRICH	MR. ANTHES
DER LANDGRAF RUDOLF	MR. BISPHAM
EIN HAUSIRER	MR. BLASS
PETER	MR. MUHLMANN
ERSTER JÄGER	MR. DUFRICHE
EIN BURSCHE	MR. MAESTRI
Conductor	MR. ALFRED HERTZ

Incidental Dance by the Corps de Ballet.

SCENE—A FOREST.

Followed by

IL TROVATORE
(Only Performance this Season.)
OPERA IN FOUR ACTS,
AND EIGHT TABLEAUX.
MUSIC by VERDI.
Book by Salvatore Cammarano.

LEONORA	MME. NORDICA
INEZ	MLLE. BAUERMEISTER
AZUCENA	MME. LOUISE HOMER
MANRICO	MR. DE MARCHI
IL CONTE DI LUNA	MR. CAMPANARI
FERRANDO	MR. JOURNET
RUIZ	MR. VANNI
Conductor	MR. MANCINELLI
Stage Director	MR. ALMANZ

Illustrations

Ethel Smyth as a young woman	ii
Earl of Bristol's *Farewell* written out by Elizabeth	v
Ethel Smyth and Mary Hunter as young women	vi
Der Wald	viii
Four of the Smyth family children	xii
George Moore to Phyllis Williamson	xiv, xv
Letter from Violet Paget to Mrs Hunter	xvi, xvii
Hill Hall guest list May 15th, 1915	xviii
Accounts	xix
Elizabeth Williamson	xxi
Mary Hunter, Elizabeth Williamson and guests at Hill Hall	xxiii
Elizabeth Williamson playing chess at Hill Hall	xxv
From the Hill House Guest Book	xxvii, xxix, xxx
Letter from Philip Burne-Jones	xxxiii
Letter from John Singer Sargent	xxxiv
Hill Hall, an Elizabethan mansion, near Epping, Essex	3
Dedication in Harry Brewster's *The Theory of Anarchy and Law*	5
Page of music with a song from *Taormina*	11
Comment on the fly-leaf of ES's copy of *Through the Shadows with O. Henry* by A I Jennings	12
Hill Hall	17
One of many damaged letters from Ethel Smyth to Elizabeth	26
Cast List for *The "Teraph"*	31
Elizabeth Williamson, by John Singer Sargent	37
Ethel Smyth with one of the Pans	47
The last of the guests at Hill Hall	49
Ethel Smyth's note in her own copy of *Inordinate (?) Affection*	51
Ethel Smyth with Pan III	60
Elizabeth to Ethel, August 1928	76
Ethel Smyth's plan to use the fragment	98
Suffragette handbill	103
With Pan	104

George Moore to Phyllis Williamson	107
Elizabeth with Golfing Friends	117
Flier for Ethel Smyth's Concert June 29th, 1930	121
Ethel Smyth's "Calendar" for Virginia Woolf's visit	123
Memorial volume for Hilda Matheson	124
Dedication by Toch (i.e. Anna de Noailles)	131
Bob Smyth - letter from Abbassia Barracks	157
In ES's copy of *The Village in the Jungle*, given by Leonard Woolf	171
Book plate in the copy of *Marius the Epicurean*	175
Dedication in ES's copy of Anna de Noailles' collection of poems.	231
Ethel Smyth's Notes on the *Bo'sun's Mate*	234
Ethel Smyth - Rehearsal	237
First page of letter from Elizabeth	243
Dedication from Vita Sackville-West in *Collected Poems*	252
A letter of Ethel's Smyth to Mary Hunter from Holloway	257
British Women's Symphony Orchestra A G M 1934	261-62
George Moore's Verse on Beecham's Pills	297
ES in Violet's copy of *The Statuette*	305
Ottoline Morrell's dedication in *Murder in the Cathedral*	322
An early page from Ethel Smyth's Book Catalogue	344
Dedication in *My Medley of Days* by Lady Maud Warrender	368
Edith Somerville to Phyllis Williamson, after ES's death	373
Edith Somerville, in memory of ES.	375

Introduction

It might be said that it is unnecessary to publish any of Ethel's Smyth enormous output of letters, since she wrote her own very vivid autobiography in several volumes; there is also the excellent biography *Ethel Smyth* by her friend Christopher St John, with additional chapters by Vita Sackville-West and Kathleen Dale, published in London, 1959.

The letters here, however, show another side of Ethel Smyth. They are written to her much loved great-niece, Elizabeth Mary Williamson, the granddaughter of her elder sister, Mary Hunter, whose story and some of whose correspondence were published in *MH*, Seville 2002. As *MH* makes clear, the two sisters had a difficult and competitive relationship – wealthy and conservative social hostess versus "penniless" composer and suffragette - and it clearly gave Ethel Smyth great pleasure to find that it was she who had more in common intellectually with Elizabeth and, perhaps, greater influence over her.

Because of the wealth of autobiographical material available, very little needs to be said here about Ethel Smyth's life, beyond the following brief description of her family to explain references to various members in the letters. She was very fond – although sometimes critical – of her siblings and some of her letters to her younger brother Robert (Bob) have been added, where the ones to Elizabeth are missing, in order to round out a story.

Her father, General John Hall Smyth, was in the Indian Army and letters of his survive describing the Indian Mutiny (Rebellion) of 1857. His first three children, Alice, Johnny and Mary, were born in India; Ethel, Nina, Violet, Ellinor (Nellie) and Robert, after his return to England. General Smyth was appointed to the command of the Artillery at Aldershot, but the failure of the Agra Bank in 1866 left him impoverished and he was very concerned as to how he would provide for his family.

Mary and Ethel, being the closest in age, were often bracketed together and it is clear that their rivalries that went back to childhood. Nevertheless, their upbringing seems to have been remarkably un-Victorian, judging

Four of the Smyth family children

by Mary's teenage diary and Ethel's reminiscences. Certainly, General Smyth encouraged sport of all kinds, especially riding, which was to be one of Ethel's great pleasures.

The family's social life at Farnborough altered when, to their regret, their next door neighbours, the Longman family, left Farnborough Hill. They were replaced by the Empress Eugénie, the exiled widow of Napoleon III of France, who soon became not only a family friend, but also a great support to Ethel, as she set out on a musical career of which her father disapproved.

In 1875, Ethel's sister Mary married Charles Hunter. Initially, the young couple had a relatively modest life-style – General Smyth feared that the young man would not be able to support his daughter and hesitated to give his consent – and moved in circles more interested in "huntin', shootin' and fishin'" than in art, literature and music. They had three daughters: Kathleen (Kitty), Phyllis and Sylvia.

Unlike most of the Smyths, Mary did not care for hunting and was a nervous rider, but it was perhaps through a friend of her husband, Sir William Eden — who was not only a fine sportsman, but also an amateur painter with a passion for the arts; his nine-year feud with Whistler over a portrait he had commissioned became a *cause celèbre* recorded in *The Baronet and the Butterfly* — that she came to be introduced to the artistic world of London. The contact seems to have begun with John Singer Sargent in about 1895, two or three years before he painted the portrait of her now in the Tate, which she donated after his death "in memory of a great artist and a great friend". Gradually, he introduced her to his circle – Henry James, George Moore, Monet, Rodin, Edith Wharton, Mancini, Henry Tonks....to name a few.

Charles Hunter was by now making a considerable fortune, particularly from collieries at Whitburn, and, in order to have a suitable house at which to entertain his wife's new friends, acquired Hill Hall at Theydon Bois outside London. The Hunters' life-style was lavish and all the people named above were frequent visitors. Sargent's portrait of *The Misses Hunter*, also now in the Tate, was commissioned in 1902.

In 1900, Phyllis Hunter married Frederick "Fritz" Williamson. They had three children, of whom Elizabeth was the eldest, followed by Charles and William. In 1907, Fritz Williamson died, aged 34, leaving his wife very badly off; Phyllis went back to live with her parents at Hill. It must have been a difficult situation, economically dependant and always outshone by her ebullient mother, but she had little choice.

> Read this   June 15   1920
> Ebury Street 121
>
> My dear Phyllis,
>
> Your letters are always full of humanity and are therefore admirable; and to this merit is added a manner of writing entirely your own — one that springs out of an individual mind; you see life from a special angle and are ~~~~ — highly qualified, I know nobody more so, I might have said truthfully, as highly qualified as yourself to write a book — not necessarily a novel. Why don't you write one? You wrote of for

George Moore to Phyllis Williamson

another baby but as you might ward
of yourself, circumstances were
against you. So it is with your
disappointment in mind that
I suggest the alternative, a book: a
book is a creation, quite as much
as as many ~~babies~~ Gabies, as long lived and
much less expensive. Try the alternative
I shall be mystified if it doesn't
succeed. (not for publication)

Begin here My life passes by in Loneliness and
Composition. I see hardly anybody
no body for long but my secretary
to whom I dictate from 1500 to 2000
words daily. Héloïse and Abelard

IL PALMERINO,
MAIANO,
FLORENCE

Dear Ethel is very
nearly heartbroken
because... I have
asked Mr Brooks
to keep me posted
about it. I am a good
deal more excited than
I ever am about my
own work: it's
Ethel's prose which
shakes me up.
I am hoping it

I hear Ethel is very nearly through with the opera. I have asked the Brewsters to kep me posted about it. I am a good deal more excited than I ever am about my own work: it is Ethel's power which shakes me up. I am hoping to have Violet Hippisley here towards the end of the month. How I wish you would come this way, too. Believe me, dear Mrs Hunter, Yours sincerely, V. Paget.

Hill Hall, Epping Essex

15th May 1915.   House Party.
Mrs Charles Hunter - Mrs Williamson
                              & family

Guests
George Moore. Réjane - Gerald Kelly
Robert Horton. H. Clifford Smith
Cora, Countess of Strafford.
Grace Countess of Wemyss.
The Honble Lady Johnstone & her Son Mr. Harcourt Johnstone
Miss Violet Keppel.
Mrs Hickinley, (Mrs Hunter's sister)

Hill Hall Visitors' Book, May 15th, 1915

<u>Sales</u> x <u>Takings of performances</u> (see p 3) 15

1915 (X means "have applied")

June 24. Sold 1. Quartett   1.6. p⁴
Sep 1. Recᵈ for B.M.O. Albert Hall in June f. & Baylis 15/- pᵈ
~~Aug~~. B.M. Queen's Hall x   15/- pᵈ
~~Oct~~ 71   " Manchester (Sir H. Wood) x
~~[struck through]~~
Dec 9ᵗʰ   "   Dan Godfrey   (nothing!)   "   "
Nov ~~####~~ 4 1) Sleepless Dreams } 40 sets at 6ᵈ
              2) Hey nonny no   } Manchester x
          Hire 1) £1.1. 2)   Hallé 3.5.0
                            post of Material 4/6
Dec 7ᵗʰ T.B. Birmingham (Hallé Och) x
"Nov 11ᵗʰ Manchester (E.S.) (Hallé) x
                                          pᵈ
(Spring 1915) Mus Festival 3 songs (paid in £3.10
                                    Chester Bill
Dec 21ˢᵗ Glasgow Ch. Union x B.M.O. 15/- pᵈ
Jan 15ᵗʰ Manchester (B.M. Overture) p Hallé settled
March " B. Male ~~Liverpool~~ Nottingham (Hallé
3.5.0 Hey nonny at 4ᵈ = 116/8
  "   "   "   3ᵈ = 87/6

A page from Ethel Smyth's red accounts notebook

For Elizabeth it was an idyllic Edwardian childhood, passed in beautiful surroundings and with every comfort and luxury, including brilliant and intelligent company.

Later, there would be an element of tug-of-war over Elizabeth, who adored her grandmother, but did not enjoy the formal social life with its "marriage market" aspect still current immediately after World War I; and indeed she never married. Educated by governesses, she developed a passion for mathematics, astronomy and classical Greek and announced her wish to go to university. She was warmly encouraged by her great-aunt, but her grandmother, who had no time for women's liberation, having always got exactly what she wanted without it, was appalled. She had not been pleased or impressed by her younger sister's suffragette activities, although she supported her loyally in practical ways, when Ethel Smyth ended up in Holloway. Eventually, however, persuaded by George Moore and by Tonks, Mary Hunter gave her permission – as long as Elizabeth was always chaperoned to lectures by her elderly ladies-maid. So, Elizabeth got her degree and went on to translate Ptolemy's *Almagest* and work at the University of London Observatory. Her great-aunt clearly felt at several levels that she had won a battle.

Ethel Smyth, unlike her sister, led a modest life in her cottage at Woking, counting pennies, battling to get her work performed and fighting ceaselessly for the fair treatment of women on the musical scene. She considered herself the truly artistic one of the family and rather resented her sister poaching on her territory, as she perceived it, through money rather than any real sensitivity to painting or music. This was unfair, but family rivalries rooted in childhood often are, and Mary Hunter's casual "charity" must often have been galling. Part of this rivalry was played out in their relationship to Elizabeth, whose loyalties were often uncomfortably divided, as this correspondence makes clear.

The letters – Elizabeth kept all of her great-aunt's, whereas Ethel Smyth kept only a selection of her great-niece's – were returned at some stage to Ethel Smyth when she was writing a volume of her memoirs and some have notations made by her at that date. Although all were kept, in their envelopes, tied up in neat bundles with the thin string that Elizabeth always had on her desk for such purposes, not all have survived and some bundles are too damaged to be safely opened and read. The series begins with a few letters from 1922, when Elizabeth would have been 21. From the late '20s until the mid '30s the two women kept up a very frequent exchange, which slows to almost nothing in the '40s – perhaps because of Ethel Smyth's age, the difficulties of the war and Elizabeth's work, or

Elizabeth Williamson, c. 1904

through the various waves of destruction mentioned below. There is no reason to think that they became less close as the years went on, although it is perhaps significant that while, by the time I knew her, Elizabeth spoke frequently of her much-loved grandmother and told numerous stories about her, she barely mentioned Ethel Smyth.

Nevertheless, apart from a few letters from Virginia Woolf, Ethel Smyth's were the only letters of her own that Elizabeth kept - although she preserved some of Mary Hunter's correspondence – an indication of how highly she valued the relationship. It was her habit to open her mail immediately upon arrival, answer all personal letters and tear them up. Bills always were paid at once, the cheques often being written within minutes of receipt, and sent off by return of post; business letters and paperwork were dealt with and filed. No doubt because of her grandmother's bankruptcy, she had a horror of debts remaining unpaid for even a matter of hours.

Elizabeth was not musical. Later in her life, encroaching deafness made both composition and listening to music difficult for Ethel Smyth; their correspondence was largely on other matters – books and current affairs, their personal philosophies and family matters. The range of their interests is striking, particularly in the case of Ethel Smyth who, with indefatigable energy, remained abreast of new developments well into her eighties.

There is another more personal aspect to the wish to publish the letters. They were clearly something valued by Elizabeth, but they have already come very close to destruction on three occasions. The first was during the Blitz, when family possessions stored with the Pantechnicon Company were "severely damaged by water" when one of their premises was struck and all the windows broken. Later, Elizabeth kept many of her books and papers in the cellars at Trumpeters' House, once the site of Richmond Palace, and when tides were high along the Thames, water crept up the great lawn and flooded the book room. I remember on more than one occasion as a child dashing downstairs to help move the contents to safety – but not before the damp rising up the wooden book shelves had had serious consequences. After her death, I inherited her books and papers and moved them to my house in Seville, once part of the convent founded by St Teresa of Avila. During a particularly rainy winter, while I was away, a blocked gutter flooded the house and for the third time letters and books were "severely damaged by water". It seemed to me that there was much to be said for preserving at least some of them in a more permanent form. The bulk of the collection is now in the Beinecke Library at Yale.

Ethel Smyth's letters are quite often repetitive – descriptions of her dogs' maladies, for example, or travel arrangements of no particular

Mary Hunter (seated centre), Elizabeth Williamson (standing behind her) and unidentified guests at Hill Hall.

interest. *A very brief summary of what has been omitted is given in square brackets [ ].*

She also frequently used initials for names that she mentioned often. Harry Brewster was always HB; Maurice Baring was generally MB; Virginia Woolf was V or VW; FG was her opera *Fête Galante*; MM was Mount Mascal Farm where Elizabeth was living during the 1930s, and so on. Similarly, if she had already written a name out once she would generally refer to it by initials at the next mention within the same letter. The full name has been added in square brackets only where it seems unclear, for example T[homas] B[eecham].

I have also referred to the main characters by their initials in my notes: ES – Ethel Smyth; EMW – Elizabeth Williamson; MH – Mary Hunter, etc.

Ethel Smyth also tended to use abbreviations – "Imps" for the volume of her autobiography *Impressions that Remain,* but her intention is usually clear from the context. Other abbreviations "wd" for would or "yest" for yesterday have similarly been left in order to avoid flattening out her style. Unfortunately, typography makes it impossible to reproduce most of her very expressive underlinings, or her habit of writing particularly important words double the size of the rest of the sentence.

Since Ethel Smyth had acquaintances in a great variety of circles, notes accompanying the letters include brief biographies of many of the people mentioned, on the grounds that a reader familiar with Hilda Matheson, for example, may happen to know less about Joyce Wethered. In the case of figures repeatedly mentioned, such as John Singer Sargent or Maurice Baring, brief biographies follow, mainly to explain the relationship with Ethel Smyth and her family.

Paul Lunde, to whom this book is dedicated, perhaps through being American, was very struck by the denseness of the web of relationships connecting the aristocratic, political, academic, literary and occasionally business worlds, even when they might not have been expected to have much to say to each other. Something of this has also been indicated in the notes.

Some bibliography has been added for further reading.

The letters were transcribed in Cambridge c.2010, edited in Kerala, 2013 and the book given its final form in Cambridge and Seville in 2017.

Elizabeth Williamson playing chess at Hill Hall, with Mary Hunter seated left.
Sargent's portrait *The Misses Hunter* is just visible behind, as are the columns he allegedly marbled

The von Herzogenberg Family

Ethel Smyth went out to Leipzig to study music and in about 1878, while working with Heinrich von Herzogenberg, fell in love with his wife, Elizabeth "Lisl" von Herzogenberg. She lived with the family for seven years in a strange "mother-daughter" relationship, which she describes in Ch.xx of *Impressions that Remain*.

In 1882-3 she made the first of several trips to Florence, where she had an introduction to Lisl's elder sister Julia and her husband, Henry Brewster (q.v.). Elizabeth fell in love with Julia, but also flirted with friends of theirs, the Hildebrands. Meanwhile, Brewster was much attracted to Ethel. Lisl, appalled by the situation Ethel Smyth had created in her family, broke with her. Ethel Smyth never really accepted responsibility for the emotional chaos she had caused, indeed with repercussions echoing back to her own family in the form of her mother's reaction.

Johannes Brahms: the Herzogenberg Correspondence, ed. Max Kalbeck, tr. Hannah Bryant, New York, 1909

Henry B. Brewster (1850-1908)

An expatriate American, a philosopher and author, a friend of Henry James, Brewster was the one male love of Ethel Smyth's life. Born in Europe and identifying as "cosmopolitan", he nevertheless retained American nationality. He despised both the low-church ethic and the commercialism of America, which nevertheless provided him with independent means, so that he never needed to work. In 1873, he married Julia von Stockhausen, eleven years his senior, in whose parents' house he had lodged while at university in Dresden, and for a number of years they lived a highly reclusive life studying philosophy together.

After meeting Ethel Smyth in 1884, Brewster naïvely imagined they could create a *ménage à trois* – at which point both women left him. In 1890, Ethel Smyth and Henry Brewster met again, but it was not until the death of Lisl von Herzogenberg *(supra)* in 1892 and Julia in 1895, that they finally consummated their affair; but Ethel resolutely refused to marry him.

Henry Brewster wrote several philosophical works, which were well regarded, for example by Henry James and his brother William, himself an eminent philosopher, but which seem quite unreadable today. He also provided the libretto for Ethel Smyth's opera *The Wreckers*. In the wake of Ethel Smyth's musical settings, his book *The Prison* was reissued in 1931 with the addition of her Memoir of him. She always felt that he was

A page from the Hill Hall Visitors' Book

the one person who had provided her with unfailing encouragement and support in her musical career and for the rest of her life continued to cite him as an authority on all kinds of subjects.

Brewster's daughter, Clotilde, an artist and architect, is mentioned several times, not always kindly, about the period at which she had been recently widowed. Her daughter Susan was married to Major-General Hugh Hibbert, presumably the disapproving son-in-law of one of the letters. The younger Henry Brewster, also mentioned, did not, as Ethel Smyth predicted, make a name as a poet, but was later involved in editing his grandfather's works. He also wrote several books about the world in which he grew up and was said by Martin Halpern (see below) to be preparing an edition of family letters, but it seems never to have materialised.

Ethel Smyth's relations with both Brewster and the von Herzogenberg family are described at some length in her volumes of autobiography, especially *Impressions that Remain* and *As Time Went On*.

"The Smyth-Brewster Correspondence: A Fresh Look at the Hidden Romantic World of Ethel Smyth" by Amanda Harris, *Women and Music: A Journal of Gender and Culture*, Vol 14, 2010, pp. 72-94

"Henry B. Brewster (1850-1908): An Introduction," Martin Halpern, *American Quarterly*, Vol. 14, No. 3 (Autumn, 1962), pp. 464-482

The Cosmopolites, Henry C. Brewster, London, 1993

The Benson Family

This is not the place to describe the extraordinary soap opera of Benson family life, but here again Ethel Smyth was to wreak havoc within the family circle. On her return to England in 1885, having alienated most of her German friends and temporarily unable to compose, she sought comfort from Mary Benson, wife of the Archbishop of Canterbury, but trouble arose as her affections swung between mother and daughter - Margaret Benson, the first woman to carry out archaeological excavations in Egypt.

It is perhaps worth mentioning the casualness of the Victorian and Edwardian approach to lesbianism. After the death of her husband in 1896, Mary Benson lived quite openly with the daughter of his predecessor, Archbishop Tait; it was common knowledge that they shared a bed – but apparently nobody much commented or cared. One wonders whether today they would be so lucky.

Mary Benson was sister-in-law to the Balfours (q.v.). She was the mother of the novelist Edward Frederick (E.F.) Benson, best known for the *Mapp and Lucia* series and later to portray Ethel Smyth in his satirical

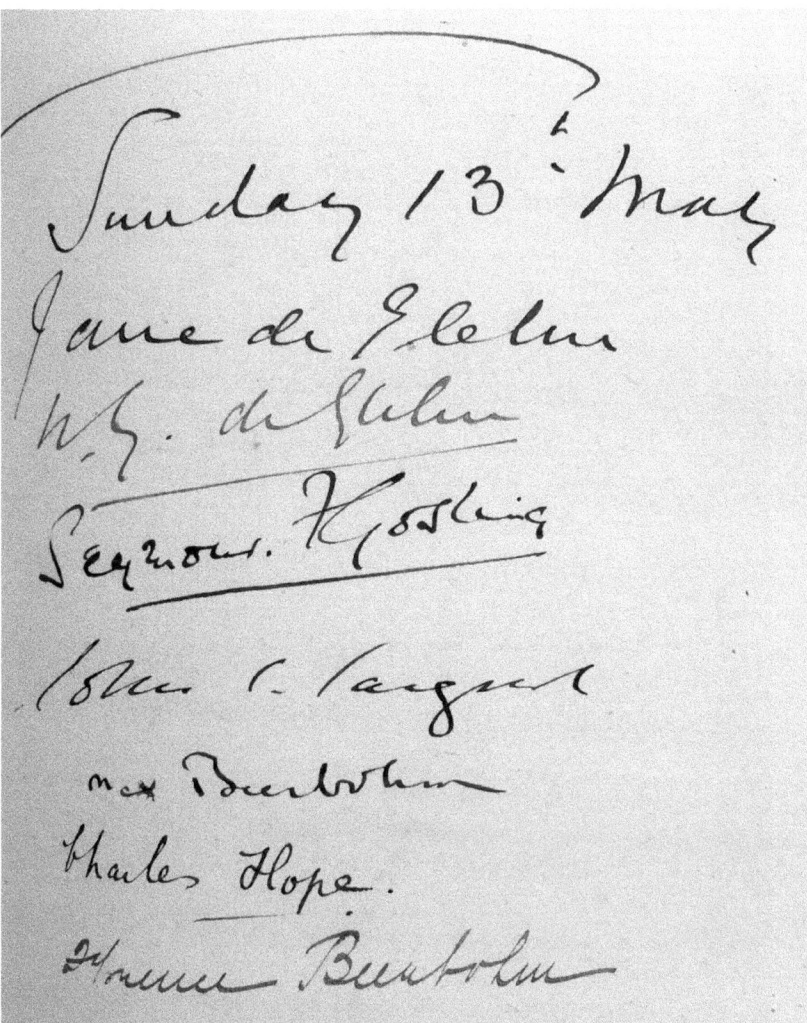

From the Hill House Guest Book

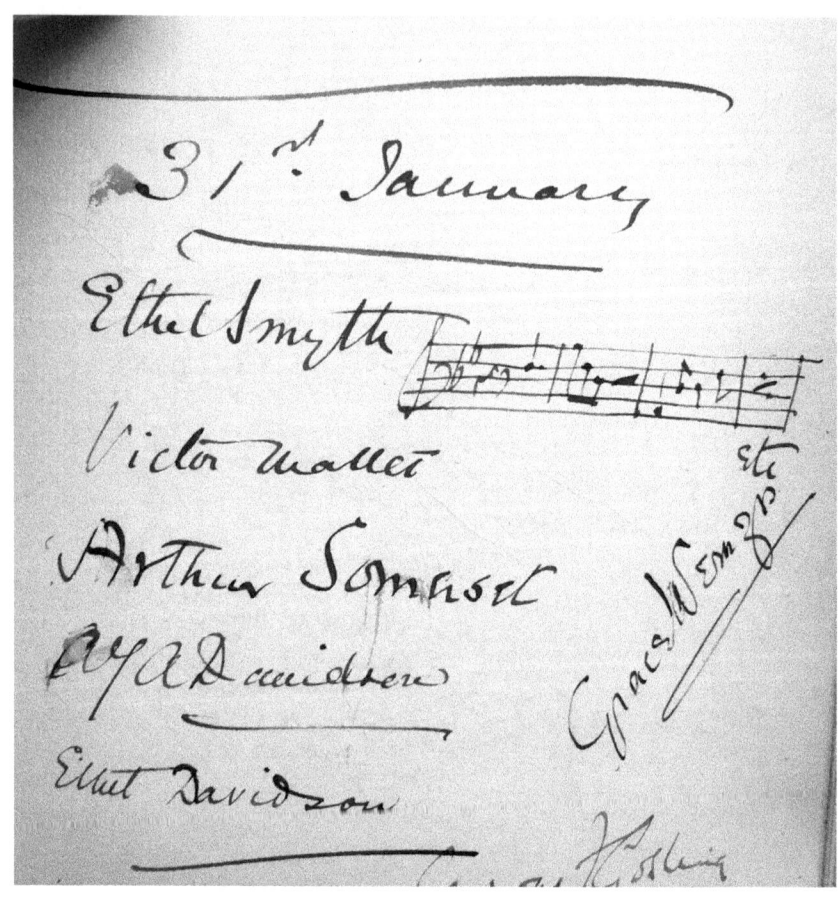

From the Hill House Guest Book

novel *Dodo* (1893). He was a great friend of the family and "Fred" is frequently mentioned in the letters, as is his home, Rye House, previously inhabited by Henry James and subsequently by Rumer Godden.

Intimate Friends: Women Who Loved Women, 1778-1928, Martha Vicinus, University of Chicago Press, 2004

The Ponsonby Family

The Ponsonbys were another military family and had a long-standing friendship with the Smyths, perhaps through the Empress Eugénie. Ethel Smyth seems to have first met Mary Elizabeth, the wife of Sir Henry Ponsonby, Queen Victoria's private secretary, in 1891. After her husband's death, Lady Ponsonby maintained a stormy emotional relationship with Ethel Smyth, which they apparently both enjoyed.

Sir Henry's son, Frederick "Fritz" Ponsonby, who was again both a soldier and a courtier, and his wife Victoria "Ria", became great friends of the Smyth family. Both of them were lively and active. Never very well off, the money from her cookery book *Lady Sysonby's Cook Book* (1935) and his posthumously published *Recollections of Three Reigns* (1951) and other works, was very welcome, even though their daughter Loelia, often mentioned in the letters, had married the Duke of Westminster, one of the richest men in the world.

Henry Ponsonby, Queen Victoria's Private Secretary: His Life from His Letters, Arthur Ponsonby, London, 1942
Grace and Favour: The Memoirs of Loelia, Duchess of Westminster, London, 1961

Maurice Baring (1874-1945)

Born into a wealthy banking family, Maurice Baring had a varied career. He served briefly in the diplomatic, was an officer in the Royal Air Force, acted as war correspondent reporting on the Russo-Japanese War and was subsequently based in Russia and the Balkans. Baring spoke Russian and had great sympathy for the people, in spite of political differences, and his books on Russia and *Letters from the Near East* are still an interesting source for the period (1905-1914), which he witnessed at first hand. Financially independent after the death of his grandfather, Baring began writing novels in 1921 and these had a considerable success at the time, although they have little appeal today. His autobiography, *The Puppet Show of Memory* (1922), however, continued to be read and *The Oxford Book of Russian Verse* (1924), chosen by him, went into a number of editions and was still being reprinted in the 1970s.

In 1909, he converted to Catholicism, to Ethel Smyth's everlasting disapproval, and with Hilaire Belloc and G.K. Chesterton, formed a triumvirate of Catholic writers, immortalized in James Gunn's *Conversation Piece*, now in the National Portrait Gallery. He and Ethel Smyth were, however, great friends and he supported her in many ways, including, on various occasions, financially. In 1938, having already written about him as a novelist, she published *Maurice Baring*, largely a literary biography. From the early 1930s, Baring was increasingly incapacitated by Parkinson's Disease and wrote much less, apart from a little poetry, including verses to Ethel Smyth. His last years were spent in Scotland at a house belonging to the Lovat family, again very old friends, where Laura Lovat nursed him until his death.

Maurice Baring, Ethel Smyth, London, 1938
Maurice Baring: A Postscript by Laura Lovat with Some Letters and Verse, Laura Lovat, London, 1947
Maurice Baring: Letters, ed. Joyce Hillgarth, London, 2007

Edith Somerville (1858-1949)

An Anglo-Irish author of numerous books, written with her cousin and companion, Violet Martin (1862-1915), who used the pseudonym Martin Ross. After Ross' death, Edith Somerville went on publishing under their joint names, convinced that their collaboration was continuing through spiritualist séances. She was also extremely active running a farm and working for social welfare in her part of Cork.

Edith Somerville and Ethel Smyth met in Ireland in 1919 and became life-long friends, drawn together, among other things, by the suffrage movement. They shared many interests, including a passion for horses and hunting, as well as Edith Somerville's love of traditional folk music. Ethel often visited her in Ireland until the Second World War – and old age – made travel impossible and it is Edith who is given the last word on Ethel in this book.

Much of their voluminous correspondence, which covers a wide range of subjects, from their personal lives and work to politics and travel is preserved at Queen's University, Belfast: www.qub.ac.uk/specialcollections and there is further material at the *Edith Œnone Somerville Archive* in Drishane.

Somerville and Ross: a biography, Maurice Collis, London, 1968
Edith Somerville: a biography, Gifford Lewis, Dublin, 2005

Letter from Philip Burne-Jones

Letter from John Singer Sargent

John Singer Sargent (1856-1925)

Sargent is too well-known to need a general biographical note. He and Mary Hunter seem to have met about 1895, perhaps introduced by Sir William Eden, sportsman, connoisseur of painting and amateur artist. It was at this period that Charles Hunter was making his fortune and his wife was increasingly drawn into the literary and artistic world of London.

Through Sargent, who became a close friend, Mary Hunter was introduced to his circle, many of whom became regular visitors when the Hunters acquired Hill Hall. Sargent painted family portraits and, according to family tradition, did the marbling on the columns in the great drawing room at Hill. Later, when he ceased painting society portraits in oils and would only do chalk on paper, he drew the well-known picture - which she hated - of Ethel Smyth playing the piano and singing (now in the National Portrait Gallery) and the sketch of Elizabeth Williamson mentioned in the letters, here reproduced on page 37.

Mary Hunter was certainly a very close friend – one of the few admitted to the intimacy of Sargent's family circle centred on his mother's house – and after the death of Charles Hunter gossip had it that they might marry, a rumour that they were at considerable pains to quash and which Ethel considered ridiculous and offensive. Mary never really recovered from her husband's sudden death.

The Balfours

Gerald Balfour (1853-1945), a distinguished conservative politician, married Elizabeth "Betty" Bulwer-Lytton, daughter of Lord Lytton, Viceroy of India, responsible for the disastrous 2nd Afghan War, in 1887. The Balfours, with their six children, were neighbours of Ethel Smyth at Woking, living at Fisher's Hill House, built for them by their brother-in-law, Edwin Lutyens, one of the architects of New Delhi. The gardens were designed by Ethel's friend Gertrude Jekyll. Betty Balfour was to become a close friend of Ethel's and a great support on numerous occasions, as the letters indicate.

Notes on the format

The convention is to refer to Ethel Smyth as ES, and to the editor as CS. A date in square brackets means the letter was undated, but the year can be assumed from the context.

> The correspondence, to and from ES, has been indented slightly and set in this typeface with additional features to represent the ebullient style of the handwriting of ES. The headers and valedictions have been standardised.

Editorial material is set thus, in this type.

Notes by ES appear set like this

Notes by CS appear thus

A very brief summary of what, if anything, has been omitted from the text of a letter is given in square brackets [ ] and set like this.

1922

The first surviving letter seems to be the following from Ethel to Elizabeth, although there were certainly earlier ones. Elizabeth's first surviving letter, a thank you note to her Grandmother, was written when she was five. Although this one makes little sense in isolation, it touches on several themes that were to reoccur frequently in their correspondence, especially the views of Henry Brewster[1] (always abbreviated in her letters to H.B.) and philosophy.

1 Henry Brewster – see Introduction.

January 12th, 1922

Dearest Elizabeth I think if you'd known H.B. as I did when he was 33 – just emerging from <u>absolutely nothing but metaphysics all his life</u> and with a still-more-so wife you'd understand that nursery gov[ernesses]s. and blithe peasants were inevitable. In theory at least. As a matter of fact he liked all sorts – only was more sympathetic towards mediocrity than most of us are.

[On H.B.'s loathing of Catholics, especially priests; ES's difficulties in reading philosophy]

1923

Unless otherwise indicated, all letters for 1923 are from Coign – at Hook Heath, in Woking – to Hill Hall. They are often in bad condition, having been affected by damp.

Hill Hall, an Elizabethan mansion, near Epping, Essex.

January 8th, 1923

[Reading The Legacy of Greece *et al.]*

I'm glad I may read it slowly for I have but little time – am constructing my new libretto all day and writing lyrics which I think will please you! Of course the great point is the rhythms I have in mind with them – but here's the refrain of the love song of the orderly who's been blamed for "irregularities".... (You must drum on the table in equal beats at the red places.)
Pfftt!!..(he blows on his fingers)
Do see if you can whack out the rhythm and see how it goes? Rather an interesting sort of cuneiform experiment - to do it without notes-values....

[On reading matter; her admiration for Dean Inge[1]: "I'd far rather you were a bigoted anti-Catholic than any other sort of bigot." On her health, golf and family meetings]

1 William Inge (1860-1954), Dean of St Paul's, Professor of Theology at Cambridge and prolific author.

Harry Brewster was clearly much in Ethel's mind, for on January 12th she wrote again on his philosophical ideas and a few days later returned to the subject and the question of his publications.

January 21st, 1923

Dearest Elizabeth – your letter about Anarchy and Law[1] quite delighted me. Do you know it is a curious thing that Harry B himself always said a time <u>might</u> come when people would not insist upon monism, and be content to admit relativity in religious beliefs or moral codes. I have always held that 9 out of 10 people can't get on without believing (or pretending to believe) that the way they solve problems, or try to, is the only way. And I still am of that opinion. Yet it is curious how, apparently, the march of science has been working with him. I dare say people are much more disposed

To his latest & best reader
Elizabeth Williamson

from Ethel Smyth

New Year 1923

THE THEORIES OF ANARCHY AND OF LAW.

Dedication in Harry Brewster's *The Theory of Anarchy and Law* now to allow that what we see is not a solid body, but just a particular disposition of screens......The Theories of Anarchy and Law was really written to explain the Harold [?] rôle in the cosmos (and in their own case) to his wife. She herself – a terrific metaphysician – had always been strong on the Anarchist as Real Lover of Humanity. But when it came to conducting life on those principles – actually, and not only in theory – the completest revulsion set in. I don't think this was wholly what is called "human nature" (in its least pleasant sense). It is partly on these grounds that I don't believe humanity will ever work to its own comfort except under dogmatic sway. In practice the other air will be too rareified for it. This is of course why the Roman Church will never make concessions to fallibility. It bides its time, thinking that when a wave of intelligence and independence has spent itself, people will long for certainty again. Yet how can one imagine the N of Europe or the Anglo Saxons re-embracing R.Catholicism?

When I come again I shall bring my old copy and we will compare notes on what we like. By the way what copy have you been reading? I have a spare uncut one. And if you'd like it wd love to give it to you – a jolly link between 3 generations. H.B. wd be so delighted! By the way Dick Hippisley[2] was saying he thought the time had come for re-printing those books[3]. I wonder? I had thought of it, and that it should be done, perhaps with a sort of biographical note. But that wd be difficult for me to do. Oh well, I don't know. It wd take some doing – but perhaps be possible. Anyhow I rather wish you wd write to Williams and Norgate# (who must have had many applications) and ask how it is with these books? – if they still have any? I know that H.B. paid for the printing so the copyright must be safe and belong to the children[4]. Do you know I think his greatest work is his correspondence! I often wish I cd face the task of editing his letters – I may when I'm quite gaga perhaps! I have left them to Maurice [Baring][5] but think that my life is perhaps better than his tho' I'm more than 20 years older (I think). I shall leave them to you afterwards!

Your loving E

If I wrote they'd smell a rat and make difficulties, perhaps.

The second page is headed: "(Later) 11.30 am)".

[On her health; more on her reading]

I think - inspired by you, I shall try Plato again, but I don't take to abstract thought as I do, for instance, to ethnology, or history, or geography. I think my feeling has always been that that side is busy with music. And as Geoffrey Toye[6] was saying here the other day "Was ever such an appalling job as ours? The ink, the paper – tons of it – to fix a phrase that is over in 6½ [61½] seconds" – And if like me you have no natural facility! All I can do has come so slowly. Fast in some ways, but technically so slowly.

[Politics; her sister Alice's views]

1 Harry Brewster, *Theories of Anarchy and Law. A Midnight Debate,* Williams and Norgate, London, 1887.
2 Richard Hippisley – the husband of Ethel's sister Violet - see Introduction.
3 In fact, they still seem not to have been reprinted.
4 Harry Brewster's children - see Introduction.
5 Maurice Baring – see Introduction.
6 Geoffrey Toye (1889-1942) Conductor and composer, governor of the Old Vic and Sadler's Wells, and director of the D'Oyly Carte Opera company.

February 23rd, 1923

Dearest Elizabeth I have got Vol II of the Outspoken Essay[1] - but now tell me this truly. The other day I put the book down on my knee not knowing that Pan, who had laid his head there a few minutes previously, had been drinking. Consequence – the cover got a little dabbled. Of course I want to send you my new Edit and had it packed when it suddenly occurred to me to look up the last page – and there I found "4th Edit." Query wd you rather have your own 1st Edit back? And if so will you ever forgive the slightly waterstained cover? -------- Tell me......

Tell your Mother to get and read "Hassan" by J.Flecker[2]. A play publ. by Heinemann. Most arresting. <u>That</u> leaves an after exaltation of a queer kind – or so I find.

Your loving
E

I lunched with Rutland Broughton³ yesterday....He is wholly un-elated by his "success" and <u>really</u> doubting himself because "fools flock"!! But he accounts for it mainly (as do I) by the fact that people having lost religion want something "mystic" – (rather what I elicited from Fred Benson⁴ as to his "14 times"). I think too R.B.'s complete absorption of the folk style blended with his own utter musicalness has a great deal to do with it. He <u>is</u> a queer creature – like a child with dear traits and horrible traits but something incorruptible in the regions that matter (for me) art and moral courage. At this moment he is behaving quite atrociously to the woman (a dear) whom he has lived with and called Mrs R.. for 16 years and had children by. She is producing Fenelon⁵ [?] at the Vic the day I conduct B.[oatswain's]. Mate (1st March 7.30). I come first and am excited by Fenelon.

1 *Outspoken Essays* (Vol.II 1922) by William Ralph Inge.
2 James Elroy Flecker (1884-1915) *Hassan: The Story of Hassan of Baghdad and How he Came to Make the Golden Journey to Samarkand* was published in 1922 and first performed in September 1923 with incidental music written by Delius in 1920.
3 Rutland Broughton (1878-1960) composer, particularly of operas and choral music, many with historic or Arthurian themes. His socialist sympathies brought him into contact with such men as George Bernard Shaw and one of his ambitions was to establish a summer music festival. His most famous work was choral-drama *The Immortal Hour* (1914).
4 E.F. Benson (1867-1940) – see Introduction.
5 Conceivably François Fénelon (1651-1715), the French priest, writer and advocate of Quietism, whose *The Adventures of Telemachus*, an impassioned attack on the divine right of kings, inspired a number of works, including Mozart's *Idomeneo*.

March 8th, 1923

Dearest Elizabeth,
I half hoped ere long to appear with Edith Somerville¹ at Hill – but she is over for such a short time and so tied up in business that I fear it wont be possible....Do tell yr

grandmother in case I haven't time to write. It's a huge disapp. to E. – she wd have loved to go and is so grateful for having been asked.

Well – about the Immortal Hour². You would never get a huge run with a work of art on the first line – clean, objective, unmingled with side issues – like Carmen or "Figaro" because a run of this kind depends on various people going there again and again, who must have the second rate quality of liking something because of something else. In old days English people only liked music because of religion (oratorio etc). Now, I think, as regards the I.H. what makes people go 10 times (which is a form of opium eating) is owing to the mysticism – a sort of substitute for religion (which no longer possesses the floor). It's a vague state of something or other – it's emotionalism of a kind that is never induced by art pure and simple....but it is by religion. No work of Beethoven, of Mozart's could ever impel people to go and see it 15 times. You may love the music – (so do I) but if you went 10 times it wd be because the music is only a factor in inducing the opium state of enjoyment – something as different to the ecstatic bracing triumphant feeling great art gives as the feelings you have galloping after hounds on a gorgeous day differs from the opium bliss. R.B. is quite justified in half disbelieving in himself since he has managed to make himself a "stunt" – only, as I said, it is not his fault; it's the chance mingling of his music and Fiona McLeod's idea – (which make in their way a perfect brew). I must confess however that hearing some of it by chance for the 3rd time (I have only heard it straight through once, but have nipped in now and then when bent on business at the Regal) it was born in upon me that the music will not bear investigation let alone frequent hearing. Its unequal – like the work of a talented child. The Beggars Opera holds by virtue of an unique thing – exquisite tunes (the pick of the output of a country then at its musical apogee) a most amusing plot and so on. But only in a mawkish country, intellectually lazy, and adoring that least artistic of things, a long run, would it be possible to find hundreds of people who are willing to go 20-30 times – and be proud of it. It's the mentally uneducated who like to hear the same story ten times over. Did you read the article of mine (the 1st or 2) on music and mawk? – Now no one would go and hear Holst's Hymn of Jesus 20 times! As things in that attitude never get into the region of being the fashion. "The Lost Chord" does, Chu Chin Chow[3] does... and alas! The Immortal Hour does - There is something about work on the first line that prevents it producing that particular effect. It lasts for ever and people go on flocking to hear it ... But it will not lend itself to sentimental misuse....

[On reading matter, social commitments and personal news]

1 Edith Somerville – see Introduction.
2 An opera with a theme of the fairy world by the English composer and founder of the Glastonbury Festival, Rutland Broughton, adapted from the work of Fiona MacLeod (William Sharp 1855-1905). It was first performed in London in 1914 and ran for 216 consecutive performances in London in 1922 and for 160 in 1923.
3 A musical comedy on the story of Ali Baba by Oscar Asche with music by Frederic Norton. From August 3rd, 1916 it ran for 2238 performances.

April 6th, 1923

[On EMW's health]

The concert was fairly all right, only Dan G.[1] let me down over the previous trying out of the songs and I only had a scramble through. But my singer was splendidly safe and secure, and so warm and jolly in her delivery that the last two songs went quite well....as they wd have with 15 minutes more rehearsal. But those 15 mins were unattainable. The whole festival[2] is ridiculously large and things cant be rehearsed. The whole system is rotten and "What the army is coming to
   I'd really be afraid to guess"
   (Extract from "Irregulariters" – song by Corporal Erb Iggins)
   While here, now that the concert is over, I'm immersed in every sort of musical arrangement.

1 Dan Godfrey (1868-1939) conductor and founder of the Bournemouth Municipal Orchestra. He was knighted in 1922, in part thanks to the efforts of ES.
2 From 1922-1940, there was a Bournemouth Easter Festival of Music, in 1927 devoted to music by English women composers.

April 13th, 1923

"Dearest Eliz - Thank you for your loathed offspring[1] – yes – I want to try again. It may be easier in print...."

Ethel continues, springing, as so often, chamois-like from subject to subject: A lost letter, reading matter, on religion: "....the English, rightly or wrongly, hate logic and hard and fast lives....I think convert R.C.s are very childlike..." "Date your letters. It's a good habit to acquire", and on failing to welcome a painter friend, who had come to visit all the way from Taormina.

[1] Not clear what this refers to – perhaps an article by EMW on relativity.

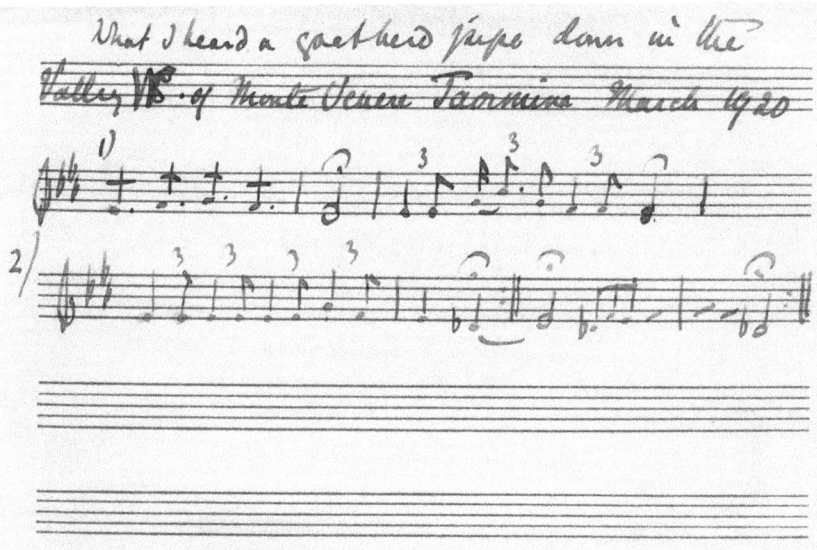

Page of music with a song from Taormina.

November 22nd, 1923

One small headed page enclosing a double page letter from Joyce Wethered[1]

Tigbourne Court,[2]
Witley, Surrey

Ethel Smyth
April 23 - 1923

A birthday present to herself.

Comment on the fly-leaf of ES's copy of *Through the Shadows with O. Henry* by A I Jennings.

Dear Dame Ethel

I was so sorry I had to leave after the concert yesterday and could not come to tea at the Langham. I did not realize how late it would be and had promised to pick my brother up some where at half past five. It was kind of you to have both mother and me. I enjoyed your concert enormously – especially your songs. I thought Ann Thursfield sang the second one too beautifully for words. I am so glad I was able to come and I loved it all. I only saw Elizabeth for a second – she seemed very frightened of her proffessors [sic] and dared not stay!
Thank you again for such a delightful afternoon.

Yrs sincerely
Joyce Wethered

[On some gadget, unspecified]

Isnt this a nice letter fr Joyce Wethered? I've implored her if she comes (ever) over to [?] or Wok[ing] to golf like an ordinary mortal to come here to lunch instead of eating muck at the Club – I do wish it wd come off.

[On her pleasure at EMW attending her concert]

You were **such dears** all of you to come – tell your relations so, will you? By the by the givers of the concert made exactly the same sum people always do whether the place is crammed (as it usually is) with free tickets or whether they are barred, as this time !!! That is they will have lost about £40, I think – <u>as they expected</u>. (All I did was pay £12.12 to the artists, on my own). Fives into £40 makes a loss of £8 pounds each – but to them it was worth it.

Many thanks, again
Yours loving E

---

1 Joyce Wethered - Lady Heathcote-Amory (1901-1997) – one of the greatest women golf champions of all time, at this date was at the height of her fame. She was a friend of Ethel's, as well as her coach. Quoting from His Honour Judge Simon Brown, QC's letter to *The Times*, August 8th, 2012: " Arguably the two greatest golfers were the 1930 grand slam winner [Bobby] Jones and the women's champion Joyce Wethered from Great Britain. On May 23, 1930, Wethered played a four ball match at St Andrews with Jones, T.A. Bourn, the English champion and her brother Roger..." After this date, she more or less retired from competitive golf, but her *Golfing Memories and Methods* was published by Hutchinson, London, 1933.
2 Tigbourne Court, one of Edwin Lutyens' (1869-1944) best known country houses, built between 1899-1901 with gardens designed by Gertrude Jekyll (1843-1932).

December 11th, 1923

Dearest Elizabeth do you think I shd grasp Lewes's[1] Hist. of Philosophy? I remember H.B. saying just what you do - that it was quite as irritating as his Life of G[oethe] <u>and I possess the book!</u>....relic of the days (I suppose) when I discussed Comte[2] with Willie Wilde[3] and was sick immediately afterwards – proof that philosophy disagrees with me. Almost everything Lewes wrote (except Actors and the Art of Acting) has that tiresome tone – but even there it is perceptible. Rereading the Life of G. in a German translation (!) picked up at a jumble sale at Castle Townsend[4] Co.Cork (!! For 6d (!!!) the style is less provoking. Have you got to the bit about Beethoven at Marienbad that made me laugh so that I woke Pan? (Only it cant be quite so funny in English....)

[On Lewes and Goethe]

When first I went to Weimar (in 1880 I think) I saw one of Goethe's grandchildren[5] - they lived in the Goethe haus and were two tiny shy little abnormalities in snuff-coloured clothes who only went out at night for fear of being pointed out as Goethe's grandchildren. Of course they never married. Goethe adored them as children, but one could not believe they had ever been children.

[On EMW learning German and on reading Goethe – including his mother's letters[5]: "She is simply the most adorable person in literature"]

1 George Henry Lewes (1817-1878) philosopher, theatre critic and long-term companion of George Eliot; he was much interested in the work of Auguste Comte. *The Life of Goethe* (1855) was his best known book.
2 Auguste Comte (1798-1857) French philosopher founder of the doctrine of Positivism. He had considerable influence in the 19th c., among others on George Eliot.
3 William Wilde (1852-1899), an Irish journalist, Oscar Wilde's elder brother. ES claims elsewhere that he proposed to her on the Irish packet and that she was sick on that occasion as well.
4 Castletownsend near Skibbereen on the southwest coast of Ireland was the home of ES's great friend Edith Somerville and she often visited her there.
5 Presumably Walther and Wolfgang. The Goethe family house was in Frankfurt.
6 Katharina Elizabeth Goethe (1731-1808) was an important intellectual influence on her son and said to be of a very lively and joyous disposition. An edition of her letters was published in 1889.

The last letter of the year was written on Christmas Eve. Later, after the family had left Hill Hall, where Christmas was celebrated on a very lavish scale, this was to become the traditional season for a particularly lively exchange of letters. This one, however is quite short, mostly in German and largely about Ethel's reading.

1924

Hill Hall

January 3rd, 1924

The first surviving letter from Elizabeth to Ethel seems to be the following, although there must have been a good number over the preceding years.

> Hill Hall
> Theydon Mount
> Epping
>
> Telephone 21 Epping Station and Telegraph Office
> Epping 3 miles

Dearest Aunt Ethel,

My heart does indeed bleed for you about the shoes. In spite of the deepest sympathy I laughed uproariously at your illustration and comments thereon! Mine certainly have no such ridge. I keep them stretched tightly on trees because being made of that soft leather with no stitching or broguing of any sort they are apt to lose their shape. Is the ridge in yours a new development? I will certainly produce mine and confront them if you like. I have to wear them on Saturday as I am rather short of golf shoes, otherwise and after that I could spare them easily. I hope you have not been done: my shoes only cost 50/-, and this in spite of being twice the size of yours! I feel rather like George (in the Cautionary Tales) "who was in part to blame" etc. for having induced you to buy them!

[Discussion of a book on Goethe and his attitude to science]

A strenuous day is before us tomorrow, a school treat which I always revel in and a fancy dress ball which I abhor...

> Your loving
> Elizabeth

Friday, February 8th, 1924

The second was written to congratulate Ethel on her *Mass in D*, which had been performed for the first time in 31 years in Birmingham on the previous day.

The Royal Institute,
21, Albemarle Street,
London W.1

Dearest Aunt Ethel,

You will have to bear with more overflowing about the Mass than I had opportunity for last night. I always feel like a barbarian an outcast in musical matters but if one has ardent love for music and no knowledge and no standards there is the advantage that it takes more than a bad orchestra to spoil one's fun! Also the direct and straightforward impressiveness of the piece seems to me "to be easily understood of the people" i.e. the likes of me. The thing that struck me was that the mixture of strength, conviction, richness of feeling and warmness is so exactly like you yourself. This sounds sloppy perhaps but it is true so why not say it? Anyway the whole thing was an overpowering enjoyment to me from beginning to end. I exult in having deserted the spheres in such a cause and glory in unrepentance.

"Gott war so schön, ach war so lieb"!!!

I wish to goodness I could unearth from my faith a feeling like your thundering

Credo in unum dominum Jesum Christum

I feel less behindhand with the Spiritu Sanctu!!

[Description of a dinner party]

I had a short confabulation with Miss Bayliss[1] [sic] mostly a duet on the inspiring theme "Gloria in excelsis Ethelo Smytho". I bemoaned not having seen Henry VIII and said how you praised it and she said "Oh but you know she sees us through rose coloured spectacles and don't you set any store by what she says." I replied that your spectacles were always clear whatever their colour. She was a dear.

We were all completely unstrung this morning after the emotions of the night before. Aunt Kitty and I were in the helpless giggling state, and talked German all the way down in the train and the mournful limitations of my vocabulary increased our mirth. She then gave the porter one half penny instead of 1/- and his furious face set us off again!

I went for a brisk walk round the noble city of Birmingham after breakfast and had a look at Millais' Blind Girl to see what Gran meant about them not sitting properly on the ground. I bow to her opinion in these spheres but I don't see it myself as I think they are more or less leaning in the way one does on a steep bank.

I must bring back my scattered energies to the integration of inverse hyperbolic functions. The worst of Sin is that it lasts i.e. the disturbing effects are more far reaching than just the event.

Your loving,
Elizabeth

1 Lilian Baylis (1874-1937), manager and producer, was arguably the most important figure in reviving English theatre, opera and ballet in the first half of the 20th c. With her aunt, an associate of Octavia Hill, she brought into being the Old Vic – initially intended to improve the quality of life in one of the more deprived areas of London – and then Sadlers' Wells and what were to become the Royal Ballet and the English National Opera. Ethel Smyth greatly admired her.

Elizabeth's mother, Phyllis Williamson, also wrote to congratulate her aunt:

> Darling Ethel,
> Just a line to thank you for another proud and pleasant evening. Of course the goodness of the music got through, in spite of the drawbacks of that particular production, and after all they were not caused by you but by your interpreters....

Sunday, March 9th, 1924

Dearest Aunt,

Gloria in excelsis Deo.

What an afternoon. I have never felt such exultant enjoyment. I am never tired as a rule but last night was so limp with "emotional" exhaustion that I could not have turned my head for a total eclipse of the moon! It was most odd and I have never felt like that before. It is the frightful excitement of the Mass. And not just being carried away by the noise and the occasion, because I feel just as excited sitting here now when I think of it. There was such a feeling of tenseness about it all. You had only to look at the chorus to see that they were under the spell of something that completely mastered them. I noticed this particularly – rows and rows of men and women with wrapt [sic] faces of intense concentration. I know the face (and the feeling!) They are unmistakeable. And how they sang their words. You could hear every line. Of course for me it was hearing the thing for the first time. I <u>understand</u> about your feelings at Birmingham now. I don't believe life contains such another afternoon but what matter? Of course you are the most wonderful person in the world. This is not exactly a new idea to me but one's convictions can be enforced!!! I am sorry to "go on" (vide G[eorge].M[oore]. and you!) like this but you can't give people such potent drink and expect them to remain cool headed and self controlled about it!

[On other people who did, or did not, attend the Mass]

With love to Miss Somerville M.W.S.V.
Yrs Elizabeth

Saturday, March 15th, 1924

Hill Hall
Epping

Dearest Aunt Ethel,

[The Mass]

I have got hold of an Italian book on Goethe by Benedetto Croce[1]. Very interesting as far as I have got but I was switched off by innumerable events crowding upon me, and I haven't read a word of it for over a week. I am also reading at the R.I. at short and infrequent moments an enchanting book by Aristarchus of Samos on the distances of the Sun and the Moon. It is Greek and English side by side, and rather easy Greek being in the curt style of mathematical exposition – rather like Euclid. It is not one of Aristarchus' best books (they are almost entirely lost) and in fact contains most of his few bad shots! He was one of the best astronomers ever! It is well established from fragments and references to him in contemporaries and commentators that he had the Copernican system complete. He adopted this late in life – his early books being still geo-centric in treatment. It is typical of the divine Greeks that they carefully considered the question of the earth turning on its' axis and round the sun. The reason why they rejected it after weighing the evidence was due to a fundamental mistake of their dynamics. They couldn't believe the earth to have a surface velocity of 1000 miles per hour [?] because they didn't realize that force is measured by acceleration and not velocity and that it doesn't require force to <u>keep</u> a body moving only to start and stop it. I have found a new and most humiliating incentive to learn German viz that Newton's Optics is translated from the original Latin into German and <u>not into English</u>. Isn't this scandalous? I think I shall suggest this as a life work for Billy[2] who is quite good at Latin and optics! Newton delivered these epoch making lectures on his discoveries of the composite nature of light in Latin to "one or two students" at Trin. Coll. Cambridge. The bare thought of this makes me quake with excitement!

The girl who does astronomy with us is most intelligent about you and your works, lives in Oxford – her father being boss of a college – and she has asked me to stay the weekend in June that your things are done by the Old Vic.

Great excitements have been going on. That angel Ld. Islington returned good for evil after me beating him 7 & 6 at golf by inviting the Astronomer Royal to lunch on purpose for my benefit. He was a darling to me and the affair was a great success. I am going down to Greenwich next Tuesday afternoon. Joy. Triumph. I am taking the young lady mentioned above as a reward for her kind invitation. She will be most helpful in making intelligent remarks and gasps of admiration at the right moment.

To turn from the Muses to "gymnastic" (in the best Platonic tradition)....

[On golf; someone's suggestions re orchestration "!!!!!!"]

When are you coming back and <u>are you coming to</u> Sandwich <u>as promised</u> from April 4th – 15th??

What an appalling length this letter has reached. I do apologize. I always ramble on so to you. You can always read it in separate instalments as a soporific after your bath.

Gran and Ma have gone to Cambridge....

Ys
Elizabeth

1 Benedetto Croce (1866-1952) – an influential Italian intellectual, philosopher and author. His book *Goethe* was published in English in 1923, although EMW, who read Italian easily, may have had it in the original.
2 EMW's younger brother – see Introduction for EMW's family.

Friday, July 11th, 1924

Hill Hall,
Epping

My dearest Aunt,

I am sending back "Catullus", not that I have finished it all, but because I am so inundated with things that he is lying idle. I wonder what becomes of the mythical days of which one says "After July – th I shall have "plenty of time" to read such and such!"? It is all illusion. I am ploughing along through the Republic and am within 3 pages of the end of Book I. It is very slow and laborious but huge fun. I make an average speed of 3 pages an hour.

Gran is very well and in good spirits. An instance, of similar nature to H.B. and Lord Haldane[1], is too good not to tell you. I asked her this morning how she had liked "C". She had written mark you full of enthusiasm while in the middle that "his writing fascinates me". She now said: "Oh I thought the first part very dull, the whole thing too long, and then his writing is very amateurish. I don't think it at all well written."!! And then the illuminating remark making all clear "<u>Edith Wharton</u> can't bear it"!!!!!

I see by the papers that a man I used to know called Coxhas brought out a marvellous edition of Sappho with two translations 1 literal and 1 verse. The review I read was a paean of praise. It is an outrageous price £2 something so I shall hope to scan its pages in the R.I.[2]

I took down your "Impressions" to look for something the other day and of course began at Page 1 and devoured the whole thing again. I read all the letters with more intelligence than before when I was a fool and galloping on to know what happened next. I am still gasping. I must stop about this or I shall go on for hours. I can't read vol II with the detachment with which it is written. It is terrific.

I look nervously through this for glaring mistakes in spelling. I am now convinced about being a bad speller since finding an angry scrawl across a page of fruitless and prolonged mathematics consisting of one word

"wrotten!"
Yr loving
<u>E.</u>

1 Richard Burdon Haldane (1856-1928). 1st Viscount Haldane of Cloane – politician, lawyer and author of a number of philosophical works. Uncle of J.B.S. Haldane and Naomi Mitchison. Was actively involved in the founding of both L.S.E. and Imperial College.
2 The Royal Institution, founded 1799, aimed to teach and disseminate scientific and technological discoveries, particularly with a view to practical applications.

July 15th, 1924

Dearest Aunt,

I. Exhaustive search has failed to locate your linen coat on these premises. Ethel says you brought two linen skirts and one coat; that the coat and one skirt went to the laundry and came back and that she packed them. I said it seemed strange that the coat got out of the trunk between here and Woking, but the argument did not impress her.

II. [*More about clothes*]

It is inexplicable to me that Mrs Wharton should not think Impressions better than Streaks. I put it down to that disintegrating mania for "shortness" on preference to length in every case which seems to be the worst sign of the wrottenness of this age and the death of the arts. I am stung to these remarks by the eternal wrangles over St Joan which go on unabated here, It is surely a hopeless and meaningless criticism that if a thing is good throughout it shouldn't be long. Just think of the Greeks who sat at the theatre the whole day in the sun on marble steps!!!! We are a weak-kneed (or perhaps weak-seated would be more apt) lot and self indulgent and intellectually slothful.

I am so interested in what you say about the purging effect of writing. I doubt if it be applicable to the ordinary mortal. I mean that the faculty of exteriorizing personal experience is the peculiarity of the artist, isn't it, and makes the difference between them and ordinary people? This particularly in reference to your religious beliefs and the Mass.

[On a life of Sir Isaac Newton, one of Elizabeth's great heroes]

One thing especially delighted me. When the Principia was in the press under direction of the Royal Society, Halley writes

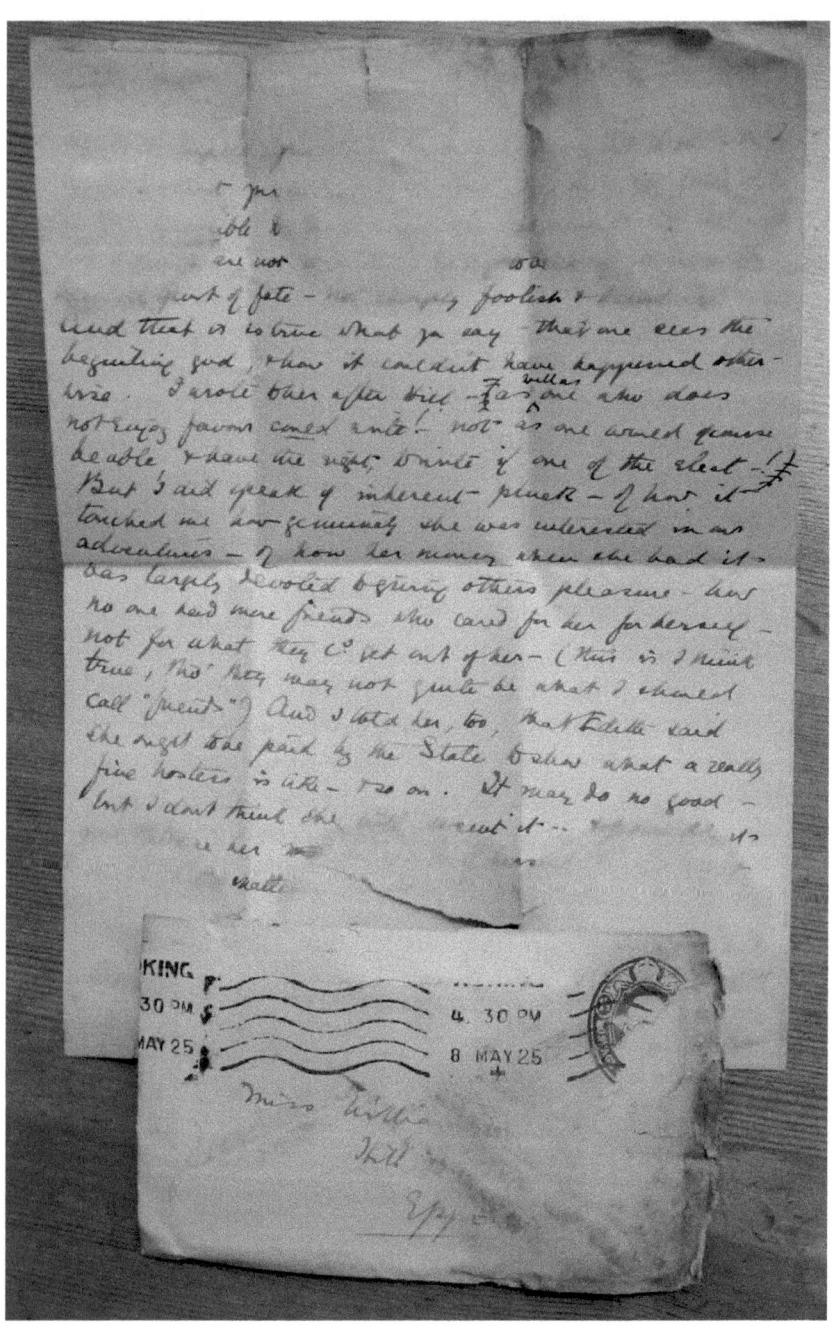

One of many damaged letters from Ethel Smyth to Elizabeth

to Newton explaining a delay "by reason of the presidents attendance on the King, and the absence of the vice-president whom the good weather has drawn out of town"!!!! This is what the world-shaking Principia had to wait for!

[On gardening and her reading in Greek]

Yr
E

Already in 1924, Ethel's elder sister, Mary Hunter, was beginning to suffer economic problems. Ethel wrote to her brother:

September 30th, 1924

Coign. Woking
Telephone:Woking 467
Telegrams: Smyth.Mayford

My dear Bob ....

I had a killing 4 days at Hill – Mary buying gowns at rate of 2 per week; Billy and Eliz over inclined if anything to economy and Charles not extravagant. Visit from agent and after that a dramatic scene at each meal, with wonderful angelic tones and wavings of hands "all I say is my dear boys, I do implore you don't get into debt at Oxford – for if you do I cant help you. We shall be beggars – no coals – no nothing – and if you do get into trouble you must just go to prison....for I cant bail you out." – All this because she wanted to have a flat in London this winter besides Hill, and, the daughter had said, if coals are to fail in May, this is awful extravagance.

Phyllis: You mean have a flat and let Hill?? In the winter?
M. with heroism: Yes!! If it must be! I'm ready!!
P: But no one will take Hill in the winter....
Eliz.calmly: If we are going to live in rooms at Epping may I know now so as to say the new telescope stand is to be sent there not here?
At this point I broke down....at last
Mary (gravely): You may laugh but it is not a laughing

matter.

<u>Ethel</u>: I only laughed because the idea of rooms <u>in Epping</u> is so very fantastic.

(There M. laughed herself)

Your loving
E.

In later years, when Elizabeth used to spend Christmas and New Year with her mother and grandmother at Cromer, Ethel and she would exchange very long letters, perhaps in part to combat the boredom of the occasion. In 1924, only two random pages have emerged, one on the subject of paintings. Ethel regretted that Phyllis did not buy one of the pictures at an exhibition and much admired another one "under Laura Lovat's[1] picture". She went on to encourage Elizabeth to learn German: "I believe if you got a foundation in a month, Berlitz wd get you along in no time".

1 Laura Lovat, the wife of Simon Fraser, 16th Lord Lovat, nursed Ethel's great friend, Maurice Baring, towards the end of his life and wrote a memoir of him: *Maurice Baring: a Postscript*, 1947.

1925

This bundle was similar to the others, tied with thin string; some of the envelopes grubby, and with more water damage than other years – indeed a number of the envelopes were almost unopenable and best left for someone with more technical skill, while a number of pages were so mildewed as to be illegible. Unlike most of the packets, these letters were out of order, although the string had clearly never been untied, hence the most damaged are not necessarily consecutive.

Many of the letters from the first half of 1925 are about Ethel and Elizabeth's long-held plan to visit Greece. Elizabeth's passion for the country had begun years before, when in her teens she fought to break with the usual pattern of a "young lady's education" and learn classical Greek. But, although she was to visit it again many times before the Colonels seized power in 1967, this journey with Ethel was to be one of the high-points of her life. It was to result in Ethel's *A Three-Legged Tour in Greece*, published in 1927. Elizabeth's own copy carries the dedication: "To my beloved yokefellow Elizabeth from Ethel Smyth" March 5, 1927. As always, they exchanged notes on their reading and on New Year's Day 1925, Ethel wrote that she had begun Herodotus and was enclosing some notes on practical matters now missing. She was also battling to finish work for publication and arrange for various performances of *Fête Galante* and *Entente Cordiale*:

January 1st, 1925

I was so sorry abt Mid. Nights Dream but I was panting to get back to work and can't leave it just yet a while – just certain finishing touches of a delicate order requiring happy thoughts...and one doesn't have them – at least my light weight brain hasn't – except at home...

January 3rd, 1925

Elizabeth replied in answer to a letter now missing:

Dearest Aunt,
Ha. Ha. I have got to the Battle of Plataea....
The story of Miss Somerville's[1] engineer is very good. Rather like a nursery governess of ours who when sacked by Mother for neglect of us said that her trouble was that she disliked children!! I feel for her deeply, but still!
I am so glad Bob thought the acting entertainment good. Sir Fritz Ponsonby[2] is a rock of great strength on these occasions. Simon Elwes[3], a beautiful young papist, was also worth his keep and more.

Your loving
Elizabeth

1 ES had had one of her passionate friendships with Edith Somerville. Much of their correspondence is in the Somerville Ross Collection at Queen's University Belfast.
2 Frederick (Fritz) Ponsonby is often mentioned in these letters. He was a great friend of the family, had held many court positions and was the father of Loelia (Lelia) – see August 1st, 1930.
3 Simon Elwes (1902-1975) - portrait painter, joined the Welsh Guards and served in North Africa in WWI, becoming an unofficial war-artist. The Elweses were a Catholic recusant family and friends of the Williamson clan.

The Smyth family and indeed the Williamsons had a passion for dressing up and theatre of all kinds, and the family letters are filled with references to them. One of Mary Hunter's proudest moments was performing in Hedworth Williamson's play *The "Teraph"* at the Court Theatre in 1900. It was advertised in *The Times*, 17th May, 1900, p.8. and harshly criticized in the *New York Dramatic Mirror* on June 2nd.

THE "TERAPH"

*A Classical Play
in Blank Verse
by*
HEDWORTH WILLIAMSON

Phalena (*Queen Regent*) Mrs. Charles Hunter
Itylus ⎰ *her* ⎱ Miss Jaqueline Hope
Selene ⎱ *Step-children* ⎰ Miss Kathleen Hunter
Nitocris (*Phalena's Attendant*)
  Miss Margaret Birkbeck
Heliodora (*Nurse to Itylus*) Mr. Geoffrey Birkbeck
Johannes (*a Christian*) Sir Rennell Rodd, k.c.m.g.
Life ⎰ *Mummers* ⎱ Miss Norah Burdon
Death ⎱ ⎰ Mr. Hedworth Williamson
Centurian - Mr. Edward Mitchell-Innes
Aglaïa (*a Dancer*) Miss Helen Henschel
Myro (*a Singer*) - Miss Norah Burdon
The Teraph (*Mummified Head of Hyperion*)
  Mr. Hedworth Williamson

Court Attendants, Dancers, Soldiers, &c.

The Hon. Mrs. R. Parker, Lady Rodd,
Mrs. Macpherson-Grant, Mrs. Edward Herbert,
Mrs. George Batten, Mrs. George Swinton,
Miss Amy Troubridge, Miss Clare Davies,
Miss Phyllis Hunter, Miss Sylvia Hunter,
and Miss Gwendoline Gardner.

Mr. Denzil Cope, Mr. Charles Goetz,
Mr. Montagu Wood and Mr. Edward Behr.

Cast List for *The "Teraph"*

January 7th, 1925

Dearest Aunt

[On Tempe]

Just imagine meeting eagles, snakes and tortoises out walking. I fear the longing for Greece will burn me to ashes before we get there. I pray you not to fade away from lack of food, liver or not!

I suppose I shall turn to Urania again with the old ardour next when I "set down" to it but at the moment the Greek fever is absolutely devouring.

Your loving
'Ηλιξαβεθ

January 8th, 1925

The following day, Ethel replied, discussing books to read on Greece, etc., *Paradise Lost* - a poem for which Elizabeth had an absolute passion - as well as musical plans and how she does not want to let them interfere with Greece. This would have been something of a dilemma, given Ethel's endless battles to have her work performed.

Elizabeth! I dared not tell you yesdy – Tomorrow there is a session at the Roll. Which I attend "to consider the feasibility of performing F.G. [*Fête Galante*] <u>this term</u>", Now it may be that as Sir H[1] is in love with E.C. [*Entente Cordiale*] which he means to do in the summer, he will suggest to me to do both operas in the summer term (about July) and this is what I shall urge – as together they are only two hours music.

On the other hand, it is probably absolutely possible for me to say: "I cant be there from March 25 to Ap. 23rd – indeed they will probably say (or think) what H.B. did when I told him the mechanism of the harp was so clumsy that you cant play f natural with one hand and f# with the other: "I consider that a perfect blessing."

---

1 Presumably Sir Hugh Allen (1869-1946) conductor, academic and Director of the Royal College of Music from 1918 to 1937.

January 9th, 1925

Dearest Aunt,

[On tracing a Greek quotation]

I long to hear the result of your session at the R. Coll. I don't quite gather what the verdict most favourable to our Greek plans will be. But I assure you truthfully that if given time for prayer I could attain the
"Thy way not mine oh Dame
 However dark it be"
frame of mind, if it is an urgent matter that you postpone Greece until the autumn...!! The thought freezes the heart I confess but after all I profess to follow the Muses too and we know that their service is fraught with suffering. So don't <u>on any account</u> put me into the balance when you weigh the pros and cons.

My quotation about Tempe is from Shelley's Hymn of Pan. The cabalistic signature is only Elizabeth in Greek letters!

There is a passage in Paradise Lost that I can't resist transcribing for you. Its' sentiment is so beautiful. Adam is giving Eve a discourse on the wonders of astronomy and the power of God (Aurora Borealis type).

And Eve says:
"My author and disposer, what thou bidst
Unargued I obey: So God ordains;
God is thy law; thou mine: To know no more
Is woman's happiest knowledge and her praise."

And so on in the same vein. Adam is <u>the</u> most awful prig, and I always think of Ned Mitchell Innes[1] wandering about a garden with nothing on!....But the passages about the stars and the heavenly host far outweigh all this, viz.
"Then came still evening on...
And o'er the dark her silver mantle threw."
Was anything more lovely ever?

Ys <u>E.</u>

On the same day, Ethel sent a postcard to reassure Elizabeth that there would not be a disastrous clash between music and travel:

All well thank goodness abt F[ête].G[*alante*]. The performance will be <u>quite</u> early in March...and they are going to repeat it together with the new opus in the summer term (abt July) Great doings, aren't they! But oh! I have my work cut out for me till March 23rd!!

1 Several members of the Innes family are mentioned in passing. This perhaps refers to Edward Mitchell-Innes (1863-1932), a lawyer.

January 11th, 1925

She pursues the same theme a couple of days later:

...I think I should die if we don't go this spring – our date is perfect.

If Sir Hugh will do Entente Cordiale in the half term of Midsummer (from 15th June to 25th July) I am perfectly safe. All hangs on that – and on my working now – persistently, blindly, without looking up.

The whole business of printing and proofs – of all that is the horror. I am going to try and get it published in London – not by the U[niversity of] E[dinburgh] (my real people). That wd knock Greece on the head indeed!...

February 2nd, 1925

At this date, Ethel Smyth was almost 67 and, although she had always been a very active sportswoman – riding, mountaineering, tennis and, latterly, golf – she worried whether she would be up to the trip.

...I dread being a drag on you that way – on the other hand I feel so frightfully well on expeditions, and feel that mules <u>are</u> the solution. (All this time I have quietly been building breeches and have invented a gaiter to wear <u>over</u> golf shoes! riding and walking! Am trying it on Thursday – momentous day!

My only other trouble (tho' am writing to look for routes today) that... if you cant start till 25 March and must be back April 21 it is an almost too tight fit! It will leave only a day or two over a fortnight for "seeing Greece!" As regards myself, I feel that if your Mother objected to your returning alone (<u>rot!</u> I travelled everywhere alone after my 19th year!) one could find someone to convoy you back – and I could stay on a week or so. If I were back by May 5th it would be loads of time. But what I want to know is, as you are not a resident College, <u>would</u> the world come to an end if you missed the beginning of term?? I do thoro'ly appreciate your hatred of the very thought, yet honestly I don't see how you are ever going to be free for a classical and sublime lark of this kind unless you violate first principles. I do think it wd be an <u>awful</u> rush. Of course with motors and charabancs (which doubtless are to be had) much can be done and we musn't think of expense. The only question is how much fragrance one loses by rushing? This is what I want to get out of Sir R.R.[1]- and incidentally I feel sure a dragoman is a good investment....I do feel E.C. may go to blazes – tho' I am working on and on like a lunatic at it and now am certain that all the material for study will be corrected by me (printed proofs) before I go...

Almost every day there would be a postcard or letter on the question of guidebooks, dealings with Cook's, general plans, and complicated calculations relating to railway timetables and fares. Some days there were more than one and Ethel might add as many as half a dozen PSs in red ink with exuberant underlings, garnishing the bottom of the page and both sides of the envelope. Besides golf, the other recurring topic was the struggle to finish everything she had in hand before their departure. Ethel Smyth generally wrote her own librettos and the following presumably refers to *Entente Cordiale* on which she was working at the time.

... However all will end well – and the frightful joy of having turned out, in one fell swoop – without a single hold up for lack of oil – a really good lyric, - (which means that every bit of printed stuff will be read by me before we depart) is what really matters. You will like it! So will the great J.S.S.[2] and it will make such a good start – the 1st singing number it will be – and tune people up into the proper key. I think its one of the best numbers of the lot...

As a younger woman Ethel had been a passionate and competent horsewoman but now, she had various rheumatic complaints and had not ridden for a number of years. In March, she was writing:

> Gaiters arrived and tomorrow I sally forth on a very lamblike animal all alone!!
> (This is the hardest thing I have ever done let me tell you) Kathleen says "it has such an easy gallop". Gallop forsooth -

And a few days later:

> Ride quite a success – 1½ hours and shant I be stiff tomorrow. Very mild animals – lips made of hairpins – action to match. I didn't <u>dare</u> canter or go off the high road but did much painful trotting and felt <u>quite at home</u> (in a <u>not</u> very comfortable home either)

Meanwhile, Elizabeth was concerned less with health and the details of travel - "..am taking my smoked glasses as a precaution.." or "Is it burdening your memory too much to ask you to get me an umbrella ring?.." - than with family finances and whether she should leave her mother alone to deal with the problems.

1 James Rennell Rodd (1858-1941) was a classical scholar and diplomat. FMW had a copy of his translations from *The Greek Anthology*. Ambassador to Italy from 1908-1919, he felt that Britain was ignorant of Italy's part in World War I and invited Rudyard Kipling out to the Italian Front to write articles about the fighting in the Dolomites and along the Isonzo (www.kipling.org.uk/rg_mountains_intro.htm).
Rodd's daughter, Gloria, married Simon Elwes, a friend of the Williamson family.
2 John Singer Sargent (1856-1925) – see Introduction.

March 14th, 1925

Dearest Aunt Ethel,
I hear from Mother that she has told you of the predicaments of the families' finances and the fact of leaving here and so on. I thought at first and am inclined still to think it shirking on

Elizabeth Williamson, by John Singer Sargent

my part to go to Greece and leave mother to cope with Gran. I know it doesn't make any difference really – I mean my being here in the flesh does not alter the fact of it being Mother who in the nature of things has practically all the coping to do and it is this that inclines me to think it all right. But I do not see the thing at all clearly. People say that one does in crises but I don't seem to. It is not the financial aspect that strikes me so much because I can pay Mother back and also that this crisis is somewhat different from the previous ones (!!!) in being not so much a question of ready cash <u>now</u> as a change of one's whole style of life.

It is interesting to see the reaction of the theatrical temperament of the central figure to all this. But it is also a strain on the less theatrical temperaments of the household.

Your loving E

Descriptions of their preparations continue, based on advice given by them by Sargent and Rennell Rodd. The contrast with Ryanair-style travel today is amusing:

The things recommended by Sir R we yet lack are <u>Citronella</u> and <u>the Super Keating</u> [which I hope to get the name of out of Miss Peel today when she returns to London. O how I <u>hate</u> erratic people!!] and <u>Maggi</u>. I have a small store of <u>quinine, Calomel, Aspirin and Epsom Salts</u> – also <u>Lysol</u> (for gargling) – All this takes no room.

Food (<u>for Salomea Larissa journey of which I have grave doubts!)</u> butter, figs and a flask of whiskey – and condensed milk + 2½ pounds of tea.

My plan of luggage is this – a cabin trunk for registering straight thro' to Athens from London and (with me) a Gladstone bag, a leather bag (built for me by H.B. for books etc.) and a parcel of rugs, fur coats, etc and the donkey bags which will go to Larissa with us.....

So glad you are taking Prison as I can plan out my H.B. Requiem an old dream...and my <u>strong</u> dreams come true![1] Am going to Woking to buy a small tin opener and corkscrew. I think <u>sardines</u> wd be a good thing to take - but am not sure because oil is so very indiscrete...."

And there were last moment preparations:

> Casson says dragomen and dogs are the only drawbacks in Greece! I hope this is so!

Ethel Smyth's opera *The Prison* was finally composed in 1930 and Virginia Woolf was to write a description of one of the rehearsals:

> On Monday I went to hear her rehearse. A vast Portland Place house with the cold wedding cake Adams plaster: shabby red carpets; flat surfaces washed with dull greens. The rehearsal was in a long room with a bow window looking on, in fact in, to other houses ... a barren brick outlook ... Ethel stood at the piano in the window, in her battered felt, her jersey and short skirt, conducting with a pencil. There was a drop at the end of her nose ... Ethel's pince nez rode nearer and nearer the tip of her nose. She sang now and then; and once, taking the bass, made a cat squalling sound -- but everything she does with such forthrightness, directness, that there is nothing ridiculous ... As she strides and turns and wheels about to us perched mute on chairs she thinks this is about the most important event now taking place in London. And perhaps it is.[1]

1 Cited in *Ethel Smyth: A Biography*, Christopher St John, Longmans. London, New York and Toronto, 1959, p.225.

For the next weeks there were no letters, because Ethel and Elizabeth were together in Greece from March 24th to May 4th, 1925. It was, on the whole a wonderful period, with the exception of one event. ES writes:

> At Athens a great shock awaited – news of the death of J.S. Sargent, the great painter, who had been a close friend of many in my family for a quarter of a century. He had drawn E's portrait just before we started for Greece, and had specially urged us at the cost of any effort to see Meteora. Our letters to my sister – E's grandmother – had interested and excited him to such a degree that he declared that he must go to Greece again by-and-by! Curiously enough, this portrait being intended as a birthday present for E., it was antedated by him: "15th April" – the day after his own death!

One cannot conceive of a more wonderful end than his. As full of energy, as completely master of his powers, whether as creator or participator in life, to have just finished and personally superintended the shipment of the work of his which, I always think, interested him more than any other, the decorations for the Boston Library; and then, on the eve, almost, of following his work to America, to be found one morning early by his servant, to all appearance quietly asleep in his bed, a volume of Voltaire still in his hand...Who can desire a more perfect death for himself or others?[1]

1 *A Three-Legged Tour in Greece*, London 1927, p.122

Both Ethel and Elizabeth were very careful over accounts, Ethel because she had never had much money and Elizabeth because she had seen the dire consequences of her beloved grandmother's thoughtless extravagance. Details of their expenditure on the Greek trip appear in a brief note dated May 7th and on the back of a letter from the Press Club, very water stained and mildewed.

Elizabeth ended up owing Ethel £11. Their expenses were remarkably modest, especially as regards buying souvenirs – Ethel spent a few shillings on a parasol and a scarf as presents and Elizabeth paid rather less for a cushion. Ethel seems to have spent c.£88 for the trip and Elizabeth £64.7.3.

The Press Club letter sent on April 5th, 1925 from St Bride's House (it is still at more or less the same address) invites Ethel to a "Ladies Dinner" on April 25th adding:

"On these occasions we always like to entertain women who have distinguished themselves in some branch of art or in public life, and if we can by your presence pay our humble tribute to the art of Music we shall be very happy.

Later the same day – Elizabeth must have already been at the University of London – a postcard added more details to their complicated calculations:

However the mere sight of your Premises in Bloomsbury gives me confidence that you will work out the bill in masterly fashion.

And crossed in red ink:

Is by any chance my white handled knife in your dinner knife case?

Elizabeth, however, had been plunged straight back into the family's financial crisis:

Thursday [*sic*, but actually Tuesday]**, May 7th, [1925]**

Hill Hall

Most beloved Aunt,
Herewith the French money. I think of you with awe as I might of Newton applying his latest researches to the planetary motions.

I think Gran has more or less come down to the truth about the future – at least more than we thought. She dwells constantly on the smallness of the house in London and the necessity for ruthless throwing away. Also she has accepted the fact of having no car.

[Details of Mary Hunter's health]

She has just rattled off to London fortified by a terrifying amount of brandy in black tea! She firmly declined either G^1. or me going with her. She talks of either Sargent or plans the whole time, as Mother said. But I think that so much part of the childishness in her that we agree about – she just talks about what is in her mind. She reads nothing but letters from her friends about Sargent – over and over again. It cuts one to the heart. I don't know why I tell you all this which is useless and harrowing – but I feel very strongly how you and I coming back into the middle of things are in a different stage about it all than the others. I cannot feel the faintest degree of anger and "She brought it on herself" mood. Even in moments of coldest reason and sentiment banished there is a grand style about the summit and the fall – something Helen-like that makes me see the beguiling "Poor shameless me."

She is lunching with Sir Philip Sassoon. I heap blessings on his head. He is a friend to her.

Work!!!!

Yr loving
E

I have sent you a (much reduced in size – be comforted) photograph of the Sargent drawing of me, with some compunction, as I regard littering peoples houses one of the major sins.

[On other photographs from their tour of Greece, some of which were eventually used as illustrations in A Three-Legged Tour*].*

Later, she wrote again:

1 Griselda Grant Lawson (born 1905), known as Grizzie, was Elizabeth's cousin and the daughter of ES's niece, Sylvia.

Thursday [sic, but actually Tuesday] night, May 7th [1925]

My dearest Aunt,

I wrote this morning in a moment of intense depression about Gran and am remorseful and think I may have been exaggerating and morbid and harrowing you to no purpose. She came back from London looking better – not so fading away looking – and in better spirits too. She had found a house – the right size and that she liked and this has given a spurt of the old zest and interest in things that seemed utterly absent last night and this morning. She was very pleased by a letter from you which she got on her way to London – and talked of you in a very soft strain last night.

I saw Dr Erskine (Epping doctor) today and asked him what he thought. He says her blood pressure is inclined to be high and that she ought not to do so much. But how to stop her!?

I disposed of the potted meats and "our old soup" to Mr Stanley for distribution to the deserving poor!

I miss you infernally.

Yr loving E

At this point among Ethel's papers, there was a very short note from Mary Hunter – the only thing in her hand that has come to light, apart from her girlhood diary of 1871-2. Ethel describes their diary craze in *Impressions that Remain* and their parents' disapproval of the habit, which eventually led to her burning hers.

Thursday [sic, but actually Tuesday], 7th May [1925]

Darling Ethel – Bless you for your dear letter.

Elizabeth is a most charming sympathetic and understanding companion and how she enjoyed her trip with you – such a perfect 6 weeks falls to the lot of few people.

I am too busy to worry – and for the future. Hope is the only possibility – or Death.

Ys. M

The following day, Ethel wrote Elizabeth a long and interesting letter on her relationship with her elder sister, unfortunately very damaged with water and mildew so that much is illegible. Their feelings for each other were complex. As she tells in *Impressions that Remain*, Ethel had always felt a measure of jealousy for Mary's greater charms and had the sense that she was much less important to Mary than Mary was to her. In adulthood the rivalry took on another dimension. Ethel had fought and struggled for her musical education and career, and had always had to count every penny, while Mary had effortlessly drifted into the position of "patron of the arts" and was perhaps too casual in her generosity: "After all it is only money". These resentments became far more acute when an impoverished Mary Hunter seemed incapable of forgoing luxuries her sister had never had and looked like becoming an impossible burden on the rest of the family.

May 8th, 1925

[*Four lines illegible.*]

"....been the sport of fate – not simply foolish and blind. And that is so true what you say – that one sees the beguiling god, and how it couldn't have happened otherwise. I wrote to her after Hill – as well as one who does not enjoy favour <u>could</u> write! – not of course as one would be able, and have the right, to write if one of the elect! But I did speak of inherent – pluck – of how it touched me how genuinely she was interested in our adventures – of how her money when she had it was largely devoted to giving others pleasure – how no one had more friends who cared for her for herself not for what they cd get out of her – (this is I think true, tho' they may not be quite what I should call "friends") And I told her, too, that Edith[1] said she ought to be paid by the State to show what a really fine hostess is like – and so on. It may do no good – but I don't think she will resent it...and possible it may please her....."

[10 lines illegible]

"...did you? Tho' it's a very good likeness" (!!) – To proceed. The only thing that fusses me is the terrifying lot of stimulant. Do the doctors know about that? <u>Because I think they should?</u> It is frightfully bad for her – or anyone.

I send you the last issue of the Grecian Accts at £1=118 lira and including return of 145 francs today – I find it makes a difference of exactly 10/- in total! – Really our tour was cheap £110 each for 41 days – [2]

I'm just going out to plough round with a card as I want to play in the Spring Meeting on Tues next. If I don't tie myself up thus I shant play at all. Shant be able to begin orchestrating until tomorrow – ....F.Galante...."

[4 lines at the bottom of the page illegible.]

Later the same day, she wrote again, this time about Greece and her work:

By the way do send me our Greek programme. I think you handed it to me in Athens and I wisely refused to have it then

– begging you to keep it – I am putting all the M.S. together till time permits for <u>the</u> Opus. I <u>have not begun to orchestrate yet</u>!!!

A couple of days later, Ethel responded to Elizabeth's concerns about her Grandmother, but in a letter so water-stained that only part can be read:

> Dearest Eliz I don't think you were a bit morbid and on the contrary it is a comfort to me that you see things as I do and that we can express our feeling to each other. I had a <u>dear</u> letter from yr Gr.mother and feel that choked pipes have been sluiced (what a pretty metaphor freshly inspired by ?). It is good news that she has got to bed rock in her visions of the future – how I wish the Hill affair cd be settled and done for. But patience is never a commodity easy to lay yr hand on....

Indeed, Ethel found the difficulty of restraining her sister from extravagance deeply frustrating. On May 23rd, after her thoughts on Greece and accounts of her latest games of tennis and golf - a feature of her letters for many years – she wrote:

> You are a dear to keep the BM [*Bosun's Mate*] for me – and I think I shall have done my scoring sooner than expected – perhaps about June 2nd or 4th ! So you wont have to wait long. - What your mother wrote is that unless the situation is faced it is a case of bankruptcy <u>after</u> yr Gr's death – if not sooner – and <u>if the expenditure goes on</u> (parties etc etc) she will not be party to what is dishonesty and will withdraw the W. family from a situation of apparent connivance You say "<u>what's the use of remonstrating?</u>" But it is of use. The cumulative pressure gets through – finally – and I consider the proposal to Lady H. (to let) is one result of it - ! When [people] (on principle) wont listen and yet know their bluff does no more good, they eventually do begin to listen <u>if y. go on enough.</u> That is why I have always been urging to face up to the dilemma – I think indeed it's a matter of probity to do so and to all say "we all <u>know</u> its not the coal trade[3] - and intend to see things put as straight as can be, or else part company." That old testament thing about "Jehovah

hardening the kings heart" etc. or stopping up his ears – is so true. The god you have worshipped does see your continual faithfulness in this manner – and nothing but hammering away one outside shell of bluff and pretence after another can do any good. I am sure the seeming acquiescence which has been your unfortunate mother's role for so long is all wrong. No one should acquiesce in such situations. – I shall try and get Vernon's last book[4] – By the by I don't know when you posted (or who posted yr letter of the 20th but it only arrived this morning with the other of May 23rd from the R.I....[5]

A number of letters are missing, but Elizabeth had clearly tried to defend her to Ethel, pointing out her stoicism at being forced to change her entire way of life at the age of 70, as well as leave her much-loved Hill Hall. Ethel replied:

Yes – I quite agree – Your Gran is magnificent in her courage.
O if you are sorry for me in my homecoming I am still sadder for you in your home leaving. And most for yr Mother.

And as a PS:

Do you think it wd be decent to ask them to spare you just now? I rather fear not.

Elizabeth perhaps felt the catastrophe less than she might otherwise have done, as she was beginning to do well in her career; a public lecture she had given was a success, she was considering the possibility of publications. But departure was imminent:

Tell me when you all go where? Ethel enquired

And tell your family I have succeeded in getting E. Cordiale put off (as to quasi public performance, but not as to study) till the beginning of next term. (I do wonder when it begins at Colleges).

As well as finishing work on *Entente Cordiale*, Ethel was beginning to plan out a book on their Greek travels and reported excitedly:

I've had a huge packet of Greek photos – his own snapshots, sent me by a young man I met on the train coming from Gloucester!!

Although, for once she was not wresting with deadlines:

It will be too odd – for the first time in years I shall have an epoch with no chores and pistols at head – just freedom....
"PS: New Pan a little duck.

Ethel Smyth with one of the Pans

The puppy was one in Ethel's series of Old English Sheepdogs, all called Pan and, as she remarks a two or three days later, far from perfectly behaved:

> ...The puppy is adorable – but fearfully fond of turning out the wastepaper basket and as I am correcting orchestral parts I expect a "O Diamond Diamond" [6] incident shortly.

Ethel was over-optimistic about her rhythm of work slackening. A couple of days later, she was inviting Elizabeth to the dress rehearsals for *Fête Galante* and for what was to be the first performance of *Entente Cordiale*, on which she had been working since their return from Greece. She adds a complicated and exhausting schedule of rehearsals, broadcasts, performances – and trains:

> It's a hideous bit of life – planned without mercy for horse-flesh by Sir Hugh Allen[7] who has no idea of what the execution of his wishes really means. It is like some people's ignorance of the value of money!

In the end, the performances went well – although normal typography will not do justice to Ethel's underlinings:

> The second perf. was splendid..... The orchestra accompanied as it has never been known to do!! As C. Benck said (and he knows me for a dragon on rhythm) "we felt they were afraid of you!!..."

1 The family had several friends called Edith. This could refer to Edith Wharton, a frequent visitor at Hill Hall who, indeed, at one time considered buying a neighbouring property, or possibly Edith Somerville.
2 In fact, although done in an extremely economical way for the time, the trip was not cheap by modern standards. www.measuringworth.com estimates £110 in 1925 as having the purchasing power of £4,890.00 in 2010, according to their most conservative estimate.
3 The reference is not clear, although the family had mining interests in northern England and much of their wealth came from coal.
4 Vernon Lee, pen-name of Violet Paget (1856-1935) author and friend of Ethel Smyth and cousin of Sargent. The volume in question was probably *Proteus or The Future of Intelligence*, which was published in 1925.
5 ES occasionally comments on the inefficiency of the post, when letters have taken more than 24 hrs to arrive.

6 The quote refers to the famous – although perhaps apocryphal - remark by Isaac Newton: "Oh Diamond! Diamond! Thou little knowst what mischief thou hast done." when his pet dog overturned a candle and burned his papers with notes on many years of research.

7 Hugh Allen (1869-1946) – musician, academic and conductor. At this date, he was director of the Royal College of Music, as well as holding the chair of music at Oxford.

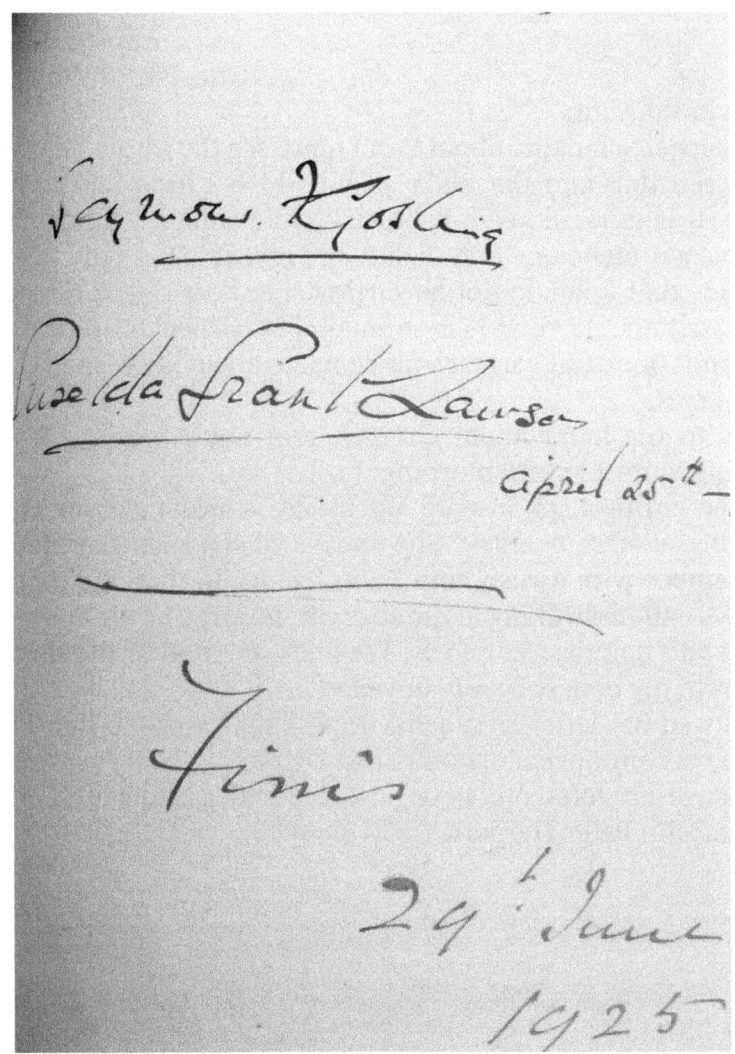

Seymour Gosling and Griselda Grant Lawson, the last of the guests at Hill Hall

Letters of Ethel's seem to be missing at this point, but two or three weeks later, Elizabeth wrote:

August 18th [1925]

Appley Hall
Ryde, Isle of Whyte

Beloved Aunt,

Deepest sympathy about Pan I quite see the whole relation between that and the Blake poem which I have before me now. It is miraculous in its' divine childishness I think, and the way it melts one and makes one cry. It is the only poem I know that I should not be surprised to hear Christ himself had written. Do you? It is so much his particular spirit and reminds one of all his heavenly remarks about lilies, sparrows and taxes.

As to the letter about Greece[1], that made me cry. I am having quite a tearful morning! [....]

Her enthusiasm worked up in me a nostalgia for that darling austere country. She speaks of its' silence which I remember with a rush, and I can feel again that "tightened up" strenuous walking in the sun with no large meals and soft beds and <u>pointless</u> comforts. We knew the best of life then I knew in my bones. Beauty unveiled.

I loved her letter so much I think I shall write to her. She didn't see my apricot moon rise at Delphi.

I have my telescope here now and star gaze to the small hours with Peter Herbert.

Yr lv
E

1 Sender unidentified.

Ethel's dog, Pan III had turned savage and had to be put down. She tells the saga of her many dogs in *Inordinate (?) Affection* and describes this particular incident on pp.40-1:

The whole business preyed strangely on my mind, the more so because in two cases I knew about of dogs that had turned savage, the post mortem had revealed advanced heart disease; and O how well I remember that the only comfort was supplied by my great-niece Elizabeth Williamson, who introduced me to Blake's wonderful poem 'Night'. I learned it by heart and never have been able to say it to myself aloud without breaking down as one visualised the angels stealing to and fro at night among the wild beasts trying – alas! Not always successfully – to turn their hungry thoughts away from the defenceless sheep....

Ethel Smyth's note in her own copy of *Inordinate (?) Affection:*

By September, Mary Hunter had found somewhere to live in London – 2 Gloucester Square - but Ethel feared, rightly as it transpired, that her sister would be incapable of making sufficiently stringent cuts to her budget so as to avoid ruin:

> I think No.2 enchanting but I well see that mints of money are being spent. Philip Sassoon[1] who as you know loves her, says the worth of money is a thing she has less idea of than any one he has ever met!!

1 Philip Sassoon (1888-1939) – politician, collector and well-known host, cousin of the poet Siegfried Sassoon, painted by Sargent, who may have introduced him to the Hunters.

September 29th, 1925

A long letter to Elizabeth, who was staying with her mother at her house at Cromer - Morden House, Cliff Avenue - exemplifies the wonderful mixture of subjects so typical of Ethel:

- her reading, including "Pausanius Baedeker"
- "I always wanted to ask you exactly who Charles Darwin is – whether grandson of <u>the</u> Darwin...." – perhaps the physicist Charles Darwin (1887-1962), brother of Gwen Ravarat and brother-in-law of Geoffrey Keynes, Maynard's brother
- on the meaning of the phrase "Dutch mustering"
- family news
- enjoying a book by "Lunn" : "I suppose he is a son of the "Tours". Shall we give Lunn a chance instead of Cook next time?"
- her views of Belloc, Knox and Chesterton
- health

And then, she returns to a subject that always interested her passionately: making music, both training and performances, more easily accessible to the public, and also increasing women's opportunities, particularly for playing in orchestras:

> The crisis is merely the formulation of a scheme – a brilliant inspiration of mine that, germinating for years, has suddenly leapt Athena-like from my head. If it is not put through it will be because men <u>cannot</u> think or act clearly and sharply – always compromising – always wondering if one need go quite so far as that. Anyhow I've roughed it out for them (the objective is a repertory opera house in London, Suburbs, built up of the ex-students of the Mus. Colls., where <u>art</u> shall be generated and will see it through – I being the only person as they all allow, who <u>could</u> get a subsidy. But if they want to hedge, and try less drastic measures I shall say "All right" and go back with a sigh of relief to my own work – I've not got all the data I want –but the "1st Paper" has been typed and sent to wobblers – all their stupid objections and difficulties foreseen and answered in it...

- plans for meeting: "I do want you to see my new little Pan – he is all legs of course (rising 6 months) but too enchanting…"
- more on her reading

>   Maurice [Baring] wrote the other day that he wont make a will as he has nothing to leave but will 'give away'…now… at any time. Yesty arrived 2 gigantic <u>uncut</u> vols 'Memoirs of Count Kayserling'[1]. I felt rather blue – haven't thanked him yet.

1 Hermann Alexander Graf von Keyserling (1880-1946), philosopher, who aimed at the intellectual reorientation of Germany from militarism to democracy.

Elizabeth was again at Cromer for Christmas.

December 31st, 1925

On New Year's Eve, Ethel wrote her another long varied letter – probably intending to cheer her up. Cromer in the winter is a dispiriting place and the family atmosphere could hardly have been very lively.

- on a fine photograph of MH
- Christmas parties
- family news
- trouble with one of her choruses and suggestions on how they could be emended plans

..
>   I went in the bus with Gerald Balfour[1] the day before he went back to Scotland and thought bitterly of Mrs Pankhurst on the subject of how men abandon themselves to their infirmity…

On the back of the envelope:

>   Rebecca Clarke[2] came down here yesty. She's a perfect darling – and a lady. She was so enchanted at the Seal Man having found such favour. She's very very gifted and I loved the 2 songs (S.M.) was one she brought down. I cant remember which of you liked it so. I think your Grandmother.

1 See Introduction.
2 Rebecca Clarke (1886-1979) was a violinist and composer. She played a groundbreaking role in the acceptance of women in the world of professional music. Although talented and productive, she ceased writing, in part because she preferred to dedicate herself to her family. Her remark as regards composition would certainly have found an echo with Ethel: "I can't do it unless it's the first thing I think of every morning when I wake and the last thing I think of every night before I go to sleep." *The Seal Man* by John Masefield was set to music by Rebecca Clarke in 1922 and published in 1926.

1926

For some reason, no letters from Elizabeth and only two from Ethel have survived from this year, but one of Ethel's is of particular interest since it concerns her receiving an Honorary Degree at Oxford.

May 22nd, 1926

Hotel des Baignols,
Dax (Landes)

Do you see that the greatest poseur in Paris (Jean Cocteau) – a type only Paris can produce, has just been "converted" and I daresay will soon have the event filmed or put on a marionette theatre with dernier-cri music. I'll send you a little article in the *Temps* about it. I once met him just as he was entering on the siege of Paris, and he was holding forth on some theme or other, illustrating with astronomical illustrations so inaccurate that even I was constrained to say things like "But it's Saturn not Jupiter that has rings" etc. etc. This was at Clary's bedside and before one or two of Cocteau's adoring lady friends. Cocteau was quite knocked out pro tem, much to Clary's delight. This is the man who now has done Rome the honour!

After the death of Radiguet in 1923, Jean Cocteau had become seriously addicted to opium, but in 1925 worked to overcome it and somewhat clamorously (and temporarily) turned to the Catholic Church. Artistically, it was an extremely active period; writing, drawing and collaborating with Stravinsky on *Oedipus Rex*.

June 25th, 1926

City of Cork Steam Packet Cpy Limited

My dearest E. I loved your Warden who sent you his love and bemoaned your not being there. I said I was very glad you weren't – an austere touch which astonished him, It was really great fun tho' I was in physical misery – But mercifully the lumps confined themselves to my lower limbs and it was not until the next morning that I had one swelled cheek. Austin [sic] Chamberlain[1] came up to me which was dear of him and we had a great talk. We had a great reception at the

Encoenia [sic][2] which really was a lovely sight, the sun blazing through the S. windows of the Sheldonian – and I told him (which I hold) it was because the man in the street feels about him – sound and straight – as much as I do. The Master of Balliol[3] took me in – a youngish man with an awfully nice face but whose election caused heartburnings because he is a Communist. I avoided the Scylla of political discourse (we talked German literature all the time nearly) to fall into the Charybdis of ....R.C. polemics with my other neighbour, a professor with a Spanish name whose last word to me was "you see we happen to have the truth"!! He is a mad R.C... Spanish papa and English 'vert mama! imagine! And the whole thing arose through my asking where Campion Hall lay. I talked for ages and made friends with Sir John Simon[4] who looked splendid in his robes – ditto Lord Reading[5] whom I reminded that the last time I saw him he was trying me. He said "Ah! I hated having to administer the law against the militants because I had such deep admiration and sympathy for them." And when I said I thought the militant movement the most miraculous proof of the survival of idealism in a world supposed to be all materialistic combined with English practical sense he said "That is exactly it...." And I saw he meant it. Certainly the 2 Israelites were the best looking among the honored. Of my dear Sir M. Sadler[6] I saw nothing hardly – because thinking he was going to take me in to lunch I didn't seek him out specially...and he was not at the party. But Lord Lane [?] I loved and had discourse with. He told me no one recommended me...I was his own choice "tho' of course I consulted musicians". He said (I think) that there was "another suggestion" – but I think he meant just for honours – and that it was Vernon. Anyway next year the Warden of All Souls (your man) will be the Vice Chancellor and we must get in Vernon. I hear he will be very influential on that list, whereas this time it was the Chancellor's own list and it has been rubbed in that it has been a great honor that has been done me. The Mus.Docs come last and I was the only one, at the tail of the procession, so doubt if I shall be much to the fore in the photographs. They probably took one for the housekeeper or a female Bedel. But I saw myself in the

"Times" group sitting next Sir A. Chamberlain. There was a great search for Sir J. Barrie, but he couldn't be found, so the photographer said to Lord C. "Shall we carry on with what we have got?" They are priceless people.

I was very happy at Somerville College. The principal is a granddaughter of "Mrs Markham" (!!) [7] and her father whom Sargent painted – do you remember a man rather like Lord Wemyss? – was "little Mary' (!!) the youngest of the 3 – for "Mrs Markham" (i.e.Penrose) had no female child and felt the feminine touch was needed in that group!!! I like contemplating little Mary's gigantic whiskers.[8] Miss Penrose[9] is the last person to be my hostess, you'd think; tho' I believe she is an excellent Principal – by the way she was recently made a D.C.L. and Emily Sargent presented her with Sargent's gown [?]. She was so pleased and proud, as also at E.Sargent saying he had so particularly enjoyed painting her father, who was the first head (or perhaps founder?) of the British School at Athens. Miss P. learned modern Greek to help him (she's a great ancient Greek scholar) and won my heart in spite of very conventional manners by her adoration of Greece and her lovely paintings of Nauplia, the Parthenon, Crete and so on.

I made greatest pals at the dinner for me [?] and the Dk of Atholl[10] at Lady Margt Hall with the Greek Tutor, such a goodlooking woman about 30, who went and fetched various translations of Theocritus to compare the passage I love so in the "Two Fishermen" Idyll which Leconte Delille [sic] translates (referring to nets and fish spears) as "les instruments de leur fatigue". The only one who brought in that touch was Calverley. She fetched the original and his transl. bore out what she had said of his marvellous skill as translator. Two or 3 of his Horace odes are masterly. One about the Fountain of Bandusia and a gorgeous one about a ship. At that place I felt most deeply that a chief aim of your life should be to master ancient Greek. The forehand drive is important but O, Eliz! With your gift of tongues, gather, gather that rosebud while you are young! Later on languages become much more difficult. Miss Penrose talks it fluently and was urging even me to begin! But Mr Sidgwick who mysteriously turned up for that dinner (<u>not</u> for the Encoenia! [sic]) explained that my life was very <u>full</u>.....Poor Miss Penrose who is well over 60 and very tall, fell flat on her face on the asphalt crossing the Broad – can't think how she did it on the way home between Lunch and Garden Party. I said I hoped she wd rest for ½ hour at least...and she said "yes, I am feeling rather flushed after my fall."

Lunch at Mabel Price's – Present the <u>late</u> head of the B School at Athens, Wace, who left before we came and a very great archaeologist young and cross looking called...heavens I forget! Well he and Wace had never heard of the Minoan road from Sandy Pylos – looked more than superior abt it and broke to me that doubt exists whether the real Pylos is not one near <u>Olympia</u>! Isn't that a blow. I must look at the map to see if it simplifies the route of our charioteer. Am now writing in train to Skibbereen and it is too difficult so shall stop. Both my hands look like inflated hot water bottles....Am going to see a Dr at Skibbereen.

Yr loving
E

1 Austen Chamberlain (1863-1937) – half-brother of Neville Chamberlain, statesman and one of the recipients of the Nobel Prize for Peace in 1925.
2 Encaenia - the ceremony at which the University of Oxford confers honorary degrees and commemorates its benefactors. It usually takes place about mid-June.
3 Alexander Dunlop Lindsay (1879-1952) later Vice-Chancellor of the University.
4 John Simon (1873-1954) - Politician and Lord Chancellor.
5 Rufus Daniel Isaacs (1860-1935) - Lawyer, jurist and politician: Viceroy of India 1921-6.
6 Michael Sadler (1861-1943)- Historian and university administrator.
7 "Mrs Markham" was the pseudonym of Elizabeth Penrose, who wrote a number of very popular history books for children and other educational works.
8 The portrait is at RIBA and shows a grizzly looking old man with the most extraordinary vast "mutton chops" – but for Sargent he was probably a welcome change from society beauties.
9 Dame Emily Penrose (1858-1942) was Principal of Somerville from 1907-1926. A distinguished Classical scholar, she fought ceaselessly for the recognition of women within the University of Oxford. In 1920, they were admitted to full degrees, largely as a result of her endeavours and the Somerville alumna, Helen Waddell, poet and scholar, paid tribute to her in 1925, saying: "We feel it was you who made it inevitable that women should be recognised in the university".
10 Katherine Stewart-Murray, Duchess of Atholl (1874-1960) – politician and keen composer, nicknamed "the Red Duchess" for her active support of the Republicans in the Spanish Civil War, although in 1931 she published "The Conscription of the People" in protest against the abuse of rights in the USSR.
11 Alan John Bayard Wace, Director from 1913 to 1923.

Ethel Smyth with Pan III – This was one of a series of portrait postcards issued to celebrate the Fiftieth Season of the People's Concert Society, 11 Lincoln's Inn Fields, London, W.C.2.

1927

A small collection of letters and cards in poorer condition than average. Elizabeth's address is 2 Gloucester Square, Hyde Park, London, W2, unless otherwise given.

In Ethel's first surviving letter of the year on the 16th of January, she describes herself as being in bed with "the family cold". Other topics are her financial situation, the hope that Elizabeth will not have to accompany her grandmother back to Cromer, her reading and, in particular, her passion for Anatole France.

January 19th, 1927

Dearest E...

[On reading her letter]

Your mother is so human that I expect it is a comfort to have you – tho' I am sure to have your Gran would <u>not</u> be. (By the by I cant make out why your letter inscribed Mon.17th only got here today Wed. 19th)...

[Family and health; on sacrifices to one's chosen work]

It suddenly occurs to me how I adore Ethel Davidson[1] and how difficult it would be to explain to some people I love deeply, like your mother, why I adore E. with such a very high quality of adoration. I think you would understand if I expounded it to you – but them despite your many crimes, you <u>are</u> rather intelligent, you know.

I've chosen an <u>orange</u> cover for "3 legged tour" – <u>Very loud indeed</u>. But I had next to no hesitation.

Your loving
E

On the back of the envelope, rather obscure:

I have been paralyzed with horror over the book "Nigger Heaven"[2] and glad to think that Abbott has this thing to cope with. I <u>felt</u> it all in jazz but this completed realisation makes one swoon.

---

1 There seem to have been two Ethel Davidsons in the family of ES's elder sister, Alice.
2 The highly controversial novel, *Nigger Heaven*, by Carl van Vechten (1880-1964) had come out in 1926 with the Harlem renaissance as its theme.

March 30th, 1927

Dearest Elizabeth I do indeed congratulate you on following the admirable example of your great aunt and adopting two professions. And, as in her case, what may be called the second string will probably prove the more profitable of the two. I feel sure that as Gamp one can earn more than as plucker of the hairs of the sun.[1] Ediths vicious comment was "well....I hope that will put her off matrimony!" How she considers the world is to be kept going round by spinsters and bachelors I do not know but these are her views. Did I tell you I find C and H [?] did much of our tour but with a dragoman and all the peasants were then (1901) in costume! I was then deep in "Der Wald" and had forgotten this voyage. C was just as mad abt it all as we were but I doubt her finding 7/6 to buy the book! It is having glorious reviews (2 more today) and I hope will sell a bit, after all. I hear Desmond Macarthy[2] spoke of and praised it in his fortnightly outpourings and my lecture will take place (B.B.C.) in abt 10 days I think – that again shd help sale. Tell all this to yr Gran and your mother. I thought the former looked so white and feeble – alas!

Your loving E

[A long PS on correspondence with a Greek lady about the tour]

1 EMW had presumably been nursing some member of the family in addition to lecturing on astronomy.
2 Desmond MacCarthy (1877-1952) English literary critic and journalist.

April 18th, 1927

Dearest E - I send you this *[missing]* which surpasses anything I ever read (and was worth the 5d I had to pay on it!). It is in answer to my letter saying that our ideal is not the personally conducted motor tour!

[Family news; more on the offending letter; Greece]

I will not disguise from you that in reply to a letter from R Storrs[1] asking "when are you coming" I enquired what Cyprus is like in the autumn! In fact I feel I shall go...When are you free?? Let us dogear some such page of the future

Your E

1 Ronald Storrs (1881-1955) was a very senior official in the British Colonial Service. At this date he had just left the post of Governor of Cyprus. A friend of T.E. Lawrence, he was to be one of his pall-bearers. His own memoirs, *Orientations*, which shed much light on the Middle Eastern politics of the period, came out in 1937 and the inscribed proof copy that he gave Ethel is marked, as was her custom, with a number of comments.

May 6th, 1927

My dearest Eliz I expect you went out by the side door. I was in the house all the 2nd interval talking about what can be done to save the exquisite Mozart show at the Court, whereby much hangs. There may be a letter of mine (I corrected the proof on Wed) anytime from today onwards in the Times – and one tomorrow in the M.P. And all that fits in with Walters' remarks in the D. Mail. Music in England is doomed unless it gets official support – that's a fact. You can't <u>improvise</u> an art. ...I've just been sent a book "Ride thro' the Balkans"[1] on behalf of the author who is in Irak. One Sir Martin Conway writes the Preface. The journey took place in 1914 just before the war...I only got it an hour ago so can't say more. But "2 ladies" seem to have been the travellers....

[Criticism of some points in the book; on some experiments made by Elizabeth: "Your letters are, you are, in every sense stimulating to the intelligence"; tennis and health]

Reviews continue to be brilliant – but sale only at 1250 so far.

Your E

1 Agnes Conway (1885-1950), historian and archaeologist, had travelled through Greece and the Balkans, covering some of the same ground as Ethel and Elizabeth, in 1914 with a Newnham friend, Evelyn Radford, and published *A Ride Through the Balkans, on Classic Ground with a Camera* in 1917. It was this trip to Iraq that was to launch her on her career as an archaeologist. Her father, academic and mountaineer, was first Director-General of the Imperial War Museum.

Three or four days later, Ethel wrote hopefully of her letter to *The Times*:

> Johnston-Douglas[1] (of "Cosi") tells me that my letter <u>may</u> brighten up the attendance this last week and make their salary for 8 weeks pan out at....£20 each!

1 Walter Johnston-Douglas was founder and director of the Webber-Douglas School of Singing and Dramatic Art. A production of Mozart's *Cosi fan Tutte* by Walter Johnston-Douglas opened at the Kingsway Theatre, London, on 23 March, transferring to the Court on 18 April.

On the 20th, she met Vita Sackville-West for lunch and they went together to *Fidelio*:

> Yes – it makes me sick – people who think it is modern and smart intellectually to pooh pooh Fidelio because it is not something quite different. These people don't love music and they have, as we agree, something wrong in their equipment if they are not moved to the depths by the dungeon scene...

And the following day:

> This will rather thrill you (destroy) – Vita will deposit me in her car about 4.45. Shall I try to make her come in for tea at your house?...

July 22nd, 1927

Dearest Eliz

[On dashing up and down to London; on EMW missing a party]

> As Maurice said that sort of party – a few musicians and... The Smart [Set] – is devastating. All the people I most hate were there. Cunard, Rutland, Mary Crawshay[1] (I don't hate <u>her</u>...but she is one of the "old friends" I never "really liked") and several well known whores...

[On EMW's appreciation of H.B.]

1 Nancy Cunard (1896-1965); perhaps Violet Manners, Duchess of Rutland (1856-1937) an artist and member of the "Souls"; Mary Crawshay unidentified.

July 29th, 1927

Do you know I find "Seducers in Equador"[1] very arresting – fantastic to a degree and really very touching. But you have to admit the premises – to step over to the angle of the teller. It is real stuff like all she does – and a scope such as Teheran, the Land and that is rather amazing E.

[Arrangements to meet]

1 By Vita Sackville-West, Hogarth Press, 1924. *Passenger to Teheran* and her poem *The Land* had been published in 1926.

August 7th, 1927

St Andrews House
Droitwich[1]

Dearest E I have the honour of telling you that with no adequate words at my command to express a loathing so deep, so frantic, yet I must nevertheless tell you, how I abominate Paradise Lost. I have it with me from Book VII and have not come upon <u>one single line</u> to redeem it....to lift it for one second out of the bog of boredom (a boredom that sets out to be revenged on other people by making <u>them scream</u> with boredom) in which it was conceived and brought forth.....

[More on Paradise Lost; her deafness perhaps due to tonsils; dates of concerts and broadcasting]

Imagine – Enthusiastic letter from a man who did the Peleponnese trip in the other sense and heard rumours of us, to which, when he read my book, he was able to give a name! He said he signed the Nun's book just below us at Mistra. But he says he did it all with a rucksack and on foot!...(<u>I</u> said that wouldn't work) But here's his letter (Tear it up) .... He doesn't say if he speaks modern Greek, but I daresay he'll tell me as I asked him (because of a man from Australia who is going to Greece and took my word for it that that sort of rucksack travelling wouldnt work).

[On the cure]

The guests here are like a Lambeth Garden Party crowd[2]. One asked me whether she shd leave her magazine for me when she departs. I said "what is it?" and she (aged about 60) said "The Girls' Own".

Your loving E

[Golf]

1 Droitwich Spa in Worcestershire. The hotel still exists.
2 Lambeth Palace, the London residence of the Archbishop of Canterbury was – and is – a favourite venue for church groups, charities, etc. to hold garden parties, etc.

August 10th, 1927

Appley Hall
Ryde
Isle of Wight

Dearest Aunt,
I am in a great stew about your tonsils...

[Medical details and advice]

I revelled in your diatribes against Paradise Lost. I haven't got the work at hand and I daren't go downstairs to look for it for terror of being caught and made to play booby tennis before tea. But I do say there are gorgeous things about the stars in it and shall never agree that it is boring. All the bits about Archangels flying down beams of light, the Creation etc. are to my mind "slashing stuff". As for the bits about Adam and Eve they place the work in the first rank of humorous literature as well as all its' other virtues. Ned Mitchell [?] with no clothes on teaching Eve her true place in the world is sublimely funny I think....

[A long quote from the end of Book VII of Paradise Lost *beginning: "He through Heaven/That opened wide her blazing portals..." - remarkably accurate, unless she had managed to creep downstairs and get hold of a copy]*

Bill knows some other choice bits about phalanxes of angels but he is playing tennis. However I hope some nice tale out of the Girls' Own Paper[1] will be a change for you!!!

I have just begun Maurice's [Baring] new book². I contrive to do some work here and the 2 bad weeks of real scrimmage and social glitter are over....

[Plans etc.]

Yours lv
E.

1 Besides the obvious joke about literary taste, the family often teased ES about her preparedness to write for <u>any</u> publication that would pay. As far as I know, this did not include *Girls' Own Paper*.
2 This was presumably his novel, *Tinker's Leave*.

In August Ethel was at Droitwich. In common with many of her generation, she was a great believer in spas and was probably there to bathe in the waters, considered beneficial for a range of rheumatic complaints, as well as to try a treatment for her deafness.

August 16th, 1927

[Travel arrangements and family correspondence]

My ridiculous little operation – operations have become very insignificant. Anyhow I now have a reply from my Dwich doctor who wires that his pet surgeon comes back fr holiday on 23rd and he feels sure he can arrange for operation in the week 29th and onwards but not sure if he'll do it for 15 gns! The blackguard. I trust he will tho'!

August 17th, 1927

Droitwich

Dearest E if I didn't write to you yesty to tell you how I hang on your reports, it is because when I got home from my walk (taken during 2 rare hours of sunshine) I found the usual <u>awful</u> musical confusion. Flew to the P.O.; sent a very restrained but really furious wire -; then back here wrote a letter in same sense, pelted down again to P.O....and by that time all was over – no time even for a p[ost].c[ard].

[Her health; concern for EMW's mother]

I think it <u>magnificent</u> of yr grandmother <u>not</u> rushing off to the sick bed. Really heroic. She has learned something – and that is as much as we can hope to do at our ages!

September 1st, 1927

Dearest Elizabeth, The account of the D mail aeroplane man is simply overwhelming....as for the pilot – he was, as we see, too good for this world...[1]

[Plans for six weeks in Wales; her music enthusiastically received: "The concerto was <u>fine</u> – and the public really yelled." Correcting the story that she had made a speech: "Tell yr grandmother she should <u>not</u> read the papers unless she disbelieves them!" and adding that this "connects with a Press campaign against the B.B.C."; preparing to rehearse The Wreckers]

I enclose a letter from Ronald Storr[2] which really pleases me. He being my friend speaks of '<u>Your</u> luck in your companion'; your friends, I should hope, speak of <u>my</u> luck. And both are right. We were a well assorted couple. Send back R.S. and don't think me fatuous for sending it. I want your grandmother to see it....

Your E

1 It is not clear to whom ES is referring. In early May Charles Nungesser and François Coli vanished while attempting to fly cross the Atlantic. A couple of weeks later, Charles Lindberg succeeded.
2 Sir Ronald Henry Amherst Storrs KCMG CBE was an official in the British Foreign and Colonial Office. He served as Oriental Secretary in Cairo, Military Governor of Jerusalem, Governor of Cyprus, and Governor of Northern Rhodesia

Later in the month, Ethel was in Wales and apparently again trying some treatment for the increasing deafness, which was effectively putting an end to her musical career:

September 16th, 1927

The Noyadd,
Llagattock-Crickhowell

Dearest E I am so immersed in shaping stuff for the new Vol. of Streaks that I never look up...

[Family news]

I feel <u>sure</u> this treatment will do me good. I doubted it till 4 days ago because my left Eustachian tube evidently came into contact with a piece of furniture when I was on my way into this world. When my Mother came home from a visit, tired and cross, as people generally are after visits, she always used to alter the places of all the heaviest bits of furniture in the house. My E.T. consequently has a kink in it which the doctor is only now successfully circumventing. It is rather fun when the catheter wriggles successfully round the rock [?] and the poison-gas rushes in with a roar and you and the doctor cry simultaneously "that's got it"! but till that moment arrives it is rather unpleasant. What is amusing is inventing new facial contortions to open up the tube. The best is to try and yawn as you do just before you're sea-sick. This favourably relaxes the "soft palate" but I can't look very pretty while doing it. And I admire the doctor for keeping his countenance. But Oh! Isn't the technique of anything enthralling?

[Family news and travel plans]

September 26th, 1927

[On books, both reading and writing them + a snippet cut from a friend's letter]

"Pidd[1] has tried <u>Gertude Bell</u>[2] and discarded it as too badly written, and <u>all interesting</u> things left out." I must tell you Pidd, always a captious and capricious reader, is now ill, and only equal to P.G. Woodhouse. I have seen <u>one</u> letter of G

Bell's quoted – superb in thought and expression too…Fred Benson who adores his aunt Norah, says the <u>minds</u> of the clever ones shd be put down by the inspector of nuisances. I love them all 3, but really, really….!"

[On her current reading]

Your handwriting is getting awful; I constantly have to think "What is that word" and this distresses me deeply. Do mind your ps and qs, I beseech you – also your k's (a weak point of mine), your y's, your g's, you're a's – in fact all your alphabet except your d's which are a godsend to your reader ("Ho! A sail!")….

[Health and travel plans]

On the envelope:

This was written days ago but [?] 1) under the valance of an armchair (I hate valances) 2) under several papers on my table where it had been replaced by the nice girl who picked it up and did not know the floor system with letters.

1 Probably John Piddington, President of the Society for Psychical Research (1924-5), a position held by other friends of the Smyth family, notably William James.
2 Gertrude Bell (1868-1926) - writer, traveller and political officer, whose activities served to shape the Middle East in the 20th century, and who opposed women's suffrage. *The Letters of Gertrude Bell, selected and edited by Lady Bell* (her stepmother) appeared in 1927.

October 1st, 1927

My dearest E

[On some correspondence]

The question is of Miss Agnes Conway whose letter I have lost and whose letter I have forgotten, but enough of it has come back to me – <u>suddenly</u> – to risk a letter, with her Papa's name writ large on the envelope….thus (tho' as feminist it irks me)

Miss Agnes Conway
c/o Sir Martin Conway etc. etc.
Allingham ? Castle
Maidstone

The castle may be Allinton or Allington[1] or anything. But there cant be many tri-syllabic castles beginning with A near Maidstone. Anyhow she's coming down to lunch with me during yr golf week, walk out to the Golf Course and have tea with us (at Coign) afterwards. I wonder if we shall like her? Or put off by her mouth going round (as I'm told it does) like the needle of a weighing machine (when, stepping on to it, you put a penny in the slot) – each time you ask her a question? - Vita told me this and it may be exaggeration. Anyhow it'll be great fun her coming.

[Domestic matters; her pleasure at being in Wales]

Where is your grandmother? She has vanished into space as far as I am concerned.

Yr E

[1] It is Allington.

October 23rd, 1927

Elizabeth dearest you mustnt think it necessary to write me a Collins![1] I adore having you more than most things in life! Joyce [Wethered] was a great dear on Thursday and played – Lord! how she played!

[On golf]

After Mary Hunter left Hill Hall, she and Phyllis Williamson tended to spent Christmas at Cromer; Elizabeth and other members of the family were expected to join them there. Ethel considered Cromer bleak, so she often refused to take part in these family gatherings, but there would usually be a particularly lively exchange of letters about this time of year.

1 Slang of the period for a "thank-you" letter, after the obsequious Mr Collins in *Pride and Prejudice.*

December 21st, 1927

Dearest Eliz

[On Lord Birkenhead's[1] letter to The Times: "the cleverest utterance about the Prayer Book farce I ever read"; on the Church of England: "That's why I admire and adore it – the truth is not black and white and heaven knows Christ was a compromiser in some ways..."]

I am writing in a fog bound train – anchored between Vauxhall and Waterloo. (Let me say how glad I am you liked the choruses – I wish we'd had a talk about them. We were badly seated and Kennedy Scott[2] was on my mind. He has been good to me and was sad about Life in general and I wanted to comfort him. He wrote a dear letter next day. (We are moving on at last) (We have stopped again)...No!!! WE are again crawling on!! The frost was 20° last night and I staggered to Woking this morning on foot (no cars cd travel) with nailed boots and many an escape from death – in my heavy fur coat with 2 lots of proofs!!!

1 F. E. Smith, Earl of Birkenhead (1872-1930) statesman, lawyer, Lord Chancellor 1919-1922 and friend of Winston Churchill. A flamboyant figure, he fought – among other causes – to prevent the proposed criminalization of lesbianism.
2 Charles Kennedy Scott (1878-1965) – organist and choral conductor, worked tirelessly for the performance of choral music in England founding the Philharmonic Choir in 1919. He had been involved in productions of ES's work, such as *The Prison*.

December 29th, 1927 [?]

Dearest Elizabeth - Do you know that the first orchestral piece I ever wrote was an overture to Anthony and Cleopatra (Maurice still talks about it and my father said it was "very pleasing"!!) I simply cant make out what you mean about A and C being cads! I never saw them as anything but as world compellers and the lovers of the world. I think it is of all his plays my favourite – the molten love outpourings of both....

[On her favourite lines in A and C; on EMW learning Greek; a performance of her Mass at Bristol and problems with a concert in London]

I go to London tomorrow to cope with things. The whole thing costs (will cost me, I mean) about £90 to start with! <u>but I knew that</u> and have earned the money all right. Theres something I wanted to say but cant remember it and post is departing. The cold is bearable but today when I walked (a cat on nutshells) to Woking I bought and stepped into a 2nd pair of knickers....

Your loving E

1928

As for the year 1926, almost nothing seems to have survived from 1928. One letter is dated January 3rd, while the other undated – which is unusual for Ethel – is in a scruffy envelope numbered 22 with an illegible postmark and comes from a packet predominantly from 1934. The former was mostly on her impressions of *Antony and Cleopatra* – especially Cleopatra.

And a PS: "Nina[1] has had both lungs filled with liquid. I am anxious given this mad exodus."

In the other undated letter, she returns to the subject of Cleopatra:

In haste for post 7 p.m.

No….not a desert island chum but she really was a great Queen in her way and what I think so wonderful is that she valued that part so immensely and was quite capable, if Caesar had cared to leave her a scope of action to carry on. She had had many love affairs and evidently her motto "tout lasse, tout casse, tout passe" was followed up as in Sarah's[2] case with the <u>ultimate</u> one "Quand meme!" Both of them were potentates and I don't think she should be asked to behave like Juliet (all for love). Love was to her [?] a grand streak in her life, I expect, always. In fact she was (I feel certain) an inspired prostitute by vocation. If Sarah had been of that epoch I can see her doing all Cleopatra's tricks – But, as a woman oneself, I quite agree one would not choose C. for a pal – nor wd she have any use for any woman – I feel sure – anymore than Sarah had, as far as I know. I believe women friendships existed only Ionia and England!

Your loving E

I <u>do</u> hope you are revelling in golf!

[Her sister Nina's health]

Aug. 22nd 1928

Summing up our v. relation

APPLEY HALL
RYDE, I OF W.

Beloved Aunt

I wrote to Mrs Braun! I agree that Greek maniacs must be tolerant of their fellow maniacs outpourings. And her letter did really awaken hot flames from ever smouldering ashes in me!

I will read more Humbert Wolfe on your word alone. There is none here — H. W. only likes de la Mare of modern poets. I did read Wolfe's "Requiem" & didn't fall to it at all. But I always feel guilty, legs — for loving poetry as I do, not to search the moderns for hope here. I get morbidly depressed

Elizabeth to Ethel, August 1928

1 Ethel Smyth's' sister Nina Hollings, with her friend Helena Gleichen, had run an X-ray Unit on the Italian Front in World War I and since in those days no precautions were taken, had seriously damaged her health. The "mad exodus" probably refers to their purchase of a fine Tudor House that they could not really afford: Hellens'. See Helena Gleichen, *Contacts and Contrasts*, London 1940, reprinted by Hardinge Simpole, 2013, with an introduction by CS.
2 Sarah Bernhardt (c.1844-1923) was considered one of the greatest actresses of all time. ES knew her through her Parisian group of friends. In fact, Bernhardt did have close women friends, notably the impressionist painter, Louise Abbéma, her life-long friend and perhaps – in view of a dedicatory note accompanying a painting of them together: "Peint par Louise Abbéma, le jour anniversaire de leur liaison amoureuse." – lover. Cleopatra was one of her favourite roles.

At the top of the following letter *(see reproduction on opposite page)*, Ethel wrote in pencil: "Summing up our relation"

August 22nd, 1928

Appley Hall

Beloved Aunt.

[re "Greek maniacs"]

I will read more Humbert Wolfe[1] on your word alone. There is none here – H[edworth] W[illiamson] only likes de la Mare of the modern poets. I did read Wolfe's "Requiem" and didn't fall to it at all. But I always feel guiltily lazy – loving poetry as I do, not to search the moderns for <u>hope</u> more often. I get morbidly depressed thoughts about art being dead which I quite realize is not fair until one has looked to see.

[On Blake and Christopher Smart]

I have read very little and made slow progress with Homer. I have been thinking a lot about art and the realism in the Classics. Also I have been "stock taking". Thinking more personally than I usually do about my own life and the values in it. I am emboldened by your dear remarks about me to say in black and white what you must know already - <u>How MUCH</u> you are in my life. Phyllis and Billy and you are the only people I love all through. When I first grew up you made me see what sort of life I really wanted. "There is a great difference between Music and Astronomy"!!

But a life lived intensely in a medium too big for one is the blessed happiness of the servants of the Muses. Once on the tennis court at Hill I said something about comets moving in parabolic orbits from infinity to infinity and you said I had no business to be playing tennis! You probably don't remember. 6 months after, I began to learn mathematics. You have always been a sort of standard of a mental integrity and inner sternness with oneself to me. That began before the enchanting friendship and companionship in literature leading to Greece and such delights. I hope you don't mind this "weighing up". It is very accurate and I am all for conscious appreciation and deep rooted influence.

I think Gran is going to Gloucester and I should have gone with her but Bill and I are going with Phyllis and Martin to Austria. They have taken a shoot. It will be wonderful fun – wild and lovely and comfortless.

[Travel plans]

Yr. l.
E

1 Humbert Wolfe (1885-1940) – poet, translator of Heinrich Heine and others, and civil servant.

Another surviving letter is on rather bright sugar-bag blue paper, which was a great favourite with Elizabeth, but which Ethel loathed.

Friday, December 28th, 1928

13 Cliff Avenue
Cromer

Beloved Aunt,

I am so glad you are back and fixed in one place to be written to. First I must let off pent up squeals of joy about your concert having such a triumph. I read Maurice [Baring]'s account of it which he wrote to Gran a few days ago. It was thrilling. To think of Robin missing it when he might so easily have gone! But if you go about with millionaire dagos in aeroplanes these things happen. Give me the poor middle class life in planes [?trains] and buses!

I liked Hulton's[1] book and letter (thanks for sending it). I have finished the book but will wait to send it back till all Christmas arrangements are over. I suppose you didn't enter into any arguments about his Elgin complex. I must say I have a very shy and uncomfortable feeling about the Caryatid from the Erechtheion. I was looking at them all, the day I came down here and that particular one made me squirm.

His remarks about the Olympia Hermes rather surprised me though I see his point of view. But that thing has the same untouchable perfection to me that the Parthenon has – a feeling of the last word being said and the soul in peace. I have reached the point of thinking it is the only sort of peace in the world for the soul. I mean that religiously too, the peace of God that passeth all understanding is aesthetic. There is <u>no</u> peace for the mind as a speculative instrument, only as a contemplator of beauty - the beauty of Holiness and mathematical form and all the beauty perceived with the senses as well. That beauty exists objectively I take to be the soul of Platonism and the only rock I possess, in comparison with the many rafts one pushes out on a different times. Do you remember that raft bit in the Phaedo?

[On plans to meet.... "But bear in mind the house is <u>really</u> warm..."]

I am in a fever of energy and slogging through the tedious mechanical preliminaries to a job which I dare say will come to nothing, but I want to have a shot at it. The great enemy is sleep! In this place being out all day and drinking beer and burgundy....! The stars are attacking my Greek activities but I am reading grammar solidly. The awful part is I don't believe it sticks to a mind so bereft of training in that line. My Greek professor says my last Greek letter rivalled the 4th century rhetoricians in elegance though!!

[Family news..."Gran is unusually peaceful and looks very well."]

I haven't read Haldane's book "Possible Worlds" but heard it was very good[2]. When I read anything again if ever, I have Eddington's "Nature of the Physical World" 1st on the list....

Do you know they had a bad fire at Mount Mascal about 4 weeks ago. A very narrow escape, and a lot of damage done. But it is all fairly concentrated in area, so life goes on there much the same.

Yr lv E

1 Unidentified.
2 John Burdon Sanderson (J.B.S.) Haldane (1892-1964) was a British-born Indian scientist known for his work in the study of physiology, genetics, evolutionary biology, and in mathematics, where he made innovative contributions to the fields of statistics and biostatistics. He was the son of the equally famous John Scott Haldane, nephew of Richard Burdon Haldane (q.v.) and brother of Naomi Mitchison. He was a professed socialist, Marxist, atheist, and humanist whose political dissent led him to leave England in 1956 and live in India, becoming a naturalised Indian citizen in 1961.
He was a brilliant populariser, whose essays *Possible Worlds* postulated future scientific developments, not necessarily in line with modern political correctness: "…if you desire to check the increase of any population or section of the population, either massacre it or force upon it the greatest practicable amount of liberty, education and wealth. Civilisation stands in real danger from over-production of 'undermen'. But if it perishes from this cause it will be because its governing class cared more for wealth than for justice."

< > This passage is heavily marked by ES in red pencil. Clearly something she thought was important and perhaps was considering including in one of her volumes of autobiography.

1929

This packet lay next to 1925 in the box where it was found and is damaged in a very similar way. Only two letters from Elizabeth dated 1929 have surfaced and there is very little other related material.

At the beginning of the year, Elizabeth was, as usual, with the family at Cromer for the holidays and Ethel wrote a long letter on a wide variety of subjects, including the eternal question of the return of the Elgin marbles.

January 2nd, 1929

Darling Elizabeth I've been wanting to write to you ever since getting the letter you wrote to me on the 28th – but I have been coping, despite groggy thumb (which nothing but golf does real good to) with Berlin aftermath, such as a lightening article about German orchestra playing music with the exact quality of <u>attention</u> that English artists display on the football field – (there I was able to fire my poisoned arrow into the first group of H.Wood's[1] enemies). In short a lot of farewell effort has to be made on <u>the</u> two themes, H.W., and women in orchestra – and then peace, perfect peace – and contemplation unbroken of my own sodden-ness of spirit – result of prolonged collar work, and nothing-at-all-ness now.

No – I didn't discuss Elgin matters with Hutton; of course I quite see his point of view – who wouldn't? But even about the caryatid I feel the ethics of the matter are decided by earthquakes. When you consider that hideous Corinth as we saw it is no more*....![2] By the by in Berlin I went to see the Pergamon Altar[3], by special permission for it is being built up – or rather built in – to a complex that more or less makes the whole thing convincing. I had little time that day and a heavy cold, but I saw some of the most exquisite Egyptian things – new acquisitions, that beggar description. Hugo Wach[4] told me that we have as good, but I can hardly credit it...little exquisite heads that might be by any already famous youthful Parisian sculptor of today – the image, too, of so many of ones friends! The planetarium was quite close to my hotel and I thought of you but never went beyond that. There are fine Greek things in the Museum and I did obeisance before a certain Stele as I fled past it, but let me tell you that I do <u>not</u> see Hutton's point of view about the Olympia Hermes – and feel just as you do abt. it – that here the last word is said.

I rather envy you in holding that the only peace in the world for the soul is aesthetic. Of course I see that the mind as speculative instrument cannot give it – but being perhaps so frenetically [?] engined - (perhaps overengined) – in the region of personality...having such a fierce will, and in my youth such a fierce desire for the things I wanted, the only peace I have ever found is in acquiescence...resignation, submission, a relaxation of the mind and soul that makes floating on the sea of time possible instead of being submerged by your own violent desire to float....

I'm just going to look up the Phaedo for what you refer to – I've been reading things that I don't think are in your line, but one very exquisite book – a masterpiece – you must read if you haven't already read it "The Diary of a Foxhunting Man." Edith's indignation at the name, tho' she liked the book, amused me "It ought to be 'memoirs of a youth with a turn for sport – goaded into hunting by a wish to stand well with his groom'"[5]. That adored person is coming to London for 5 weeks from next Satdy (5th) and I have no doubt I shall be in London some day next week to try on (O Lord) a garment concerning which I can't even say what it is to be, eventually. So I hope to see you all – and, if the worst comes to the worst, for love of you, I'll make it not lunch but tea – winter tho' it be – and bleak Woking buses a terrifying thought. I have just been trying to recommence golf by 5 or 6 holes with a neighbour. But the N. wind blew so appallingly that...we actually picked up our balls in the middle of the [?] and fled home – Pleasure and pain are not the same thing any more than music and astronomy.

I forget if I told you that I got my £600[6] all right, and as the newspapers (Times etc.) will be publishing any day from next Satdy onwards, the list of subscribers will be in the January 11th number ("Time and Tide" its rather a surprising record) – "Lady Juliet Lowther £5 and so on! – people one doesn't know, hardly, to speak to, but who apparently were approvers.

I am deeply sorry about yr Mother and her knee – but if the weather is as cruelly Arctic with you as here she is not missing much (remarkable how the recently discovered new verse in the Ancient Mariner meets the case; but I think see and sea a little too easy for a really brilliant rhyme. Perhaps that's why he left the verse out?) Do tell your Mother that her Mother and everyone raves about the charm and the warmth (which in [?] is ¾ of the word "charm" for me) of W.13. I am dying to see it and hope it may be pulled off, only Tovey[7] and all that Edinburgh group is so madly unbusinesslike. I have come back more in love with musical Germany than ever and feel that I am like the young man who wouldn't push forth with Christ....A cottage and a sheepdog are my undoing ------------------Heaven wont let me off and I shall do no more good work...Well....What matter?....Bless you my dears all –

Your loving E

* "Lost Corinth may resist no more"...Don't you wonder who that's by?

Henry Wood had supported both Ethel Smyth and the British Women's Symphony Orchestra, encouraging women, including the cellist Guilhermina Suggia, to conduct. Critics of the time disapproved. *The Times*, on June 27th, 1924 had remarked that:

> There is no reason why women should not make good conductors, but Miss Gwynne Kimpton and Mme Suggia and, to some extent Dame Ethel Smyth, all hindered rather than helped the orchestra.

The Daily Mail indicates a curious blankness about the purpose of a conductor and a depressingly stereotyped view of women. In August, its comment ran:

> It is strange that in conducting men are more graceful than women. I remember the first time I saw Ethel Smyth conduct I was disappointed in her style, though she got the effect she wanted. I must say, though, that I have only seen Dame Ethel wielding Sir Henry Wood's baton, which is an outsize in such things. It seems to fit him very well, but I dare say Miss Smyth would have felt more comfortable with a stick a foot or so shorter.

Mme Suggia reaped greater approval as being more graceful and, as the Augustus John portrait finished in the same year bears witness, she was extremely good looking. Ethel's anger and depression at the treatment of women musicians was not simply paranoia.

1 Henry Wood (1869-1944) - conductor, especially known for his association with the BBC and as one of the founders of the "Proms", which he conducted for almost fifty years, as well as his support of new or little-known composers – he conducted the premieres of some 700 pieces of music.
2 Totally destroyed by an earthquake in 1858 and again 1928. The quote comes from Lord Byron, *The Siege of Corinth*, (1816) canto XXIX, a poem on the sack of Corinth by the Ottomans in 1715, at which time the city was held by the Venetians.
3 The Pergamon Altar (2nd c.B.C.), a monumental and very important structure from Asia Minor, was ceded to Berlin by the Turkish government in the late 19th century. In 1930 the new museum to house it was finally completed, only to close

again in 1939. The Altar has had extremely varied fortunes in the 20th century and major restoration work was urgently required before it could be put back on display in 2004.

4 Hugo Wach (1872-1939), engineer and architect associated with the Pergamon Museum, Berlin.

5 This refers to Siegfried Sassoon's (1897-1988) largely autobiographical *Memoirs of a Fox-Hunting Man*, published by Faber in 1928 and immediately hailed as a classic; Edith Sitwell (1887-1964) was a friend of ES.

6 Perhaps for *A Final Burning of Boats*, published the previous year.

7 Sir Donald Francis Tovey (1881-1965), composer and musicologist, Reid Professor of Music at Edinburgh. His opera *The Bride of Dionysius* was first performed in 1929.

January 4th, 1929

13 Cliff Avenue
Cromer

Beloved Aunt,

Don't stay in London until teatime on my account as I can easily arrange to come back to luncheon. The only impossible day for me is Thursday as I lecture at 2. On Wednesdays we have a conclave with the professor over work, and that is uncertain in its' duration but only on rare occasions exceeds an hour, and I get away at 1. So it is really just as easy for me to lunch at G.Sq. as tea as I should not normally leave there until after 6.

[Plans to meet; on Coleridge, golf and some now irretrievable family joke]

Gran seems to know the Siege of Corinth[1] too! She began reciting it flowingly at luncheon yesterday. You must have a competition one day!

The cold has been intense and still is. Golf is hopeless and only pain. I am therefore having a most amusing wallow in Greek grammar, having finished off my 2719 stars. (I was doing a preliminary classification before a job I wanted to do.) My "Advanced Greek Prose composition" is the most inspired and thrilling book I ever struck. It has opened unhoped-for doors! I think I am learning a lot, apart from using it as a crib to weave Greek letters to Elinor Vaughn[2]. Anyhow the latter writes that I have "grown from a puling Thracian babe into a cultured Athenian gentlewoman in 10 days." And that some goddess has wrought a marvel!! In another 20 years I believe I shall know some Greek.

Yes, I mean to read the fox-hunting book. I love Miss S's amended title!³ Billy read it and adored it and so did Mother.

I can imagine what you feel about Germany and music. It must be like a Greek living among barbarians for musicians here.

< I think at bottom we mean the same thing about personality and the peace of the soul. Only not having a very urgent one, resignation does not come into my problem. To me the idea of personality drops out of the spiritual. It seems to me that in every spiritual activity it is transcended – in aesthetics, in prayer, in scientific contemplation, in everything. It is for me the fence that hedges in one's spiritual inside and only exists as a relationship with one's environment, and to God one has none. All philosophy that leads one up to personality as the final affirmation with arguments about the "Personality of God" has no response from me. I mean that if you and I stand in front of Demeter of Knidos we meet there without our personalities and they only reassert themselves when we turn away and think about where we shall have luncheon! This is my version of Christ's words about losing one's life to find it. I should be less sure of not talking nonsense if He hadn't said it and it didn't fair [?] so well. What would one do if one hadn't Christ to refer one's speculations to? I honestly cannot imagine what one's mind would be like if one abstracted Him entirely, can you? >

Yr lvg
E

1 See page 84, note 2. On one of the battles between the Venetians and the Ottomans, still a favourite poem that children were made to learn in school in the 1950s. It begins:
>Many a vanished year and age,
>And tempest's breath, and battle's rage
>Have swept o'er Corinth; yet she stands
>A fortress formed to Freedom's hands....

2 A classicist and very close friend of EMW.
3 See ES to EMW 2.1.1929

< > Heavily marked in red by ES.

One of Ethel and Elizabeth's pleasures was to go to the theatre – something Elizabeth continued to enjoy throughout her life. In January, Ethel enquired whether she would like to see Macbeth again: "I am – furiously disposed…." And the following month she enquired whether: "… anyone would like to go to see The Merry Wives of Windsor?"

February 25th, 1929

Darling Eliz I send you the 3 tickets I have secured No.4 (yours being 5.6.7). I have paid for them 5/- each which you can give me when we meet. If it suits yr Grand. I might come to lunch, as the pictures are hopeless on Sat (- as I found out last Sat) – I am sure your Grand. will be delighted – and you too if I told you abt. it – to hear that I found my dear gold watch in the pocket of a seldom used coat! I quite gave it up for lost and this is like a gift, of course. I hear you were asked to take a **very great** lecture for your boss but won't congratulate you till I know more (!) I am reading a book which rivets me by Professor Herford[1] of Manchester. It is called "The Postwar Mind of Germany" – and even that, on the philosophy side, might interest you….."

[On Triggs Lock in the frost]

1 Charles Harold Herford (1853-1931) was an English literary scholar and critic. He was Professor of English Literature at Victoria University of Manchester from 1901 to 1921.
Published in 1927, these six essays analyze the plight of Germany in the years after World War I, a period that was, as one reviewer pointed out: "..a continuation of the war against a disarmed people." This was a subject that interested Ethel Smyth passionately, knowing Germany as she did. She had already been maintaining for many years that the humiliation of Germany and its reduction to beggary was extremely dangerous and liable to produce a very violent reaction and a dramatic renewal of hostilities, as soon as the right combination of circumstances arose.

April 7th, 1929

Darling Elizabeth I think Paradise Lost[1] the most odious work I have ever struck and can think of nothing more calculated to make you loath God, Christ, the scheme, human nature, the whole bag of tricks (except Satan) . Of course there are purple patches – (but <u>very</u> few) – and fine tags eg about the mind being "its own place" etc. – I cant find (anyhow never noticed) about the archangel coming down on a beam (except in the "hymn" of course where someone does it) and I cant find a fine line or two you once showed me – something about the stars. There! A lovely place about the moon sitting arbitress overhead and nearer to the earth wheeling her pale course (I think to look at the fairies[2]) – another amusing one about the "lab'ring moon eclipsing at the sight of the charms of the Lapland witches (rather Shakespearean that) and the fight in heaven is a very fine battle piece – But otherwise the lines "how came still evening on" are alone in their glory ... (tho' followed by a lovely speech of Eve about "nights solemn bird" (spoilt at the end by the usual statement that <u>only</u> in Adam's company can these things be enjoyed!!!)

No – I think it is the most overrated thing in literature – <u>a shameful production</u> in fact. And if you followed (which I am not doing myself by the by, but I catch bits of it with the corner of my eye now and again) the correspondence in the M. Post about women teachers you would see how deeply Miltons lessons sank into the heart of the British male – and how it still is the foundation stone of the outlook of ¾ of them.

Let me know the final result of the competition "pray, please, dear" and think of me on Thursday 11th when I shall be showing Pan at the Crystal Palace[3]. I stay that night at 40 Moore St.

Your loving
E

Tell yr mother that I wrote to her but foolishly put the letter in Eothen[4] which I cant post (Sunday) in the letter box – It will go tomorrow.

1 *Paradise Lost* was one of EMWs great literary passions not, on the whole, shared by those around her.
2 ES was quite correct: "Faery elves"
3 A favourite venue for dog shows until destroyed by fire in 1936. No picture has been found of ES at the Crystal Palace, but British Pathé News has some wonderful clips of such occasions at www.britishpathe.com
4 by Alexander Kinglake (1809-1891). This work (1844) seems to have been popular with all the family, perhaps because of John Sargent's travels in the Near East.

May 31st, 1929

On May 31st, Ethel was at Hotel Mercédés, Aix les Bains and writing to Elizabeth at the Cambridge Nursing Home, Dorset Square

[Much sympathy to EMW for some – presumably - medical misfortune; her own medical problems; nightingales – for which she had a passion; Belloc¹ and the Catholic Church]

ES disapproved of both these last, but in spite of various criticisms:

> But the book is <u>enormously</u> well worth reading ....Pan caused me to treat part of one page of the 'Reformation' with Iodine oil (he also gnawed the title off the Library edition of Clarissa Harlowe!! The only 1 vol copy in England) – a fearful affair. He found the parcel in the porch and forthwith the devil entered him). For this reason I left both books at home – and as I want you to read the Reformation first (if you will be so <u>very</u> kind!) I won't send you the other now."

[1] Hilaire Belloc (1870-1953) – writer and political activist. *How the Reformation Happened* was published the previous year.

June 26th, 1929

Darling Eliz I'm going to lunch with yr. Gran. tomorrow in a fond - and I wish it were a sure and certain hope – of seeing you and your mother tomorrow, Thurs.... I'll get the Bishop of Durham on disestablishment[1] - the idea thrills me. Ethel comes here to lunch today and I shall be keen to know what <u>my</u> "wisest man" – Archbp Davidson[2] – says.

I am longing to see you as soon as an awful tragedy has been rectified which now necessitates my sleeping in the spare bed. No – I have not "wetted" in mine, but an officious Woking tradesman who was to merely re-cover my beloved box mattress has seen fit to put in springs that would do well for a large Pullman car – but on which my form makes no impression. Nothing but a man of Sargents build bouncing about as if in delirium for a fortnight could soften its character – I am sending it back today.

Your E

1 The campaign to disestablish the Church of England as the state religion was being particularly hotly debated in Parliament in 1929 with the aim of preventing political interference in matters of worship. Four Church of England dioceses in Wales had already been disestablished some years earlier.
2 Randall Davidson, Archbishop of Canterbury 1903-1928.

July 2nd, 1929

Darling E. I confess this seems to me unanswerable! I had no idea that England contains but 3 000 000 Anglicans. I wonder what Archbishop D wd say to it??

The bed *[problem struck out]* crisis will be over by Sat next I hope (Joyce is suddenly away) and I am glad it occurred for I found the spare bed had sagged badly – I always dimly felt I ought to take a night in it, and having done so I deeply apologise to all my guests. The man who conveyed away the bed to have its heart softened wound it up etc and now it is very very comfortable (I mean the spare bed)

Yr loving
E

Most of Ethel's correspondence during July was concerned with family arrangements to meet:

Yr Gran.r. is coming to lunch today and I shall take her to Triggs Lock Poor dear! She must be hard up for amusement to come here!"

And indeed, judging by modern photos Triggs Lock would not have offered someone with Mary Hunter's tastes much in the way of entertainment. There was also the on-going saga of her spare bed and various lost or desired items of clothing – like Virginia Woolf, Ethel always had a difficult relationship with her wardrobe:

> …do you have any <u>musk </u>(grey) fur you want to get rid of? I seem to remember your saying you too had surplus furs and your mother sent some musk – but not enough.

One letter enclosed two sheets of striking blue paper from Tigbourne Court, signed "Joyce" [Wethered] and explaining that her mother's ill-health and an imminent a fête were making visits difficult. The letter is, very understandably, marked "<u>tear up</u>".
Towards the end of the month, Elizabeth went to stay at Coign and this time it was her items of clothing that had to be got back to her. Ethel was also very anxious to get in touch with Vernon Lee and her repeated requests show her at her most insistent.

July 25th, 1929

> Dearest Elizabeth if I discourse at great length on….say… your memory, what sort of memory I mean and so on, please realise it is because Pan chewed up, as I think I told you, my 17/6 fountain pen, and at this moment I have all Watermans' shop on my table owing to the fact that one of the young ladies at "Pen Corner" sang in the Albert Hall on the occasion of the Royal Mass. Of course my object is to test the lot and for that there is nothing like unchecked verbosity. For example what more to the point than to say I have just discovered that according to a new valuation, valid for 5 years of rates and taxes my yearly contribution will be £33 instead of £27[1] and that I am lodging a protest of a vigorous order.
>
> Well: I suppose re Vernon, I should have said "don't leave it to your Grandmother to tell me the 2 things I want to find out a) where Vernon is staying b) if and when she has arranged for us to met at No.2 <u>because of course yr Grandm. will forget all about it </u>but get the information from her and send me a p.c. <u>yourself</u>."

As a matter of fact I did ask you to let me know. It wd never occur to me to ask you or anyone to take any other step, if it is a case of getting any mortal thing out of your Grandmother. I know too well how the matter would

Scatter in liquid dust, and drift
To death among the dusty sand[2]

Mind I am an overorganiser and inclined to see the last turn of the screw everywhere. So I <u>think</u> in yr case I shd have written to Coign "Vernon is staying with E Sargent and Gr. <u>says</u> she will ring you up this afternoon <u>when she will know</u> about [?] – meanwhile I gather that Vernon is seedy and impossible to pin down to anything"....

Now....you see I wanted to make <u>plans</u> (as ever) when one faces going to London – well – in what an admirable (2nd new pen came in here) position I should have been to do so if you had sent me a p.c.!...See?

I dont think though this is a case of short <u>memory</u>...and if you had realized enough how much I wanted to know (which you did to a certain extent but not enough to make you act as above....which <u>I</u> certainly shd have done because of my personal twist...what Bob calls butting in) you would have sent that p.c.

[The letter continues with more on the subject of her pen; social events; Belloc; her health and – related – the misdemeanors of her maid, Mary. "Irish people can't help lying and it is no good charging her with it or being angry…"]

1 £33 and £27 in 1929 = roughly £1633.5 and £1336.5 in 2010.
2 from Arthur Symonds (1865-1945) *Silhouettes*.

A couple of days later Ethel wrote again, jumping from one topic to another: the problems of choosing a pen, different types of writing paper; still nagging Elizabeth about Vernon's address: " Yes, I think your Vernon sin was laziness - not forgetfulness….", before going on to Belloc and the Catholic Church and why English Catholics were so much more militant than those in Latin countries. Unusually, there is no salutation at beginning or end. This was something characteristic of her nieces, including Elizabeth's mother, Phyllis, that makes it very hard to sort out who was writing to whom, since they all had very similar handwriting. Subsequent letters continued with the theme of her disapproval of the Catholic Church with their "tawdry decorations" and, according to Ethel, objection to any kind of fun or pleasure, including music – which seems a little unfair.

There is then a gap of a couple of months before the correspondence begins again, with Ethel complaining of health troubles, especially a rheumatic shoulder. Her trip to Bath, a town of which she was fond and where she went in early August, was largely for medical reasons. She mentions a visit from Maurice Baring, who was planning to write about Ethel's beloved H.B.

> Maurice came down and took away some of H.B.'s letters to refresh his memory about Rome in 1901-2...He wrote today "O what a marvellous book one cd make of extracts from those letters!" No one wrote such letters, you know...

October 23rd, 1929

2 Gloucester Square
W2

Beloved Aunt,

[Miscellaneous plans]

I am very busy but in a rather restless way and seem always rushing about but not doing much. I have not got into my stride with my lecturing and have had a difficulty fitting it in to give me whole days at Hendon[1], and to suit everyone concerned. I have 7 for my own lecture. My new lecture is disappointing. I was looking forward to declaiming then but the audience = 1 so it is really more like coaching and not such fun.

[On various concerts]

Another problem I am wrestling with is a spiritual one. I won't inflict you with it, but it is beastly. Having basked in the Lord's grace for months to a degree quite exceptional for me, He has turned away His face.[2]

Today is the first "open to the public" afternoon at the observatory. We don't know whether there will be hordes of eager enquirers or no one at all!

Yr lng
E

1 EMW was working at the University of London Mill Hill Observatory at Hendon.
2 This paragraph was heavily marked in red pencil by ES.

October 25th, 1929

33 Brock St, Bath

Darling Elizabeth – I cant write the freestepping letter to which my spirit is O so disposed because my arm is steadily getting worse (I think) tho' X ray shows how right the bone setter was – nothing distinctly resembling arthritis. But...I think it's a torn tendon that has got stuck and is now a complex of rheumatism. Time I think will help...as happens with all neuritic things but meanwhile everything hurts it – to write, not write, to blow my nose, to go in a car and so on and I am certain – after trying this and that – that Lord Melbourne's word is the only solution "Cant you let it alone?"[1]

Alice, Ethel and Nina left yesterday - - all were such dears – but I want to go straight to your letter because if I can get it off in ¾ hour it will reach you in London. As I told you, why D[elius].[2] provokes you is that you instinctively feel and resent the planless brain. This meandering of an exquisite musical organisation makes all his charm and attitude enjoyable to me – always has – and is just what attracts T[homas]B[eecham].[3] Of that I am certain. I think some of his short things (the Cuckoo) lovely and from what I heard thro' the wireless (for I never heard it really) on the 18th I feel sure I shd enjoy the concerts...Lots of Sea Drift is lovely – but the Invertebrate spinal cord if one can say such a thing runs thro' all – and you feel he doesn't know when he is meandering and that it may happen any moment. This and the monotony and greyness, is the reason why he has never quite caught on and he shd have if you could edit him – tho' conductors like conducting him and tho' he is very well known in Germany where he ranks as a German!! His publisher said to me in the summer "but why is D. an <u>Englishman</u> in England?" I said "George III advised Haendel to be <u>naturalised</u> and since then he is chez nous Handel and counts as an Englishman. Geo III and T.B. were both very wise about their master passion [?]." He was much amused. Most of D. makes me want to scream after about 5 mins and O his opera!!! Lovely bits... but...well – you can imagine. By the way there was a beautiful performance of Hey Nonny[4] at Belfast and wild press and other appreciation...its never been <u>well</u> done in London! But I shall try to achieve something when I return - tho' not for this season – Why you love Brahms is the reason why Tschaikowsky – a clever, superficial spirit (see my Vol II – Imps) – loathed him. He is as constructive and as brainy as Beethoven – the most satisfying of composers in the long run – or at least as regards the depth of his thought. He hasn't the exuberant melody of Schubert and the sort of invention that goes with irrepressible melodious inspiration. But he has the sort of inspiration that goes with the power of moving ever so deep under the surface without being crushed by the weight of the water. – It is that slow, massive, inexorably grim brain movement of his that is unlike anyone else and his claim to immortality. At least I think so – slow titanic wrestlings and accents that remind one of Goethe's Prometheus ------- O by the by Maurice [Baring] sent me a book of a desperate character for a cure by J.W. Allen late Prof of Hist at Bedford College London University "Political Thought in the 16th Century". I told him I cd not see the wood for the trees and that if as M. says he is a brilliant lecturer I wish he cd be a little more snappy in this tome. "Shd I send it on to someone else...someone like Dean Inge or Bishop Hewson?" But M. implored me to "pick out the plums" such as Knox, Calvin, Henry VIII. Etc. The modern mind. I am keeping this pc (lest I miss the plums when I come across them) and am starting again full of hope and determination – <u>but in the middle! Tell me about him</u>? Is he an RC? (I haven't read enough to hazard a guess!)

I am so sorry for your being spiritually in the desert (tho' I myself am there too). This I am certain of that these periods of aridity (Eli, Eli, etc) are part of every blessed game we are called on to play. I expect great financiers have periods when bulls and bears or whatever they are called seem to them dream creatures – like dodos and unicorns. But that it is so in things of the spirit is the deadest of certainties – and O it is beastly – and the younger you are the more beastly. All my sympathy------------

I don't expect to be home until 1st week of November – I loved you and the telescope. You had the air of a slim properly detached young don. Very chic was that aloofness and also that anonymity for no one cd see who was who.

> Bless you darling.
> Your E

1 Famous dictum of William Lamb, 2nd Viscount Melbourne (1779-1848), British politician and Whig Prime minister, generally opposed to change for change's sake.
2 Frederick Delius (1862-1934) – English composer. *On Hearing the First Cuckoo in Spring*, 1912-13; *Sea Drift* – for baritone choir and orchestra, 1903-4.
3 Thomas Beecham, (1879-1961), conductor and impresario, founder of the London Philharmonic and Royal Philharmonic Orchestras, a major figure in the English musical world and a great supporter of Delius.
4 *Hey Nonny No* by ES, chorus and orchestra, 1910, dedicated to the harpsichordist Violet Gordon Woodhouse.

November 3rd, 1929

33 Brock St, Bath

Darling Eliz I want you to hear Tovey. I have tickets for the Wigmore Hall concert on the 16th November Sat. 3 pm. What if you came with me and if we went off to Coign together? Are you free? It's a <u>very</u> interesting concert – [Adela] Fachiri - and they play a Brahms Sonata (not my favourite alas!) 2 new Hindemith[1] Sonatas (the man whose career I foresaw and wrote about in 1922 "Music in Germany") and also they play either a Mozart or a Beeth, sonata. A good article on Schnabel[2], Delius etc. in the New Statesman of yest.y. but Tovey is as great as Schnabel any day and for the same reason.

[Various social arrangements]

1 Paul Hindemith (1895-1963) German composer and violinist, who taught composition at Berlin from 1927. His work was original and controversial. He also had a complicated relationship with Nazism and in the 1930s spent time in Turkey reorganizing Turkish musical education. It is not clear to which sonatas ES refers.
2 Artur Schnabel (1882-1951) German pianist and composer. He taught at Berlin 1925-1933, and had a specially devotion to the classical German composers.

25th November, 1929

The next letter, from Coign, has one or more pages missing:

"His back showed dolphin-like above his pleasures" is the phrase I think – substitute "Her" and "labours"and there you are![1] Darling you need <u>never</u> write me Collinses - I believe you like coming when you can as I like having you. I am so glad I played you bits of the Opus – it gets more and more difficult....one has to avoid so desperately carefully <u>monotony</u>, before you get to the "What are they waiting for?" and after that, not to spend too much capital over "<u>Go then...pass on immortal ones</u> – etc. etc.

This must be weighed against the following chorus "The laughter you have laughed" and the colour of the Souls soul-o (a joke) "For years you have been conning your lesson" a sort of subdued glow ("milky way", etc.)...ending in "<u>now someone says 'taste also death'</u>"

From there (<u>Banners and Music</u>) I see the shape, the bulk all right – but its coming right depends on the awfully hard bit I am doing now. When I come from Lincoln shall tackle "Go then pass on" after deep thought in a <u>1st class carriage</u> (Yes!) later on (T.O.) I would so like the next Vol. of Thucydides – it is enthralling. Imagine – my bed book just now is the Trial of Socrates !! So there's hope for me!

[1] A somewhat confused paraphrase of *Antony and Cleopatra*, Act V, scene 2: "… his delights/Were dolphin-like, they showed his back above/The element they lived in….."

December 9th, 1929

Darling Eliz I must tell you my wild excitement – As I told you I was wondering how to treat the 6 lines about the syrinx and the kisses and all that. Well! I have fitted the words [?] too gloriously to two of the fragments – One the <u>Aidin inscription</u>[1] is I think well known – the Phrygian mode and the diatonic genus (!!) (I don't know what the Greek words mean but will find out). The other, the "Ajax fragment"[2] is, may it please you, "a mixture of the Ionan, Hyperionan and Hyperaeolian Keys" – modal scale is "Lydian tetrachord joined to a Dorian chromatic tetrachord" (!) and is a form of the Mixolydian (what Beethoven used in a divine later quartett)[3]. Sounds nice doesn't it? Of course all Gregorian music is simply these modes. I was singing (nasally) the Ajax fragment, fitting it to the words, and Pan gently howled[4] and finally came and licked my nose in distress, so I think it will be effective – I have slightly displaced (or rather transposed) H.B's lines and have them thus:

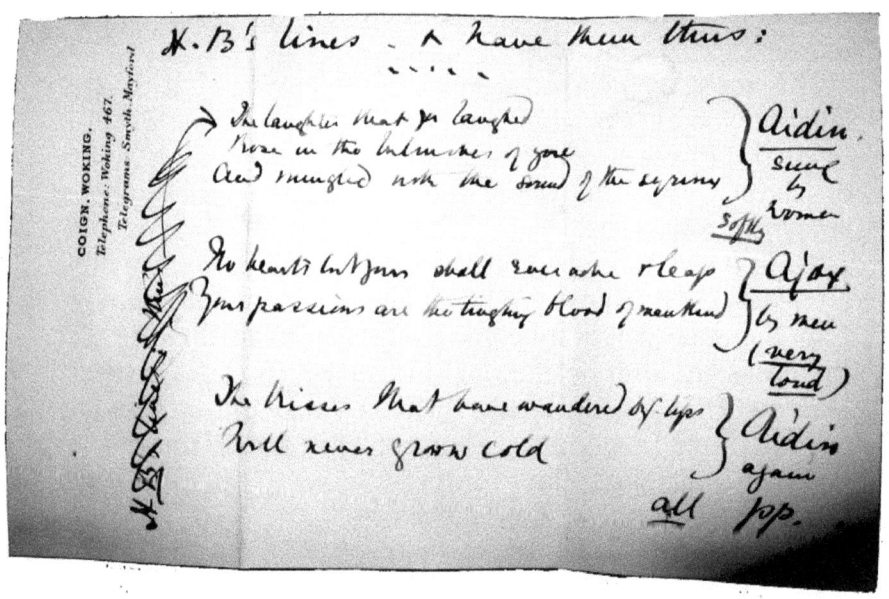

Ethel Smyth's plan to use the fragment

I am awfully excited at this. Of course people have used these modes before (Holst, in the "Hymn of Jesus" the whole beautiful "Pane something" as embodied in the Russian Mass)[5] But the point is if these things happen unsuitably or are dragged in (It is fine in Holst).

Your lov.g
E

1 The Seikilos epitaph (c.100 B.C.-100 A.D.), with notes as well as words, was found on a funeral stele at Aidin (Aydın), near Ephesus, in Turkey and is believed to be the first complete composition to have survived:
    Ὅσον ζῆς, φαίνου,
    Hoson zês, phainou,
    While you live, shine,
    μηδὲν ὅλως σὺ λυποῦ·
    mêden holôs su lupou;
    don't suffer anything at all;
    πρὸς ὀλίγον ἐστὶ τὸ ζῆν,
    pros oligon esti to zên,
    life exists only a short while,
    τὸ τέλος ὁ χρόνος ἀπαιτεῖ.
    to telos ho chronos apaitei.
    and time demands its toll.
2 The Ajax fragment from Berlin papyrus 6870, dated to c.2nd c. A.D., seems to be the *threnos* of Tecmessa from Aeschylus' *Ajax*.
3 For these technical terms see any standard source e.g. *Ancient Greek Music*, Martin Litchfield West, Oxford U.P., 1992; or relevant Wikipedia entries.
4 "growled" crossed out.
5 Possibly ES is referring to *Panis angelicus*, part of St Thomas Aquinas' *Sacris solemniis*, a hymn for the feast of Corpus Christi, much less celebrated in the Orthodox Church, however, than in the Catholic.

December 11th, 1929

On December 11th, Ethel surpassed herself in communicativeness, writing three times in one day:

> Darling Eliz. I meant to write to you but there was no time…and isn't about Budge – I know it is narrow of me but I think one <u>must</u> be very careful abt using archaic diction. If 100 years ago Shelley and Keats could say "<u>squanders</u>" surely "squandereth" and all the "eth" family are a nuisance (all except Eth-el I hope). Also I wonder if you can <u>squander a bed with rosy hues</u> - ?? I thought the most you could do was squander rosy hues about or on yr bed?
>
> I know the worth to you of yr Sat freedom but those puppet shows of Simonds[1] are quite unique. Great art – Shakespeare's England as surviving today in Glos: etc. I'm lunching on Saturday with your Gran.r. This lest she forgets to tell you.
>   Yr E

1William Simmonds (Constantinople 1876 – Gloucestershire 1968), was a prominent member of the Arts and Crafts Movement and a well-known maker and operator of puppets, as well as a sculptor. ES might have seen *The Woodland* with its cast of nymphs, fawns etc.

December 11th, 1929

The second letter was a request that Elizabeth obtain a translation of the Seikilos Epitaph for her, while the third contained:

Two queries
1) Wd you like to write to Vittoria Sermoneta[1] and go there with yr friend to lunch? Its a lovely palace and she is the greatest dear – very intelligent and has always been a family friend. She's very sound on art and things and wl give you some good tips. If so let me know when you go and I'll write. She is going immediately after the Royal Wedding – (or was) that is January 8th to Africa.

2) Can your professor translate for me (they are quite short) literally, the words of the Aidin Inscription and the words of the Ajax fragment? Or what wd do as well tell me where I can find a translation? The book I have them in I wd send with greatest pleasure."New Chapters in Greek Literature" (1929) 2nd Series edited by J.U. Powell and E.A. Barker.

Only as it's a library book I shd have to have it sent back – such a bore. And I expect any Greek scholar has access to such a book the fragments are in Chapter IV "The Arts" and give the musical analysis etc. – (thrilling only most of it beyond me) – but no translations ever. It wd thrill me to know what lots of the words mean – that of the so-called Xtian Hymn.[2] But these editors are too grand to stoop to translation. Am sparing arm when I can (!) for work.

E

P.O.

I fear the editing is too recent to be very current – tho' the Aidin inscription was found in 1883. They took squeezes - and well they did for when Smyrna was burnt in 1922[3] this stone perished!! ("Picture it — think of it, Dissolute man! Lave in it, drink of it, Then, if you can!")[4] The inscrip has been discussed by people like Cousins, Reinach and R. Wagner (! not Richard!). It is thought to be 1st cent Xtian era. The Ajax fragment is a papyrus – the poem itself reasonably thought to be an excerpt from a tragedy (it is 4 lines only...mutilated)

Your E

1 Vittoria Colonna, Duchess of Sermoneta (1880-1954), famous beauty and amateur of literature and the arts. She published a number of books, including *Things Past*, London and N.Y., 1929 and her description of Ethel Smyth taken from it is given above.
2 This is what is believed to be perhaps the first surviving Christian hymn from the Oxyrynchus papyrus, 3rd c. A.D., P.Oxy.XV 1786 in the Sackler Library Oxford, published in 1922.
3 On the 13th September, 1922, the Turkish forces set fire to Smyrna, massacring many of the Christian inhabitants and driving out the rest, in order to rid Turkey of what was called *Gavur Izmir* – infidel Smyrna, on account of its large Greek, Armenian and Jewish populations. The fire, the massacres and the deportations were recorded by numerous eyewitnesses of various nationalities, including Turkish. Smyrna was largely destroyed. The stele eventually resurfaced, damaged, in the house of a Turkish woman and is now in the National Museum of Denmark.
4 Rather an odd quotation in the context, taken from Thomas Hood, *The Bridge of Sighs* (1844) on a homeless young woman who had committed suicide by throwing herself from Waterloo Bridge.

The following is an impression of ES by Vittoria Colonna[1]:

Amongst the neighbours whom we saw most of was the celebrated Dame Ethel Smyth, the composer, who has spoken charmingly of the Empress[2] and the Farnborough Hill *milieu* in the memoirs she has published.

We all delighted in her, for she was always entertaining and cheered us up with her great vitality and ready wit. Her friendship with the Empress was most curious, as two more different natures can hardly be imagined, but the Empress appreciated her clever brain though she sometimes shook her head and murmured: "*Elle est vraiment trop bataillère.*"

Ethel Smyth often dines at Farnborough Hill and it was her custom to bicycle over from her cottage, take up a good strategic position behind some bushes when once in the park, and proceed to change into evening clothes, after which she would run up to the front door and ring the bell. After this had gone on for some months the Empress got to hear of it and was rather upset, so in future a carriage was sent for her guest. I am sure my old friend will forgive me saying – and will also agree with me – that this innovation did not make any difference in her personal appearance, her great charm being an utter lack of feminine vanity.

I remember once she turned up rather late for dinner and the Empress was already in the drawing-room. This was contrary to Farnborough etiquette, which demanded that all the guests should be assembled before the Empress made her appearance. Ethel advanced towards her hostess, running and curtseying at the same time, the result being a series of kangaroo leaps. A minute later my aunt beckoned to me and whispered: "*Emmène Miss Smyth et arrange un peu sa robe.*"

Whereupon I obeyed, and a certain amount of hitching up went on in the long gallery outside.

"My dear", said the great musician, still breathless and wriggling, "I'll tell you what's the matter. I bought a new pair of stays at the grocer's and I believe he sold me a birdcage by mistake."

Later on she neglected her music for a time and became a militant Suffragette, which thrilled us much more as none of us was particularly musical and we all preferred excitement. We never tired of telling her to tell us her experiences; how she was arrested and what prison was like. I can still see her sitting on the grass under an oak tree on a golden summer evening, surrounded by an admiring ring of young Spaniards and Italians. She invariably wore a rough tweed skirt, a man's shirt with a stiff collar and a coloured tie and a hard straw sailor hat, and smoked like a chimney. "I was in Berkeley Square," she told us, "and I said to the policeman, 'Which is Mr Harcourt's house?' He answered, 'I don't know' and I said '*Don't* you? Then I'll show you!' and I threw the stone I had in my muff and smashed the window to smithereens." (We all gasped with delight.) "The policeman said, 'I felt it coming! Will you go quietly, Miss?'"

We were all rather disappointed to hear she *did* go quietly.

In prison Ethel was put to sew policemen's trousers. As she had never held a needle in her life, she pointed out to the authorities that it was pretty rough on the policemen, but she had to do it all the same."

1 Vittoria Colonna, Duchess of Sermoneta, *Things Past*, London, 1929, pp.129-30.
2 The Empress Eugénie de Montijo (1826-1920) of France; in exile, she was a neighbour at Farnborough, a friend of the Smyth family and a great supporter of ES's musical ambitions, as well as a firm advocate of women's right to work.

Hampstead Women's Social and Political Union,
178, FINCHLEY ROAD, N.W.

WINDOW BREAKING
AND
INCITEMENT
TO
MUTINY.

For Breaking Windows as a Political protest, Women are now in H.M. Gaols serving sentences of
Four and Six months imprisonment.

For Inciting Soldiers to Disobey Orders, a much more serious crime, known to the law as a felony, and punishable by penal servitude, the Publishers of the "Syndicalist," were sentenced to nine months hard labour, and the Printers of the paper to six months hard labour.

The Government under the pressure of men with votes reduced this sentence on the Publishers to
Six months imprisonment without hard labour,

and the sentence on the Printers to
One month without hard labour.

IS THIS JUSTICE TO VOTELESS WOMEN ?

Suffragette handbill

With Pan

1930

A bundle similar to the others, tied with thin string; some of the envelopes grubby, and with more water damage than some other years. Unless otherwise mentioned the letters are from Coign to Elizabeth at 2 Gloucester Square or Mount Mascal (MM), where she was staying with her cousins. Mount Mascal Farm now seems to be a livery stable and warden for the Woodland Trust of the local woods, all of which would have given Elizabeth great pleasure.

Many of Ethel's letters to Elizabeth contain elaborate plans for meeting, sometimes including complicated train and bus timetables. Arrangements for playing golf was a another favourite topic of which this is fairly standard example:

February 4th, 1930

Darling Eliz if your party is on Tues February 25th I simply will come to it as I am quite free. But even if it were on the 3rd when I am haranguing the Universe for ½ hour it might be possible....But the 25th is perfect. I am immersed in work... but I won't miss this chance of identifying myself with my "gifted young niece" as Grace Wemyss[1] called you yest.y. Of course it is, (O dear) an evening affair and what to wear I can't think. But we'll see to that on Sat. Tell me would you like to have a very good foursome? The swell Illingworth[2] is here – he gives his Pa (whom I love) a half. Women may start at 11.30 if with club members and we'd fix meals (slight lunch at 11.30 and proper feed at 2 accordingly). Tell if you'd like this (a foursome) or rather stay quiet? Or wd you prefer a single with a woman? – I played 12 holes today. Am weak but dead sound. I think I shall play rather better than before by and by!! I feel so very supple (relatively) at the shoulders. Cd you let me know by return abt Sunday? Perhaps quiet a.m. and perhaps just dodder with me or walk wd be best for you. But tell me so that the I[llingworth]'s may not tie themselves up. Yr E

On the outside of the envelope: "Mahler's thing is of course magnificent"

1 Grace, Countess of Wemyss and March (c.1857-1946).
2 Probably Albert Illingworth (1865-1942) - Liberal politician.

Read this

June 15 1920
Ebury Street 121

My dear Phyllis,

Your letters are always full of humanity and are therefore admirable; and to this merit is added a manner of writing entirely your own — one that springs out of an individual mind; you see life from a special angle and are ~~Tiyalefeel~~ — highly qualified, I know nobody more so, I might have said truthfully, as highly qualified as yourself ~~to~~ write a book — not necessarily a novel. Why don't you write one? You wished for

George Moore to Phyllis Williamson

another baby too. As you might ward off yourself, circumstances were against you. It is with your disappointment in mind that I suggest the alternative, a book. A book is a creation, quite as much so as many ~~babies~~ Babies, as long lived and much less expensive. Try the alternative I shall be mystified if it doesn't succeed. (not for publication)

Begin ~~hop~~ my life passes by in loneliness and composition. I see hardly anybody, nobody for long but my secretary to whom I dictate from 1500 to 200 words daily. Héloise and Abélard

February 19th, 1930

The 19th of February brought more complicated travel arrangements, as well as problems of what to wear - a recurring issue:

> Darling E We are told not to dress and certainly the plays will be suitable to assist at in ordinary day clothes. I shall bring some old tea gown or other (for I have <u>no</u> betwixt and between garments) for supper, which is to be afterwards in Miss S's office. Just ourselves. About trains – that's right the 1.15 arr. at 3 when the school taxi will meet us. I feel certain the only way to get to Brighton is to go back to Padd. and across to Victoria. But couldn't you find that out as you are in London? Ring up [Thomas] Cook? I am sure the safest thing is to take to Bath what we shall want at R.....I am feeling depressed at the thought of my wig. But I probably wont wear it. It was touching at Henschel's[1] today"

1 George Henschel (1850-1934) - British musician, composer and conductor; February 18th would have been his 80th birthday.

May 16th, 1930

On May 16th, Ethel wrote that she had to go to Manchester, adding:

> Virginia[1] keen on inviting you to dinner. Says she shall do so but I doubt if she knows your address. As however I'm not sure when you go to Middlethorpe perhaps we'd better leave it (she is more than vague and helpless about dates, etc.)...

[Other plans; tennis and golf]

1 Ethel Smyth and Virginia Woolf met in February 1930 and ES immediately fell in love and began to overwhelm VW with demands. (See Quentin Bell, *Virginia Woolf: A Biography*, London: Hogarth Press, 1972 vol. II pp.151-2). VW was at the time desperately trying to finish *The Waves*. Their friendship was tumultuous, as VW's letters and diaries make clear, but continued, although with decreasing intensity, until her suicide in 1941.

June 3rd, 1930

On her return, a couple of weeks later ES details her numerous engagements, work commitments and travel plans. Her energy was amazing: after all she was 72 and her means did not allow her to take taxis or do anything to make her constant running around less tiring.

Darling Eliz – Having so gloriously heard the bird[1] (and probably I shall do so again tonight) I think I will escape 2 journeys at Whitsun and go straight home from London on Thursday morning – (you know I am going up to Toscanini[2] tomorrow – dining with V.W.) P[hyllis] quite agrees this is common sense. I believe tomorrow is a bad day with you. But if not I wonder if you could come after yr labours are ended to 40 Moore St to tea? (Sloane Sq the station). I go up in time to hear my records at Petty France (Westminster) and at about 4.30 shall deposit myself and luggage at Moore St. Of course your letter has not come yet and I doubt not it will be thrilling – but there are dozens of questions one wd love to ask.

Do ring up "Mrs Daly" at 40 (Kens.5523) and just say "tell Dame E I can (or I can't) come to tea."

I shall fly down home first thing – I really am getting terrified about my work…no more long jaws to V.W. –no more "pleasure of any sort" (that's one comfort).

Yr loving E

1 ES had a passion for nightingales and went to considerable trouble to hear them whenever possible.
2 Arturo Toscanini (1867-1957) – Italian conductor, then touring Europe with the New York Philharmonic.

The same day, Elizabeth sent her great-aunt a fairly detailed account of dinner with Virginia Woolf:

June 3rd, 1930

Darling Aunt,
The telephone is no good as the fact of concentrating on the vocal problem completely paralyses my wits and I was <u>shouting.</u>

During dinner we talked of politics and Mosley's brush with his party[1]. V. was rather silent and abstracted during this. We had a delicious meal of cold fish, roast chicken and asparagus – then fruit and coffee and we all 4 smoked cigars and adjourned downstairs simultaneously. We talked of balls and parties, of the modern v. the old social machine. V. thought we have much more fun and that the formality and the decorum which Henry James so loved and which he wouldn't find now, is more than compensated for by our greater intimacy. She says she admires H.J. very much but hardly reads him for fun ever. She knew him quite well – at least that is what she said it was quite impossible to do, through all his endearments; "My dear child...." And so on. We talked of George Moore (Hutchinson[2] knows him very well), Tonks, Steer[3] and all that galère, and they asked me a lot about old days at Hill. V. seemed amused by my tales of the long war time visit of the Rodins. I can't quite remember the transition, but next came up people and their interest. H. said how endlessly he found them interesting and that was charm to him of his job. Then Woolf began about astronomy and there was an argument. V. and I were against L.W. and H. was hedging. L.W. said that contemplating the stars must make all human affairs seem of no importance whatsoever, or if not that, then, that looked at from a human point of view, the cosmos was an imbecile affair, [??] silly. We said, at least I said and V. agreed, that to judge the external world, Nature, in terms of a human scale of importance was impossible. I said we only had a mental construction built up from sense impressions by thought (about which nobody knew anything) and to assign importance or value to it was impossible. That to my mind to say a "nebula" is more "important" than Hamlet is to talk illogically. V. said a pain in her finger was not affected by the distance of the stars. This argument lasted only about 5 mins. and fizzled out. V. said she thought of the moon as she had seen it in the Nicholson's small telescope. We then talked about words and whether a word called up the thing it represented visually or not. V. said that when we said ROSE we probably saw a rose but her first feeling was of a short hard word to go in among other words. She then said what a waste of impressions and emotions it was never for one moment to get behind another person's eyes and see with them. Then somehow the talk got on to the Royal Family. V. seemed very interested in these strange beings and we contributed from a meagre store of royal impressions. H. knew some of them and I described the process of the annual visit of the Queen to Appley and she asked a lot of questions. At length H. went away to a party to look after his daughter. I made civil motions to go. They wouldn't let me – at least she wouldn't, but he I am sure wanted me to! We talked a little more and then I went. She asked me about your house and how far away the Balfours were. She asked me about golf, whether you played well, whether I played well, and what there was that made it amusing and was Billy Jones the best in the world. She said she had a great love for cricket in her youth and could have got mad keen at it.

That is about what the evening was. She seemed worried about her cook[4] who is having an operation I think today. She looked entrancing in a long rather stiff brocade coat I think. I went according to your orders in "the old green"! L.W. didn't dress, and H. was in party rig.

They seemed to think Vita's text "very readable"[5], and are making a great success from the sale point of view I gathered.

So glad you have heard the nightingale.

Yr loving
E

1 Oswald Mosley's (1896-1980) drastic proposals - the "Mosley Memorandum" - for relieving unemployment, including an extensive programme of public works, was applauded by the liberal press, but rejected by the Labour government, and Mosley resigned in May 1930.
2 St John Hutchinson KC (1884-1942) – a prominent barrister and supporter of the arts. His wife Mary was a cousin of Lytton Strachey and they had numerous friends and contacts among both Bloomsbury and the wider world of English artists and intellectuals.
3 Philip Wilson Steer OM (1860-1942) was a British painter of landscapes, seascapes plus portraits and figure studies. He was also an influential art teacher.
4 The cook, Nelly, with whom the Woolfs had a very long and somewhat wearing relationship (see *Mrs Woolf and the Servants*, Alison Light, Penguin, 2008) had had an operation in May 1930. In August, VW became very ill (Bell II p.154).
5 Vita Sackville-West, *The Edwardians*.

June 4th, 1930

Ethel answered the next day in pencil on some scraps of paper:

> Darling Eliz you wrote a noble account of yr evening – really an awfully good summary....
> What I wanted to ask you was
> 1) Did you broach the subject of dining at W2 (I think she might like it if told she might come in her coat – the one she had on!) Query – will the end of the world prevent the coming off of this plan?
> 2) *[Golf]*
> 3) I sh'd have liked to know from what point of view she enquired about Coign – dimensionally or the Scale of Life there, or what?
> 4) Did you describe the Balfour ménage – the Clever Ones, Mr S and all that – and did you tell her what a prize dear Betty[1] is?
> 5) *[Golf]*
> 6) Was she <u>at all</u> impressed by your remarks and comparing the Milky Way with Hamlet? I think they were excellent and want to shake her faith (if she has any) in his very German-materialistic ways of thought.
> 7) Yes, I expect he wanted her to go to bed when H went – but she loves talk and <u>not</u> going to bed. She does too much.
> 8) Did H realise you and I are relations (I learned too late that he was the nephew of the man who made me loathe Evangelism – or is it Evangelicalism?)
> I am dead tired ...[health]...O what triumph abt the nightingales! Again last night we went and sat under the very bush the bird was singing in. I heard another far off but Phyllis heard 4 – a concert. Each night bed at 1 and I'm worn out and don't feel concertish. I think the H's so adorable that I cant hold forth [?] about it. Her capability delights me – the way she led us oer moor and fen oer crag and torrent in a bee line to the bird she had selected was marvellous. (I did <u>heaps</u> of work – really worked all the time); we had roaringly gay meals.
> I think there is something a trifle don-ish about L.W. Do you? Yet I feel it is only skin deep. I don't think he is cold,

really, but I think he has a don-like respect for...well, you know.

I wonder if on a further acquaintance you have an increased, or lessened, impression of V's frailty? Did she strike you as <u>tired</u>? (I think the cook affair has worried her a lot – Tho' she would say "I am very very good about hospitals and all that." I don't like to think of her having to cope with situations of that kind –

Your E

1 Elizabeth "Betty" Balfour (1867-1942) - see introduction.
Her sister, Constance Bulwer-Lytton (1869-1923), was a militant suffragette and campaigner for women's rights, prison reform and birth control. On her arrest in 1910, she posed as an ordinary seamstress in order to avoid special privileges as a member of the ruling class. It is thought that her treatment in gaol, particularly forced feeding, caused the strokes that led to her relatively early death.

June 7th, 1930

On the 7th, Virginia Woolf wrote to Elizabeth:

Dear Elizabeth
(and I think you might call me Virginia) I don't see why you should thank me – it seemed to me great goodness on your and Jack Hutchinson's part to put up with that stingy feast. (After cooking it my poor old char collapsed – smashed several tumblers, lost all her keys and complained of violent pains in the toes rather an excessive tribute I thought to the excellence of the dinner). But I enjoyed seeing you all the same. I never meant – how could she, I be such a fool? – that I don't enjoy every atom of admiration, only when people like you and your Aunt are too generous, then I begin to mumble and jumble. Suppose someone told you that you were a great mathematician?

We shall be very pleased to look at stars. Will you rig something up? I have forgotten your address. I rather think you are with Dame Ethel in Kent: but it is safer to send to London.

Please give her my love and tell her I shall give a full account of you one day. At the moment my mind is like a litter of broken glass: I almost said puppies; but they are composed and coherent compared to me. Why is it that contact with servants, servants sisters, with servants young men, doctors, kidneys, insurance societies, and charwomen has such an overwhelming effect. So I cant begin to describe you yet.

Yours,
Virginia Woolf

This was soon forwarded to Ethel:

> Darling Aunt,
> I enclose V's letter. She thought we were still together you see. Will you send it back as I shall hoard it. I enclose envelope as I am sure you are very busy.
>
> *[On reading a novel, apparently by Harry Brewster]*
>
> I wish I could confine my philosophic range to H.B.'s humanistic ground. Reading him is like being in a garden compared to being lost in a wilderness which is my own recurring state when not wholly engaged with my top (A better image for my particular pursuit could not be found – turning spheres with processional gyration.) It is a far more arid world in which I wander. The tormenting problems of the perception of the external world, and whether space and time are mental constructions or the very principle of the coherence of the physical world ....

June 9th, 1930

On the following day, Ethel replied that she had to come up to London for work, adding with the wildest underlinings, exclamation marks and words written large.

> Will you be at No.2 at lunch or at tea time unless (which is very unlikely) V. can see me then – but I'm sure it won't be possible. Anyhow I'll keep in touch with you and long to see her letter – She phoned to me that she liked you so much and hoped to see more of you. I think you'll be <u>SO</u> good for them.
> I have <u>found out what was wrong</u> (rheumatism stiffness

etc) and can now drive **miles** farther than <u>ever in my life</u> !!! wildly excited, Cant write. Work daily fr 6.30 a,m, to 11.

E

P.S. I was at the 11th tee – driving <u>with ease</u> balls right up to the bunker. Betty [Balfour] and Mrs Tennant advanced (Pan out of sight) and Mrs T. said "Lets keep well to the left – there's a girl slashing away in a murderous manner straight at us - (I was that girl!!)

Thursday, June 12th [1930]

Darling Aunt

I am afraid I shan't be here or anywhere available tomorrow. I am busy in the morning and going away in the early afternoon with <u>8</u> learned friends (!) from U.C. to a pub in the New Forest to play very bad golf. The Professor of Philosophy is among them with whom I am much in love as he has a brown beard and an entrancing mind, but married of course – always a girl's luck!

I am overjoyed about your <u>driving</u>.

Phyllis failed to read The Lighthouse and it was too hot for me to try to explain "<u>what anyone could possibly like in it</u>?" I only laughed and laughed.

Yr lv <u>E</u>

Saturday night, June 14th, 1930

Darling Eliz I had a delightful visit to V.W. today and took her up some carnations – We have arranged that you and L.W. are [to] arrange for them to come down here in their car. <u>Programme</u>: tea at Fishers Hill[1]....then (if I can get her!) Joyce to come over and do a few shots to show V. perfection!!

Elizabeth with Golfing Friends

You shall be whipping boy – play a hole or two together for V's edification!! (I must write to Joyce and ask her when she will be about) Then supper here – we will have Maurice [Baring] and Ronald [Storrs] and borrow plates and glasses from Betty – you are to be brought down by then in their car... [and incidentally we will hit off Trigg's Lock en route]

Virginia says I am to tell you please <u>to come to dinner</u> with them (just you 3) <u>at once</u>. I said "but you must invite her!" and then all details of our party can be settled. I shall now tell her I have told <u>you</u> to write to her <u>and say I told you to do so</u> and you are writing merely to say your <u>good</u> days are so and so...and any time etc. etc. you will be delighted to come. L.W. smiled his slow smile and said "I should like to upset her faith" (!) and evidently thinks it will be an <u>easy task</u>!!!

V. hopes you will fall in love with the beard you are now golfing with! Am longing to hear about your adventures.

The first stage of my work – coping with the Leeds crisis – is over – and although I find I am just ½ way through my (whole) job and hope to get done by the end of August

It is rather jolly having a solid mountain of work to bore yr way through.

V says you exaggerate the badness of Vita's book[2] – I say I'm sure you don't. (A flaming puff in Time and Tide today).

Yr loving E

1 Fishers Hill House, very close to Coign in Woking, was designed by Edward Lutyens in 1900-1 with gardens by Gertrude Jekyll, for ES's great friends the Balfours.
2 *The Edwardians* (1930)

June 16th, 1930

Two days later, she wrote again detailing plans in a way that must have irritated Leonard Woolf, while Virginia would probably have been sardonic, and it is to be doubted whether they would have been impressed by Joyce Wethered's eminence in her own field. The letter shows Ethel's schoolgirlish, somewhat pathetic enthusiasm.

Darling Eliz.

Joyce <u>enchanted</u>! Proposes <u>Mon.23rd</u> to start with and I have just sent LW this news and Betty's free days. Maurice and Ronald must fit in as they can when I've settled things. Joyce wd come over after tea – and stay to supper – [or to tea...anyway the point is that she can.... And what we hope and pray is that you will hit better shots now and again than J! Joyce says this she can guarantee <u>will</u> happen!!] I think even Lord B[alfour] will come out and witness the scene. Well: I've sent L.W. a duplicate of the paper I enclose and I've told him you will ring him up about 2 tomorrow Monday and ask if you shall come round to fix things up – or do it by phone or what? And then you'll let me know. Anyhow Monday 23rd is the first available day – and if the Woolfs are going to Rodmell[1] next Sunday (22nd) a later date <u>might</u> suit them better. But July 1st is far off and I am all for the 23rd!!

Yr.lv E

1 Rodmell in East Sussex, where V and LW had their country home, Monk's House.

June 24th, 1930

An amazing letter from V. about her past. I cant part with it but it is about you. I had sent her letters from you on religion "I send back E's very remarkable letters. What a terse and muscular mind she has – and it is this muscular mind that believes in God. I shall try to see her alone if I can and try to rake her mind with my erratic harrow, for she must be sown [?] with all sorts of seeds. I can't finish this image – I see her mind and I see my mind – but I am so hot so sleepy. I must leave it there." (pause). That's all abt you. I wrote to her a bit of our talk at breakfast – that I had said to you "they don't see that it may be a lack in them like thinking poetry all nonsense" – and I told V. she <u>must</u> see you alone – that I hoped you (E) wd put up a fight as I think the harrowing ought to be mutual.

Yr E

[PS: On a letter lost by the P.O.]

June 24th, 1930

Darling E <u>you know</u> how I value your weekend fresh air – but if I find Virginia (and the Bells whom I want you to know – by the Bells I mean Vanessa and D[uncan] Grant) are coming to this, would you care to come. I know <u>no one</u> else coming and we'll just have tea together us 6. I'll give you a ticket. (I'm forgoing all royalties and tipping them – so all is well and I can have as many tickets as I want).

I forgot to tell you that after supper when we were discussing character Virginia said "I <u>will</u> know – which do you like best, me or Vanessa." I said "Vanessa. She's a human being – flesh and blood like myself – but you!! God knows what you are!" And that very child-like genius, walking with me to Euston Rd said quite gravely and slightly perturbed "I know you do – or will like Vanessa the best!!" at which I laughed. All that and much else reminds me of our German Governess who used to say "What age have you? Answer 3 years."

Your E

had inspiration all along as to colour and I don't disguise from you that I feel as Jehovah did at the end of his job. All the same I don't forget that as in his case the final verdict may be far from unanimous. Do you remember the woman in "Histoire Contemporaine" who had no wish for a next world: "Vous me dîtes que celui qui l'a créé est le même qui a créé ce monde-ci?...Je ne connais que trop comme il travaille." But I think what I think all the same...and here it is.

I've been subterraneously conscious of you for all these weeks (or months is it?) since my head was in a bag. I had got an impression that you were not happy. I did not know why and wouldn't think about it as I could do nothing. Was it this world? or the other world? Well: no more of that till I see you but I am always always preoccupied with you, my dear. That's all.

[Pan's health]

My friendship with Virginia who I haven't seen for 3 weeks – she's at Rodmell – progresses and I get marvellous letters at intervals. She says Vita doesn't like even to think of her book[2] but cant help being glad of ability to flaunt money in the face of "that greedy old peasant woman, her mother". I don't know what about the party to celebrate the finish of the Prison – and V says she's in a blessed swoon – strolling on the downs and not an engagement in sight. Leonard W did say they might contrive (as they have to be in London a day or two) something about the middle of August – but I feel languid about it – even I....in this blessed swoon of work done!"

[The BBC and broadcasting; plans to meet; Pan]

...I proposed a meeting between Pinka (the Woolf's yellow dog who has just had a litter of coal black puppies) and Pan the resultant race to be called <u>Woking Wolf Hound</u>. Brilliant. What?

1 ES's setting, written in 1907, for Anacreon's (c.582-485 B.C.) 9th Ode for mezzo-soprano and chamber orchestra.
2 Presumably *The Edwardians*, 1930. A portrait of upper class life in the Edwardian period, it sold well, especially in the States, but there were reservations about its literary merit.

GROSVENOR HOUSE
PARK LANE
SUNDAY TEA-TIME
CHAMBER MUSIC CONCERTS
In the Ballroom (Grill Room Entrance)

LAST CONCERT THIS SEASON
JUNE 29th

Programme of compositions by
ETHEL SMYTH

String Quartet - - - - *(Curwen)*
      Allegretto lirico
      Allegro molto leggiero
      Andante
      Allegro energico

Song, - - Chrysilla - - *(Novello)*
    (arrangement for Voice, Piano and Violin)

Trio for Violin, Horn and Piano - - *(Curwen)*
      Allegro moderato
      Elegy (in memoriam)
      Allegro

The Cadenza in the last movement was specially written for Aubrey Brain. The Horn part can be played by Viola or Violoncello.

Herbert Heyner, *baritone*; Marjorie Hayward, Pierre Tas, *violins*; Rebecca Clarke, *viola*; May Mukle, *'cello*; Aubrey Brain, *horn*; Kathleen Long, *piano*;

Blüthner Pianoforte

TEA from 4.30—5.30   CONCERT 5.30—6.30   6/- inclusive
Smoking permitted.   Tables may be reserved.   Gros. 6363

Flier for Ethel Smyth's Concert June 29th, 1930

Elizabeth's letter and that of Virginia have both vanished from these packets, but the next day, Ethel wrote with some excitement:

June 26th, 1930

Here's the precious doc. I love you to see it but return it quick. How magnificently worded – her bit of autobiography. I <u>am</u> sorry you can't come on Sunday.

Haste – post write abt the review when you have time.

Your letter about isolation thrilled me. I have much to say but no time.

E

July 1st, 1930

Darling Eliz. Leonard thinks Virginia will be quite fit – but I am ringing him up tomorrow (Weds) at 9.15 a.m. to make sure. Blessed Hilda [Matheson][1] is seeing about the food for me (Harrods).

I wrote to Leonard that I hope he will bring Billy too – and that he and you must fix up where to meet. I expect they'd rather pick you up – I expect about 4.30.

[Detailed driving instructions]

Do <u>utterly</u> refuse to talk to V. coming down. I am terrified about knocking her up and you <u>have to be firm with her</u>. Say "I know you have been knocking yourself up recently and I really <u>wont</u> talk."

Go so far as saying you yourself have laryngitis (which can mysteriously get well here!)

Isn't it fun Vittoria [Colonna] is coming? I suggested to her the 5 pm fr Waterloo. I hope to bundle Virginia out of house at 9.15 (her great need is to get to bed early and her greatest desire, always, not to go to bed until morning.) You two can and must stay on – there's a convenient bus that catches the 10.34 at Woking (11.16 Waterloo). Joyce says she cant hit a ball and it's a shame to send you both down to the 10th tee which it is my inexorable intention to do – (such a capital place to sit and watch). She says it's the hardest hole in the course! I said "Good! Then Eliz will beat you" however she is quite sure that will happen any way! I told her Billy will caddy for her because otherwise we might get a crowd – O what fun!

["Do you know I ended by loving Maurice Baring's biography Robert Peckham[2]..."; on a film: "Nothing (as you say) is so entrancing as comic catastrophe – like the picnic at Kenwood in Vanessa's car"].

1 Hilda Matheson (1888-1940), was an important influence in forming BBC broadcasts and, as Director of Talks, invited many leading intellectuals to speak. Her left-wing views offended John Reith, the head of the BBC, and she resigned in 1931. From 1926, she and Vita Sackville-West were lovers and from c. 1932 she began a long-term relationship with the poet Dorothy Wellesley, Duchess of Wellington.. See also below, May 15th, 1935.
2 A historical novel, published 1930, inspired by an inscription on a tombstone in Rome which, translated, read: "Here lies Robert Peckham, Englishman and Catholic, who, after England's break with the Church, left England not being able to live without the faith and who, coming to Rome, died not being able to live without his country."

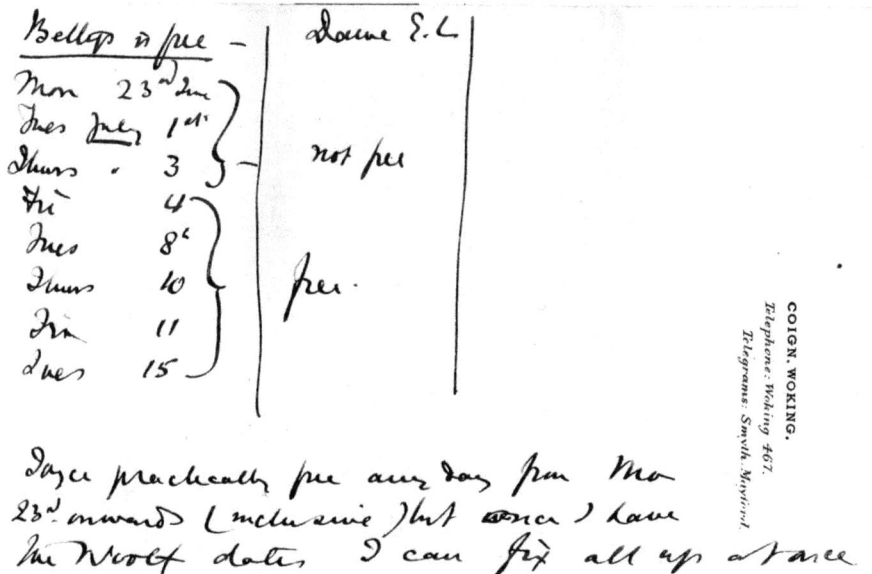

Ethel Smyth's "Calendar" for Virginia Woolf's visit

HILDA MATHESON

Born June 7th, 1888,
Died October 30th, 1940

THE HOGARTH PRESS
PIXMORE AVENUE
LETCHWORTH, HERTS
1941

Memorial volume for Hilda Matheson (inset) to which Ethel Smyth contributed

July 6th, 1930

[On meeting; a disappointing film; unsure where EMW is living]

I did so enjoy my party and had a priceless letter from Maurice [Baring] about it. Will show it to you. Anything fouler than that oil-broth I never ate but these are not the things that matter. I am in love now with Leonard Woolf – and quite understand Virginia selecting him. (The difficulty in that milieu seems to have been to pick a fiancé who was not a Sodomite – and L.W. was up to sample on that point for one thing). I wish you had not borrowed my form (golf) – and as things were it was idiotic not to ask darling Joyce to put down a doz. balls and show us approach shots. However, I know that Woolf (and I think Virginia) grasped her godlike attributes. I am so glad Maurice and she seemed to hit it off – and do you know I think V. really will come here sooner or later. You backed me up re the charms of Coign, like a true friend.

Clotilde[1] and all her brood came here yesty and eat the remains of the feast (strawberries, melon, foie gras etc for tea). As Nelly who came to meet her remarked, only a hot bath and a scrubbing brush wd now meet the case. There were rings of filth round her neck and she cant have washed her hands for days and days. It really is <u>awful</u>! No wonder the son in law looked like a walking thundercloud – having to pilot her about the Barrack Square (!!)

Someday I'll show the poetry of Harry Brewster Junior.... such a dear boy but he doesn't know English and wishes to protest against purple patches... and so he remarks of the Lion of Cheronea[2] (for instance):

"He looks somewhat grim and I don't know why
And is old as much as you can bet"

Yr E

As a PS:

Pan now reminds me of Aldous Huxley – he has been rolling in something.

---

1 Clotilde had recently been widowed. Her daughter Susan was married to Major-General Hugh Hibbert, presumably the disapproving son-in-law of the letter.

Later, as a devout Anglican, he must have been even more disapproving when his son Giles, "one of the brood", joined the Dominicans and was extremely outspoken on a number of issues, including support of Gay Rights. See Introduction for HB's family.

2 The Lion of Cheronea was a monument to the Sacred Band of Thebes annihilated by Philip of Macedon and his son Alexander in 338 BC at the Battle of Chaeronea. In the 2nd c A.D., Pausanius wrote in his *Description of Greece*: "As you approach the city you see a common grave of the Thebans who were killed in the struggle against Philip. It has no inscription, but is surmounted by a lion, probably a reference to the spirit of the men." The statue Harry Brewster would have seen is a 19th century reconstruction. The young man did not make a name as a poet, but was later involved in editing his grandfather's works.

July 10th, 1930

[Apologies for not having time to go and see a friend of Elizabeth's]

You can imagine what straits I am in! I literally cant take on any mortal thing (give information that <u>wd want looking up</u>) – or, above all, stir from this spot. But if he (the man) will come here all is well.

[Plans to meet]

I don't think I work slower than I used to...but I know more about orchestration I fancy. And this thing needs that (the atmosphere) <u>most awfully</u>. T.[homas] B.[eecham] really <u>is</u> playing up abt the Mass! And I hope we'll pull it off. But...he has woke up abt it late – alas!

I sent Joyce Virginia's party letter (a most generous tribute!) as Leonard W (whom I now adore) said such delirious far-seeing things about Joyce to V. who passed them on. And I think compliments (on human side) do J. good! I shall have the letter back by Sat. E

August 1st, 1930

Do let me know all about Loelia[1]– I am in a sort of trance of work[2]...am just now on "There is nothing that is yours but a name" a sort of soft rather crackly dance (tambourines even going) I see Odysseus ghost – also the wraiths of the prostitutes who danced in Hey Nonny – dancing in a mist – fainter and fainter they get – I must go back to them...

[On her reading]

1 Loelia Mary Ponsonby (1802-1993) was the daughter of Sir Fredrick and Lady Ponsonby, great friends of the Smyth family – see Introduction. In 1930 Loelia had married the Duke of Westminster, one of the richest men in England. It was a disaster almost from the beginning, as she was to relate in her autobiography *Grace and Favour* (1961) and, although they were not divorced until 1947, it was said they rarely spent more than two nights under the same roof. Fortunately they had a number of roofs to choose from. At one stage, Loelia was living at Send Grove near ES in Woking.
2 At this date ES was working primarily on *The Prison*.

August 11th, 1930

Elizabeth I've done! And tomorrow I take all the MSS. up to London – 18 days before the presented pistol would have been fired at my head...

[General plans and family meetings]

Next plans? Mild work here till Sep. 4th when I conduct the *Anacreontic Ode*[1] at a Prom and then 3 weeks in Bath (Norman Barnett) – I've worked gloriously – simply all day for the last 3 weeks or more – with perhaps 2 hours off which covered a) light much-masticated meals b) ½ hour savage motor [?] 3) signing a few cheques 4) a short toddle on the links....

[Excessively intimate details of Pan's health]

I began my work vetting what I had done the day before, in bed (always) at 6.30 up at 7.30, retired for the night at 11. It is a comfort and joy to me beyond words that I can concentrate and go on and on as when I was young. And I've

September 13th, 1930

On the 13th of September, Ethel wrote from the Lansdown Grove Hotel in Bath to Elizabeth in Munich.

[On Elizabeth's Tyrol tour; the discomfort of chairs in Bath and the badness of the golf course]

I had most amusing tennis yest.y Ethel Steel and one girl against me and another. She's a "good 'has been' rather in my style", so it is the greatest fun. And she has a bought a Kum Bak[1] but I fear hasn't a covered place high enough to take it. And taking it in and out is such a bore.

[Her own and her brother Bob's hearing problems]

He [unnamed friend] is just beginning what he says must be according to reviewers Dean Inge's[2] masterpiece... apparently an analysis of Christ's character and pointing out how the gentle dove-like Pale Face clung to by sentimentalists is an outrage to a heroic figure at once fierce, ironical, tender and everything else (Like the "Lady with the Lamp" business which no doubt Inge would consider very right and proper).

I am still engulphed *[sic]* in The Economic Prosperity of the B.Empire[3] which I think the most engrossing book I have ever struck. Which reminds me I wrote to Prof MacMurray [4] but so far have no answer.

Clothilde is quite hopeless and I am tackling "the Prison" business myself as I always knew I shd have to in the end. Blackwell of Oxford suggested to her to try if Lund Humphries and Co would not republish on their own (not on commission) and I am in correspondence with them...letters full of MacMurray possibilities, my "Prison" shows and every kind of ginger...

Your todten mal[5] letter was so thrilling that I sent it on to Virginia. I fear (a fortnight after the attack) she [VW] is still very sub-normal, lying about, sleeping and playing at work – Anyhow I feel sure that to see people when they step off the boat at Newhaven 8 a.m. (which was her undoing that day – Vita and the boys having thus turned up unexpectedly) would be quite the wrong thing for her – In fact, between ourselves, unless she stays on at Monks House over October 1, I expect we'll have to see it another year – unless, as might be quite possible (and that's what I shd suggest to her if I were you) you cd run down there from London before you go North. But Lor! I don't know what your plans are and speak as a child. She always wants to do things and will no doubt declare that she will come to Bath, or to V. Woodhouse[6] at the end of the month just as if she hadn't had this heat stroke. But L. won't allow it, of course. She gave a horrible description of her back (!) a series of knots of every one of which she is conscious, and over it a net that sags and twitches and then suddenly becomes blissfully quiescent.! These literary geniuses are terrors at describing their symptoms (I remember Anna de Noailles[7] and her "trances").

I think Elinor is right about Germans always saying they are ruined – but for ought we know it may be true for part of the population. Think of people like the Rütgens at Leipzig after the war. Still I don't see why the Germans shd have a monopoly of financial grousing and why I too should not say I feel blue about Argentina from which half my income derives! Martin says it will come all right and I'm sure it will – but mean time its all wrong and there's no time like the present -

I have gaily written thus far when it suddenly occurs to me "but this letter may never arrive".

Not one word more will I utter except to say how I envy you that Schubert Concert. Yes, there are days when a special benediction takes charge –

Your loving
E

1 The Kum Bak Tennis Trainer for practising solo was a very popular gadget at the time, patented c.1928.
2 Dean Inge was distinctly conservative in his views, although not actually anti-feminist – hence Ethel's dig that he would like the sentimental image of Florence Nightingale.
3 By Stephen Leacock, published 1930.
4 Prof John Macmurray (1891-1976), Philosopher and Quaker, he wrote on returning Christianity to its communitarian origins, by action rather than theory.
5 This appears to be what ES says, but in any case the letter is missing.
6 Violet Gordon-Woodhouse (1872-1948) harpsichordist and clavichordist, notorious for her unconventional private life and aunt of the cookery writer Elizabeth David. ES had dedicated *Hey Nonny No* to her c.1910.

7 Anna de Noailles (1876-1933), Princess Anna Elisabeth Bibesco-Bassaraba de Brancovan was a Rumanian-French poet, novelist and glamorous society figure, who moved in the artistic circles occasionally frequented by ES. ES was not convinced that the nerves and ill-health of which Anna de Noailles frequently complained were genuine.

October 15th, 1930

[A detailed account of golf with Joyce Wethered and others; on trying to read a postcard from her doctor [NB]: "his writing is a disgrace", "the dentist's report" "sounds ghastly" – an enclosed typed note describes some hair-raising dental treatment]

I told Barnett [the doctor] I fancied Phyllis was going to Venice and as NB had told me you needed "bracing" (and feeding up) I imagine Venice wd not meet his views....Also I don't think it a good plan for 2 invalids to go off together and brutally said so straight out to Phyllis!.

[On the therapeutic value of UV rays, at this date considered unqualifiedly health giving]

October 21st, 1930

Darling Eliz I am on strict economy, so I don't ring up – and am sick [?] with work and don't write....

[Mostly about golf, Joyce Wethered: "By the by Joyce lives on religion"; health, especially the danger of septic tonsils]

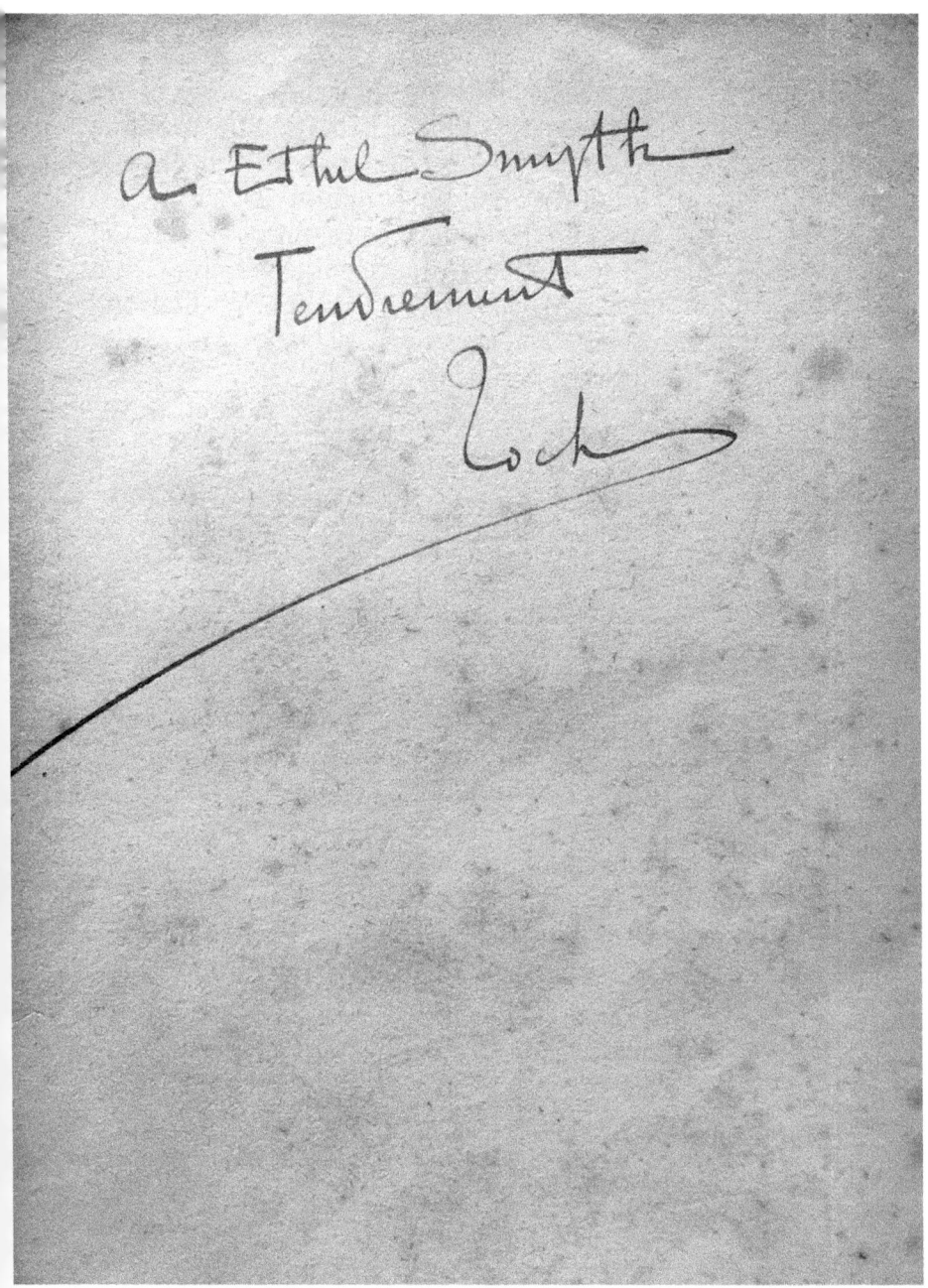

Dedication by Toch (i.e. Anna de Noailles)

October 24th, 1930

Darling Eliz. Your news delights me. I've been working like fury – (too hard) finished my memoirs (it's good!) take it up 10 tomorrow to Waterloo – meet typist there – back here 12.30 to have tooth out – Shall be in calm in a week – then hope to meet. I send you these glorious things of V's (it's out of print in England so look out) All are gorgeous save Green to Blue and Monday or Tuesday (mad: that's why she won't reprint) But O the Haunted House – Mark on the Wall – Kew Garden Unwritten Novel (amazing!)

Your E

November 6th, 1930

Darling E send back when done with, wretched script tho' it be. I have come home rather shattered by my cold but all is well. Squire takes the Memoir (February 1st)[1] I am (or shall be tomorrow) looking up a letter or two more of HB's and generally polishing memoir. Billy was wild at the Concerto last night but the Sea Symphony[2] is ghastly. I heard a delicious viola concerto of Hindermit's [sic][3] today. If I can get a ticket tomorrow and am not too ill I'd give my head to hear it again. That fellow has something to say.

Your E

1 ES was writing a Memoir of Henry Brewster to preface the new edition of *The Prison*.
2 By Ralph Vaughan Williams (1872-1958).
3 Paul Hindemith. The piece was perhaps *Kammermusik No.6*.

November 9th, 1930

In bed...and had for once to take my temperature! Touchingly uniform with yours! 99! Am in bed - awful head – that's why don't write E

A mysterious postcard, undated and with no postmark appears at this point in the packet. There are no clues as to what it is about, but Ethel refers on a number of occasions to packets of letters being sent or lent to friends or relatives, some of which were apparently never returned.

> <u>Thrilling letter</u> of yours. Fri: 6 p.m. I searching HB's letters (all day) In the Vernon dinner party I have found splendours (1901-3) but not <u>it</u>. Am writing to Maurice and wonder if it was in a letter to him or whether perhaps he opened other packets? I told him to do so if he wanted to. That is why cant write today.

Ten days later, she was still unwell, although on the mend, and deeply disappointed at missing Elizabeth, who had come to visit and was turned away by Mary, the maid, owing to a misunderstanding.

> Edith [Somerville] is in London and secretly delighted to believe it is better not to come down because she is rooting at the B.Museum – going to write a life of Lord Ch Justice Bushe her great grandfather[1]. I think she is too ignorant of history to do it well – but that's her look out! Meanwhile she threatened to send me, "<u>when you are well enough to read it</u>" a genuine autobiographical story of....a Red Indian Chief!![2] I wrote back that I never shd be well enough to read it.
>
> Your letter thrilled me and I will tell [?] V. who I hope is coming down here on Sunday with Leonard and <u>Pinka</u> who will have got over her childbed taint and have less charm (I hope) in consequence for Pan.
>
> *[Health]*
>
> I have ordered (1st time in my life) a bottle of burgundy and am imbibing strychnine.
>
> *[On friends; pruning a tree]*
>
> I've been working all through this illness; <u>had to</u>. But in a day or two shall have peace...Give yr mother my unending devotion and blessings on her misguided (because Baldwinian) politics! Clotilde is being <u>maddening!</u> O she <u>is</u> like her grandmother... no inward discipline, no common sense wherewith to check vain alarms unworthy of a child!
>
>   Yr E

1 Chief Justice Charles Kendal Bushe (1767-1843), noted for his oratory, his charm and his honesty. Somerville and Ross had already written his biography in 1906 with the title *An Incorruptible Irishman*.
2 This was presumably "Chief Buffalo Child Long Lance's" bestselling autobiography *Long Lance*, published in 1928. Long Lance claimed to be a Blackfoot Indian, but was in fact a journalist from North Carolina, although he had Indian blood.

November 30th, 1930

At the end of November, she was still not well:

> I'm back but still an awful wreck and while I was at Eastbourne a sort of collapse came on! I felt too languid even to read let alone write.

[Her own and Elizabeth's health]

> I wish I knew when you think of coming home? I don't believe I shall ever see <u>anyone</u> again for I have come to the conclusion to <u>walk</u> a lot and not go at all in trains and underground will be my tip for the next 2½ months (till after the Prison) At this time tomorrow I shall be listening; - and am mildly excited but really too languid to be very keen. All my mind is bent on <u>The 2 H.B. memoirs</u> and all that part of the enterprise – and Clotilde has quite returned under the sway of reason – so that worry is over.
>
> I shall so dreadfully be wanting to know – how is finance going at Cromer? I fear things are in a very bad way and that all my nieces will have to let their houses and come and live in a <u>very nice</u> house which is to let in Hook Heath Road!¹
>
> Your loving E

On the back of the envelope:

> One is quite cut off from No 2 by that awful phone. Cant you <u>young ones</u> make Yr Gr do something about it? It wont cost <u>her</u> anything but a display of firmness with the P.O.

1 Round the corner from Ethel in Woking, very close to the golf course.

1931

This bundle of letters from the second half of 1931 and 1932, were not in order and tied up – almost certainly by Elizabeth – with thin string. They are in particularly bad condition having got damp, probably in the cellars at Trumpeters' House and apparently having been mildly nibbled by a mouse. The paper of some letters is very brittle. As usual the addresses are from Coign to Elizabeth at Mount Mascal, unless otherwise stated.

Because of the poor condition of some of the letters from the first months of 1931, some of Ethel's letters to her brother Bob have been added for continuity and where they give additional – or a different – perspective of events. They largely concern family matters, especially the bankruptcy of their oldest sister, Mary Hunter, and its effect on the rest of the family. As in other years, a few of the surviving letters from Elizabeth have been put in as well. They were clearly ones picked out by Ethel and often marked as especially important to her,

It was also about this date that Elizabeth's acquaintance with Virginia Woolf began to develop, independently of Ethel's passionate interest. Some of Virginia's letters to Elizabeth have therefore been included, to give an idea of the relationship between the three women, and also Virginia Woolf's less than kindly impressions of Mary Hunter on what must have been one of the worst days of her life.

At Christmas Elizabeth was, as usual, with her mother and grandmother at Cromer – an occasion that Ethel tended to avoid, in spite of the opportunities for golf.

January 4th, 1931

(my parents wedding day)

Darling Elizabeth That wretch Virginia has not sent back your letter on Sin – which, as it happens, is just the sort of thing which will engross her. However Leonard and she went for the day to London on the 2nd to broadcast and I know she's feeling awfully under the weather, so probably has held on to the letter. Meanwhile to my joy I have yours about St Paul and will at once look up your points....

Before reading it up as you suggest, I must say that I have often felt, in the days when religion was my chief preoccupation, the debt owed by St Paul for saving Christ... and of course his lava-like outpourings...swept one away. But it is more of late years that I have come to feel sickened by the Church angle on sex (I feel I shall yet commit terrible deeds in T[ime] & T[ide] on this theme!). All that has come to a head in this world depression and the line of the R.C.'s to birth control and so on; the absolutely ostrich-like outlook as to what they call "pleasure"......What is the use of ignoring the fact that the senses are and always will be a source of delight? And why, as Leonard says, adopt views on "purity" of a savage Asiatic tribe whose only achievement (he doesn't say this but I do) was the evolution of the monotheistic idea, and who made the most hideous mess of what after all we have to deal with: life in this Vale of Woe?

[On various points of dogma and her reaction to them]

... I love what you say about the wind of the spirit blowing through the arches of temples in spite of clerical screens and curtains. Only at times when I think 1) of Alice D.[1] writing to say she feels that Jack was fitter for the next world because he was so good 2) of a letter then arriving to say that without consulting her he had made Ethel (who he <u>well</u> <u>knew</u> would say "no") guardian of the 4 children 3) that a further letter arrives that he hastily begot a 5th child before leaving the world and putting all these responsibilities on others....then I remember that the male self-indulgence, and fecklessness, and declining to profit by modern sciences in this question, is encouraged by the Church and called purity, and the sacredness of the marriage bond....(whereas in the matter of drains and [?] water to disregard science's rescripts is considered even by the Church as criminal) then my blood boils and begin to hate the Church.

[On Anglican dogma]

I wrote on Fri or Sat to Virginia and implored her to send back your letters but though she never loses things and may be trusted with any sort of M.S. in any sort of dilapidated condition (an inherited literary conscience). I know she is ill-ish – and to get up and look for a thing and put it in an envelope is an effort sometimes. But I'm so longing to have those letters back and to reply to them line by line.

Betty [Balfour] is very bad – influenza – and I feel my illness and her faithful visits to me when she ought to have been in bed did her harm. I'm now going to take over to her your letter about the beano which made me howl with laughter. I'd rather have seen your Grandm.trying to laugh about Charlie C[haplin] and the whistle[2] than most things in life... the resurrection [?][3]...the desire for aristocratic company... O Lord, she is a wonder! But poor old thing, I do rejoice in her having had you two dears all to herself like that.

[A detailed description of the Victorian guessing and acting games played by Betty and her eight grandchildren over Christmas, and an analysis of her favourite scenes from Dickens]

....O Eliz! I am posting back Marius[4] to M.M.!! I am absolutely defeated. Screaming boredom is what happens when I try it again ! [V. says it was her favourite book when she was a girl]. Don't give me up because of Marius! Yr E

---

1 Unclear. The dates are wrong for Alice Davidson, ES's eldest sister (1848-1933). Her husband John Henry Davidson had died in 1917 and they had four children.
2 Charlie Chaplin's *City Lights*, 1931. A silent film, but with certain sound effects, notably when the Tramp swallows a penny whistle.
3 Perhaps referring to Mary Hunter's remarkable recovery of spirits even after realising that she was about to be made bankrupt.
4 *Marius the Epicurean* by Walter Pater, 1885 a historical novel set in the middle of the 2nd century A.D. with long debates on aesthetics, Stoic philosophy and the role of religion.

January 7th, 1931

On January 7th, she sent Elizabeth a postcard.

> I am thrilled by your thrill at Orlando – which again proves that Maurice is always right – He told me "She <u>has</u> pulled it off – try it again." I have now asked her to send it to me – and will try it again. Poor V. has been having a dragging on of influenza but goes back to warmth today. 16th cent. cottages are no good at Xmas. Give me my villa....

Later in the month, she was back in London and on January 15th wrote:

> What if I come to lunch on Thursday next 19th (I have to be at the B.B.C. 3.15 and talk abt Orlando etc.). Virginia says I shant understand one word of The Waves if I find as I do certain bits of Orlando hard to connect up...
>
> *[A list of queries about* Orlando*]*
>
> Thus leap grasshoppers and V.
>
> Your E

The back of the envelope was as so often, a mass of PSs:

> - When V has done with it you must read Rodds[1] Memoir. It interested me a lot.
> - Why don't you ask V if you may go and see her? To tea (?) some day? I've ask[ed] her to keep next Mon. for me. She mayn't dine out I'm glad to say.
> - Am writing to yr G.mother to tell her abt. a meeting at which V and I are speaking Wed 21st (8pm) wd you like to come??

---

1 Rennell Rodd's memoirs: *Social and Diplomatic Memories*, published in three volumes, 1922-5. See also January 11th, 1925.

January 17th, 1931

Ethel's prime concern during the spring of 1931 was her sister Mary, whose financial affairs had entered their last desperate phase.
Her bankruptcy was to entail the sale of all her lovingly collected possessions, after which she would be left penniless at the age of 75.

> Darling Elizabeth I am glad to say that owing to having lost my own Orlando (which I have found again, after realising it is a yellow book – not a blue one!) and to Virginia refusing to take back the copy she gave me instead, mine is very much at your disposal and I have written your name in it and packed it up – but it wont go of course till Monday. I was practising with "The Prisoner" all day so couldn't take steps about it and….its Sat.y. There are marks of mine (in your copy) and a list at the end of the bits I have Ethel'd over and bits I love. This list wont bother you – may amuse you even. The marginal marks I painfully transferred from the V. copy thinking she ought to have it back (both are 1st editions and of value) into my old one – now yours – and rubbed them out of her gift – Orlando! Then finding she didn't want (wouldn't have back) the gift Orlando and wanted me to give my old one to somebody, I said (phoned) I'd give it to you who certainly deserved it and left the marks. –
> She's ill-ish again. I thought her below the mark (physically) on Wed last and she said she had a slight temp – and she was still coughing. Well! – it appears that writing her speech for next Wed (we are both going to read) gave her one of her headaches again – in fact I doubt if she will be fit on Wed. Anyway it will be very bad for her and I wish that party were at the bottom of the sea for that reason. Going down to Rodmell in that awful cold there was at Xmas did her in. She said only 1 room cd be warmed and all the rest of the house was icy. O give me my villa in winter…not a 16th century cottage uninhabited during the winter, madly repaired to for Xmas! I cant understand such foolishness. I shd never love Orlando as I do Jacob, the Lighthouse, Mon or Tues, and A Room of One's Own, Mark on the Wall, etc, but the inspiration in it – the bold utterly controlled imagination – the easy stride… all this staggers me. And spots of authentic Virginia beauty every 6th page. Yr loving E

April 5th, 1931

Easter Sunday

Darling E. I'm keeping your Eddington[1] a little longer. It is amusing how very violent L.Woolf is on this theme; he reminds me of the old prophets on the theme of Baal and I felt that he pro tem rather disliked me for flaunting E[ddington] and Haldane Jr[2] and all that lot in his face. I can't quite understand this anti-God fury, but I suppose he feels about it as I should, for instance, if literary dogmas were propagated on the "take care of the sounds and the sense will take care of itself" line –

I cannot tell you how foul Bath is. Just E wind that has (here) the peculiarity of blowing also from the W.....And the hotel chock-a-block for Easter with the homeless, I suppose – among them any amount of old military men to whom their wives yield as a matter of course the best arm chairs...

[On various medical treatments and the advantages of having young male relatives competent in the latest technology]

I have just been writing to your unfortunate Grandmother. She had sent Alice pictures of Nina and my father saying she now had no home of her own. I cannot help feeling Micawber feelings about "something turning up"!! and I have written to your mother about Charles and the diamonds. I think he ought to give them back! But...to your Mother to sell to finance the family until better times! If he is, as you all say, so generous, that would seem a fairly reasonable thing to do – and after all it was your Gran's ruthless and maddening energy that hoofed Charles out there...(and Billy into Dead Men's Shoes!)[3].

[Medical treatment and musical research]

I've just had a letter from Virginia that makes me laugh. You know her life is a round of dreads and horrors of all sorts (which I don't think she exaggerates) and she says I give her "protection", so far as she is "capable of it". – "I look at you and, being blind to most things except violent impressions, think: if Ethel can be so downright and plain spoken and on the spot, I need not fear instant dismemberment by wild horses" – (!!) Poor V.! How glad I am I am not built on those lines – and you may be equally glad.

I've read and loath "The Man Who Lost Himself"[4]– shall never try O.Sitwell again...

[More on her reading and travel plans]

1 Arthur Eddington (1882-1944) – astrophysicist and popularizer of science. His book *Why I Believe in God: Science and Religion, as a Scientist Sees It* came out in 1930.
2 J.B.S.Haldane
3 Elizabeth's brothers. The elder, Charles, had been found a place in the diplomatic service; the (Williamson) family diamonds had gone to him on his marriage. William (Bill), the younger, was at one stage working in the Williamson family business.
4 Osbert Sitwell (1892-1965) – his second novel, *The Man Who Lost Himself*, came out in 1929 and was not received with much enthusiasm.

April 14th, 1931

On April 14th, Ethel was still in Bath, hating the weather and complaining of her state of health, but determined to stay for another ten days. As usual, she lists her reading matter:

...Poor Eliz[1] Russell's "Father"...!! O!!!

And immediately after:

Pan only got a Very Highly Commended – Mary says he had very bad conduct in the ring – and Miss Taylor[2] says he's a <u>bad</u> ring dog (!...)

1 Elizabeth von Arnim (1866-1941), cousin of Katherine Mansfield and author of *Elizabeth and her German Garden* was, by her second marriage to Bertrand Russell's elder brother, Countess Russell. He had died the previous month hence, presumably, "poor" – although they had long been separated. *Father* had just been published and, unlike *Elizabeth*, which went into twenty editions in its first year, was not a success.
2 A neighbour and occasional assistant to a local sheepdog breeder – see *Inordinate (?) Affection* for full story of ES's dogs.

April 15th, 1931

Ethel wrote to her brother from Lansdown on 15th April, 1931.

    I can't get Mary out of my head and am longing to be back within reach of her tho' what she is doing, exactly, I don't know – whether with Kitty[1] – or just going into London to tear up papers or what. And I don't know when the sale is but have written to K asking for details - and am writing a lot to Mary – slightly complicated by not knowing where to address to. Kitty wrote to Phyllis that she is awfully changed since the pow wow a month ago – that her arms and legs seem too feeble to do their work. I think then for the first time she was really faced by the situation – couldn't look the other way. And the last bluff (that the house and furniture, etc. were <u>not</u> pledged...she had stuck to that tho' none really believed it!) was formally broken down by the lawyer before them all. (Phyllis says he was <u>most</u> merciful and gentle all through) Poor poor old thing! I wish myself she could die.... Meanwhile, she rushed up from Kitty's to go to a <u>wedding</u>!
    Your loving E

1 ES's niece, EMW's aunt - see Introduction.

April 18th, 1931

    My darling Elizabeth I've just heard Tuesday 12 May is the sale and had news from Kitty that the rest and boredom of Bournemouth had improved yr Gran's health. I shall go home on the 25th - only one day of Mrs Austen who to me is really like cholera or yellow fever, in that one flies a town in which she is raging...[details]...I am aware that my own state of mind inflames her less attractive sides...excites her to loud statistics about the size of "Naomi's" magnolias, the old masters N's husband has bought, and many anecdotes of a jocularity that more nearly make me burst into tears than anything I have suffered since I had double pneumonia in 1918.

[On her health and weather in Bath]

    A letter from Mary says that Pan did so badly (so Miss Taylor says) because of "the shocking conduct he had 'in the ring'" and for that reason alone. "<u>That</u> done it" she says "not his coat or his neck...and it will amuse me to have an account of it from Aubrey Taylor when I get back – of Mary's horrorstruck helplessness. O I see it all. But I'm very sorry for her.

[Social and medical affairs]

    Virginia and L. are motoring in France for a fortnight and I had an enchanting letter from her just as they were starting – And shall expect another from the balcony of the Inn at la Rochelle where all the sails are purple and green (with the white foam that makes up W.S.P.U.[1] colours). I think her letters as masterly, as unique as anything she does – Vanessa says her "real genius". And my genius is to provoke [?] them....

    "Je sais l'art d'évoquer les minutes heureuses

    Et revis mon passé"[2] etc. Do you know that? I think it is the most beautiful love poem in the world except 1 or 2 of the Sonnets.

    I must stop and I have much to say. About God. I am absolutely out of touch – only consoled by Prof Alexander saying he is frequently that way. (Pazienza.). And I need God hideously just now. Yr E

1 Women's Social and Political Union – the Suffragettes' organization.
2 From "Le balcon", Charles Baudelaire, *Fleurs du Mal.*

April 27th, 1931

    Darling E

[On a leaf from Vale of Tempe*]*

    Your Gm ! was too tired to come here yesty so I buzzed up to London. She was in bed and looked very beautiful, but ill, and above all awfully sad. It does tear ones heart to ribbons – and I am sure this particular moment seeing her dreams of financial recovery can never come true and, mainly for the sale, is the worst she will have to go through. It is like waiting for your head to be cut off after you have persistently cherished hopes of a reprieve and know at last that it is not to be.

[On Edith Somerville and troubles with her treatment at Bath]

Your loving
E

PS....Virginia is mad with joy – motoring in France, sitting in Montaigne's armchair, etc.

Ethel had been trying in all sorts of ways to ameliorate her sister's situation – for example by appealing to friends for contributions to her upkeep, something which both Mary Hunter and Elizabeth must have found profoundly humiliating.

May 9th, 1931

According to a note in the *Diaries*, the Woolfs went to view the contents of MH's house at 2 Gloucester Square on the 8th of May and to the sale on the premises on the 14th. Virginia Woolf wrote:

> Yesterday I went to Mrs Hunter's sale, & before I had been in the room 5 minutes had bought through Mr Marchment of Shepherds Bush a large old rosewood & satinwood secretaire for £6.16. Heavens! The wood alone was worth that. It was a sordid, emulative, exciting, depressing scene. The trade was there in force. Jews, smoking pipes. Many winks & nods interchanged. Poor old Mrs Hunter's odds and ends were peered at and snatched; everybody seemed to be finding out flaws, & offering the least money. Marchment kept saying to me "Buy it – buy it – it'll grow into money." Thus solicited I did buy a shawl for 35/- & a little cabinet for £3.15. This I regretted; & I let slip – oh never mind. One must take these bargains and slips philosophically, in order to attain the perfectly buoyant & energized life which is now my aim.....
> The faces of Mrs H.'s rich friends disgusted me. Nothing is quite so coarse, cruel, meaningless, & sensual as a fashionable

woman's face, who is about 50: has done nothing but scavenge about London in cars; eating & drinking; marrying; coveting; tittle tattling. The Smyth-Hunter circle centers I think round the shires; the golf courses; the purlieus of the Bath Club & Whites. They are horsey, dressy; but not aristocratic, not distinguished. They are very well off; but lose money largely – or so at least I diagnose them. But their philosophy requires them to take tumbles bravely. When we went in on Friday to look at the things, Mrs H. was sitting at the desk which I wanted to buy, as cool and self-possessed as if she were giving a house warming, instead of seeing all her possessions, beds & blankets, paper knives & pen trays, all go for two or three shillings. "I see you so seldom. Do sit down for a moment & talk!" And what was I to say, to a woman old enough to be my mother, in that predicament?[1]

1 *The Diary of Virginia Woolf*, vol.IV, London, 1982, pp. 25-6

June 5th, 1931

Darling E – I am sorry to say my efforts have not been crowned with success and that the help I tried for is not forthcoming – and I have informed all concerned that this is so.

I got however some information out of Whiteley [the solicitor] which rather cheered me: 1) that Fred said there will be a dividend yet to come 2) that your grandm.'s income, when premium's are paid, is <u>over £2000</u> – only this includes her marriage settlement of £526 or some such sum per ann., which the creditors will certainly have 3) that deducting the £3000 of the sale her debts are only (!) £9500[1] 4) that Sir J.D.'s sol[icitor] said the pictures might – sold with care – realise "a few thousands". I gather her Insurance and Bank Loan together amount to £3900 and I am glad to say Betty takes my view that no doctor wd consider yr granm. fit to be cross-examined, and if she is (as she will be, I suppose) made bankrupt, the thing that will come out (like her theory that the furniture was not pledged) will go to prove what I am certain is the case – that she is not, and for many years has not been, responsible. Only...no one could stop her! – She doesn't now in the least realise her position, yr aunt P says. But when one thinks of the "few thousands" for the pictures and the possible sale of the diamonds to reduce the £9500 it looks as if creditors might take ½ a loaf! The ghastly thing is (according to Wilfred S.) that yr gramps will is so drawn up by the precious Whiteley that creditors (themselves included perhaps??) can have access to capital. But I don't think this <u>can</u> be. Your E.

[PS: enquiries after and messages to Mrs F – see below]

I am so sorry your entrance into ideal conditions is marred by all this horror and uncertainty. But if it gives your brain a twist in the direction of possible earnings I shan't wholly regret it. You know I have always had these views about a must (to be created if one hasn't got one imposed on one) being an influence that works like manure, and athletics and all those things for mental and moral well-being. One doesn't realise this so much when one is young – or even youngish.... but O lord – you do later! Still I am so awfully sorry for you all – and begged Bill (to whom I was most unjust I think) as I begged you, to forgive me my fierceness. I didn't know you three dears had stumped up for your mother's present needs which was the essential. Let this be a lesson to Dames not to take headers like that; only your Mother's plight did distress me so. As it is I think she was unduly agitated since Fred and Wilfred S were on the job as to her future situation and as you 3 had seen to her present needs.

1 As always, it is far harder to give the present-day value in real terms. www.measuringworth.com suggest a purchasing power in the order of half a million pounds, but considerably more if the sum be calculated in terms of labour costs, etc.

June 8th, 1931

Darling Eliz – I was of course thrilled about the nightingale. O what bliss to lie in bed and be serenaded...

[On Mrs F – in French to avoid hurting her feelings should she see the letter – see note below]

I can read nothing but Montaigne though I sometimes find the French more archaic than I can cope with. Surely except Shakespeare, there never was so richly endowed a nature; he ravishes my soul - and it is such fun finding again and agreeing with one's scratchings of 25 years ago. I'm also reading Roger Casement's Life and Death[1] – a most curious mentality made of fire and sentimentality and vitriol and what not....

1 By Dennis Gwynn, Casement's first biographer - *The Life and Death of Roger Casement* was published in 1930.

June 18th, 1931

[On wanting a copy of the Antigone*]*

You know the Prison is <u>settled</u> for November 11 – self conducting – and I'm choosing cantatas (Bach) to go with it, also meeting a German Stage Manager about how to rig up a cheap and not nasty last act décor for the Wreckers (useful thing to have up one's sleeve).

[On going to stay with EMW and her domestic arrangements]

Mrs F[1] never I think addressed me voluntarily during the 16 years we were together (see A Fresh Start!). With help from Above I will bring along Einstein's letter[2] for you to see his squirmy and hideous little signature. Everyone says he is <u>adorable</u> and passionately musical. Betty [Balfour] thinks my article on Mus. Criticism very good (unanswerable and funny). It will cause agitation in the seats of the scornful. Of course it is <u>wholly</u> non-personal. E

What fun, what fun lies before us and I am so glad there are several shelves for my clean collar!

1 Mrs F was "...one of the supreme people I have met in my life, the servant who was with me for 16 years, wonderful adorable Mrs Faulkner." After leaving ES for reasons of health, she took on occasional jobs when she could. See *Streaks of Life*, pp.81-9.
2 Albert Einstein (1879-1955) had indeed a passionate interest in music. The letter in question – June 8th, 1931 – is now in the William Ready division of the McMaster University Library: www.library.mcmaster.ca

June 26th, 1931

[On how much she enjoyed a visit to EMW and some household hints]:

As for the fish I think you shd <u>perhaps</u> give up fish that is <u>round</u> (whiting!) as that is more difficult to breadcrumb successfully. Filet of plaice (equally cheap) or a cutlet of hake <u>do</u> – the last wants no breadcrumbs and all are more manageable...

June 29th, 1931

[On a matinée much enjoyed and on leaving her luggage: "..will deposit tomorrow 1) coat 2) knickers 3) cushion..."]

I have not really got over Antigone yet!! Got a real chill inside and felt that I might die someday if sufficiently bored, of boredom – poison. <u>That music</u>!! Its appallingly jauntiness as contrast with the deadly slowness of the speakers....and Antigone's chin (also Cleon's) – they all had upliftedness in their chins – their idea of dignity, I suppose. I cannot think that Lucrece[1] will equal Noë[2] - the story of Noë is so gorgeous as you saw....

<u>Do do</u> write to Virginia and say that you want to dine with her in the week that begins 6th July for instance. You <u>have</u> to give her the office [?] however much she wants a thing. It is a sort of infirmity of will. She likes my article – says it's in my best style. And my jokes please her – as she put it "Your Smythian pleasantries" Your E

1 Uncertain which version this was. André Obey's *Le viol de Lucrèce* on which Britten's opera was later based was first performed in 1931.
2 The last opera of Fromental Halévy (1799-1862), eventually completed by Bizet, his son-in-law.

It was in many ways a difficult year. Besides her grandmother's bankruptcy, Elizabeth's closest friend was not only getting married, but leaving for India. In a very personal letter, which Ethel had marked "Destroy" and then, apparently, changed her mind, Elizabeth describes her feelings.

Monday, August 4th [1931]

Appley Hall
Ryde
Isle of Wight

My darling Aunt,
19 people in the house with wireless and footling card games and all the horrors of pointless "entertaining" is in full swing. Your letter was a drop of water in a thirsty land – to be reminded of silence, work and a sane life! I am not protesting – I rather enjoy it as an amazing interlude but I am very dazed and numbed inside for a reason I will tell you later.

[On questions of health]

I shall certainly try to twiddle the infernal machine round to your concert. I wish I were there "in the body".

[On being in the mood for Kant and metaphysics rather than poetry]

I read Bolitho[1] with intense interest and as always was moved to boundless admiration of the Queen. That unerring way she was always <u>right</u>, and her sense of the sacredness of her constitutional trust moves me so

The state of the World now. What will happen. My heart is leaden when I think how 5 years ago I really thought peace and <u>sense</u> would make some headway. It is the awful stupidity and hysteria of nations compared to individuals that makes world betterment an illusion I think. If I didn't feel that Christ had overcome the world I should die of misery. He knew it was hopeless I think and only gave his peace in a personal sense to individuals and never "loved humanity" as sentimentalists like to think.

As well as bottomless depression about the world I am summoning up powers to stand a pretty shattering personal blow in that Elinor is engaged to be married and will depart to India for 5 years. (This is a secret for the moment but there is no point in not telling you). However one tries to suppress personal and selfish feelings on such occasions love is selfish and a separation like that absolutely desolating.

I wonder again and again as I stare at life how people go on through it without God. A man like Greg planted in the world with no defence or comfort. If one has no treasure in heaven, no source of inexhaustible strength and consolation coming from the very depths of reality. That is a profoundly lovely phrase in the psalms about God keeping your tears in a bottle[2]. It is extraordinary how some simple and familiar sentence scattered into one's memory will return with healing and mercy when one most needs it.

I was nearly finishing without telling you of the most interesting meeting I have had – Paul Robeson[3] the negro singer. He came over with his wife to see the garden after we had met at a concert he gave on the island. They are paragons of charm and learning both of them and he is a great artist as I was certain on seeing his Othello[4] and as one can tell by some spiritual quality in a great person even meeting in a garden. I hope to renew the acquaintance in London as they come to U.C. for various studies they both work on.

I must go and pour out tea for 24.

YrL
E

We had the Queen on Friday.

1 Perhaps an edition by Hector Bolitho of the letters of Lady Augusta Stanley, including many unpublished letters by Queen Victoria, which had come out the previous year.
2 Psalm 56 v.8.
3 Paul Robeson (1898-1976) – singer, actor and political activist.
4 With Peggy Ashcroft in 1930.

Ethel's letters which are mentioned do not seem to have survived, but on August 10th, she wrote to her brother, Bob

August 10th, 1931

....Of course everything is overshadowed by the Mary tragedy. Kitty tells me she remarked the other day that if she hadn't been a "damned fool" this appeal – (or these appeals) would never have been necessary! It is the first time she has been known to take any other line than that of a blameless victim of Fate! Kitty told me when she went to Alice she had £18 between herself and charity. It is bad luck that this year, for the first time in my life, I set my teeth and determined to spend what amounts to ¼ of my life's savings to save "The Prison" – It is of course shameful that such things as my paying for a hearing shd be – however if the Wreckers kindles the public (Blois says he doesn't care about the <u>Press</u> if the public catch on) that will help matters. But, as I said, what I chiefly regret is that it cripples me as regards Mary. For I see very bad times ahead of us all. – and one insolvent Smyth is enough. Can you understand such a thing as that poor rake's progress?? Well yes....there have always been people like that. And when I think how, by that same refusal to see things she preferred to ignore, she snapped my life in two, who can wonder that she has equally done for herself? I think an appeal later to the many people who practically lived at Hill could be made as in the case of Mrs Asquith[1]. People are under the impression that M. is very generous (which I think she never was, really) and that is all to the good ......

1 Margot Asquith (1864-1945) was a society figure and author of numerous autobiographies. After the death of her husband, Herbert Asquith, the Prime Minister, in 1928, she was left in relative penury. Dorothy Parker said of her: "The affair between Margot Asquith and Margot Asquith will live as one of the prettiest love stories in all literature".

Monday, August 10th

Appley Hall [1931?]
Ryde
Isle of Wight

My darling Aunt,

How <u>splendid</u> about The Prison. I am so delighted and above all that Beecham should do it again in the wonderful way he does and not some new person who might or might not give satisfaction.

I don't know much about E's man and have never seen him. She met him at Oxford whither she went as delegate from U.C. for some conference. He never left her side from that instant and when I saw her last she knew that he was very much in love but had come to no decision herself. He is a physicist and a swell in India, will probably be made Director of Education of a whole province. I wrote to him and had a <u>charming</u> letter back. I shall meet him next month. He goes back in October and the idea is that E, should join him in January and marry out there (one comfort!). I am really as full of faith as one can be that she will be happy because hers in an instrument on which the marriage tune should play well and she has always said so. I think one knows that sort of thing about people just as I know my instrument is constructed for solo playing!! I am not an unduly possessive friend, and Phyllis'[1] marriage was all joy to me, but of course in this case it is the inevitable separation, so huge in time and space, that constitutes the unavoidable losing [?] for me personally. I have a tough proposition before me in not obtruding this on them too much. Thank you for your sympathy my darling aunt.

I will write to you again re the World![2]

Yr
E

1 Probably Elizabeth's cousin.
2 See letter of August 4th.

August 15th, 1931

[On dates of performances of The Wreckers*]*

Anyhow there will be no hideous T[homas] B[eecham] shifting of dates regardless of the effect on the work. Get your grandmother to tell you the amusing little incident about Avis[1] No.1 – always my elect Avis. Beloved of the Director (late Guardsman – a dear), she is touring in Canada, having taken the part with her, and does not return till the 11th hour. This holds up piano rehearsals rather – and meanwhile a 1st class little understudy, an obscure member of the troupe whose Papa I knew – (a German Jew called Grünbaum – a conductor at the R.Coll) has been filling the gap so brilliantly that had I ever heard of her I shd have plumped for her at once in the 1st instance. Now as the lover was forever bewailing to me the fact of Avis No.1 (Miss Odette de Foras[2] whose real name is Olive Forrest) having too much to do and wondering whether she could possibly take on Avis , I wrote to him in his Cornish Fastness, the joyful news of Avis 2[3] Needless to say, he now finds the transfer impossible (!...) You see all these singers are Bottom the Weaver – also as well take butter out of a dog's mouth as, out of consideration etc., relieve them of a rôle!! Meanwhile I'm coaching No.2 (whose stage-name, a perfect track-effacer as she considers – is <u>Gruhn</u>) and shall make an ace of trumps of her. This will anyhow prevent the other, who, "they" say, is the object of favouritism – I wonder why? – having airs and graces...if such be her tendency. And I have never known a young singer in her position who doesn't – it is one of the things opera writers have to contend with. As for Directors, in such cases they'd far rather wreck the opera than disappoint the lady who however in this case really is A1. But I suspect, as dramatic force, Gruhn wd beat Odette. I am having lots of preliminary fun – pott[er]ing about among properties, discussing costumes with a wardrobe mistress who has not the slightest inclination to dress these Wreckers like the Pirates of Penzance – a capital and intelligent woman. The Producer, whom I like awfully, comes back on August 24th and we have great correspondences (he's ½ Italian and has a villa on the Lake of Lugano) – and I prowl in the Scenic Artists premises – the topmost floor of the Opera House and a place as huge as a church – and study models of my scenery: and tell him behind the chapel there must be room for 3 concealed brass instrument-players and so on. Mating Pan tomorrow and tennis every other day fills in the gaps.

[Domestic arrangements; on EMW's Greek reading; health]

A long paragraph on Mary Hunter's financial arrangements marked with green crosses, so that EMW would know <u>not</u> to read it aloud to other members of the family:

....Seriously, so many people habitually went to Hill and I think if even £1000 or so could be raised among them it wd mean £40 per ann. anyway. I hope you keep a list of these standard guests, Chas. Hope and Co – adding names as you remember them. <u>Do do that</u>.

What beats me is what is to happen if your Grandmother leads a Flying Dutchman existence for as long as she can work it (staying about etc.) Will your mother get in temporary help when she's there? I suppose so; people seem to live that way nowadays. Bob[4] is overdrawn and has to commute 50% of his pension as security for his overdraft!! I put in these chalk crosses in case you feel disposed to read the rest to yr Grandmother.

Yr E

1 The Lighthouse Keeper's daughter – a soprano.
2 Odette de Foras (1895-1976) - Canadian soprano, who sang at Covent Garden 1927-1935.
3 ES's forceful letter on the subject of the "second string" is online at the Royal Academy of Music website: www.ram.ac.uk
4 ES's younger brother - see Introduction.

September 2nd, 1931

Darling Eliz

[On meeting]

I don't yet know when the final perf. is but I hope <u>late</u> in October as I fancy then there will be a better chance of H.M. All is going splendidly except that that horrid scamp

CAVALRY BARRACKS,
ABBASSIA,
CAIRO.

She showed us round when I tried. & has certainly the best blood in Egypt. It was a pleasure to see them. One of her stallions a grey was better than any I have seen here. It was very badly run - on arab lines & with all her knowledge & love of it the management was very poor -

Bob Smyth - letter from Abbassia Barracks re Lady Anne Blunt de Foras who as you know is beloved by nice Col. Blois, has been allowed by him to stay away until 5th September!! This is absolutely disgraceful and I am not at all sure whether the other girl ought not definitely to do the part. I have left it to poor B [?] and the guilty lover to settle among themselves – writing to Blois to say so. Before writing, my prayers contained a clause: "Please God don't let me tell Col. B that de Foras is a dirty little bitch" – but I feel it will slip out viva voce one day if I'm not careful...All the rest working like niggers <u>for a month</u> and this wretch starring in Canada!! Shameful. O my dear Elizabeth – classical works are full of the dire workings of love....I cant write – defrauded of tennis by rain I must go and comb Pan's mats out and jot down a few incidents...

[On a long walk, the gift of a gold watch by Mary Dodge[1] and a copy of Sir Thomas Browne]

Wreckers is (I think) rather a good opus – and I find the best (Harrods) ¼ bottles of champagne cost only 2/9 each. Again, Betty [Balfour] came back yesterday to my delight and told me the inside story of the financial crisis which made me gasp. A. Henderson[2] ought to be whipped! – there's a "leader"!

Your Grandmother seems to me much as she has been of late years – quite on the spot only you mustn't change the subject too quickly. She was very dear at the Wreckers and had been thrilled by Frimhurst. There was a marvellous moment: as she rose to go; Violet absently took up my <u>filthy</u> blue serge office coat and prepared to envelope her aunt M in it! Lord how we laughed, but she of course did not see anything to laugh at. Perhaps as you said about my stockings at Hill such a garment was beneath her notice....

1 Mary Dodge (1861-1934) an American heiress and patroness of the arts, who lived much of her life in London, where her friends included Henry James and John Sargent. Theosophy was among her many interests and she commissioned Lutyens to design their headquarters in Tavistock Square. She was extremely generous and helped numerous artists, for example hiring a theatre and paying all costs for six performances of *The Wreckers*.

2 Arthur Henderson (1863-1935), from a genuinely humble background, was three times Leader of the Labour Party and winner of the Nobel Prize for Peace in 1934. The Labour Party was torn in 1931 by battles over how to remedy the economic crisis and Henderson's position was unpopular. His remaining years were spent trying to avert war.

September 2nd, 1931

The same day, Ethel wrote to her brother Bob describing Mary's visit and it is interesting to compare the tone of her letter to him with the one to Elizabeth, who would have been hurt and angered by some of the comments about her grandmother.

Coign
(writing early in bed – forgive scrawl)

Dearest Bob I want you to tell me what you contributed to Mary's fund, or promised to do? Because I have had a windfall and think I can give you back some of it ......
<u>The Wreckers:</u>......I have seen about the dresses, more or less, and my ambition is not to cost the syndicate a penny as regards that. The male Wardrobe man – an old fellow who has had a stroke was rather wedded in spite of p.c. hints from me to the Pirates of Penzance idea, but the wardrobe mistress caught on " - ! that pink shirt is not mucky enough for you" (Exactly).

Mary came with Nelly and Violet to tea and seemed very serene and quite on the spot (as much as she has been of late years and when not wound up) looked very handsome, but with rheumatic toes crammed into slippers for a foot 17 years old and of course can hardly walk. Who shall say if she grasps the situation? She is "artful" (as Mary Stapleton puts it) that you never can tell whether it isn't that she has adopted what she thinks is the best line – to pretend nothing has happened, including the fact she is living on the money of poor relations!! – Amusing to think how if you have been the rich relation long enough the poor relations go on being negligible even when they are your only resource!! There was a superb moment when she got up to go and Violet dreaming took up and held out my filthy blue serge "office coat" as I call it which was lying on the sofa !!! We three howled with laughter but Mary as usual did not catch the joke.....

September 28th, 1931

Darling Eliz – No luck for you!! Mary went today on holiday.....<u>Also no wine is my regime</u> - ! only whiskey and <u>water</u> (not even soda water) <u>but</u> we can get a bottle of beer for you...and I'll get a tongue à la Vita at Harrods....

[Plans]

Where I shall be between the Acts (tho'I may be delayed) is in the glass Gallery over the Portico – on the right at the top of the "Grand" staircase. And I shall be at the staircase end of it. The sad thing is night after night the place is not 1/3 filled – People are too rattled to go in for anything new like this autumn season. There were, I think, more at the Wreckers than at any other opera except La Bohème. It is hard luck for the Syndicate!

Your loving
E

October 5th [?], 1931

Do tell me where you found Earl Bristol [1]? What an exquisite lyric! I've just had a killing letter from Virginia describing a visit (sprung upon her) by an E.Kent Schoolmaster and his family. I laughed until I was sick over it and <u>may</u> send it to you! She begins by saying when she finds herself in a ridiculous situation she vividly recalls me "for I am making a new image of you, bearing a new [?], and she, the new Ethel, is sardonic, brutal, truculent, savage – an irredeemable love of reality in its least flattering guise; but my new Ethel is not finished yet" (!!) E

I love to think of you and your fruit trees! It reminds me of the Delphi scene.

Not surprisingly, money problems were uppermost in Ethel's mind at this period. In a long letter to Bob, she comments on his financial situation - and that of Lady Balfour - and then returns to the family.

[1] see Frontispiece

October 6th, 1931

...I always tell Mary <u>little</u> economies are all people with small incomes can achieve. For instance I have, as you see, all my address on one stamp <u>which saves half the stamping of my note paper</u>. And so on. No – I have no jackets or files but a sort of rough and ready system like Papa. I'm just going to settle down to an examination of the cost of note paper – one can save a lot by bothering about that and I have samples etc which there is now time to tackle. I find drinking whiskey an economy (I don't like it at all) instead of wine. I hope I shall succeed in heading off Mary H[unter] from another trip [?] south for the 14th. What <u>do</u> you think of this? The other day, <u>to rub in facts</u>, I said....but first let me tell you what she said: "I suppose now The Wreckers" is such a success you wont have to pay for some concert or other you are giving' (!) I said "The Wreckers <u>may</u> bring me in £10 all told (a fact!) and that has nothing to do with <u>The Prison</u> which I am financing on November 11th with the Philharmonic Choir" and I went on to say "I am doing this because of H.B. – as well as myself; I didn't choose that our foul Press shd kill a thing every bit as good as The Wreckers... and Walter quite agreed with me that it is just to do things like that that one saves money" – "O" said M. "Did he say that?" "Yes" said I "All the same had I known what was going to happen about you I shd probably not have done it – for £170 of my savings devoted to that leaves me <u>less able to do as much as I wanted to for you</u>." (I sent them £50 as a matter of fact). Well....hereupon Mary said airily "O of course <u>I</u> shall pay for that £170" (!!!).

When I wrote to her about not facing up to her situation I could not help saying "That remark of yours terrified and shocked me – for you must know <u>what we all know</u>: that but for chance donations (I believe someone has put a pocket-money sum into Fred Hunter's hands for her) "you have not 170 <u>shillings</u> of your own in the world!!!" And I added that even gentle Alice said she didn't think she [MH] realises what her daughters are doing for her (and others). As I said to her, pluck and courage are good things – but going on as if nothing had happened is the very thing Snowden[1] warned the country against! <u>That's</u> not courage!...

An undated note, hastily scribbled and tucked inside a later letter must be from shortly after October 8th, the actual date of publication of *The Waves*.

> Virginia's book is out today (13th) and there's a jolly article of hers in this week's Good House Keeping (1/-) also one by me – a rather good one.
> But I ask myself whether the high pay makes that awful style of being published bearable!

1 Philip Snowden, 1st Viscount Snowden PC (1864 – 1937), who came from a family of weavers and mill workers, was at the time Labour Chancellor of the Exchequer. His economic policies, including his opposition to borrowing and belief in a balanced budget, were highly controversial.

October 11th, 1931

> Darling E[lizabeth] – I am panting to know what you think of the Waves – surely the most amazing of V's productions. It overwhelms me, frightens me, and I don't know that such a work is not destructive of life, and whether therefore it ought to be written - incidentally I think the last paragraph one of the most beautiful things ever written. Some of it (Rhoda) I don't quite grasp but think I shall by and by. After you have read it life is not quite the same...and at present I am waiting for these terrific waves to settle and stop tossing me up and down [?]
>
> Your loving
E

Thursday, October 15th [1931]

University of London
University College

On a performance of The Wreckers – *to which EMW reacted with great, but as she herself says, untutored enthusiasm]*

The letter ends:

I have finished the Waves. <u>My God</u>!
I can't go on as I have a lecture.

Yr
E[lizabeth]

October 16th, 1931

Darling Eliz – of course I was delighted at the improvement in Act III for which I worked like a nigger (I'd like to shoot Muir [?] - stupid obstinate <u>owl</u> – as I have always heard) but I thought the singer and Barbirolli[1] tired and overworked – lacking in bite as people generally are at a 2nd rehearsal! Only this was at a 3rd.

[On The Waves]

However I'm tired and not on a judicial mood at the moment – also <u>racing</u> for the post

Yr E

[1] John Barbirolli (1899-1970) – British conductor and cellist, particularly associated with British composers of the period.

October 18th, 1931

Darling Eliz. I'm sure you'll be glad to hear there is no deterioration really. You know how awfully fond I am of Mary S.[1]

After all the regular wage she gets is £34 per ann[2] and I do think she has a right to 17/6 board that being so. And yet she offered to take 15/- ! It was just that the chimney wanted sweeping (this is figurative!!) and all is more than well, now. A roaring draught.

I am working to madness getting the new Wreckers Edit. out (very complicated) so I shant write at length about the Waves – nor in such an original opus have I come to a final opinion.

Here are some vague impressions;

1) I think it <u>is</u> morbid and lowers my vitality.

2) The personages are too undifferentiated. She works them out all right as general lines, but pokes in remarks that don't fit and which blur the outline. A lack of sanity I think.

3) I don't think it wd ever be one of my most beloved books because I know I care supremely for normality – bed-rock normality as basis (Shakespeare! Keats!) and fancy my first impression about the Waves (a sort of tumbling back into the formula: I like V best when she's tied by one foot to mother earth; in the Lighthouse it was her family, in "A Room" a thesis, in criticism the person or the theme she is elaborating) may be a final one. If you have time, do write at length about it.

Your E

1 ES's Irish maid, Mary Stapleton.
2 A purchasing power of £2,083 in 2017. This would have been high for the late 19th c. In the 20th c. wages rose, especially after World War I, but dropped back sharply in the depression of the '30s. In 1931, the minimum wage for a male labourer was c. £1/10/0 for a 51 hour week. A woman living in and so receiving board, lodging and probably uniform would have expected substantially less.

Monday, October 29th [1931]

My darling Aunt,

I am so glad you sent me this letter which I was much moved by. It expresses with almost exact parallelism my own feelings, and it is a great support to me to see that you took the same line as me about not obtruding your misery on P. It was the most devilish and bitter struggle – I say "was" because I got through the worst I think at Appley – I didn't say anything about that to you because I was so in the midst of it and filled with that bitter self detestation that turns life to ashes – at least to people like us who care for the inner life and its integrity. To find oneself eaten into by a vile ungenerous longing to say "Damn you – you <u>shall</u> realize what I suffer" – and to think one has got it beaten by prayer and then for it to come sliding back like a cat jumping neatly and silently into one's lap! Phyllis thought that I was over harsh with myself but I know I am right and am confirmed by you – I am much better now. In fact I read the letter this morning in E[linor]'s presence and no impulse but a fleeting one to say anything about it! I expect she wondered what I was reading that moved me so! It is odd how distinct and separable are the ingredients in a trouble of this sort and how the facts themselves supply the natural and only-to-be-endured part of the same, and how one's own temperament supplies the bitter part and the part one can and MUST overcome. I found that the most helpful way of enduring oneself as a companion at all was to keep hold of the feeling of one's real self being in some way behind and above one's "states of mind" at any particular moment. I am certain that the practice of prayer gives one unerring [?] skill in this at times very difficult feat, and that one does by Divine Grace so build up a spare self as it were to live with when one can't endure one's more familiar personality. You may smile when I tell you <u>Kant</u> helped me here, in the way philosophy has all through my spiritual life, by bringing into greater clearness and into the domain of the intellect a position reached much more surely by religious intuition in the first place. It is in this case a matter of using Plato's "raft' as well as the "divine word"....

[On health and plans to meet]

Yr lv
E

Elizabeth's intensely personal letter on her despair at Elinor's imminent departure from her life was marked by Ethel as one of great importance to her.

October 29th, 1931

Darling E. I think I must have missed a letter of yours – or you one of mine for I answered what you said about these people in the *Waves* having no grasp of "the Peace" etc. Although I feel about the Waves that it is a poem – but a Poem of Despair. I think I ask of a work like that some sort of moral principle – there is nothing handed to you in the Waves but a lance to combat death. Courage – Beauty – these are not enough. That is my feeling. In her other books she hitches on to things like fun, to an adorable personality (Joseph or her Mother). The despair is there, humming in ones ears, but it is mitigated, oxygenized. At first the originality, the daring (and of course the beauty) did carry me away. But….think of the [?] tastes in ones mouth left by it – and the Prison respectively!

Would you like to go to the Prison? I can give you and Grizzy[1] tickets you see.

Your loving
E

1 EMW's cousin, Griselda Grant-Lawson, born 1905.

November 11th, [1931]

Ethel was very anxious to promote the friendship between Elizabeth and the Woolfs, for a complex variety of reasons: giving pleasure to both parties, of course, but also, perhaps to consolidate her position with them by "offering" her very attractive and intelligent young relative. The following letters give an idea of how the relationship developed; the first was found taped inside a copy of the 1st US edition (1921) of *Monday or Tuesday*:

52 Tavistock Square

Dear Elizabeth,

Your aunt says you would like a copy of this little book. I am rather ashamed of it, as a matter of fact, as it is all experiment and rather wild, and should, I suspect, have been torn up. However, if you want a copy here it is. And I should be very grateful if you would tell me, one of these days, whether any of it should be reprinted, and if so what. At present, it is not to be included with the others, partly because I cannot bring myself to read it through.

I hope your Aunt is better. She says she is, but lives with such ferocity and abandonment that I cannot conceive any body standing it. No doubt it is a very good way of living all the same.

I hope you're better – the horizon is oozing out [??]. When you're in London please let me know and come and get on with the argument. I think we were in the middle of one when you got up and left.

Your
Virginia Woolf

November 20th, 1931

Darling Elizabeth – I feel I must read "After the Deluge"¹ again from cover to cover – and as it costs 15/- I don't think I can buy it! But do order it without delay from the L[ondon]. Library. I cant bear life till I know how it strikes you. If I told L. how deeply it impresses me he'd be horrified. How tiresome such people are! Meanwhile I do wish Dean Inge wd review it. I feel the gaps in L's mentality and temperament, yet I feel I never read more lucid convincing arguments than he brings forward to all his theses. And the style is quite entrancing – so grave, so humorous and modest.

E

1 The first volume of Leonard Woolf's Principia Politica – *After the Deluge* – had come out earlier in 1931, published by the Hogarth Press.

November 20th, 1931

On the 20th, Virginia Woolf wrote again to Elizabeth at Mount Mascal.

52 Tavistock Square
W.C.1
Telephone; Museum 2621

Dear Elizabeth,

Is there any chance you are free on Monday night (next Monday the 23rd that is) and would come and see us? I can't ask you to dine because our table is small, and already full, but any time about 9 if you would come in, as you are, with the dust of the stars in your hair – or whatever it is – unchanged, it would be a great pleasure, to see you. I'm taking this step on Ethel's swearing you won't be enraged.

Your Virginia Woolf

November 23rd, 1931

And three days later.

52 Tavistock Square
Sunday

Dear Elizabeth,

Just back from Rodmell and found your letter. So I shall expect you to dine, 8, undressed, and don't bother to ring up.

Well, I'm delighted if you like the Waves. I wonder what a mathematical mind like yours finds – I did feel rather mathematical myself though, - that's to say ruthless and abstract and savage and tight fisted while writing it. And I never expected anyone to get to the end of it so I'm very pleased that you did; - it's very nice of you to think of me in Tubes – which reminds me, may I some day look through your telescope?

But this can wait. (You see, if I light up Tubes, you must light up the stars)

Your
Virginia Woolf

Meanwhile, Ethel was reading Leonard Woolf's political works:

November 28th, 1931

Darling Eliz – Your parcel arrived and I dared not open it. Guess why! I had begun a book lent me by Leonard – his new book. I fetched it there the day we met (after a splendid interview [?] by the Soc. Of Authors] – at least I hoped to find it awaiting me in the basement of 52 and was gratified. But instead of being out, as she should have been, V. was bad again – a headache – and in bed. Perhaps only your complaint, but more likely she had been pushing her adventurous mood to extremes as L. said she was rather bad. (Poor V.) Well – this book is one of the most interesting and entrancingly written I have struck for years – It's an examination into the communal psychology that leads to peace, war, revolution, colonization, politics and everything! All the quiet mordant L. humour we know of is in it, and so far a striking absence of cocksureness. But its engrossingness is the point and apparently there are 10 vols yet to come! I am so glad. I mean to buy it, come what may, as I wish to be able to let a dab of poached egg – the carelessness of enthraldom - testify to my emotions if I choose and this you cant do with books not your own.

[Her next task will be to read Marius*; on various acquaintances, including Katherine Furse[1]]*

Yes. I thought Mrs Thesiger[2] quite an ass tho' I suspect that of being mainly "charm" put on to make people...say "How amusing Mrs T. is!" That's why I concentrated on her hat, as who should say: "Cease your funning: you know you are really a milliner and that bit I respect."

[On other bores; Triggs Lock; the beauty of the autumn leaves in the Balfour's wood; the joy of having got her work under control]

1 Katherine Furse (1875-1952), the niece of the painter Marianne North, was head of the Red Cross Voluntary Aid Detachment in World War I and later played an important role in making skiing a popular sport. In *Streaks of Life* p.74, ES wrote of Charles Furse: "....perhaps the most courageous person I have known except Katherine his wife."
2 Possibly Janet Ranken, wife of the actor Ernest Thesiger - cousin of the explorer Wilfred Thesiger - soon to appear with Boris Karloff in *The Ghoul*, and in *Bride of Frankenstein*.

The next day, Ethel wrote to her brother.

November 29th, 1931

[On the problems of The Wreckers *and* The Prison *and wrestling with a vast number of practical matters, such as copyright and the cesspit at Coign. ES was exhausted and says an "indifference born of a dislike to tackle anything ever again begets laziness, I don't much care whether the season takes place or not."]*

I think I am really am glad at the bottom of my heart at the prospect of a long spell of passivity – and, for one thing, reading of books I have been looking forward to reading for ages. One I am now so immersed in that I can hardly stop. I do wonder if you would find it as madly interesting as I do? It is by Leonard Woolf, Virginia's husband and it is a study of communal psychology called "After the Deluge". If anyone had told me just that I doubt if I'd have tried the book (!!) but in "The Listener" I read two or three chapters (on democracy) out of the broadcast last month – and tho' he never says a word you or I wd agree with, his mind is very interesting and his manner, quiet, mordant, amused and amusing, very attractive. This book is full of ideas and implications that outrage a Tory – but he never talks through his hat or indulges in sheer braininess like G.B.S[haw]. I'm not sure that it would be a good book (tho' most enthralling and readable) after a hard and long hunt – tho' that reminds me, I wonder if you have read <u>her</u> last book "The Waves". A hard nut to crack – too despairing for me – yet so gorgeously full of beauty.....

December 3rd, 1931

On December 3rd, she wrote to him again, carrying on the topic.

Leonard ….is so good for crusted Tories like us to read… Flashy books on "communal psychology: a study of" (the subtitle) like Ludwig and G.B.S[haw]. make me quite ill. But when L.W. denigrates the Xtian view of sin (which he says has poisoned life) and defends the General State even you and I can but listen! And its so delicately ironical – so lucid – The only awful thing is if this (Vol I) took him "many years" to write – when shall we get the next? I can think of nothing but Vol.II!

Your E

December 5th, 1931

Darling Elizabeth...well...truth must out! Marius is <u>not</u> my book!...[reasons]...I am so awfully sorry – I hate not liking your favourite book...

[More reasons; on buying Leonard Woolf's book and an article by Maurice Baring on Eton]

I am so provoked that I did not hear Belshazzar[1] which I could easily have done and wd have if I'd known, and had realized that it made a great impression at Leeds. I've not seen anybody to ask about it either but I am sure it is really remarkable – tho' similar things were said in 1904 about Elgar...I can never forget that!

["Hotel Dodge" and a walk to Triggs Lock]

We've had a Woking tragedy – a woman, evidently mad, about 26, walked about all night with her 11 months child and then went home and strangled it. The other two children, gnawing crusts, said cheerfully to the policeman "We saw mother do it". They are well off and up to now no explanation is forthcoming. Mary S. – harsh as ever to her own class – seems to hope she will be hanged and rejects the idea of insanity!! Strange mentality they have.

Yr loving E

1 William Walton's *Belshazzar's Feast* was first performed at the Leeds Festival October 8th, 1931; Osbert Sitwell selected the text.

December 7th, 1931

[On their lunching with Mary Dodge]

I had a sad letter from V. today. She has to lie [?] and lead an invalid's life till they go to Rodmell for Xmas; not work – has to "beat down" ideas which, she says, "swarm" – (she has 3 books in her head) – Just go out for a walk and read anything right off her own line of thought (she is keen on science) and live on the sofa – for then the pain stops. I am so awfully sorry for her. She and L. delighted in you, in your "intelligence" and V says "I doubt if L could throw her from her perch" (!) I said "He certainly couldn't but I always told you that!"

December 8th [?] 1931

[On borrowing – and mislaying – books]

The worst of it is Betty [Balfour] is always saying I am "odious" about lending books (!!! simply because I ask for them back!) Perhaps a P.G.W[odehouse] can't be a lengthy work, you had better get 2 from the Times...

[She will try again to read Marius*]*

December 10th, 1931

Darling Elizabeth – I saw V yesterday – she was on the sofa and Leonard said I could stay till 6 – but she bargained for 6.30. She again said how much she liked you and did hope you liked her nephew[1]. She was delighted with what you said – <u>she spoke a lot of you and said</u> "Would she come and see me like this? At this sort of time?" (You know 4.30 to 7.30 is Virginia's slice of the day for these sort of things. I said of course you would. And on the strength of it you might like to write to her and say I had told you what she said – and that you'd love to come when she's well enough. I think they will go to Rodmell on Friday 18th and stay there a fortnight. L. says the whole genl. election[2] <u>was</u> a bankers ramp – and that Lord Passfield[3] is publishing the truth in the January number of the Political Review. V. said you wrote her a delightful letter about the Waves. They do like you awfully – and are arrested by you. L. gave me an amazing book of his "The Village in the Jungle" – I'll send it to you when I've finished it.

Your E

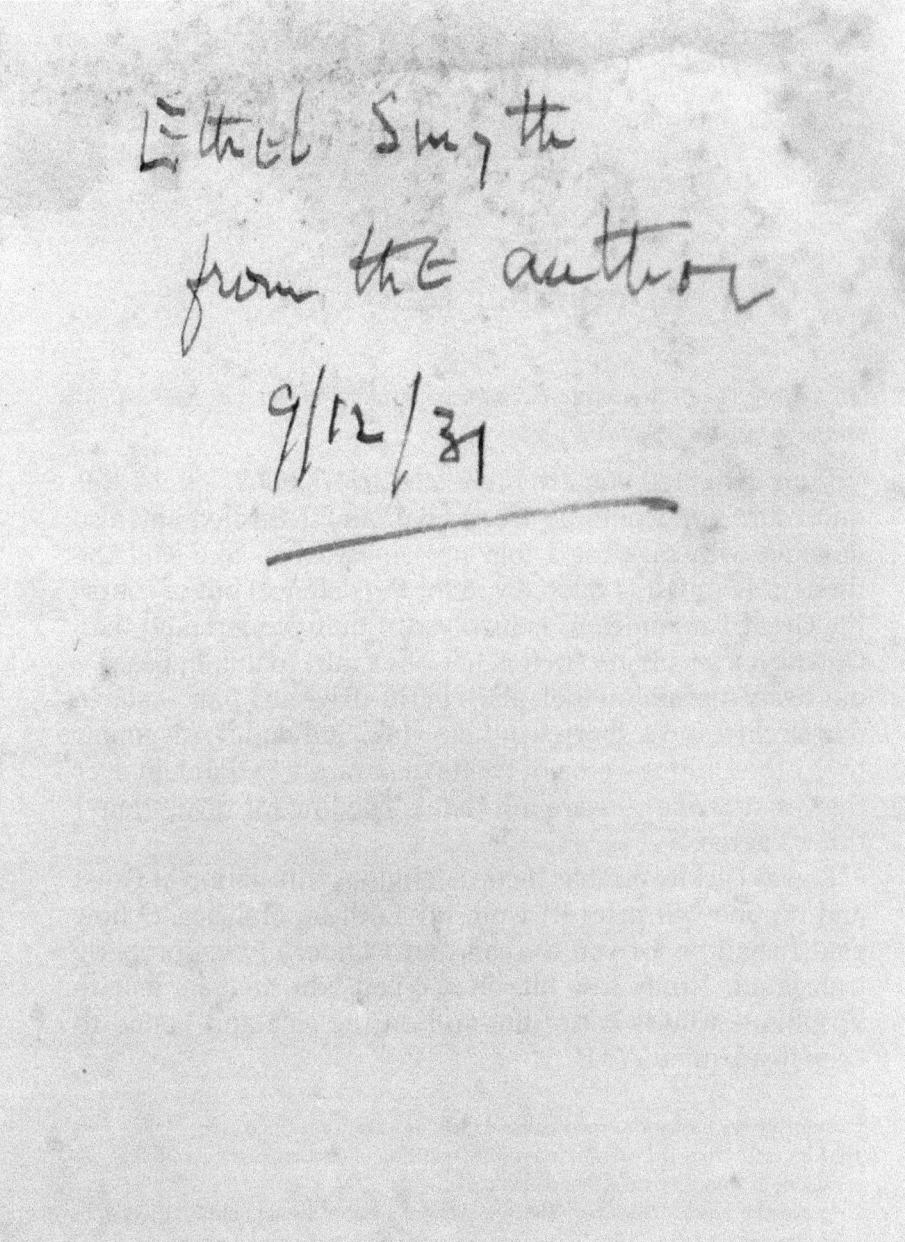

In ES's copy of *The Village in the Jungle*, given to her by Leonard Woolf

1 Julian Bell (1908-1937).
2 The General Election of October 27th, 1931 was the first since the beginning of the Great Depression and an absolute majority for the Conservatives.
3 Sidney Webb (1859-1947) socialist, economist and reformer, a pillar of the Fabian Society and co-founder of L.S.E., had been warning about the imminent death of capitalism for many years.

December 14th, 1931

[On finding some French and German notes and buying some half bottles of champagne: "always useful"]

I am delighted you are interested in L's book – but I was quite sure you would be. Betty [Balfour] is thrilled and also dancing with rage (as I told her she wd be). She said she thought L. unfair (I quoted you for the defence) but of course the Great Panjandrum[1] is involved! I quite understand that. One never sees Betty (that is her one fault) to talk in peace – our hasty discussion took place in the drive at 7 p.m. – she in day clothes and a sharp wind blowing. She said it was unfair to say the Unions were not trying to paralyze Parliament over the Great Strike[2] – were not that is heading for revolution. I think I agree.

Lowes Dickinson[3] has made a fabulous translation of Faust and no one will print it! I pin my faith on Maurice. O how glad I shall be for you to read that wonderful play properly translated. I only saw bits in a typed edit. that he lent to Virginia – who is better but still on the sofa and bound to keep head quiet –Yr E

1 Presumably her husband Gerald Balfour, the Conservative politician.
2 The General Strike of 1926. An interesting selection of contemporary accounts is available at www.spartacus.schoolnet.co.uk .
3 Goldsworthy Lowes Dickinson (1862 -1932) was a historian and political thinker, and a member of the Cambridge Conversazione Society, better known as the Cambridge Apostles. He wrote a number of works on politics, philosophy and religion, and was influential in forming the League of Nations in 1920. E.M. Forster was his literary executor.

Friday, December 18th [1931]

My darling Aunt,
How angelic of you to send the champagne. So to expend your treasure is an example of saintly charity I think.
[Family plans]
I have finished Leonard's book and would fain write pages on the subject but will postpone this as I am just starting for London to tidy up things at U.C. and buy my Christmas presents which are confined to Vesey[1] and Greg's children. Greg's boy has been most awfully ill and finally had a mastoid operation and will be in hospital for a month more. I thought he was done for as he had such a high temperature for so long before they operated but now he is supposed to be out of danger.

[On Bleak House; *more on the illness of one of the children in the family and regrets at not having gone to a concert of ES's: "…..was behind with my work. Not hard work, but procrastination and slowness."]*

Bitterly cold here. I rather like it except that it gives me chilblains on my feet.

I had a great day's gardening on Sunday and cut that tumble down rose bush back to the roots. It was a pergola and under the ruins I found the remains of a garden seat and yards of wire support.

Yr lv
E

---

1 Vesey Holt (1927-2001), then aged about four, was a relative of Elizabeth's – her father and his grandmother were brother and sister. He also was to be very seriously ill in 1935 and there are a number of references to his health in the letters. However, he survived and *The Telegraph* published a charming obituary of him on August 23rd, 2001. The Holt family house was Mount Mascal, where Elizabeth was currently living with Martin Holt and his family.

December 20th, 1931

Darling Elizabeth – I doubt you will get my p.c. sent today to M.M. Farm telling you of my lost letter to you. Meanwhile I want you to do me a favour; read i.e. skim thro' the book I send you which Maurice [Baring] sent me and tell me your impressions.....

The book in question was *The Miracle of Peille* by J.L. Campbell, published in 1929. It is rather surprising that this highly romantic novel – the crippled and orphaned heroine is the daughter of a mountain shepherd and a gypsy girl done to death by hostile villagers - with a strongly religious theme should have appealed to Ethel, but she "found it charming" and forwarded it to Maurice Baring, who sent back a return volume. "I know nothing about this Ste Thérèse.." wrote Ethel, "but I would be very glad to hear how it strikes you..." Most years have produced a new book on St Thérèse of Lisieux – Vita Sackville-West was to write about her a few years later, contrasting her with St Teresa of Avila – but this was probably the translation of the official Carmelite biography, published not long before. The letter goes on at some length with the scandal of a divorce among the Actons – one of the great English recusant families – and the Catholic view of the subject. Ethel longs to know whether they will be excommunicated: "Betty [Balfour] says they won't be because he's a peer.." and what would happen if it were "Mr Jones and Miss Smith (or Smyth even?)..."

"I am rather anxious and I can see Leonard is about Virginia. I've seen her twice in the last 10 days – but these headaches (they come in spells) leave her utterly played out. She lies on the sofa and mayn't work – and looks so frail that it wrings my heart. But on Tues ? they go to Rodmell for a fortnight and that always sets her up. L. says that ever since The Waves she has been rocking on her perch (even that night you dined, or didn't dine, she wasn't quite up to that mild little festivity which she <u>so</u> enjoyed (and she was anxious to know if you liked Julian Bell) and the day after crashed.

I am longing for a long letter abt "The Deluge" which I think masterly in every way – and am sure you do....."

Book plate in the copy of *Marius the Epicurean*, that EMW tried to persuade ES to read

December 23rd (Eve), 1931

Elizabeth, as usual, spent Christmas at Cromer; Ethel preferred to remain alone at Coign, but wrote her a long letter:

[On Dickens and other reading matter, including her absolute inability to get through Marius*]*

I am so glad that you were so impressed with Leonard his book – or as you say his mind – the warmth and the cold is so delightful – Like a photo I saw in Huxley's African book of snow lying in the crater of Kilimanjaro. I do think as you do about his not distinguishing enough between Christ and his followers, above all [what] the egregious St Paul made of his teaching. Still I suppose the idea that chiefly puts L. off, the insistence on sin is not to be got out of, is it? I meant to ask you. And there is no doubt either (I suppose) that Christ very definitely thought poverty, or want, and the very reverse of democratic aspiration after material happiness, generally speaking, the thing to be aimed at. That I think provoked H.B. always. But the horror of the senses, that surely there is no trace of in Christ's teaching? Do tell me.

As for his optimism about democracy perhaps sloughing conformity and working through to individuation – well, is he so optimistic? He seems to think that every group is narrow – always was – and that now unfortunately the groups number millions (owing to the Press) – in fact that it is human nature, not democracy that is to blame. I think so anyway and am frightfully interested in the revolt of the literary world against the muzzling measures of the B.B.C.[1]

In last week's T[ime] & T[ide] (December, 19) there's such an admirable article by Norman Angell[2] (one of my gods) about this. I'll send it to you...

[On other articles in the same issue]

About voting Labour – What I feel is that politics is a thing you must either study intensively or not at all – and that one party is just as blind and stupid as another – that only individuals count. But there again! Look at Lord Salisbury and the Joint Stock Company theory! (O I do delight in

Leonard's irony – don't you? He's very funny about that). Look at Norman Angell and his book written before the war[3], which seemed to one irrefutably sound and which events have proved to be only too much so! No one wd listen to him – nor to Mr Keynes about the Gold Standard! In fact I see nothing but individuals. I know I hate Fascism. I think it all wrong... but....sh'd I if I were an Italian? I never can see that Tories are any more reactionary in essentials than the Labourites are divorced from reality – and having been bred a Tory, I incline to vote Tory. Still – if I went in professionally for politics, for all I know I might be Labour – tho' I don't at all think that by voting Labour one would be helping to bring about "L's brand of socialism" – at least if he is a socialist – but I rather doubt it. He told me the Trade Union leaders are the stupidest men he has met on this planet and that to credit them with aiming at "Revolution" in the Gen[eral] Strike is a thing no one who knows them wd imagine – so stupid are they. He declares, tho', that all they did was to put on pressure just as the banks privately put pressure on the country to get a National Govt. and stop socialistic legislation by saying "You shan't have the 50 millions you want unless you have a Coalition." I do wish I could hear L and some knowledgeable person argue. Lord Eustace Cecil[4] tried to have a broadcast wrangle with him, but L. refused.

Now that you will have read the Saint book I can tell you that I found it <u>very</u> poor and provoking as literature – so poor and mawkish that I cd hardly get thro'it and told Maurice so – whereat he was <u>greatly surprised</u> (that greatly surprised me!) I also said I thought Sainte Thérèse rather detestable. The remark about "it is no doubt God's plan that Mother Gonzagues shall be so odious to me" is worthy of Esther Summerson[5].

1 Throughout the 1930s there was a general tendency towards stricter censorship – particularly of films – since it was realised that they were becoming more influential than the written word – but also at the B.B.C. and a long list of topics that could not be touched was being drawn up.

2 Norman Angell (1872-1967) – author, activist for peace and against Fascism and Labour M.P. He was awarded the Nobel Prize for Peace in 1933. His book: *Can Governments Cure Unemployment?* had come out earlier in the year and in 1928 he had produced *The Money Game*, a book with accompanying games, designed to teach school children the workings of finance and banking.

3 Perhaps *The Great Illusion: A Study of the Relation of Military Power to National Advantage* first written in 1910 and repeatedly revised – a work for which ES had great respect.
4 Lord Eustace Cecil (1834-1921) – Younger brother of Lord Salisbury (see above). A Conservative politician, he wrote comparing homelessness and prison conditions in Britain with experiences in other countries.
5 Heroine of *Bleak House*.

Christmas Day, 1931

Late in 1931 and at the beginning of 1932, Ethel and Elizabeth exchanged letters on their religious views and moral positions – something that mattered very much to both of them. Unfortunately, only a few of the letters have survived, so that the dialogue is incomplete. As has already been mentioned, this collection of letters has undergone serial vicissitudes; Ethel also both borrowed letters in order to write her volumes of autobiography, and lent her own and Elizabeth's, for example, to Virginia Woolf, to her brother Bob and to Maurice Baring. This particular series of letters from Elizabeth is numbered and it is hard to imagine that the missing ones were destroyed deliberately, since they were very important to Ethel and marked as such. For this reason, much of Elizabeth's side has been included. Her letters also serve to give a clearer picture of the quality of mind of the great-niece whom Ethel loved dearly and with whom she corresponded for some forty years, but who remains in much of the correspondence a somewhat shadowy figure. Those who are not interested in these aspects of Ethel and Elizabeth's characters can easily skip the passages in question.

The following, from an 8½ page letter by Elizabeth, was among those marked by Ethel as "very important".

Cromer

My darling Aunt
Your long letter of this morning calls for another as it is brimful of things I want to talk of.
First the Saint Book
I found the book so wholly alien to my tastes I could hardly read it but I did, word for word. But the fact that I hate it makes me resolve not to identify the saint with it. For one thing I thought she is quite impossible as a subject for a biography since the <u>whole</u> of her life was an affair of solitary spiritual adventure. If one can dare appraise anyone's sanctity

(which seems to me anyhow impossible) surely in her case there can be only one relevant document, her own book. Not having read it, I now confine my remarks to the man's own production. I thought it so <u>feeble</u> and the few anecdotes and quotations very ill chosen.

[A couple of well-reasoned pages on why she so disliked the Life *of St Thérèse of Lisieux]*

I thought it a most tiresome, sentimental and weak book, and I should think it presumptuous even to begin to form an opinion of Thèrese on anything in it.

[On Bleak House *and Thackeray]*

I followed the B.B.C. row in the Times. Both Leonard and John Macmurray[1] told me certain things about it some time ago, so the development of the row was awaited with personal interest. Macmurray is one of the committee for education and I assure you Reith's[2] self appointed divine mission of [?censure] is not confined to fiction. J.M. told me his chief hope and fellow warrior on the committee against the powers of darkness was Temple, the Archbishop of York[3]. This pleased me as I have always admired the latter's writings and printed utterances on many topics.

Of the Time and Tide dispute I only saw B.Shaw's answer to Lyttleton. I only see T & T at U.C. and even then missed the number with the beginning of it.

And now for Christ, Sin and democracy! I bewail my feeble pen but here goes with what <u>I</u> think and a personal conviction is after all the only thing that anyone, even Plato, has to offer to another. I have found it necessary to exert my imagination in a systematic way in order to satisfy myself on this question: "Is there anything in Christ's life and words that is unique, or is he one of a great company of moral teachers all saying more or less the same thing?" It struck me that modern scholarship had got into a fashion for attempting synthesis and unities [?] to such an extent that it obscures this issue. I get weary with the whole business of comparing one thing with another and always writing of "Platonism in the light of Christianity" or "Christianity in the light of Platonism" or "Buddhism in the light of Both."! (I exaggerate but the tendency is a real one) I therefore think the other way round, tried with definite concentration to read every author for himself, by himself: Job, Isaiah, the psalms, Plato, Aristotle, Plotinus, a little of Buddhism and Confucianism (but I discount my most superficial efforts there – I never have found a book that gave me confidence) and the Gospels, St Paul and Acts. With the Gospels I systematically read them all 4 yearly straight on end with the same concentrated effort to imagine I have never read them before. Well with the result I formed the opinion that in Christ something new and unique entered the world. If theologians like to interpret this in the dogma of the incarnation of the Word of God I am prepared to say Credo because it answers to my personal experience of contact with God in prayer and contact with Jesus Christ as a human life and a talker[4] I do not care for or think in terms of dogma because it seems to me a superstructure made by many minds in an attempt, bound to fail, to exteriorize and crystallize an intuitive whisper of the spirit. With the miraculous events recorded of the birth, life and death of Christ, I feel one is such a tangle of myth making on one hand, and on the other, of people who actually walked and talked with Christ and whose personal verdict was "This man was the son of God" – that I remain completely agnostic. Of course I don't think all the stories are on a level in this respect: i.e. the birth and epiphany stories have all the characteristics of myths invented afterwards, whereas miracles (?) of healing and the resurrection are much harder to explain away even for the people best at this art! I have given you this long preamble because I want to make clear that I absolutely share the point of view that the "evidence" and documents of Christianity must be examined and sifted with as much critical acumen as one possesses and that I have read with avidity as much new testament criticism as is within my scope (both as to time, and for appreciating the points of verbal criticism, with my limited knowledge of Greek)

As at the end of all this I believe quite literally that Christ is the light of the world, naturally the most important preoccupation of my religious life is to try to see things by his light, namely to realise what the essence of his view of life is and the secret of his power and the power he gave to his contemporary friends and followers. I find the essence to be in his individualism, in the way he turned his attention always on the particular question of a particular person and <u>very</u> seldom made any grand pronouncements. Even the summary of the "whole duty of man" viz "Thou shalt love the Lord thy God with all thy mind, and with all thy heart and with all thy soul, and thy neighbour as thyself" was not a command imposed by him on his followers but what he recommended to one person, the lawyer, who <u>asked</u> him what to do to inherit eternal life. There is not a single prohibition I can think of in the gospels. As far as I can see the Christian doctrine of sin is like everything in the spiritual life, an individual problem arising from an individual's aspiration to become holy. Where I do think there is a definite cleavage between Christ's teaching and the democratic ideal of "happiness" as set forward by L[eonard] W[oolf] and Bertrand Russell and such thinkers is on the question of the holy. Holiness has no meaning for a purely secular thinker and happiness will therefore be put in its' place as the goal of human life I think all believers in the underlying assumption of Christ's teaching will be at variance with this point of view. I think Christ thought and said that the destiny of man is to make himself a son of God, and that this demands a different set of values and a different goal. Once you have found a meaning in "eternal life" and the "Kingdom of God" and such phrases of Christ's I think you are concerned with a world that L.W. and B.R. are simply not considering at all. This is the world Christ was considering the <u>whole time</u> and lived in, for he was a religious and not a political thinker. This super-natural world I think a reality and I suppose L.W. thinks an illusion. For me, sin and repentance are real just as holiness and love of God are, and a philosophy that denies their existence is unreal.

    I think Christ right and democracy wrong about happiness, and to me it would be as futile to deny sin in the spiritual life as to deny pain in the physical life. I would like to substitute the word "justice" or "fair dealing" everywhere Leonard uses "happiness". I think it true to say that everyone has a right to justice, but as absurd to say anyone has a "right to happiness" as that anyone has a "right" to a good circulation or dark hair. To sum up: I believe a life where holiness is the goal and a vision of God the inspiration. Therefore I believe sin is real and that (in each individual case) that hinders the vision of God. I believe the secular outlook to be limited, perfectly valid within its' limits, but not to be compared to Christ's for depth and correspondence to what human life is really like.

I have taken a long time to sketch the sort of thing I mean, and perhaps you disagree, or more probably, approach these awesome questions differently. We are babes crying in the dark, with our little minds trying to understand God philosophically I am sure, but religiously speaking I am not an agnostic. Nor do I think all teachers on a level but Christ, as a revelation of God, unique and therefore I am prepared to call him anything the Church likes as long as I don't let the Church do me out of the necessity of thinking out his attitude to life myself.

Yr Lv
E

ES's note: "No.1 copied"

1 John Macmurray (1891-1976) was a Scots philosopher who, after a distinguished military career in World War I, was so shocked by his congregation's unchristian reaction to his sermon pleading for reconciliation rather than vengeance that, although devoutly Christian, he decided to have no more to do with the established churches and eventually became a Quaker.
2 John Reith (1889-1971) - first Director General of the B.B.C. and founder of the Reith Lectures. A complex and controversial figure, he frequently found himself battling the Government. In spite of a decidedly autocratic streak, an admiration for fascism, and certain puritan attitudes, he was instrumental in establishing the B.B.C.'s reputation for unbiased reporting.
3 William Temple (1881-1944) – Archbishop of York and later of Canterbury was deeply concerned with social theology and wrote extensively on what would constitute a just society and how it could be achieved.
4 "Teacher" would seem a more likely reading, it is fairly clearly "talker".

Tuesday, December 29th, [1931]

Cromer

My darling Aunt,
How beastly you being ill. When you are restored do write and say so. I had no idea you had the 'flu and had missed Christmas reunions and so on.

[More on Bleak House *and Thackeray]*

The weather here after being unnaturally warm is now reverting to type. A very strong N.E. wind and no golf. Tonight Bill and I are going on a shooting expedition to Blakeney Marshes. You go out about 10 (when the moon obliges) and wait for dusk and wild geese, returning about 2 AM. Great fun. Very beautiful and agonizingly and unbelievably cold. We have done it before. I love it, never shoot anything and should dislike it if I did! You either walk out over the marshes and wait by the shore, or hunt through the creeks on a punt. I have never done the latter.

Yr
E

ES's note: "No.2" – apparently referring to a series of letters she considered particularly significant.

On the 30th, she sent a hastily scribbled note on a small sheet of lined paper, principally on borrowing/lending each other volumes of Proust.

1932

New Year's Day, 1932

Darling Elizabeth – Your analysis of the Christ figure absolutely enthralled me – and above all your reading of the sin problem which, by the way, is curiously like H.B.'s. Virginia was so enthralled by the whole business – I mean your preoccupation with all these questions and I was so frightfully sorry for her in her long drawn agony about Lytton Strachey[1] (do you know that I have new and astounding lights on V's inside [?]) that I sent the letters and the long Dickens one, to her. And I greatly fear she will sit on them and hatch them in spite of my imploring.

What most arrests me is your declaring Christ is unique – O my, how I long to see you...

[On plans for meeting, her illness and on sending EW's letters to VW]

But V. has had headache and consequent inactivity of brain since they left London – aggravated by daily dread of hearing of L.S.'s death – and I was so awfully sorry for her.

But O Eliz what can we do about the whole hideous erection built up by the Church? The dreadful legacy of a sexless epileptic? The whole sea of hypocrisy in which the race prospers so amazingly. Isn't it terrible that tho' modern science can collect and keep pure for human consumption a mountain stream, this cannot be done for a divine teacher's words?

[Her admiration for Dickens, and again health and plans]

Yr devoted E

1 Died 21st January, 1932.

January 2nd, 1932

Cromer

My darling Aunt,

I agree that the distortion of Christ's attitude to life by the Churches is the saddest thing in the world. Sometimes the whole thing sweeps over my spirit in a wave of anguish and I find my attachment to the Church (belonging to a very different compartment in my mind) is a bad compromise and not a good one. I have never yet really made up my mind about this. But in less acute and more everyday moods I lead my spiritual life more happily outside than inside the Church and I think that on the whole high church Anglicanism is the least baneful of the compromises. But I <u>do</u> think you are unfair to St Paul. He was so mighty a force that I admit he left his stamp on Christianity but I can never forget that he also saved it from its first and most deadly peril, a lapse into Judaism. In fact he rescued Christ from the Jews on behalf of the Gentiles. Do read again his own story of the fight in the Epistle to the Galatians. It only takes 20 mins or so. It moves me more than any of his writings by its heat and personal devouring passion. When you think what was at stake and what would have happened if he had not "withstood Peter to his face"! and vindicated the "liberty with which Christ has made us free." Remember too that the crabbed rather churchy remarks about wives and husbands, fathers, children, bishops, etc. in the so-called Pastoral Epistles (Titus, Timothy, etc.) are <u>more</u> than probably not his at all. The short late epistles are thought not to be by him. Of course the Epistle to the Hebrews isn't. It is very beautiful, I think, the most philosophical writing in the N.T. but utterly un-Pauline.

If you are spellbound as I am by the miracle of those early days and the point of transition between the failure and despair which the crucifixion must have plunged the little flock into, and then the sudden appearance of a world conquering religion as triumph and hope, I think you must reckon with Paul as something more than a "sexless epileptic" (I am now developing Miss E.W.'s theories in New Testament criticism so don't think what follows has any learned authority. I have learned a lot from books on the N.T. but have never been discouraged by them in basing my version of the growth of dogma on my own reading of the N.T, itself. Where expert opinion is so helpful in tracing this is in fixing in one's mind the sequence of the writings, the dates.)

Well, Paul's epistles are the earliest of all Christian documents. In them you find the substance of the "Gospel" preached to the Gentiles and I am of the opinion that the key to the door leading from Christ on the shore of the sea at Galilee talking to his friends, to the Church Militant with its' simple but very definite dogmatic theology is to be found in Paul's personal history. There is a very sudden break. You have this show [ES's "?"] in Jerusalem bossed [ES's "?"] by Peter and James (see 1st few chapters of Acts before Paul comes in) in which the little community lived on memories of Jesus as a human being and the hopes, based on the fact (fact for them anyhow) of his resurrection, of his imminent reappearance to reign in Jerusalem. Paul was not in contact with this environment at all. Then 3 years later out of the blue comes Paul to Jerusalem, not to ask about Jesus' history and to put himself under tuition from Jesus' intimate friends, but already "fully grown in Christ". That is with a blazing revelation burned on his vision of the Risen Lord. (Paul's own statement of his attitude to the apostles who saw the Lord in the flesh is very clearly put in the epistle to the Galatians). From that point the resurrection as a dogma because the pivot of Paul's own (and his particular little group's) missionizing. He put the cosmic element into what was the story of an individual and made the Incarnation, Passion and Resurrection into great mystic events embracing the whole World and God's plans for it. That he influenced the actual form in which the 4 canonical gospels were written I am not so sure. I am engaged now in an attempt to sift this idea. It struck me that the one to find traces of theology in would be Luke. (It is pretty certain I think that the evangelist Luke was the same as the Acts Luke and certainly a companion of Paul.) But at the moment I see no trace of this influence. We may really [?] in the Gospels, I think, their consistency being so much more striking than their divergences, and the fact that Mark represents Peter's version of Christ's life and therefore an eyewitness account. The much more expanded Matthew and Luke are so close together when they depart from Mark that the so called "Q" passages point to a very early and authentic source. But I must not wander in the labyrinth of gospel arguments but return to Paul. What I see is this: 1) that it was the resurrection dogma and not the holy life and words of Christ that converted the world. 2) That this came about because Paul did not know Christ in the flesh but threw his whole <u>colossal</u> strength of character into preaching Christ at the right hand of God in Heaven (which was where he did see him) and not Christ walking about in Galilee.

I think it useless to repine at the subsequent dogmatic developments. Beauty, goodness and wisdom have no "universal value" in the biological sense, whereas human institutions because they are rigid are also strong. The spirit bloweth where it listeth and certainly has blown through the arches of the temples made with hands inspite of the efforts of clerics to shut out the draught! Also that strange jumble of writings bound up together, with such doubtful origins and precarious history, <u>do</u> give a steady light and justify the title of "Holy Scriptures". At least I think so. I don't always read the N.T. in the spirit of this letter, shaking it like a dog does a rat. But I have found that reading it with a (metaphorical) magnifying glass, a Greek dictionary and a notebook makes me more and not less inclined to read it on my knees at other times.

The duck shoot was literally and metaphorically a wild goose chase. The moon kept clouding over and we never saw a winged creature. We each took a stretch of marsh behind the bank that runs along the rear side of Blakeney golf course and padded up and down for an hour or more but the feeble moon played us false and we had to chuck it. We were in by midnight. The fisherman Will Long, a charmer, wisely remained eating his supper with his family and refused to budge. They looked so smug. There was a terrific wind blowing and the rush over that waste of waters was very lovely. Bill has now gone away with his fowling pieces so that sport is over for me.

I shall look forward (how much) to your comments on my letters. It does rather shatter me that you send these lengthy scrawls to Virginia! I find it hard to conceive of her wanting to read them but she must blame you for sending them rather than me for writing them. What fun it is writing to you my most beloved aunt.

Yr
E

On the back, Ethel noted "No.3 January 2nd St Paul (copied) a magnificent letter." She replied:

January 8th, 1932

4 St John's Mansions, Eastbourne

It appears to me that there is a fate against my writing to you about Sin – I had put aside tea-time by which hour I am rather more intelligent than before 4.30 – animals are just the same; when ill, that is the moment of renaissance.

[On reading Dean Inge]

By the by Virginia agrees with all your remarks on Dickens. Also – on the Bottom the Weaver note as usual – she says re your remark at liking prolific writers "But for the nerve in my spine I shd be just as prolific as D – write day in, day out. I have 5 books in my head at this moment."

[A friend's view of The Waves]

Yr E

January 10th 1932

Eastbourne

Darling Elizabeth,

[Family news and plans to meet]

While here I came across a little book of G Lowes Dickinson which I shd have thought Leonard would disapprove of – full of profound belief in immortality and all the things that school rejects....

Monday, January 11th [1932]

University of London, University College

My darling Aunt

[Plans to meet]

We have just been to the French pictures this morning[1]....I have some preparatory jobs to do here. Instead of doing them I will answer your most interesting letter.

We seem to agree as to the fundamentals as regards sin. As I said in my last letter but one the problem of fornication versus the chaste ideal is the one point in ethics in which I am most tentative. As I have never had the slightest inclination to commit fornication I simply don't know what my reaction (religious) would be were I confronted with the problem. I would do anything without a qualm that did not prevent me partaking of Communion. I would not think I was committing sin. (The clergyman's feelings (if he knew) I should ignore.) If <u>not</u>, I think I should try to refrain from fornication. But that brings me no nearer a solution because I have not tested it! Christ in one utterance includes fornication in a list of the unclean things that proceed from the heart. But the world changes and the remarks he made about "Karban" [?] obviously have ceased to apply (dealing only with a certain puny [?] problem) and I feel <u>strongly</u> that the guidance from Christ is analogous (and push the analogy right through) to a light to examine individual problems by. If you say that fornication aids and chastity hinders your vision of God I would plump for fornication not being a sin. I think I should stick to that test throughout, in any problem that presented itself to me personally.

I think "blessedness" as used by you is what I mean by holiness. Anyhow what I mean is a certain intensity and depth of religious consciousness. A sense of the "pearl of great price" being really a thing for which one would sell all that one possessed to have. (I think the similes of Christ re "the Kingdom of Heaven is like unto..." Matthew 18 is one of the most heavenly things he said).

[On Coleridge]

I really must stop and do my job.

Yr lv
E

1 A major exhibition of French Art from 1200 onwards had opened at the Royal Academy on January 4th.

Ethel numbered this No.6, hence 4 and 5 appear to be missing and there are no more numbered letters.

January 17th, 1932

[Disapproval of an article in The Political Quarterly*]*

The only point that surprises me is that the relation of votes in 1929 was 8 million socialists to 13 million anti-soc: it was 7 to 16 in 1931. I should have expected a greater displacement of socialist votes than 1 million – (i.e.1/8 of their total). On the other hand no doubt they voted up to the hilt on both occasions, whereas the anti-socs didn't....

[Reading Keynes and Lowes Dickinson "who is good enough to want to meet me"; David Copperfield the best of Dickens' novels]

I was disgusted at having bought (urged by your Gran!) "Police at the Funeral"[1] I never knew it was a detective story – for I hate them – get bored to death!

[On a Coleridge biography; family events.]

1 By Margery Allingham, October 1931. One wonders what on earth Ethel thought it was with that title! Elizabeth loved thrillers.

January 19th, 1932

Two days later, Ethel wrote again.

[On Dickens, opinions (including H.B.'s) on Wordsworth - another passion of EMW's; plans for meeting; health and work in progress]

On the outside of the envelope.

> I was a fool not to remember that you rather like detective stories. I cannot <u>tell</u> you how they bore me. Virginia says all the Stracheys watching at Hungerford [where Lytton Strachey was dying at Ham Spray] spend the day reading them and doing crossword puzzles.

The next two days produced updates
- on her progress with David Copperfield.
   > I am (as ever) sick with crying,
- and a request for:
   > Mermaid Black Mints
   > postfree 4lb tin 5/-
- A radio broadcast;
   > I've got an awful cold again and have to get to Guildford tomorrow to plead for a new Concert Hall...
- books: her admiration for *The Prelude*; B. Russell;
- plans to reread *Elective Affinities*

Late March, 1932

In March 1932, the possibility of Elizabeth working at the Hogarth Press was discussed, presumably not very seriously, given her active career as an astronomer at University College[1]. Workers at the Press tended to come and go for reasons made clear by Richard Kennedy[2] who had left not long before and Virginia and Leonard often found themselves shorthanded, especially when they needed time for their own work[3]. No doubt for this reason, Virginia wrote in late March, 1932:

> Wednesday
52 Tavistock Square
>
> Dear Elizabeth,
> You said, I think the other day that you would like a job in the Hogarth Press. It is just possible there might be work going in the press – things have so developed suddenly. We're afraid it couldn't be definite at the moment, but we should very much like to discuss it with you 'fore we go to Greece

on Friday. Could you possibly come here tomorrow at 3.15 – downstairs to the press. Would you ring up?

Yr
Virginia Woolf

1 It was, incidentally the first British university to admit women on equal terms with men, something Elizabeth loved about it. She was also deeply attached to the observatory - see www.ulo.ucl.ac.uk - and always insisted on greeting it formally when driving past.
2 Richard Kennedy, *A Boy at the Hogarth Press*, Heinemann, London, 1972.
3 John H.Willis, *Leonard and Virginia Woolf as Publishers*: 1917-41, University Press of Virginia, 1992.

April 18th, 1932

By the following month, however, Ethel's attention was firmly claimed by economic problems. On the 18th of April she wrote from Bath, mostly about family arrangements, especially Mary Hunter's finances:

> I am certain that for £5 a week it might be possible to lodge yr grandm and feed her. People can live so much more cheaply than the class your relations belong to have any notion..... My idea is a hotel...at Bournemouth where Cordelia cd keep an eye on her and she wouldn't feel so forsaken. It's that, as Hilda says, that contracts my heart to think of.

She goes on to ask Elizabeth and her brother Billy to make up "a list of possible contributors to the Hill Hall fund"......

> Privately I think we shd hurry up before Lelia [Ponsonby] and the Duke separate!! But I hear he has settled £10 000 a year on her! So may be that's all right!
>
> Nina and Helena's house is lovely[1]

1 Hellens, in Herefordshire

Throughout the spring of 1932, Mary Hunter's situation grew more desperate and Ethel made increasingly frantic efforts to find a solution to the basic problems of where her sister was to live and how she was to be financed, and was infuriated by what she perceived as the lack of energy – or refusal to face reality – on the part of other members of the family, including Elizabeth. Her solutions included Mary Hunter living in a cheap lodging house, or boarding with an old servant. She also felt it would be "fair" to get up a subscription among the many people who had over the years enjoyed so much lavish hospitality at Hill Hall and she harassed Elizabeth in almost daily letters to get addresses and send off begging letters to friends.

Mary Hunter's humiliation and unwillingness to turn over her address book for such a purpose can very easily be imagined and, similarly, the reluctance of Elizabeth, an extremely reserved and private person, to be involved in Ethel's blatant fundraising. In Ethel's case it was very different. Not only was she more forthright by temperament and much less inhibited about practical matters of all kinds, but it is also clear that she had resented Mary's luxurious lifestyle and casual handing out of favours for many years and part of her was not altogether sorry to see her sister brought low. On the other hand, she was active, energetic, a problem solver and not over-sensitive, which made what she perceived as the dilatoriness of the rest of the family peculiarly irritating.

Naturally, this resulted in tensions. Elizabeth remonstrated gently with Ethel's over-enthusiasm and the latter in turn was offended when another of the clan insinuated that Elizabeth thought her "interfering". One possibility was that Mary Hunter would, until a better solution was found, visit different members of the family. Ethel offered to put her up, at least briefly, at Coign – which one imagines would <u>not</u> have been a success –

> ...if "Hellens" doesn't go well; and I could not swear that it will, given Nina's extravagance and Helena's very queer temper! (of which I had, in the past, experience – <u>tho' I always have liked and admired</u> her and tho' we get on now like a house on fire)...

Later on the 29th of April she was to write:

> I fancy in the end I shall have Queen Lear from 30 June to 11 July.

Elizabeth must have dreaded these letters, which show Ethel at her least attractive, each with a list of people with whom she was supposed to make contact, ranging from very old friends such as Emily Sargent and Tonks, to acquaintances of her grandmother's whom she protested that she hardly knew. Addresses of more possible subscribers to Mary Hunter's upkeep were added on the backs of the many of the envelopes in pencil. Speed, Ethel insisted, was of the essence:

> Now if we can ascertain the remainder by Monday, so much the better (we have 35 – or counting Lelia!! 36).....

This particular list included:

> Max Beerbohm ?
> Percy Lubbock?
> Mrs George Keppel (Florence)[1]
> I have <u>by stratagem</u> got Mrs Wharton and R. Norton from yr Grandmother!!

1 Alice Frederica Keppel (1868-1947) - The mistress of Edward VII, mother of EMW's friend Violet Trefusis and great grandmother of Camilla, Duchess of Cornwall, the second wife of Prince Charles.

May 10th, 1932

At the beginning of May, Elizabeth was still under siege

> I still think that you might days and days ago have found out the addresses of Max B[eerbohm]. and P. Lubbock from the publishers – simply because at the London Library or the Thames book Club you could do in 5 mins what wd take me a week of correspondence!! <u>Procedures</u> 1) "Please tell me what P.L. and M.B. latest books are and who are their publishers" 2) You then <u>ring up the publishers</u> and say you are a friend – (call yourself <u>Dame Ethel Smyth</u>) and want to send a <u>telegram</u> to them without delay.....
> Its pretty painful weather here. Pan only got 2nd reserve at the show!
>
> Your loving E

Enclosed, a note for EMW from the Medical Research Council: "I enclose some cigarettes for the Women Staff...."

By the 10th of May, her attention had, at least in part reverted to her music and Virginia.

> Darling Elizabeth......
> I enclose a divine letter from Virginia[1] who I think will be home soon – late this week. I had a scrap from Athens when she arrived, on the top of which she made a brave effort at a date, writing Wednesday the 26th May. But as it arrived on the 25 May I told her she beat Einstein hollow. Hence the reference. I then got a rotten p.c. from Nauplia which however expressed drunken rapture at its beauty. And finally this! – It only came yesty and I am loath to part with it so soon – see herein my affection for you...and Greece......I am glad those Pagans were overwhelmed by the Good Friday in Athens – Lord! how she describes it! The red words in the letter I can't read.
>
> *[A list of phrases she cannot decipher in VW's letter]*
>
> I've finished the Ballet version of F. Galante and also have written a really rather supreme short story – a true adventure of my childhood which perhaps I never told you...
>
> By the by in V's first letter she told me "Roger" thought poorly of Greek Art – as I now see with a view to a rise! I all but fell into the trap – but not quite – merely told her how glad Edith (with her workbox theory of Greek Temples) wd be to know a great expert agreed with her (!) This evidently rather dashed V! <u>What fun!</u>..
>
> *[Nightingales on the golf course; her deafness no better; more queries about VW's handwriting]*
>
>   E

---

[1] In April, The Woolfs had gone to Greece with Roger Fry and his sister Margery, who were avid sightseers and perhaps over informative for Virginia's taste.

Friday May 19th, 1932 (in garden)

[Arrangements for meeting]

And thank you for your letter about yr Gr: I too feel she will not again leave the island[1] and doubt if I shall ever see her again – as my deafness wd fatigue her. But it might be managed if an interpreter were present and supposing she picks up a bit……

[MH's poor health; meeting with the Fritz Ponsonby; financial arrangements]

Fritz [Ponsonby] seems very certain that a good sum will be forthcoming…he said perhaps £400 per ann. for her life. I don't think this <u>possible</u> and rather suspect Lelia has said "I'll make it up to that" as F. seemed so certain. He also told me that the D.[uke of Westminster] adores L. – listens to her; jealous he is, but F. says without cause he thinks. Anyhow I think it clear that L[oelia] knows how to manage him and <u>is happy</u>…

[Details of how the fund for MH could be administered]

I am writing to Fred to make sure it cant be nobbled by the creditors – F. thinks it would be good if there were some system by which she wd receive every month whatever is over of what she is allowed – so as she shd have the fun of being rewarded for economy – poor dear!

[Assorted greetings]

Your loving E

---

1 MH must have been at Appley on the Isle of Wight.

May 21st, 1932

At this point, the vague plan for Elizabeth to work at the Hogarth Press came to nothing – which must have been something of a relief for all concerned.:

52 Tavistock Square WC

Dear Elizabeth,

I'm so sorry not to have written sooner; I've been very busy, and the position has become rather complicated. When I wrote to you before we went away, it seemed possible we should want someone to take on a half time job in the Press, and it struck us that it might suit you. Since we have been back however, the position has changed, and it seems more likely now that we shall have to get a fulltime person, if possible with business training.[1]

Everything is held up at the moment because our head clerk is ill and our manager gone on holiday. I don't think we shall make any decision for two or three weeks therefore. But if there were a likelihood of work that seemed on lines that might suit you I would of course write at once. But don't of course let this influence your plans – I'm afraid that things will shape themselves the other way.

The worst of Greece is that it makes London almost intolerable – we had three perfect weeks, though, so one mustn't grumble. I'm afraid too you are being bothered with your grandmother and so on – Anyhow I hope we shall meet soon.

Yrs
Virginia Woolf

1 There had been a major shake-up at the Hogarth Press in mid-May.

June, 1932

About this time, a number of Ethel's letters are in narrow bordered mourning envelopes. No relative seems to have died, so probably she was using up an old supply. Her main subject was, of course, family finances and also the lack of nightingales:

As you know the nightingales were obdurate – not even last night the faintest twitter – that storm on Friday night washed the music out of them – and I'm not surprised. But if they pick up I may try again – it depends on what I get back from the I. Tax people. Today that darling Vita (who was not on F.P.'s list) sent me £10....

[Organizing the fund; tennis; family news]

And by the 3rd June:

Fund reached £410! Isn't it <u>marvellous</u> – I saw Fritz and Lelia and Ria – all such dears about it...

[Her enjoyment of the Derby]

While on the 7th she added:

I thought yr grandmother <u>astonishingly</u> better and do hope (and believe) she may have a spell of feeling the affection of her friends etc – I <u>so</u> disagree with the point of view that it would be "a pity" if she lives on. As she is now she certainly is <u>quite</u> capable of <u>pleasure</u> in what's going on – and I do rather rebel inwardly against "the sooner the better" theory.

It is hard to imagine that any member of the family – except perhaps Ethel herself in a moment of irritation – had suggested that Mary Hunter would be better dead.

July 8th, 1932

[Domestic upheavals various; news of friends; ES's chill and nettle rash; Lear – "hardly bearable"]

But do you know what has affected me almost as deeply – the last of Queen V's letters. That poor, poor old woman... [a list of the deaths of those close to her in her last year].. Lord Roseberry [sic] or someone who saw her in 1900 wrote that whereas in May she had been absolutely as always – full of energy and cheerfulness and decision, in November he found her shrunk to half her size and hardly recognizable. What touches one so awfully is the way that tho' in her poor journal she speaks of her health and how poorly she feels, and how "provoking" it is after a very bad night to find that she had overslept herself (!) – all this time she is dealing with public business – seeing troops and what not. It was the journey to Ireland (in April 1900) that really did for her, but she would go – The continent was being beastly about the Boer War and for that reason Ministers gave in and let her go to Ireland instead of the Riviera. As far as one sees it was the greatest success – but far on in the autumn she confesses what a "strain" it was and that it had been ("I fear") too much for her. The courage, the devotion to duty of that old woman...! I cannot tell you how the book has moved me tho' it is not as interesting and amusing from other points of view as it predecessors. In that last November, she speaks of "squeamishness" and "discomfort" so that when one Diary extract begins "Could not get to sleep last night because of the wind" I was for a moment staggered. But she was at Osborne and later recounts the damage done by the storm.

Yr loving E

Almost every letter contains an update on her reading, sometimes to be discussed with Elizabeth, sometimes simply listed. At this date she was making her way through Proust and Chaucer, both great favourites of Elizabeth's.

July 10th, 1932

On the way to Brighton

Congrats on your writing!

Darling Eliz – I on my side have been very conscious of the General Pause (a musical term) on my side it was owing to working frightfully steadily – (not too hard – I refuse to knock up) at F.Galante the scoring of which is great fun and will be done, including revision and so on, in about a fortnight

– ready for the copyist...

[Tennis; battling with Virginia Creeper and other gardening trials]

M[abel] Dodge asked me (and you) for this weekend bt I said I was too busy and might I come later? She said yes – but pity, as this weekend she is alone. Then I found out that M Keynes, brother of the K[1] – Hon Sec of Camargo (Ballet) and husband of Lopokhova - had left London for his Sussex house near Lewes and I boldly asked if I might come over (shd I be at Hove for the weekend) and discuss matters. End of it is that I am now on my way to "Wick Hall Hove" till Tues and going to tea with Keynes tomorrow...

[A friend's domestic tribulations: first servants who drank and then: "... an interim Hungarian cook who discussed Brahms clarinet 5th with her but couldn't cook. Reluctantly B had to part with her..."; reading matter]

1 There seems to be a minor confusion between John Maynard Keynes (1883-1946), economist and patron of the arts and his younger brother Geoffrey Keynes (1887-1982), distinguished surgeon and scholar. It is unclear whether ES had hoped that Keynes might sponsor a production of *Fête Galante*.

July 31st, 1932

[New glasses and the excellent effect on her tennis; her great concern at EMW's thinness – Elizabeth was indeed very lean, but gave the impression that was just how she was designed to be, in spite of a healthy appetite and a fondness for langues de chat and fudge; Elizabeth's trip to Austria]

I had what for her is a very fair judicial letter from V. but... if my friendship is not to be given up as hopeless I shall have to be awfully clever! One cant get quite ordinary facts of psychology into her head! She has got an idea that I "love a fight"...that I "insist on a scene" and so on and so on – She is worth any effort but remains the problem whether my grain is not too misleading for her – too agitating. Well – time will show

At this point, Ethel's relationship with Virginia Woolf became increasingly stormy, as she made demands that Virginia, fragile and desperately trying to work, could not meet. She countered with her own particular brand of teasing cruelty that the straight-forward Ethel was in her turn very ill-equipped to deal with. Virginia Woolf's side of the friendship is clearly expressed in her letters and diaries.

August 12th, 1932

This must have been written <u>ages</u> ago!
Darling Eliz I never saw the reverse side of your letter till today – so just hasten to say that I had a very fair letter from Virginia but 2 facts emerge –
1) That she (privately) knows she behaved badly, violently, unreasonably
2) That she has got the idea that I like a scene! and scenes make her feel degraded – which judging by the display that day I can well imagine
I think the whole question of our future depends on her getting rid of this idea ("I don't so much mind misunderstandings – it's the <u>resultant scene you insist on</u> etc.etc.)
I rather dread the dominion of ideas over her. She thinks Vanessa "lovely" [?] – told K.Furse so; and I fear once she gets an idea in her head (that I am a volcano rather looking for a chance of erupting) it may be hard to get it out. I know (<u>now!</u>) what to avoid so as not to annoy her – and shall have a plan of action ready – perhaps a "<u>good </u>heavens! A Boult[1] and I <u>have an appointment...lets finish another time</u>!" (swift exit) if I did so nevertheless! But the other thing is terrible and must destroy intercourse if it persists. It's like Mme de Brancovan's[2] fear of dogs (for her all dogs were fierce and 9 out of 10 mad) – and this phobia controlled her visiting list! Nothing but V's phobia about me could have turned what was really a gentle most loving question of mine "(if ever you think something I say looks as if I thought you something unlovely or discreditable cant you fall back on what you <u>know</u> of my sentiments and say "E <u>cant </u>mean it that way?)" into this terrific "scene"!

Friday

This was written <u>days</u> ago and hidden in my blotter till this moment. Since writing above I had another letter from Virginia – but what is really rather hopeless is that she doesn't seem to have the faintest idea of who I am! I mean she doesn't seem to me to have any real perception of the person she has been seeing and corresponding with for 2 ½ years! She feels the "value" of our friendship but I think has not the faintest clue as to one's impulses and instincts – is really bewildered and had no firm standing ground as regards me – and feels there is some fundamental incompatibility which I fear is not wholly impossible – as if I spoke one language and she another. On the other hand I had an amusing letter from Vanessa (ab. Fete Galante) in which she says – either referring to a remark of mine that "I am in V's bad books just now", or to something V said – that she cant take Virginia and my set-tos too very seriously, as she knows they'll all come right if no one interferes. Her remarks (further) were light and funny and make me feel I need not, perhaps, fash myself. I cant say I admire V's character as revealed in all this – ungenerous, unreasonable, arrogant, convinced of her being always in the right. But I never <u>was</u> fond of her because of reasons; she is most loveable – as children are – do you remember in the last letter I published of HB's in the Appendix of the Prison-reprint. What might be the exact formula to meet V's case? One never can be really <u>sincere</u> with her – (nor with children) – but I fancy that is probably everyone's case – Vanessa's too. Its not a <u>happy</u> relation exactly – but worth travail of soul – Also she is incalculable and one must be patient –

E
When do you go to Austria?

In 1930, Ethel had published a reprint of *The Prison* with a substantial Memoir of H.B. and an Appendix with several of his letters. In the one referred to here, March 1st, 1908, he says:
"......I think we ought to leave our friends free-rope to criticize us, even as we criticize them. Provided they are fond of us, all is well. Provided we are fond of them, we need not shrink from judging them in this case or that as "all wrong". Why shouldn't they be? What is the harm of being all

wrong? And perhaps they are all right and we all wrong. Nobody knows; there is no supreme court; lots of little courts that reverse each other's decisions and that re each valid within a small jurisdiction..." p.164

1 Adrian Boult (1889-1983) English conductor and founder of the BBC symphony Orchestra. He was an enthusiastic champion of British music.
2 Princess Bibesco de Brancovan, better known as Anna de Noailles (1876-1933) was part of the literary and social circle of ES's great friend, Winnaretta Singer, Princess de Polignac, and one of the founders of the Prix Fémina. See also September 3rd, 1930.

August 15th, 1932

Coign

Darling Eliz I was so glad of your good news – that you love and are forging ahead in your work – and are well. I wonder how many letters I've written you that you never get! I found one written when your domestic cataclysm occurred asking you if M.M.[Mount Mascal] was empty (as I had wildly fancied) to come here. (This letter I discovered last night - !) I am full of sympathy with you about being at the flat at such an awful moment! All I can suggest is that sometimes it is good for us to go on, for a time, being the exact reverse of what it is our nature to be – developing muscles the healthy condition of which is necessary to one's proper equipment. To be ruthless does not come natural to you but owing to the fact your Gr is <u>fond</u> of you, it may <u>have</u> to be your job just now! I am writing to Kitty to say that I do think there is nothing in the way the 2nd generation and her trustees shd not do to save her from herself – I mean something like the French conseil de famille which consists in a public announcement telling tradesmen to give no credit. There, of course the difficulty lies. Perhaps the best rope to keep her from the abyss is --- <u>her duty in common decency to Fritz P.</u>[onsonby]. I think you should <u>all</u> harp on that string for I can hit on no other that would have any power to check her.

[Her reading – Proust and "his terrible longueurs" – and Emil Ludwig's biography of Schliemann, and lending each other books]

I've had no further letter from Virginia who is at Rodmell – and indeed I asked her to meditate my last rather than reply to it. What you say is exactly the case – it is the inhumanity of her genius that makes her so difficult to deal with. Vita once said to me "she's a rather heartbreaking person to be fond of" – and again Virginia once said of Vita – "<u>of course she thinks all one does perfect</u>" This is not so really – but no doubt Vita, who is a yielding character, has no difficulty in taking that line. I think Virginia suspects in me, despite my devotion to her, a very different grain; and possibly, except in the case of Leonard (who after all has had time to study the waters of that difficult bay) intercourse with her, unless quite on the surface (which bores us both) is not possible on the only roads I can travel. She seems to me more destitute of generosity than any human being I ever met; I have never detected a sign of it anywhere – I think she must suspect she is not human, as she once told me that Clive Bell (who had been in love with her long long ago) remarked last year that if she died he wd feel that a "beautiful landscape" was gone for ever – not that a <u>person</u> had vanished from the earth. So perhaps V. is right in saying (as she did in the first letter) that she suspects that there is an incompatibility in our respective temperaments (for who so wedded to things human as I?) However I don't yet give up hope tho' the ugly thing in her is, that because of one incautious word O so lightly meant! so <u>obviously</u> a joke, all the rest is apparently of no account! Still I cant forget two things: 1) When Leonard said, smiling to me almost 3 months ago, in answer to my remark (before V) that she and I would never have another scrap "I don't think, <u>knowing Virginia</u>, I shd quite bank on that."

2) On Vanessa's remark last week. I cant think what called it forth, for I had merely said in connection with I forget what "...but I'm out of favour with V. just now" and I fancy V must have said something or other to Vanessa. What Vanessa remarked...[see letter of 12.8.1932 almost word for word]... If anyone looks on you'll enjoy it scandalously and the noise and scuffle wd be appalling."

Of course Vanessa doesn't know me and I suppose takes Virginia's reading of me as one who is always spoiling for a fight, as gospel. But it doesn't look as if Virginia were the sweet, gentle peaceable creature who never has a word with anyone which she believes herself to be!

So I am possessing my soul in patience and going to work hard at a job that amuses me – making a very cheery little suite of Entente Cordiale. It'll take some doing but what job doesn't?

Your E

August 16th, 1932

Ethel wrote again a couple of days later.

Darling E I'm sure you'll be glad to hear the rumpus is over! I had a dear letter from V....of course not acknowledging anything!! But whereas she had complained of my violence she now begs me to be a kind Xtian woman and write her a friendly letter "and don't be a sleek tabby but my old uncastrated wild cat" (!!) – Gradually one learns how to take V and I did well to cling hopefully to those words of L. and Vanessa. But oh what a curious creature she is! And how I dislike (and how careful shall I be to avoid) these crises! She again fainted in the garden that very hot Thursday but says it "wasnt her fault". She evidently can't stand heat.

[On her brother Bob's car crash: " 'The lorry did for the <u>Morris Minor</u> or the Morris Mirror' – I don't know if, you see, there is such a car as a Morris Minor!" – but he was not seriously hurt]

Yr Gr.moth is looking better than and handsomer than for years! (Alice too!) I recommend very drastic measures to save M.E.H. from herself i.e. <u>on the pretext of saving her from creditors coming down on her</u>, a published note in papers to say she has no assets – that all bills have to be paid thro' her lawyer, and that nothing shd be delivered till the bill is paid. <u>It will be the only way</u>. I'm sure of that.

Your E

August 19th, 1932

Coign

Darling Eliz You'll find the vols when you get to London. I feel I can't read Proust now – he wearies me in this heat – too detailed – In fact I always did think the Swann vols are out and out the best - but the smart French Society bores me dreadfully. The fact is the books are to my thinking long with the length of disease..."

[On reading a book on Shakespeare; plans to meet the family to be cancelled in case of heat: "...trains make me really ill in these conditions (You know I burst up my ears in Egypt by going about in late May and drinking wine)..."]

I had a very dear letter from Virginia today. Amusing how she never will say "I was wrong" or "as a matter of fact I am very fond of you" (O yes she does say that sometimes) but every letter after a bourrasque has a touch implying this or that – from one so vain and so reserved that's a good deal – But I dread this heat for her. She again fainted and lay on the grass at 9 p.m. for ½ an hour – L. putting ice under her neck. I asked her to describe what happened and it appears that her heart dashes on and then bang bang a sort of rhythmic row sets up in her head – till you'd think the pulses must break something. Yet she says both heart and pulse are masses better than 10 years ago and her heart "sound and strong and loving, as you know" (!) It makes me feel that one will only be doing right to be careful, (always) and wd be a fool to mind her vituperations when she's in a rage. But above all one must protect her from getting into rages and saying things that make her despise herself afterwards (such as one of her remarks to me that I was "a mass of melodrama" – and that it "didn't impress her in the least" and so on !).

I've been having rather a sad correspondence with poor Maurice!! Chesterton's[1] remarks on Chaucer having made me so wild!! I wrote him as nice a letter as I could today and said I do see his point – also that it is not his fault if owing to the R.C. position in England for them to talk of religion [?] or anti religion is bound to end not in praising cocoa (which I shd love) but maintaining that Houtens is the only pure brand.

Also I said "if it <u>does</u>, and shd [?] – a little poison the well – (or affect the well) of your inspiration, who shall say you were not put into this world to do just what you <u>are</u> doing. But I could not help adding that as regards every sort of perplexed person coming to him (see his letter), even so, being a great writer and a homosexual did all that clan flock round Proust – and <u>I</u> think (and so do many) made him see this brave firmament (what does Hamlet say?) as nothing but a planet full of homosexuals!

I must stop
Yr E

<u>Tennis</u>, imagine!

1 G.K.Chesterton (1874-1936). His biographical work *Chaucer* came out in 1932. Chesterton's conversion to Catholicism ten years earlier would have infuriated ES and she always objected to any group, religious or political, claiming to have the monopoly of the truth.

September, 1932

The letters of the following month are mostly concerned with ES's reading of Proust and admiration for *Little Dorritt*, as well as the usual plans and domestic comments: "I only eat one thing – fish – or macaroni at night and gin and water will do me as well as anything....."
In September, Elizabeth was in Austria. Ethel, who had great affection for German culture, was anxious for her to learn the language and, besides warmly recommending the Berlitz method, sometimes wrote to her in German. However, on the 17th she admitted: "I am too weary to write to you in German because if I do I have to turn my sentences carefully so as not to try you too high...." And added a modicum of family news: "I think your Gran. is behaving well – but I have only seen her twice since she's been in the flat – too busy to do any mortal thing...."

October 3rd, 1932

My darling Elizabeth

[Re Elizabeth's travels: "I'm enchanted at your German plans"]

On Thurs. R[onald] Storrs and his wife are bringing yr grand.m down to lunch – but I wonder if it will be too much for her. This weather is awfully trying for some of her complaints. – I shall tomorrow send you all the remaining Prousts – boring, enthralling, superb, one cant skip or put aside. Virginia says she finds the style so fatiguing that she has to read it in the translation (she's never read the later vols at all) – or did until she put it aside as too exciting. (I see her new Common Reader[1] comes out on Thurs. 13th- She says poor Vita's book[2] which also I think comes out then is bad).

By the by there are various articles of mine in October mags etc.

October 1 In Good Housekeeping (exasperating make up but they pay well) Position of Women in Music 1/- (There's also an article of Virginia's in it)

" Time and Tide "A Sicilian Reminiscence"

" London Mercury (now 1/-!) "The Hay Waggon"

I rather think that in the New Statesman of the same date (October 1) there may be my masterpiece of all "The Waterfall" but I haven't seen it.

When you've settled you must come for a week end if you can

Yr loving E

1 *The Common Reader. Second Series* seems to have come out October 13th 1932.
2 Probably *Family History*, although Vita Sackville-West published two other works in 1932.

October 17th, 1932

Throughout the autumn, Ethel was working on the dances for the production *Fête Galante*.

Darling Eliz – At the present moment, the choreographer having fallen through, they are searching for a producer (which I greatly prefer!) – just putting the dances into the dancers hands. Quite the ideal. But up to now they have not got this producer! This is "echt Camargo" – i.e. "true Camargo style"[1.]

But at this moment I'm really writing to ask if you'll come

with me to see Dido again and a new little opera which Sir Hugh says is capital, at the <u>Vic</u> on <u>30th November</u>, Beecham conducting (<u>8 p.m.</u>)[2]

[Arrangements to meet and her hectic rehearsal schedule throughout November]

1 The Camargo Ballet Society (1930-3) was founded to promote ballet and stimulate the idea of a national company. It had strong links with the Bloomsbury group through Lydia Lopokova and Maynard Keynes, as well as Vanessa Bell and Duncan Grant, who designed sets for Camargo.

2 Purcell's *Dido and Aeneas* and *The Devil Take Her* by Arthur Benjamin (1893-1960) an Australian composer.

November 8th, 1932

Darling Eliz. Thank you for finding time to write so fully when you have such a lot of reporting to do.

I am glad you are off home tonight. I wish poor V[iolet] could have a respite too but of course that's impossible. She ought to have lots of champagne – (your Gran I mean – tho' I daresay poor V. would be none the worse for it!) – It is that terrible recuperative power of the Smyth Family Robinson that makes me fear it may last a while yet. I don't think I shall try to see her. She is past taking interest in F.G. – and if she has another pull up we can always go.

[On arrangements to meet]

On the outside of the envelope.

Does the omniscient Phyllis know how to get rid of moles? I've just written a heartrending S.O.S. to the <u>Ministry of Agriculture</u>!

And a few days later as a P.S. to the problems of *Fête Galante*:

Virginia's book is out today (13th) and there's a jolly article of hers in this weeks *Good Housekeeping* (1/-) also one by me – a rather good one. But I ask myself whether the high pay makes that awful style of being printed bearable.

In another undated letter, apparently written about the same time.

["Read enclosed!!!" – alas nothing enclosed now – "I am quite unabashed and think the article shrewd, interesting; a splendid fake in fact." Without the article – apparently a hoax pretending to be by VW – most of the letter is obscure, but ES mentions a number of other "fakes" saying "1) Brahms thought my "Inventions" (a technical music term for a certain form) were by Bach."]

I think any lapse better than that of defending the Edwardians or thinking "All Passion Spent" the best Vita has done since "The Land" (! ignoring the travel book which I think as good as The Land) or thinking T Eliot's Essays[1], which I am sure are niggling pretentious constipated (never read one of them no matter!!) masterly!

A man has been about rats and moles (my 2 plagues)...His official title is Rat Officer

(Not a joke but a fact)"

[1] *Selected Essays 1917-1932* had just been published.

November 18th, 1932

A rather obscure letter – on the hoax article pretending to be by VW.

My darling Elizabeth but you see I took the "little things must hold out little hands to each other" to be a savage hit at Chapman's sentimentality! And it amused me frightfully. On examination I have found 6 phrases V. would not have written – commonplace etc. but I thought of her faintness etc. and the article as a whole, the subject of it and the sort of chaff of C. delightful – but only the <u>end</u> I thought rather faded away. That I deliberately ascribed to her being cut short by the exigencies of the tape measure. Now I come to think of it I don't think V. (or Bloomsbury) wd ever allow that J.A. letters could be anything but masterly. (For V is very like the Leipzig people used to be about Bach – Lisl [von Herzogenberg][1] wouldn't allow that even the dullest mechanical pages of Bach were not inspired and was genuinely horrified at my saying they were not). So you see the angle at which the pseudo Virginia article was written was bound to captivate me and even surprise me agreeably. But, as you say, I shall never hear the end of it! Anyhow the article is not "feeble in the extreme" as V declares it is – but I imagine she was maddened at finding someone poaching on her preserves disguised in her clothes.

How sorry I am for you getting to the end of Proust. Find the end vol desperately exciting.

Yr E

1 Elizabeth (Lisl) von Herzogenberg (1847-1892), the sister-in-law of HB, was a prominent figure in the musical world of Leipzig and a friend of Brahms and of Clara Schumann. ES met Lisl when she went to Germany aged 20 to study music and fell wildly in love. See also Introduction.

November 21st, 1932

[On rereading Proust and her growing admiration: "I feel as if a life spent in reading and rereading Proust, more especially the dull bits, would be a life well passed..." Elizabeth loved Proust and this conversion was surely due to her influence, however, she never succeeded with Milton]

You know I have been doing nothing but read 2 lives of the Emp. Eugénie and feel I never really appreciated her mental endowments. You see I think she used to be very out about English politics and that made me think that she had probably been all wrong abt. French ones. I now think she was dead right – but hampered by a sick-unto-death man (whose whole strength went into his sick unto death commerce with women – some of the lowest type) her nescience [apparently sic] was rendered ineffective – lost in irritation, fury, despair, overridingness and contempt. It is a tragedy...and O... someday I could write about it. Not a Biography but a fantasy on that theme.

[badly damp stained]

...I must send you the portrait which Virginia sent me this morning – it having been sent her by Lady Ottoline Bentinck (see back) – At first I thought the V. scribble underneath was bona fide – that the woman really was the author of the article painted in fancy dress by Lazlo or someone but now I think it is one of Virginia's jokes. Anyhow she has a look of V. and also of Vita but above all of a Jewish Sheep – (I like your joke about Woolf's clothing – it goes with this lady's style of beauty!)

I know you always like V's letters so I send you this. I've come to a great decision about her. I think she's <u>very ill</u> and the idea of being one person more in her life who wants to see her and to hear from her makes me uncomfortable, makes me feel guilty. So I've determined to let down an iron curtain between her and me till she's well again or till "time of life" which I expect has something to do with it (tho' she would be furious if one said so!) is over. I won't write and ...[badly stained] don't want to know how she is.....or that she sat up till 1.30 (with the dislike of going to bed we know of) being bored by L's Polish Count. And I've told her not to write to me – and really mean it. One cant treat her like a normal human being and I'd rather (as I did when Mrs Pankhurst was hunger striking one time after another – which determined me to go to Africa) push down the connecting switch till better times. Only I'm sorry she is, as is certainly the case, writing a still wavier 'Waves' - !!¹

[The letter continues – very badly damaged – with various plans; her music; a broadcast of some of her work; affectionate concern for EMW]

Goodbye beloved Eliz and I hope the next Vol will soon be finished – Don't <u>you</u> overwork; or if you do eat carefully.

Your E

One reason abt. V. is that I <u>fear</u> to tire her being deaf...(<u>You understand</u>) like your Gran; but I'm not afraid of tiring you!"

1 Perhaps *The Years*, which was not published until 1937.

December 11th, 1932

My darling Elizabeth Do you know it is very odd bit I have been thinking just the same thoughts about you of late. It started at the picture show when, not expecting you and suddenly catching sight of you, my joy was so violent – like a blaze of warmth from a stove when you come in out of the cold – that later on I asked myself "I wonder if E knows how I love her?" – and for every conceivable reason too...because I <u>like</u> you, because I <u>admire</u> you, because I am conscious of elements in myself that are as essential or part of your make up as they are of mine, All this besides the simple fact (it appears simple) that I love you.

It's a queer thing to have found someone of your age, belonging to my own family, who is all that to one. Yes – you did well to tell me for I think what you had to say is what one always most wants to hear – that is if it is one of the very few right people. – I've done [really] my work which I promised for tomorrow but have had a time of over strenuous work - and today am beginning to answer many letters, some of which I have not even read yet! No time. The death of Miss Jekyll[1] I mind most terribly. Thank God Nelly Cole took me over there about 2 months ago. She adored the Waterfall and I sent her other things to read (articles). There is someone I loved! And I think she loved me. It was so touching her saying that day "don't call me Miss Jekyll" and I said "O Gertrude why didn't [we] start being Ethel and Gertrude years ago?" "Well, better late than never", she answered.

Yours my darling E

1 Gertrude Jekyll (1834-1932) the gardener and garden designer had died on December 8th .

1933

As usual, at Christmas and New Year, Elizabeth was at Cromer.

A number of letters and postcards from early in the New Year record Ethel's reading, the wish to acquire a legible copy of the *Life of Dr Johnson*, reactions to her concert, her intense dislike of amateur performances and regret that Elizabeth is taking part in one - they were, incidentally something that Elizabeth enjoyed immensely – and the occasional comment on her social life, for example on her hostess's dentures, which "..I shall think of till my dying day.."

January 3rd, 1933

Ethel had written to her brother Bob, another of her regular correspondents. As was often the case, she expresses to him views about the family that she would not have shared with Elizabeth.

[News of Mary's health – "surprisingly good". ES goes on about her niece, Kitty]

...I'm rather unhappy about Kitty she seems to have become a sort of cipher – like a goose with its bill fixed on a chalk line – the line being Lincoln [her husband]. Of course its her own fault – she let him become what he is from a wrong view (I think) of Wifely Duty. And now she has a sort of glazed surface off which every arrow of conversation glances. Nothing penetrates. She doesn't listen. It makes me unhappy. The best of the 3 is now Sylvia....

January 5th, 1933

Doesn't it strike you that the problem of sexual mores has never been even approximately resolved? I don't see that Christianity or even Judaism can be blamed for spoiling something that wasn't there. Antiquity (classical) was pretty bad surely, with its social and intellectual life closed to women (at least to wives). I suppose the Romans made a rather fairer [?finer] thing of marriage than did the Greeks, and this strikes me as being a possible moral argument against the homo-sexual ideas of the Greeks. When and where do you find a tolerable state of affairs in history? Otherwise I cannot summon up the horror and repulsion that "nice' people are supposed to feel over this. To be quite honest no sexual vagaries shock me except cruelty, even incest! I feel that the capacity for instinctive repulsion is itself a sexual thing and I am without it. In all this I am extremely dubious and ready to learn of anybody because it is a topic I really feel ignorant and wholly open minded about. I think it is embraced by Christian teaching solely (and sufficiently) by the individual consideration for your neighbour. Christ's remarks about divorce seem definite but he thought the Mosaic divorce laws "hard hearted" I suspect him of thinking of some particular case of unfair treatment of women (guessing only of course).

[On her reading]

January 5th, 1933

Darling Elizabeth

[Family news]

Charles coming home is like the arrival of a whale in the duck pond of family annals. I didn't hear many details yes[terda]y tho' I went in about 12.45 to see your grandm. – for my arrival caused her to stop eating her curry and so I went.

[On everyone including Pan made sleepy by "this horrible soft weather...but today is cold enough to suit anyone only it's the wrong sort of cold. I was much amused at yr mother's idea of a nice day out – leaving Cromer at 4 a.m." On the problem of moles ".. they construct places like Piccadilly Circus and the catacombs and are practically uncatchable.."]

On Tues I rehearse at the Prom (a run through) on the stroke of 10 a.m. to 10.30 and if you want to hear the music wouldn't this be better than the evening in January? I come on at night after the interval and calculate it will be a little before 10 pm – tiresomely late. But of course I can get a couple of tickets for you and Grizzy if you like. It wont be very satisfactory I fear for first of all the rehearsal (the real one) was too far off from the concert, and secondly half the orchestra has flu – which means a lot of people reading at sight. And owing to interpolations the parts are complicated. Which reminds me I went yesty to see the girl dancer whom I want as choreographer for F[ête] G[alante]. and afterwards had tea with her and her Mama at Diana Cooper's[1] where I played F.G. through to her and broke a teacup – "not a valuable one" said the kind butler and if it's a lie may he be forgiven. It was at the Royalty...a child's holiday play, all animals - and I remembered the Empress's remark about the Jungle

Book. "Je n'aime pas qu'on fasse parler les animaux...(pause) <u>car enfin ils ne parlent pas</u>.". It was stifling and I was in the only unsold seat in the house and you can imagine "what for a seat" it was (I love that German idiom). A great waste of 8/6 for the dancing lasted 3 minutes only and the rest of the time the donkey pulled the rat's tail and so on. The child is deeply intelligent and I know she and I could make a fine thing of F.G. She says Stanley Judson would be better she thinks than Dolin[2] – only of course Dolin has the name. Well – I shall see what to aim at presently and am dolefully settling down to orchestrate my Entente Cordiale suite – working O so slowly ----- I have nearly finished Jane A's letters Vol. I and doubt if I shall order Vol.II – nor would I but V. says her literary successes brisked her up a bit. I think qua letters they are very bad indeed. Of course if she had chosen she could have written good ones – at least I suppose so – but she doesn't seem to me to have tried. In fact as I write I rather incline to think that the scaffold of a created story was necessary to her building. The detail upon detail makes me quite muzzy headed.

    I had an amazing letter from Virginia – there's someone who can write letters – and the letters are not like V. the fictioneer, nor V. the critic – but the work of a letter writer. For once she became human on the subject of the departure for America of Vita – an exquisite paragraph "And tomorrow my dear Vita sails and I shan't see her again till April. Yes – that saddens me it takes away a lamp and a glow and a shady leaf and an illuminated hall from my existence....but enough as old Lady Ponsonby used to say when she threw the soup tureen at Queen Victoria."

    And in another letter she wrote "Yes – it is curious how I miss her presence in the green fields of Kent, <u>even when I don't see her there</u>" (!) Queer secretive creature Virginia is. I don't really understand her – <u>and never shall</u>. She writes of her cruel fate now being at Rodmell she is reading 20 books at once – reading, reading, and how her passion ("the other side of the carpet to writing") is balked by the everlasting obligation in London to see people...And in the next letter she writes "After 10 days of solitude I must see some people (!) and am going up to London to a <u>party</u>. Then back here to books. Then back to society and people...Which do I really need most?" And so on. I am rather distressed about my own feelings regarding V. Sometimes I feel there are no limits to the dimensions she presents in my life – at others – this of late, I feel she is really non-existent for me. But I hope this stage – partly the result of The Waves – will wear off.

[More plans for meeting family; health]

Bless you darling
Yr E

[EMW's golf]

I've fished up and orchestrated for a 3rd number of FG a jolly old dance from der Wald, but that isn't copied out yet.

1 Lady Diana Cooper (1892-1986), English social celebrity, actress and writer.
2 Stanley Judson danced with Sadler's Wells from May 1931.
3 Anton Dolin (1904-1983,) stage name of Sydney Francis Patrick Healey-Kay, English ballet dancer and choreographer.

In a long letter, which Ethel numbered as fourth of those of particular importance to her, the discussion of different aspects of Christian ethics and morals continued - see also pp 178-183 and 187-190. After considering the origins of the desirability of asceticism and fear of the senses common to many religions, Elizabeth continued.

January 14th, 1933

Darling Elizabeth

I am truly excited about the review and abt yr having been asked to write it. Also glad that you think (<u>and allow it to me</u>!) that you know more about Greek Astronomy than the other pundits![1] It's no use asking what the review is – yet I shd like to see the article.

[On a volume of memoirs and Jane Austen's health; plans to see Così fan Tutte *at the Old Vic]*

I am rather depressed (too) about your theatricals. You see at Hill you had the brilliant Fritz – but I confess that for people like you to be, to have to be, delivered over to that sort of thing for days (and I expect weeks) seems to me an awful waste of time and strength. But then I detest – always have detested – amateur dramatic efforts and I'm certain there's <u>not talent enough</u> at M.M. to justify it. Not I mean if you are dragged in. It seems to me a mechanical and rather feverish striving after a certain sort of gaieté de coeur that makes me feel suicidal....

1 EMW's translation of Ptolemy's *Almagest* is still in manuscript in a series of black notebooks.

January 17th, 1933

But darling Eliz I didn't think you were dragged in – tho I confess I didn't realise that you adored private theatricals so whole heartedly. If you do all is well – and time is never lost under such circumstances – How odd that you weren't amused at "Cheerful Weather"[1] - I disliked it to start with and then caught on and enjoyed it thor.ly - the schoolboys! How can you not have laughed at them and Belle!! Well, well. – we know nothing is so uncertain as what will appeal to whose sense of humour.

[Other cases of this in the family]

1 *Cheerful Weather for the Wedding*, Julia Strachey, Hogarth Press, London, 1932. The heroine's name is in fact Dolly, not Belle.

January 18th, 1933

The next day, Mary Hunter died. It was not unexpected, in the sense that she had clearly been failing for some time, but the actual end came quite suddenly. The letters between Ethel and Elizabeth are missing, perhaps because they were together. However, Ethel wrote to her brother Bob.

40 Moore St, Chelsea
Wed. night

Dearest Bob,

They will have wired to you that Mary died today at 8.15[1]. I had been going to dine with Grizzy and thought it quite on the cards that I might find M. dining too – for tho' she was <u>desperately</u> ill [....?] Grizzy phoned this morning that she had a good night. I did not know that she had had heroin, and it appears that she woke up, as it were, unconscious. When I went in at 8 tonight (its now 10) I saw her for a moment but it was such a sad sight I did not stay. She looked to me as if she had had a slight stroke on the right side of her face. And as I say 10 minutes after Eliz, Grizzy and I went out to supper (for Phyllis and Kitty had by then arrived and were about to eat there) she died quite quietly. That's all I know yet awhile. I am thankful that Philip Sassoon saw her yesterday for I think his visits gave her more pleasure that anyones. I saw her afterwards but came to the conclusion that even listening was a fatigue for her – and when I peeped in and said goodnight at 7 (I was going to a concert) I did feel there could hardly be any more pull-ups. I don't know what the next move will be – and probably will go back to Coign. ....I know how you will be feeling. Nothing – no death I mean – has ever made me quite so sad.

Yr. loving
E

[1] MH died at her home, 138 Ashley Gardens.

January 21st, 1933

Virginia Woolf commented in her diary with a characteristic lack of charity.

Mrs Hunter is dead. Died standing eating drinking dressing, penniless, ruined discredited, having got through 40,000 a year, not all of her own; but they say she was a great hostess & all is forgiven – rightly, I think, though in another class she would have been in prison. Such is the price we pay for our great hostesses.[1]

[1] *The Diary of Virginia Woolf*, vol. IV: 1931-1935, London, 1982, p.144.

February 13th, 1933

Darling Elizabeth I'm horrified at my letter having perished – It was congratulating you about the lectures and asking you if they are "<u>very elementary</u>" as dear Lord B[1] most characteristically told Betty [Balfour] was probably the case - !! They are so true to type!!

[Problems with her shoulder]

Am revelling in DH Lawrence's letters and some of his books including Lady Chatterley about which (and L himself) I have not made up my mind.

[Radio performance of Fête Galante; *Gilbert Murray on Euripides]*

1 Perhaps Lord Balfour, or conceivably Lord Bertrand Russell (1872-1970), who had just inherited the title and whom ES disliked.

February 19th, 1933

My darling Elizabeth I'm so sorry I forgot to tell you about F.Galante as it seems to have got through so well, for once – but after all you never told me whether the lectures you <u>are</u> doing for your boss are elementary! Not that it matters but....well, you know. I and Betty felt we can well understand the <u>giddy</u> feeling that goes with your higher mathematics if not the rapture! I have put off my departure for Bath till Thursday – for reasons – and am meanwhile slogging away at my Brahms article (£50 for 4500 words in the Radio Times.) And have it finished, all but the clean copy for typing. Its not good because I'm forced to repeat myself in it – but no matter.

I am very much interested that you are tackling D.H.Lawrence. I saw Virginia on Thursday – still in her frozen falcon mood – and she declared DHL was non existent – that it was all a fuss about nothing and that as for his sex preoccupation, Middleton Murry[1] said that he was impotent!! I said "why take M.M.'s authority for this when you allow there is no lie he wouldn't tell about anybody and DHL had shewn him up so terrifically" (see "Jimmy and the Wild

Woman"[2]) and Aldous Huxley in "Point Counterpoint"[3]. To which V. said "I <u>don't</u> take his authority for it" (That was V's mood!) She certainly is kittle kattle to shoe – of a moodiness past description.

Well! She lent me the unexpurgated Lady Chatterley and at first I could not get a clear vision of it, so violently pornographic is it. But I am now re-reading it and think it would probably be finer in the bowdlerised edition of the libraries. Now that I don't notice the poker work (forgive my coarseness – its rather a good word) something woodland and infinitely sad is emerging and I incline to think it a very fine book. That particular vol. of short stories you mention I don't know but am going to read all there is ("Why! In God's name?" asked V. with petulance) I've ordered "Women in Love" in which he is supposed to have pilloried Lady Ottoline Morrell [4] with whom I have rather fallen in love – but now she has been sent to a nursing home, and I am sending myself to Bath. A coil. I don't think DHL is quite sane and fancy the phthisis (cant spell it) worked in him as in Katherine Mansfield to his intellectual undoing. If a man is lying, like Edgar Poe's hero, tied to a bench in a room the walls of which are gradually contracting, I don't think he could envisage the world normally, do you?

[Offer to lend EMW DHL's letters; friends who did or did not enjoy Cheerful Weather for the Wedding *– "Pid said it was not in the least funny – only <u>vulgar</u> (!)"; a confusion of football and cricket scores]*

1 John Middleton Murry (1889-1957) writer and critic was much disliked by the literary world at this date, among other reasons on account of his perceived treatment of Katherine Mansfield.
2 *Jimmy and the Desperate Woman*, 1924 – a short story by DHL based on and ridiculing JMM's second marriage.
3 *Point Counterpoint*, Aldous Huxley, 1928 – the morally extremely unattractive character, Denis Burlap, is based on JMM.
4 Lady Ottoline Morrell (1873-1938) was an English aristocrat and patron of artists and writers, notably the Bloomsbury Group; she was also an amateur decorator and designer in her own right. She wrote extensive diaries still unpublished. She is portrayed, generally unflatteringly, in several of the novels of the period.

February 22nd, 1933

My darling Elizabeth I've come to the conclusion I cant read books – huge books of peoples Collected Poems – nor have them from libraries. You cant read them through like ordinary books they hold up the traffic so I've sent for 2 little vols of Lawrence's poems. The Birds etc and also "New Poems". I think one of the loveliest poems I have read for ages is one by him in Time and Tide of this week (February 25th) called <u>Shadows</u>. I'm reading "Women in Love" but there is something to me very antipathetic in D.H.L. which is constantly turning up like grits in a pudding – Ethel Steel lunched here today – Lady Ottoline Morrell was at St Andrews with her – and after reading this book I shall still more want to know her. I think one of DHL's most beautiful letters is to her telling her she has not lived in vain. This was after they'd made it up. Virginia last time I saw her was in such a dry mood that I didn't hear enough about the split up [?]. Lord! V. can be of a dryness that is indescribable! An interesting thing was Leonard came in and said he couldn't at all understand what many modern composers were driving at. I said "Just so" and we agreed about some we really could catch an idea of – I said "A great deal of it is, I think, like cubism which I fancy has rather moved on hasn't it?" "Yes," he said "but there's still a lot of it in all the arts…and in literature…look at G. Stein (2 was it) [??] .. and <u>Virginia's doing it</u>!! (this before her). I said "at all events one can understand Virginia's grouping of her parts of speech" (her "derangement of epitaphs") and he said "well yes….but look <u>at Joyce</u>" I wonder if V's very bad mood just now is anything connected with the Foetus story? I was surprised at L. saying that. (Vernon wrote to me that she cant cope with the Waves). Arm hurts. Must stop.

E

While L said that about V she sat like a statue!

March 1st, 1933

A few days later, Ethel was at Bath for a cure.

5 Park St, Bath

[On ordering DHL's poems]

I am caught up in awful toils of 3 things that press 1) The Brahms article £50 2) The lecture for next Monday (an old one refurbished for my book later) £10.10 3) An article constructed by me of extracts from Bobs letters fr Omdurman etc. – I hope to get him a cheque from Blackwood for it (of course my editing it is simply to get more...and to get it as right as I can) All these things press – and I am not very well – these cures always tire you and the more you need them the more tiring are they. But I adored the tortoise group and adored them. Yes...he is a <u>great</u> <u>man</u> – I don't care what V. says, nor for his un-beautifulness of which we wot.

By the by the <u>cubism</u> didn't apply to Virginia but to certain modern composers and their drift. Leonard's remark was half a joke (I mean about <u>Virginia</u>) when he said "I don't know what they are driving at..." Of course V. has nothing cubic about her. But she allows she <u>makes experiments</u> – that each book of hers is that. Like Betty, Miss Steel is mad about the last Common Reader.

O I <u>must</u> stop. Yes! About yr Grandm and poetry!...You must miss the giving of that joy! And when they killed The Prison I felt it so for her – for she <u>loved</u> it. E

On the back of the envelope.

Not a word from V! I think that <u>what with admiring Lawrence</u> and letting her see that I do think she has faults (!) she has done with me!

The "faults" came in by her saying she wanted to read my "Virginia summed up" in my diary – and my replying "I think it wd infuriate you."

"Women in Love" is the most hateful book I <u>ever</u> read.

March 2nd, 1933

And the following day, she wrote a postcard in "a moment snatched from ceaseless hateful work" on poems she enjoyed and on liking John Middleton Murry's *Reminiscences of D.H.Lawrence*, which had just come out, adding a P.S.:

(Rather a dear letter from V. She thought I'd given her up!! What a psychologist!! But she does feel when something's up…a 6th sense).

March 16th, 1933

Darling Eliz: On Sat 25th at 3 pm a woman conductor whom I believe to be really "it" is conducting a Sibelius programme with the W.Sym.Orch., and, dead or alive, I mean to be there… [travel arrangements]. I have 2 tickets. Wd you care for 1?

I am reading Boswell (having forgotten to get more Library books) and cannot tell you the relief after D.H.L.!! I am now dead certain 1) that he was impotent – tho' not wholly so at first. N.Barnett says this often goes with phthisis – 2) that his refusal to accept the fact, plus his terrific creative impulse, and total lack of the Xstian virtue of humility drove him to all that Dark God and super-sensual stuff. Also I think (I wrote this to Virginia who is in divinest mood) that like St Paul the result may have been the fiercest of grips of [?] the world beyond. Hence the poems. The <u>Plumed Serpent</u> made me ill but there are fine short stories I believe. After "<u>Women in Love</u>" and the "Serpent" no more long novels of his for me.

Yr E

April 13th, 1933

For the next two or three weeks, Ethel's' letters were mainly concerned with medical matters, with the occasional variant.

The Elms
Ringwood
Hants

[Meetings with friends and family]

I've <u>lots</u> to say notably about death (In Lady Rhondda's[1] Autobiog: in her description of sinking with the Lusitania, there are remarkable sensations recorded about death when it really <u>does</u> stare you in the face). I do believe in a sort of kind of personal survival but like the Empress Augusta discussing religion during a Court Quadrille with Sir H Ponsonby "Aujourd'hui nous n'avons pu qu'effleurer la question! Demain au bal de l'Ambassadeur nous l'approfondirons!"

Yr E

---

1 Margaret Haig Mackworth, 2nd Viscountess Rhondda (1883-1958) was an active suffragette and founder of the political magazine *Time and Tide*. She survived the sinking of the Lusitania in May 1915 and her autobiography *This was My World*, had just come out, earlier in 1933. Like a number of ES's other friends, she had left her husband to live with another woman.

May 2nd, 1933

Darling Elizabeth The worst part of my long discomfort is now over. You know there has been question of a certain manifesto and projected festival of my music in the autumn which ought to have come out in September last (!) which has been dragging on all this time (tho' I am writing a section of my new book more or less connected with the subject of women in music) if it had come out **even** on my birthday, it wd have clinched various matters in the Provinces but Sir Hugh A[llen][1] is a hopeless procrastinator...and how R.Coll gets on (if it does) <u>I</u> don't know. I have had about 20 visits to London, written dozens of letters, sent dozens of wires and had 24 bilious attacks over it all....and ½ an hour ago...<u>at last</u>.... ça y est. You'll see it in Thursday's Times. All this combined with pretty bad rheumatism (a result!), interruptions, and worst of all having my mind fixed on what I spend my life forgetting – "women in music"….and writing and rewriting that chapter continuously for weeks and months…beating back an impulse to dash the cup from my lips…well – its been hell…<u>But it is over now</u> – also the chapter nearly finished only I'm awfully busy.

[Health and gardening]

O I forgot to say that this procrastination has lost me crowds of performances and a lot of money. But the worst part is having everything ready for a big blaze and then to see the effective moments passing, passing till the sticks and paper get damp and nothing (relatively) <u>can</u> happen – except I profoundly believe that this is what life really is – not the other thing – Well! You <u>are</u> going it! The Ring! I had just been re-reading the Tempest but am too deaf to go and hear it. I have been seeing Walter[2] too – whose appearance broke my heart. I think too <u>his</u> heart is really broken. He had a wild success with Leonard and Virginia at 9 p.m. one night! I took him there but wouldn't stay – went home. I had been to his dinner, been lecturing, and hurt a good deal …[details of health]…Virginia was got up to kill – all in white – and looked so **absolutely** beautiful that it hurt! They go for 3 months to Italy on Friday –

Yes I mind Anna de N's death in a way – but since Hélène[3] was killed by medical etiquette I saw her but seldom – and her French became more and more difficult for my slow brains – only one in 3 words did she actually say - leapt like a chamois over any verb or noun she doesn't think necessary to actually mention – a sort of shorthand which all her intimates quite understood but not poor Ethel. I shd like to talk to Mme de Polignac[4] about her but feel sure she is in Venice.

Maurice [Baring] writes that he has lost his greatest friend – an amazing Russian who used to write to him letters a mile long, bristling with imagination and hard common sense. He was very poor and I think had cancer so I'm glad he's gone. What terrifies one is that Mary Dodge seems very ill – Maurice says he has just had a "Mary Hunter Crash" – can give no more parties and is established at Rottingdean. I have just written to ask whether he can afford a 2 nights visit from

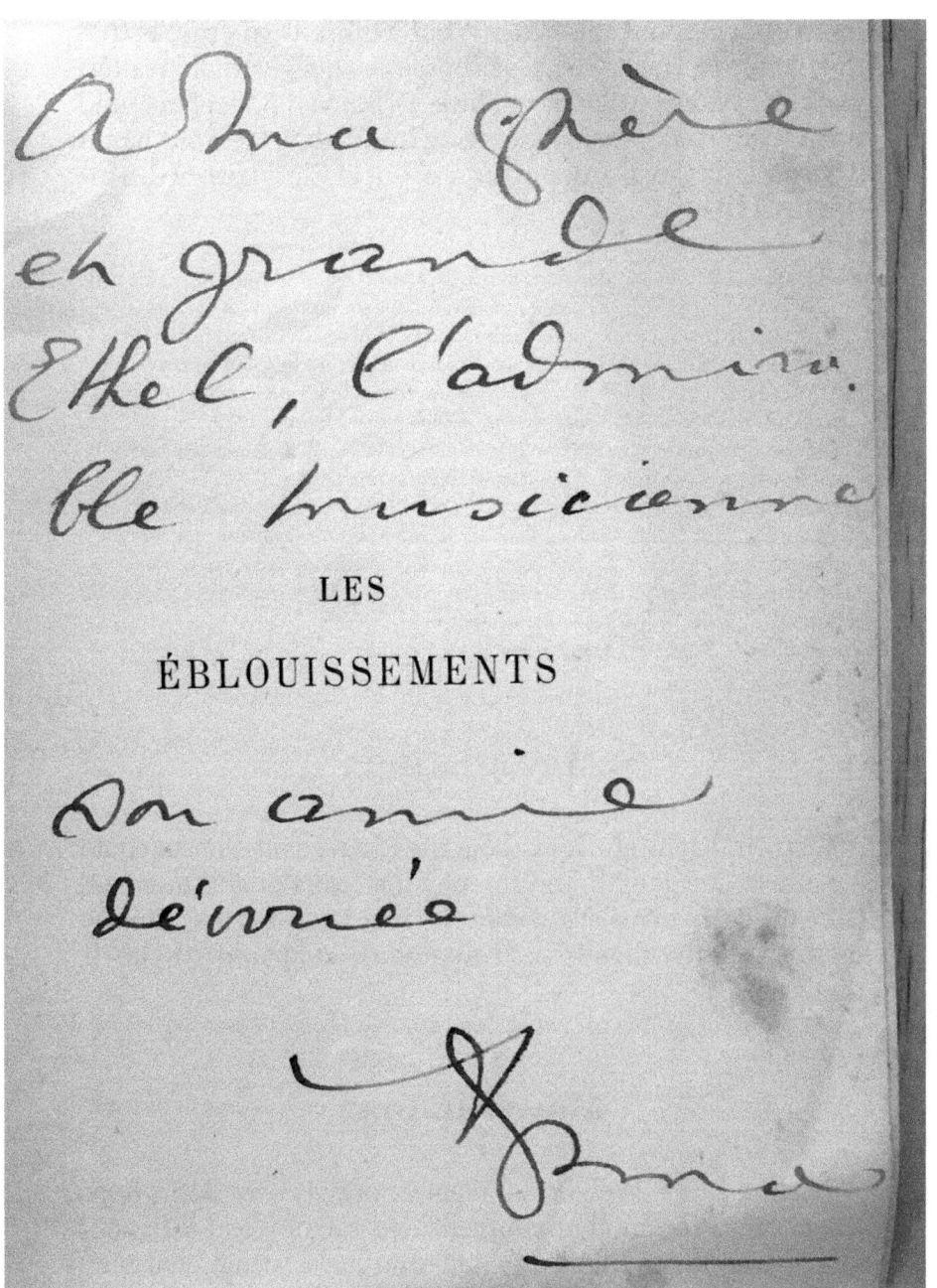

Dedication in ES's copy of Anna de Noailles' collection of poems.

me. Tell me about the Ring. What I think is so cruel is that they kept on Heger[5] who of course is cheaper than Walter, and then Walter would over shine T.[homas] B.[eecham] and poor Walter no longer lodging at the Waldorf his old haunt where all the Cov.Gard. proper are, but at Claridges. O damn damn Hitler E

1 Hugh Allen (1869-1946) conductor, musician, academic and administrator, directed the Royal College 1918-37 among numerous other commitments, including preparing the way for the creation of the Faculty of Music at Oxford in 1944.
2 Bruno Walter (1876-1962) German conductor in charge of the German seasons at Covent Garden from 1924-31. In 1933 he was forced to leave Germany and after several restless and difficult years settled in the United States in 1939.
3 Hélène de Brancovan, Princess Caraman-Chimay (1878-1929), Anna de Noailles' younger sister, was a friend of Proust and an occasional writer.
4 Winnaretta Singer, Princesse de Polignac (1865-1943), an heiress of the Singer Sewing Machine family, she held Paris' most important musical salon and was a great patroness of music. ES had been much in love with her at an earlier stage in their relationship. See *Music's Modern Muse: a Life of Winnaretta Singer*, Sylvia Kahan, University of Rochester Press, 2009.
5 Robert Heger (1886-1978). German conductor. Conducted at Covent Garden 1925-35.

May 4th, 1933

You are absolutely right about the Ring. I cant – never could – endure that length and the awful streaks of commonness (like the Walkure place where the love song begins). But no matter – Its Asia Minor (Pergamon) compared to Greek, that's all.

May 11th, 1933

Darling Eliz – Well! Your Wagner orgy is over and I hope the psychic enrichment compensated for physical fatigue. I am very depressed for Pan ...failed to mate with a charming bitch!! She is very small and has had no mating pulled off with 4 others.....but I fear Pan proves the wisdom of the celibacy of guests [?] – he really couldn't get excited this time, tho' willing to play "here we go round the gooseberry bush" with

her. And she loved him! – but naught happened –
I've fallen in love with a philosopher Frank Ramsey of Cambridge who died 1931 aged 28...[1]

[On the reasons for her admiration - complicated without following up the numerous quotations]

D[ickinson] also says of men like Ramsey...(and he might include H.B.) of people "content to know what is knowable and to reserve judgement on what is not"..."the world cd never be driven by such men, for the <u>springs of action lie deep in ignorance and madness</u>" How true! (Germany today) I want to hear a lecture of yours one day. When?

Your E

[1] Frank Ramsey (1903-1930), whose name is often linked with Keynes, Wittgenstein and Sraffa was remarkable for his contributions to mathematics, economics and philosophy. ES mistook the date of his death.

May 12th, 1933

The next day she sent Elizabeth a postcard, inviting her to:

....hear Kovssevitsky[1] (1st class) conduct <u>Prokofiev</u> (real modern music) and Sibelius Symphony...I don't get there till 11 pm as am hearing Snow Maiden at Old Vic tomorrow night. E

Re-read Mrs Dalloway – I think in some ways her best book –a <u>masterpiece</u>. I didn't like it much formerly."

[1] Serge Kossevitsky (1874-1951) Russian conductor, composer, musician and enthusiastic champion of modern music, director of the Boston Symphony Orchestra 1924-49.

May 14th, 1933

And on a postcard on the 14th:

....O I do hope he'll have Prokofiev first so I can go with you

> H. O. Sanderson   T. E. 5362/3
>
> <u>Instructions</u>   ap 21ˢᵗ
>
> (Title   The Boatswain's Mate
>   Comedy in one act and two parts
>   after W. W. Jacobs' story of that name
>
> Dramatised for music and composed by
>   <u>Ethel Smyth</u>
>
>   Persons
>
> H. B. ˣ boatswain   Tenor
> N. T. ˣ soldier   Baritone
> Mrs W. landlady of the Beehive ———   Sop:
> Mary Ann domestic servt at the Beehive   Mezzo Sop
>   (need not be a singer)
> Policeman   Bass
> Agricultural Labourers ——
> Two cats (behind the scenes)
>   Place· England____   Time Today.
>   <u>Overture</u>
> ─────────────────────────────────
>   Part I   Directions started here
> <u>Scene</u>: (as in E. Smyth's Edit.)
>   Scene I
>   (Dialogue)
> <u>Spacing</u>. Throughout dialogue — half page
>
> | Part I. The curtain etc [illegible] (says) you don't mean boar [?] so! well I think not Benn. Don't be too [?] [illegible] | Vacant |

Ethel Smyth's Notes on the *Bo'sun's Mate*

to yr lecture at 12. <u>Will you come with me to Kew in the Aft.?</u> Do....Am writing away like mad. By the by in the Keynes Book, Prof Edgeworth's "Law of Diminishing Returns" amuses me much (so good for an article writer). Epstein <u>splendid</u>.

And on the 23rd, a brief note and a flier printed on brown paper.

> The Guildford Repertory Company
> In Commemoration of Dame Ethel Smyth's 75th Birthday
> "The Bos'n's Mate"
> Etc.

June 15th, 1933

My dear Miss Baylis [crossed out] – No – my darling Elizabeth – at last one section of this really (for me) very hectic spring-summer is over. What it means getting men like Boult[1] and Hugh Allen to give the last turn of the screw is simply inconceivable – and as Beecham is much the same (tho' not this time! he saved the situation) it sets me wondering whether in England music goes with complete sanity? It doesn't seem to me to [be] a flower of an otherwise well-equipped mind [?] as in Germany, but a sort of vampire that sucks up all the rest of the victims life. Well – I finished at last, at last, and using great astuteness and still more persistence, am at the goal. All that is now necessary is an announcement in the papers to say that ES' concert (1st or 2nd week in Jan) will be conducted by Sir Thomas – Prison and all under the auspices of the <u>BBC</u> (and their band conducted by T.B.!!) the other a <u>Choral</u> affair, <u>Mass</u> Conducted by A[drian].B.[oult]. When we meet I'll tell you what measures on my part were necessary to put this through!

I have also finished "Female Pipings in Eden" and am going to have, I fear, rather a scene about it with Virginia this aft. whom I haven't seen since her return from Italy owing to heat and my illness (quite over now). You see this thing is in 3 Parts

I. Showing what music involves and how, as things are today no woman has a look in.

II. Showing that what I have achieved is only owing to the talismans I hold a) health b) fighting instinct c) an income d) a literary twist. This part is "Birdseye Autobiography", funny and objective.

III. What can be done about the situation?

Well. Virginia hinted that she'd like to see it. I was delighted as it is such a case for good balance, tact, ingenuity etc etc that suggestions can be very valuable; read it, and said "<u>Out with Part II</u>"! I explained that without my story and the revelations of how I had been hampered, and how nothing but the talismans saved me from the fate of other talented girls I have seen go down...etc. V's really angry reply is "Why then did you ask my <u>advice</u>?" (which I didn't) I think she really is annoyed but I hope to soften her heart with a bunch of Swithins [?][2].

I went down on Monday to Sissinghurst[3] which Harold and Vita are making into the most exquisite thing you ever saw – quite slow creative work. And there they sit immersed in work – no buses, no railway (nearest is Maplehurst, 5 miles off) no motor cars rushing past (they are on a field road and gradually buy up field after field). It is flat Kentish scenery – not pretty, just green fields and magnificent trees...and O the gardens they are creating. I cannot say how deeply I love Vita – her calm, her wisdom, her glow, her very great nobleness of outline. There is a person who has never been troubled by self as all Smyths are, I really believe. (That and huge behinds, are our natural snares)

[Her health]

But am coping with all this and very happy – just about to begin Mrs Pankhurst – a huge job and it must be so well done – as well as I can manage anyhow. I've had odd visits – one from a German woman composer and I sh'd say very good. She is quite content with Hitler and the herding of German women back to the three K's and is still at the point of not seeing that being herself well off, with a husband like Herzogenberg[4], a noble yet holding a professorship at the Munich Music School, does not apply to the rank and file – women also have to earn their bread. In fact I feel I can have no truck now with Germans. But she declares the driving away of people like Walter, etc. is a "passing phase – one had to clear out all Jewry, etc." I began being so incisive that I had to pull up and say, "well we wont discuss it". She said "But do! Please go on!" and I said there can be no discussion where there is no common ground. Nasty? But true.// How are your peas? Mine are good.

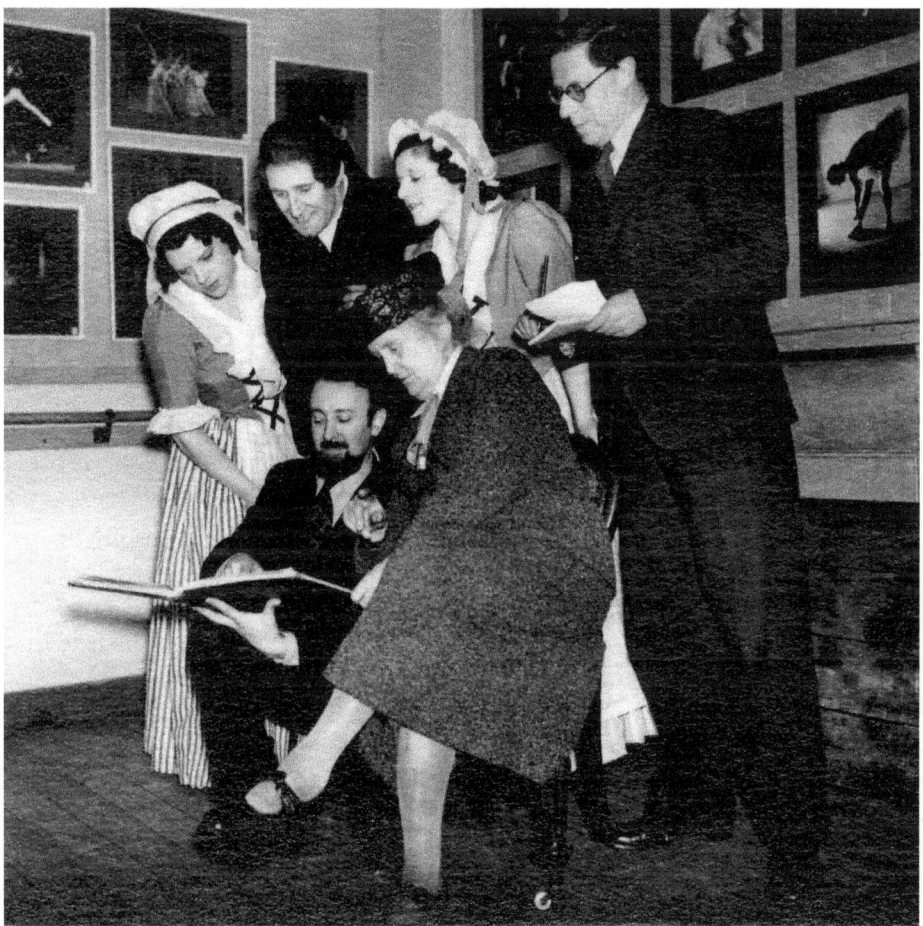

Ethel Smyth - Rehearsal

Next week I have various jaunts [?] – also this:
Tomorrow Hugh the Driver at R Coll
Saturday Hiawatha!! A thing I ought to see ere I die…at the Albert Hall

Weds. <u>The German Ballet</u> at the Savoy. A matinee.

Sat. A <u>conference</u> about the N. Women's Orchestra which Lady Howard de Walden and I take a talkative part in.

I am reading T.S. Eliot's Essays and can't get on with them. But I must persist – I think. Have just got Harold's "Peacemaking"5 – a fearful temptation. And you? ....

Yr E

This letter was followed by a spate of postcards and brief notes:

"I saw Virginia. Saintly. She's written 90 000 words...I hope its not like the Waves!"

1 Adrian Boult (1889-1993) – British conductor and promoter of British music. In 1930 he had established the BBC Symphony Orchestra.
2 Swithins would normally be apples - but they don't come in bunches and their date is July 15th.
3 Purchased by the Nicholsons in 1930.
4 Heinrich von Herzogenberg (1843-1900), composer and conductor of noble French origin. ES had studied composition under him in Leipzig. See also Introduction..
5 Harold Nicholson's *Peacemaking 1919* had just come out, earlier in 1933.

The situation for women musicians has not improved as much as might be expected in the intervening 80 years since this letter was penned. The Vienna Philharmonic has very recently (2012) – and bowing to considerable pressure – ceased to be all-male, while the ratio of men to women in British orchestras is between 2:1 and 3:1, with women soloists being yet rarer. The London Symphony Orchestra recently had a ratio of 77:22. Women conductors are more uncommon still. The numbers of women hired by major orchestras in the States was greatly increased from the 1980s with the practice of "blind" auditions.

June 27th, 1933

News of her oldest sister, Alice, whose health had been giving concern for some time.

Darling E I quite understand! I too am in a muddle with heat. Quite sad news about Alice but she doesn't know and wrote most cheerfully today. Sir L.C.[1] thinks Ethel does know. He says she is very ill, thinks it will not be long. The children are a godsend!! Keep her cheery.

[Plans to see her and meet EMW]

1 Probably Sir (George) Lenthal Cheatle (1865-1951), Lister's last assistant, eminent surgeon with a life long interest in carcinomas. Alice was Alice Davidson, ES's oldest sister, born 1851. Ethel was her daughter, ES's niece.

August 13th, 1933

In August, Elizabeth was at Appley. Ethel was planning a trip to the Shetland Islands and hoping that Elizabeth would join her.

Darling Elizabeth It really is a woe to me tho' I know you are perfectly happy where you are, that you can't come. I feel its going to be next door to Greece – the beauty I am going to see. The only thing is I cant walk as far as I could have years ago tho'at last my work is finished, I struggled up to London on Thurs. handed in the book (celebrated the event in a ¼ of Champagne that night) ....

[Medical details]

I've just been rereading the two poems of DHL you wrote out for me. God how exquisite the long lilting one is – Ah! But both are. I've made a new pal whom everyone says is very "dangerous". Vanessa said to me or wrote "Heaven help you if you're between my saintly sister and Ottoline Morrell! You'll have to fall back upon me in the end!" – She's a syren and very good to look at. V. says a liar but one she is fond of (as V. understands the term!) I talked to her about you and want to take you there. She told me a lot about DHL. and Frieda. Showed me a divine poem of his I didn't know. She was enthralled by "The Prison" and is thrall to Plotinus. How much of all this is bunkum I don't know. One never sees her except at 5 pm but alone if you wish it and she has the lovely trait of living at 10 Gower St – quite close to you.

I'm rushing down tomorrow to Mary D[odge] to lunch and may get a glimpse of V. (in Mary D's car) as she's been bad again poor dear – heat and visitors – and start on Wed.y night for Barra.

[Addresses in Scotland; concerns re Alice's health; reading matter for the journey]

August 26th, 1933

The Hotel
Creagorry
Isle of Benbecula
Inverness-shire

Darling Elizabeth behold me absolutely cut off from post, newspapers (no great matter) or anything but mutton. Very good mutton I must say – however sea-trout, brown trout (when properly cooked) and above all fresh herrings for which dear Isle of Barra – alas, behind me now - is famous make up for a good deal.

[Weather]

I am glad you were not my companion. I'm past walking now: All the back muscles are permanently hardened – not as heretofore capable of being made supple in between whiles – and an 8 mile walk is almost my limit and climbing no joy. I could do it, but so slowly and with such effort that better renounce. Which I do.

[Travel conditions, health, itinerary]

Imagine on the boat a nice but slightly inflated looking military gent accosted me as Mrs Hunter (it would make

Mary's ashes glow with shame for my get up was...as usual) whom he knew in Egypt. It turned out he was Sir Reginald Pinny[1] who knew and apparently loved "dear Rosy" tho' I don't think he was in the 21st. he had a daughter with him laden with huge tomes and working away all the 2 hours of a coasting passage when I thought it well to lie down – a jolly, cobby looking girl, very alive and modern. She is working for her degree at Univ. College and the books were worse than yours. Physics. She obviously has great powers of concentration – loathes beauty, poetry, games, the country, adores London and had never heard of Prince Charlie!! Mind [?] whose wraith haunts all these islands and it was from where I go tomorrow that Flora Macdonald took him over to Skye. She cares for nothing but science. <u>I like her immensely</u>. Quite a new type – and she only consented to accompany her father (who is here for fishing – they are [the] thing people come here for) on the condition she was not to be asked to play golf or fish. I told her to accost you at Univ. College. "Rachel Pinny[2]. Physics Student at Kings College" is her designation. Fancy someone whom history bored so utterly – in fact everything but science – that she brought her own education to an abrupt conclusion when she passed some Exam or other (?) aged 15. She is now 24 and a little reminds me of Clothilde. Quite that laugh. Not much class, physically, but attractive from vitality and receptiveness. (We discussed sex with remarkable freedom).

[Reading matter]

Being alone here I feel far more cut off from humanity than I ever did in Greece – and in some ways the experiences are not unlike – only in this case the chief joy lacking is yourself.

Yr E

---

1 Reginald Pinney (1863-1943) had a very distinguished military career and in WWI was described by Siegfried Sassoon as a "cheery old card". He was Assistant Adjutant-General of Egypt 1909-13; no doubt when he met MH.
2 Rachel Pinney (1909-1995) became a doctor and later a child therapist. She was very active in the campaign for nuclear disarmament. Although married with children, she eventually openly declared herself a lesbian.

August 27th, 1933

The following day, Ethel wrote to her brother.

> The Island of Benbecula (Outer Hebrides)

Dearest Bob on the boat from Barra hither I was accosted as....Mrs Hunter!!! Enough to make Mary turn in her grave – or her ashes glow in shame given my very Highland get up! But the accoster was an old brother officer of yours – tho' now I come to think of it I'm not sure that he was in the 21st – but he talked of you with the greatest affection – 'dear Rosy' and his present name is Sir Reginald Pinney he is stopping for fishing on the other side of the ford and has given me a letter to friends of his who have taken Stornaway Castle – for there I mean to wind up my Hebridean journeyings – crossing in quite a decent boat to Mallaig – and thence by train to spend the weekend at Bob Elwes' Pension at Fort William. He means to show me the unknown beauties of Scotland in a car without any side screens – and as it never stops blowing a gale in these parts (tho'it may be better on the mainland). I am all ready summoning my fortitude.

(Sunday morning) My lodging is not in the comfortable Creagorry Hotel where I am writing but in a little house about 1/3 of a mile off where there are only bath towels and an out door W.C. In short the conditions here are quite as primitive as in Greece. (I left my pen in my distant room and can't really write with the pens here.) At breakfast all the men sit on one side of the table all the women on the other. Up to now there have only been 3 really fine days and on those three days I saw heavenly coloring – Also Compton Mackenzie[1] (who had to pay £5000 for that affair with the W.O. [War Office] poor fellow though all he said was previously in the Greek newspapers culled from other sources) got up a luach for me – ie – 12 old women shrunk tweed by punching, pulling and patting to immemorial music. In between there were tots of whisky (I supplied one bottle) and we all made speeches and tho' the women had no English they seemed to grasp the point

August 31st 1933

Keep

My darling Aunt

APPLEY HALL
RYDE. I OF W.

I was so enchanted at hearing from you this morning. I have not attempted to write before because of the uncertainty of catching you & I imagine Mary is away & you are not having letters forwarded from home. It sounds a wonderful trip & I say with the Scotch climate would steady itself & copy us. Here the heat & perfect sun & air seem everlasting. The parties have all gone & we are a family party. Just the Trefusis 3 & Peter Herbert, brother Billy & self. We bathe & bask & I work gently. & hardly read at all except some philosophy in bed & I have been reading Spencer.
I am very interested in the new draw of the Piercy girl.

First page of letter from Elizabeth - see next page

of my speech (which was that I particularly enjoyed, thus, at the 11th hour, to get a new musical impression from <u>women</u>! This sentiment roused great enthusiasm!) I'm working up tomorrow through Harris, the coast of which is said to be very fine, to the tip top of Lewis and only wish I were 10 years younger – for I can't climb now which, in Barra, I'd have given a lot to be able to do. Lumbago has too decidedly taken charge and the effort to heave yourself up mountains is too great to be pleasurable. Yr E - I expect to be home about September6th [sic].

1 Edward Montague Compton Mackenzie (1883-1972), a prolific author and passionate Scottish nationalist, worked in counter intelligence in Greece in World War I and was decorated several times. However, in 1932 he was prosecuted under the Official Secrets act for, allegedly, quoting from secret documents in his work *Greek Memories*, which was subsequently banned and only authorized for republication 78 years later.

August 31st, 1933

And on the 31st, Elizabeth replied:

Appley Hall

My darling Aunt,

Marked by ES "Keep"

[On the weather and a trip; illustrated on page 243]

I am very interested in the picture you draw of the Pinney girl. If she is at Kings College we shall never meet as it is by the river and we never mingle – too far. But perhaps she comes to some lectures chez nous? This is unlikely though as they are self contained I think. They do no astronomy as we do no theology so in these departments we do interchange a little. It is strange indeed to be interested in nothing but physics. A sad fate I think. It is essentially abstract and deals with a closed and unreal world. A very entrancing one but <u>not enough</u>. I know the spiritual diet of individuals is infinitely variable almost, but I believe with uttermost conviction that the absolutely specialized scientist is a thin human being. If she hates poetry and beauty I suspect she has no feeling for the philosophical end of her subject. All the sciences have this one door at the end of their passage that opens into the real world but a good many scientists never open it, or slam it to avoid feeling guilty if they do so by accident! To acquire a liking for this metaphysical giddiness is the great reward of philosophy to its' children – at least I have found so. You unthink the world layer by layer by means of the analysis of the separate sciences and then hang over the Abyss. You have got to the state of pre-Creation where nothing exists except God. This is the only sense I can think of in which Time is unreal. When you let the real world flood back with all its' colour and concreteness you have so heightened your perception of the loveliness of individual things that they shake you to tears sometimes. Everything is transfigured by the renewed miracle of the uniqueness of separate objects. Bare existence is a mystery and ecstasy in such recreations of the world. Most of the religious philosophers – notably Plotinus – have dwelt on the supreme bliss of annihilating the world but are strangely silent on the subject of the return. They felt suspicious of the world and I adore it so. Do you remember Blake's verse (the best in that poem)

> Turn away no more
> Why wilt thou turn away?
> The starry floor
> The watery shore
> Is given thee till the break of day

Philosophy could never make me want to "turn away".
Goodbye darling Aunt. I shall send this to Bob.

Yr. E

September 4th, 1933

Nevis Bank
Fort William
Inverness-shire

[On problems with the writing paper]

I really think Bob is the – is well, he's Gawd's Own Masterpiece, and his angelicalness as host, in thinking out things for my comfort....

[On his car]

I am bewildered by the beauty of Scotland. It quite non plusses me. Did we see anything more beautiful in Greece? Not really....

[On the beauty of Scotland and its history]

What beats me is that highlanders tolerate being part of the B.[ritish] E.[mpire] Those rotten Irish and their Home rule. Pooh. That's all wind, froth. But the clash [?] of the clans was a real thing; and if they had known how to unite and organize and do all the things that save people from amateurishness, the Stuart cause was a real thing.

[Scottish history]

Your letter about unthinking [?rethinking] the world layer by layer by means of analyzing separate sciences and thus getting to God is strange and arresting. I think I can follow you. But above all when you explain how letting the real world flood back being almost too much to bear, given yr heightened perception, that I absolutely grasp. I wonder if the ancients are silent on that count because (as you suggest) they were "afraid and suspicious". Was it not that they had lost the knack of the other sort of commerce, as (so they say) nothing can persuade the gypsies that throng Scotland to settle down in some of the many empty crofters' cottages. They have lost the knack of dwelling behind walls – find it quite silly and pointless. Well perhaps your religious philosophers feeling is much the same only put differently. I think I can very well understand the gypsies' horror of confined space – and yet when one thinks of the gale least week – good Lord!

[On travel plans and trips, including:]

....perhaps one to Rodmell – Virginia being in a very good mood just now (she has been ill again, poor dear – sequestrated for 10 days or so). But I daresay they are back in London by now – she seems to be having a great time of inspiration and if (as I told her) the result is something wavier than the Waves, I shall bear it as I do Ben Nevis (just opposite)[?] say "O, you are beyond me nowadays" ----------------------

Miss Steel[1] has been left £300 a year and a little house at Bournemouth – I'm so glad – I trust to see you soon darling
                                                                       Yr E

1 Unidentified.

September 20th, 1933

Besides the longer letters, there were postcards.

[On failing to meet]

I think Lydia L[opokova]'s[1] Olivia rather a bit of cheek! I'm too deaf to judge really (I was at a dress rehearsal) but I thought only Sir Toby and Malvolio ....and perhaps Maria good. And I doubt if I shd like the scene even seen from the front. But I never think 12th Night <u>acted</u> is as divine as <u>read</u>....

1 Imprudent casting, it was generally felt. Lydia Lopokova played in Tyrone Guthrie's production of *Twelfth Night* at the Old Vic and although some were charmed by her performance, Virginia Woolf – predictably – savaged her both in print and in conversation.

September 22nd, 1933

Yes Myra Hess[1] is fine. Her mother told me she was just as fine aged 6!! A case of possession by some former spirit I suppose

[Plans to meet and play golf]

Do read the "Testament of Youth"[2]. The author is coming to see me, Shall I propose it while you're here? Rather fun. E

1 Myra Hess (1890-1965) British classical pianist.
2 The first part of Vera Brittain's memoirs, chronicling her experiences in WWI, was

published earlier in 1933. She was to interview ES on the Suffragettes window-breaking campaign for the BBC on March 9, 1937 – see: http://www.bbc.co.uk/archive/suffragettes/8314.shtml

October 3rd, 1933

Ethel's eldest sister Alice[1] died a few days later.

> Thank you darling for your dear letter – it <u>is</u> a rod and staff for me that she was consciously in the hand of God, and all my intercourse with her these last months – and such very adorable letters – is a source of comfort. But I do mind it more than any death I have known except mother's and HB's – mind it in an unreasonable way because after all at 82 most people are in her case. But the insanity of that very alive, keenly interested, life-hungry person being thus struck down, makes it so hard to acquiesce. With your grandmother, in a way she dug her own grave – and one could feel a sort of poetic justice in her end. But Alice!...And besides that I had such a immensely powerful <u>love</u> for her – to have laughed so much at someone, the while admiring them so passionately....! what a tie knotted round your heart....Well – Ethel shall have, and will have, all the love that hangs helplessly swaying in the air when someone you cared for like that slips out of your life. In her simplicity her courage Ethel moves me almost to tears to think of.
>
> *[On family arrangements after the funeral]*
>
> Don't you think Virginia's article very exquisite?
>
> Yr E

1 There are a number of letters to Alice from ES and other members of the family in the National Library of Scotland, Mss Division: Acc 8990 Davidson of Muirhouse.

October 11th, 1933

Darling Elizabeth I was thrilled by your report of yr visit and am certain it must be a great delight to her to have made your acquaintance. I am glad he gave in to you that the Goths were responsible for the Dark Ages, and very much interested to hear that Brett[1] is an evil woman – tho' Lady O[ttoline] began by adoring her, as she told you - ! V. says Lady O. has ever had rumpuses with her friends and lovers – and that she found DHL. such a marvellous friend in spite of being spewed forth at the latter end shows one that her view of human relationships seem rather chancy.

They seem to have been a queer crew – the Morrells, B.Russell, the Murrys, Brett and the rest – and I feel that if I cared more for probing into peoples' religious views Brussels[?] would reward investigation.

I had a delightful lunch with Maurice yesterday at Boulestin's[2] – how much nicer he is than anyone else.

[Books ES is reading]

My whole festival in the soup because of the *incredible* soft braindness and muddling ways of Hugh Allen! Maurice says all English people connected with theatre, music…etc.etc. are like that. It makes me sick.

I'm going to stay with Nina next weekend. I had a touching letter from Cheattle and he says he is <u>quite sure</u> that the x ray business prevented the suffering. Do read "Women in Love" and allow that Lady O. is a large minded woman to have made it up with him after that! Virginia is back and I had a little talk with her on the phone just now…but I feel "Flush"[3] is between us, and think I must write to say I cant catch on before I go to see her next Monday coming back from Hellens.

Yr loving E

1 Dorothy Brett (1883-1977), an artist and initially attached to the Bloomsbury Group. On making friends with Mabel Dodge and then the Lawrences, she changed allegiance, moving with them to Taos. This caused considerable ill-feeling. Her sister Sylvia married the Raja of Sarawak and was considered "dangerous", if not evil, by the Colonial Office, on account of her misdemeanours.

2 One of the most famous restaurants in London, founded in Covent Garden in 1926. In 1994, it closed and its place was taken by Pizza Hut. It has been revived in St. James's Street.

3 The biography of Elizabeth Barrett Browning's spaniel first came out in 1933.

November 16th, 1933

Golf occupied much of their correspondence in October, with Ethel describing her games shot by shot, but in November topics again diversified.

Elizabeth...what is this...? You have sent Betty £5[1] for that damned Mass concert. Darling – its too much – 5 times too much at least....

[On the same subject]

By the by on <u>January 6th</u> <u>Sat</u> (pm alas!) is my chamber music concert, <u>before a public,</u> (I won that battle) at Broadcasting House...It will be a fine performance of my 4th the Violin Sonata and the Oboe, Flute and Piano Trio "Bonny Sweet Robin". Will you be able to come and Eleanor?

[That she should invite any friends she wishes; "At present I have lost my pocket diary (taxi) and am nearly demented"; on EMW's domestic problems]

I was defrauded of the joy of conducting Land of Hope and Glory!! On the other hand have in a few short words declined another honour...viz in anticipation of another event which is impending soon, to write an obituary notice of...Elgar![2] "Nobody, I think" wrote the Ed. of the Radio Times "could write of your great colleague in a more <u>feeling</u>, a more <u>dignified</u>, and a more <u>humane</u> way, and I do not hesitate to ask you to do so" (!!!) Sancta simplicitas.

I'm too busy to turn round trying to finish the Hebrides, 2 other things, and so on. My hsp is now <u>36</u>!!

[On golf]

Virginia is being mellifluous in spite of thinking because in a letter
  a) I said I couldn't cope with "Flush" and in another
  b) that your <u>mother</u> and <u>Lady Cecil</u> delighted in it
  c) that I heard she had a <u>good Press</u> and hoped she was talking <u>in dollars</u>
  d) that I believed she had written Flush as a <u>potboiler</u>!!

Really V's knowledge of human nature is piteous! – in fact she's (as I told her) mentally deficient in some ways. (For she did think this!) Lady Ottoline loves you and implores you to propose yourself again. She and he, the daughter and the son in law[3] (who is like a nice Sheep Dog puppy) came down one Sunday aft. The heath was looking – is still looking – almost too beautiful for words; we first walked amid flying balls and then came into tea. It was delightful. She's a great dear and <u>so</u> lovely to look at.

E

1 About £250 today (2016)
2 Edward Elgar (1857-1934) was diagnosed as terminally ill in October 1933 and died at the beginning of the following year. He had composed *Land of Hope and Glory* in 1902.
3 Julian Morrell (1906-1989) the daughter of Lady Ottoline and Philip Morrell. At this date she was still married to her first husband Victor Goodman (1899-1989), Judicial Taxing Officer of the House of Commons

November 21st, 1933

Darling Elizabeth The angels Martin and Phyllis have sent a contribution to my fund!

[Her immense gratitude]

This is just to say if I didn't say it before (you see I lost my pocket diary with all notes of all kinds – but…it is found and the Lost Prop. Off. are returning it) that:
<u>On January 6th evening</u> the very nicest of my concerts takes place (all tomorrow and Thurs. I shall be rehearsing with the Quartet) and of course I shall be there, at Broadcasting House myself.

Its an <u>invitation concert</u> and I can ask anyone I please – and freely. Can you ask Eleanor, or anyone you know at U.C. to send me as soon as they can – <u>on principle</u> (but I don't believe there's such a wild hurry) names and addresses of aspirants, saying 1) or 2) tickets or more. Yourself, too, is there anyone you can think of? I expect you'll be in Cromer – dash it all – but I never quite grasp what a "vacation" means. Don't be modest. Don't let Eleanor be modest – it doesn't matter <u>how</u> many I ask – (After all the BBC has its points).

Did I tell you Virginia is quite simply appreciative of my gifts as a Biographer!! She told me she wrote Flush as an experiment

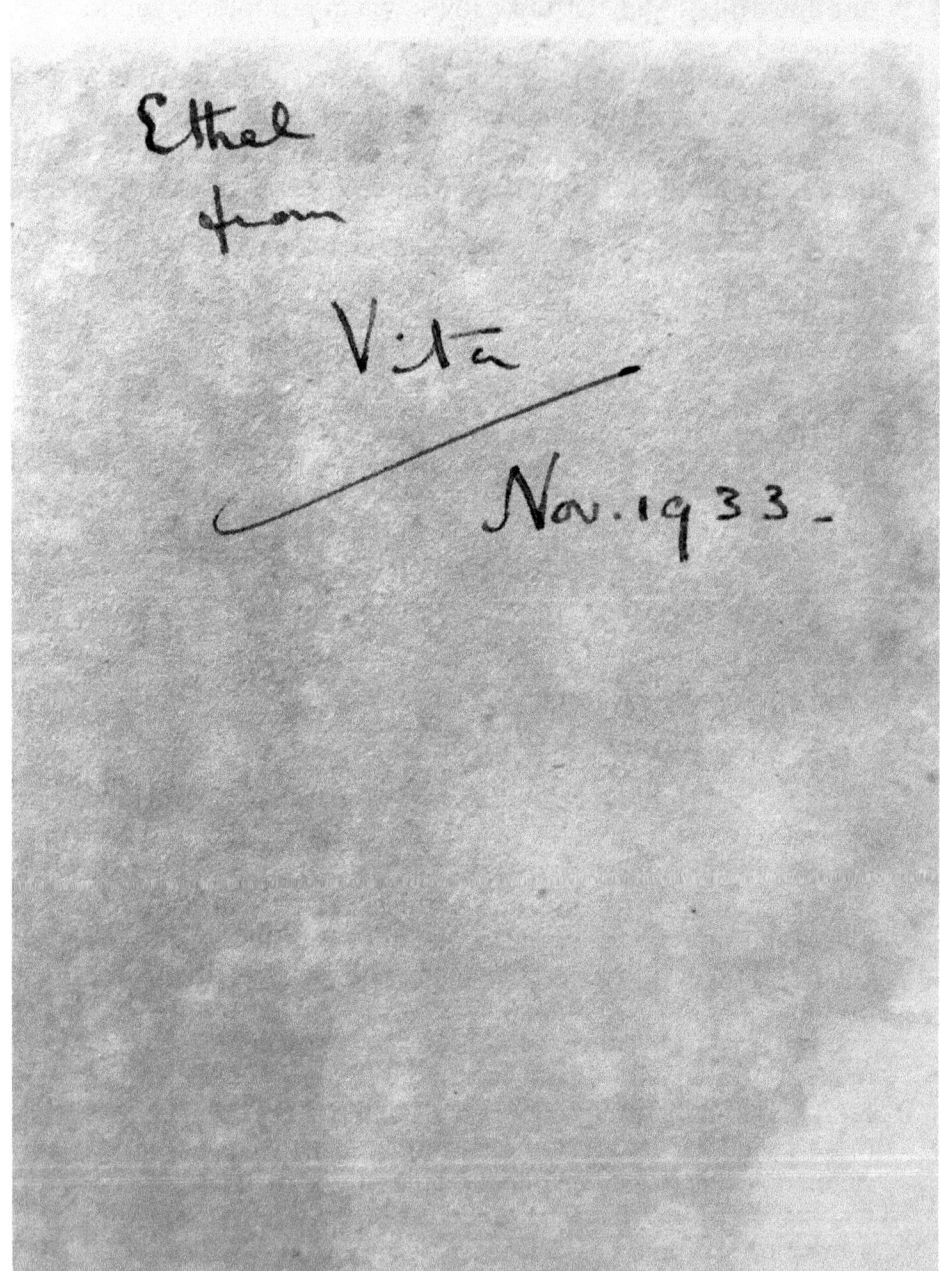

Dedication from Vita Sackville-West in *Collected Poems*

in biog: because she thinks so few people know how to do it – (only I agree with Vita it adds nothing to one's knowledge of either Browning or E[lizabeth]B[arrett]B[rowning] – at least I am sure I should if I had got further than 2 chapters!) hence it is most gratifying that she hands me these dewdrops.

Yr E

December 3rd, 1933

Darling Elizabeth. I'm submerged in an ocean of dirty water. But the last lap of something you have willed – cost what it may – is always the worst. Strange how ignorant men are of a woman's situation! For instance, in the summer a real friend, [?] a composer, Arthur Bliss[1], came here – and speaking of the impending festival he said "don't you pick up dropped stitches for them" etc. Well - if I followed that noble line the whole thing would fizzle out <u>against their own wishes</u>, and cost just as much as if it were a well run campaign - in fact more. This my friend B who is a Groove-ite [?] simply doesn't realise...and when he said to me "Why do you pack up your own parcels?" I fiercely said "because I haven't a wife to do all the dirty work as you have" His wife – present – was enchanted at this retort. I was so interested to hear of your tea-fight. I shall have to go to one (she[2] has Thursdays you know) just to see her got up to kill. It does make a difference! (Virginia, got up to mash Bruno Walter was amazing – had some sort of bandeaux arrangement to her hair). But this next week I have awful things on, a rehearsal and a dinner at the Forum!! Adrian Boult, the Woolfs and so on. Also I am to meet Rebecca West at Virginia's. I'm tidying the accumulation of years and years – letters and so on, in order to prepare for an orgie of work after Xmas.....

[On golf, and golf clubs recommended by Joyce Wethered[3]]

I've been slowly reading Vita's poems – curiously unequal (for instance the one written for me which I saw at the time delighted her as too feeble for words – and being addressed in the 2nd person is almost more than I can bear!) but some are most beautiful – for instance Sissinghurst, and the Bull and "Out with a Gun". Virginia says I shall loath her new book more than anything on earth! (By the by what do you think of Peter Davies'[4] reader attributing Orlando to <u>V Sackville-West</u>!! I had not named the author – vide my own proofs – and he repaired the omission!

I've been reading a horrible Life of Sarah Bernhardt – what a dreadful woman in private life and how wise of Maurice to say "she had no private life" (!!).

[Reading books on Russia and pre-Hitler Germany]

Oh how happy I shall be when this cup has passed – and it becomes a truly unpleasant taste when you have lost yr taste (and are too deaf to enjoy music).

Yr E

1 Arthur Bliss (1891-1975) British composer and conductor.
2 Presumably Ottoline Morell, who was well-known for her Thursday evening gatherings in Bedford Square.
3 Her *Golfing Memories and Methods* had just been published.
4 Peter Llewelyn Davies (1897-1960) – the original of Peter Pan - had founded a publishing company in 1926.

December 9th, 1933

A few days later, Elizabeth wrote her great aunt a brief but touching letter on her great affection for her. It is marked in red with a circle and a dot, surely by ES.

> My darling Aunt
> I should like to tell you that it came over me last night in a welcome wave (all waves are not sad!) how much I love you. I don't think it a waste of time to say so for I think that these odd very intense moments when the soul [?] everything else and sharp and significant are the most real ones in life, and that the rather flat "morning life" view of the world, is much less real.
> Yr lvg E

December 11th, 1933

Darling Elizabeth Moved by you, I am braving the weather, deafness and all, and going to the Old Vic matinee to see Measure for Measure on Wed next; having a seat in <u>the midst of row 1</u> I ought to hear something anyway. After that I'm going on to Peter Davies Cocktail party (Eddie Grant etc) at the Café Royal[1] at 5.45.

[On the possibility of meeting]

I've now (today) written to the BBC to ask them to arrange rehearsals I shd like to take before I go to Cromer. Beecham is away till Thurs, I think and by then I ought to see my way.

[More on plans to meet]

The great joy is the purchase of a Joyce mashie, chosen by her....I do love her.

[On golf and golf clubs]

I didn't go to Lady O's on Thurs – too cold – wanted to get home. But I lunched at Violet's[2] - Morell[3] was there and do you know I definitely <u>don't like him</u>. Very glib pleasant and all that – but there's something nasty about him. I am so sorry darling I must stop and go to bed...

[More on possibilities of meeting]

1 A restaurant in Regent Street, one of the most famous meeting places in London for the world of the arts and, to some extent, sport. Founded in 1865, it closed in 2008.
2 Violet Trefusis (1894-1972) author and friend of the Smyth family. The daughter of Edward VII's mistress, Alice Keppel, she had well publicized affairs with Vita Sackville-West, the Princesse de Polignac, etc.
3 Philip Morrell (1870-1943) liberal M.P. and pacifist; Lady Ottoline's husband.

December 12th, 1933

The next day, Ethel wrote to Bob about Emmeline Pankhurst, of whom Ethel had been extremely fond. In 1921, however, a letter from Ethel criticizing Mrs Pankhurst's adored daughter Christabel led to a rift that was never healed. Mrs Pankhurst's relationships with her other daughters, Sylvia and Adela were extremely difficult. Nevertheless, in 1930 Ethel had conducted "The March of the Women" at the dedication of the statue of Mrs Pankhurst, who had died two years earlier:

You see my telling Mrs P about the feeling everyone had about Christabel was really partly from practical motives – no one wd subscribe while Christabel was retaining room in 2 or 3 hotels and so on!! In fact she was (and is – in my opinion – and Hilda had the same impression) dotty. Poor Mrs P – with 3 daughters like that!

December 14th, 1933

[On ES's rehearsal schedule and the difficulties of getting away to Cromer. Some passages, relating to travel et al., are marked with red crosses]

I was bitterly reproached for not bringing you to the Cocktail party on a collar and lead. As things were, finding it was only 5.15 when the Vic was over I stepped straight on to a 68 bus and went first to Virginia who was in angelic mood – I wished I had thought of that at once and tried to get you there anyway. I missed Grizzy and Diana Cooper – much to my sorrow at the party, but firmly caught the 7 train at Waterloo (No dallying in this weather)

[Criticism of Measure for Measure.]

(I am herewith shewing off my critical spirit: "Must pick some holes" as an old pal of mine said who spent her life doing nothing else.)

Tuesday 26th

9/7 Darling M. I am allowed to write today — if only you have not left England! about a certain registered letter from Vienna (really from Anna Mildenburg) which came here with some others. The Governor says he sent it back to you & certainly the other ones that were with it (one from Bob — one from Clare etc) were sent back to Coign. But apparently not this one. If you have had it back you will remember it — but I am convinced you have not — & if

Dear Lizzie put it back & we have been forwarded some here again with the rest & be overhauled. If you know anything about it — a line addressed to me here c/o Matron will get through all right, as it may be important. Don't bother the Governor about it of course: quite unnecessary — I wish I knew when you are going. I'm not sure when (if ever?) I may receive visits — but will try & find out — I rather think a month after my sentence — which wd be (if they count remand time 2nd ap. or if they don't 5th) or so. I continue very fit. Fortuin Theresa has been begged to send fresh meat every time Dr. R. as they did at first — some — Of late they only send tongue, ham, galantine (too rich) & so on.

H. M. Prison Holloway

March 26th 1912.

I am now in this Prison, and am in _____ health.

Signature — [Register No.] 15534 E Smyth

I keep all right! Bless you

A letter of Ethel's Smyth to Mary Hunter from Holloway

I am told my book is selling very well and that they think its going to be a big scoop. If so it will surprise me very much because of its feministic trend all the way through and I cant really believe it.

I'm quite sad about Miss Baylis's worried face. I fear it is like Xtianity as soon as things assume certain dimensions the world gets a finger in the pie, the heyday is over.

[On meeting]

Lilian Baylis' worries at this date may have been connected with the increasing size of her commitments, or possibly with Charles Laughton, whom she had persuaded to make one of his rare stage performances at the Old Vic.

Late December, 1933

And on a postcard a few days later.

V says DHL took her friend Lady O.M's money and then wrote that <u>awful</u> book "Women in Love" in which she figures!!! Just like Roy Campbell[1] and another V. (not Virginia) What a crew!

---

1 Roy Campbell (1901-1957) poet and satirist. His wife, Mary Garman, was briefly involved with Vita Sackville-West and among his verse are satirical comments on the Bloomsbury Group with whom he was initially friends.

1934

January 1st, 1934

My darling Eliz I think your letter has made me happier than any letter I have had for years...or perhaps ever. I have to stop....Must see to things till about 11p.m. and rush to Bournemouth early to hear a girl's cello Sonata. But tho' I cant catch the post I may write later in the evening.

Yr E

January 11th, 1934

My darling Elizabeth what does one say if one of the people you love best says exactly what you most want to hear about <u>the</u> thing you have made? I mean that you find the music "inspired" and the unity of words and music attained. That's what I care for most. Also I find what you say about music "written for an idea" very arresting – I think why one can hear H.B. set to music, and inspite of its being religion, does <u>not</u> want to leave his spirit in Ridinghouse St is because Christs life was human and his human adventures are retailed – whereas the Prison is an abstraction. Do you go with that? There's no human anguish to contemplate with anguish - no horror at the stupidity and cruelty and blasphemy of the betrayal, the scourging, the crucifixion. And the odd thing is that abstract and remote as the Prison's story is, it is so much that of everyone that no one is left outside, really. It is pure and legitimate pity for themselves, merging into consolation for themselves that those Queens Hall listeners feel; a wound directly soothed by HB's voice and the plaster he offers.

Betty was saying how <u>intensely</u> she loathes Gerontius[1] with its terror, its devils, its regeneration via the Apostolic Succession and all that. Just that appeals to a common – a very very common – christian [sic], no doubt but it nauseates another type as can nothing else.

By the by keep this letter for me [heavily underlined in red]. I see in it the germ of a study on HB's Prison which I should like to write <u>first</u> <u>thing</u> when the Mass is behind me. I couldn't come up to London today – too much to do and not yet in

British Womens Symphony Orchestra.
President, Lady Howard deWalden.

Annual General Meeting held at St Pauls Church House, Tuesday June 26th 1934
Report for year ending May 31st 1933-4.

Dear Chairman and fellow members, I have much pleasure in placing before you the eleventh Annual Report of the B.W.S.O,
During the last season the orchestra has undoubtedly done very good work, the regular rehearsals with Miss Burrows have proved very beneficial, and by remarks by people who know, the detail work that has been done has been met with marked success.
The membership Twelve months ago was 75, it is now 80, we have lost 10 during the year, and elected 15 new members, several members have left London, others have given up the profession owing to the terrible slump in
The first concert of the season was an engagement in Leicester for afternoon and evening, Grace Burrows conducting, this musically was a great success, Mary was solo pianist and met with a very good reception.
Our first Queens Hall concert with the Peppin Twins Soloists, held November 25th was very successful, the pianists proving themselves quite an attraction.
The second concert January 26th was not so successful, Eda Kersey was not the attraction it was thought she would be, from a musical point it was very good.
The last concert March 17th, Chavchavadzie was the soloist, this from a box office point was not a great success, consequently we have lost heavily on the season.
Unfortunately last season it was impossible to obtain financial help from any soloist, hitherto we have always had this assistance, the first concert was broadcast for which we receive a fee of £63.0.0. more than half of this was paid out to members.
Thirty members had a weeks engagement at Harrods Musical Festival week during April, this was opened by Dame Ethel Smyth on the Monday, and proved a great attraction for the whole week, so much so that we are pormised further engagements in the early Autumn, and possibilities of other stores.
Dr Malcolm Sargent as you know was unable to do any work last season, Sir Thomas Beecham was approached also Albert Coates, but both were too busy to take more engagements, Grace Burrows has therefore conducted all the seasons work, and with very great success, and I am sure we all feel very grateful to her.
Musically the work of the orchestra has been very successful throughout the season, our Press notices have been very good, the attendances at rehearsals Have been more than the average.
The year has been very disappointing to me as far as getting work, the numerous engagements which I have hoped to secure have all unfortunately been turned down, concert promotors these days will not pay the expenses of an orchestra, the Canadian Tour, I am hoping may come off this season, it is just a question of finance the whole of the time.
If we had a few thousands at the back of us we could do much more, we are starved for the need of more advertising, we dare not launch out, we can only go on with our Queens Hall concerts, when you hear the financial statement you will know the loss on these,

This is very trivial compared to other orchestras, but unfortunately we have no guarantors, in fact I think the public imagine we are a very wealthy concern.

It has just come to my knowledge that the L.S.O. have lost £1.500 on t the season excluding the last concert which was a tremendous loss to Mr Nettlefold, but the orchestra themselves guarantee £1.000, they do not rece receive fees, we have to pay out quite a large amount.

The Birthday party organised by Miss Brightman was a great success the funds benifited to the extent of £70 0.0. it is a pity we cannot have a Birthday party every year.

I think the orchestra has had a very good season on the whole, considering the slump in music and the state of nthe profession.

We are still going through very difficult times, but if we mean to continue, and I am sure it is the wish of all present, we must all put our backs to the wall, each member be prepared to do her utmost, no matter how small to help to carry on our good work We must be alive and go ahead, we cannot afford to stand still, and it is up to every member especially the new ones who should bring new ideas and suggestions, we must not get stale but it is no use just a few pulli their weight, it is every members duty to always have the B.W.S.O. at the back of her mind, to form new friends, bring them in as patrons, talk about the orchestra, this is the only way to keep up out reputation, as stated by the press(that the orchestra was a great asset to the British Nation).

I am rather sorry not to see or hear of another member willing to take up my work, when the work is as trying as it has been, and one is feeling far from %100, it is very difficult and makes one feel that there must certainly be someone who could do better, still as long as we continue and it is your wish that I remain your Sec; then I am quite willing to do my very best.

During the season the Committee have held 16 meetings.

It has been suggested to me that we should endeavour to engage a big a artist who would be a good box office draw, but this is impossible we would like to have Bachaus, his lowest fee is 80 guineas, still if this could be found it would be very, if successful we should then realize w where our weakness was-- in not engaging first class artists.

I hope next season will be much more successful from a financial p point, and that you have all come with suggestions whereby funds can be raised.

The sound film taken at our last concert when Don Juan was recorded should bring us an amount of publicity, seeing it has been shown nearly all over the country.

I wish the orchestra and each member individually the best of luck.

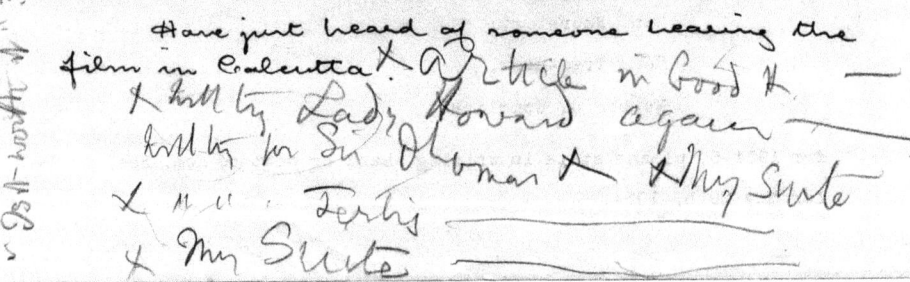

British Women's Symphony Orchestra A G M 1934 page 2

possession of knowledge ("how many string parts") which will partly motivate my going there. And O I am sickeningly busy. You will come to this lunch, wont you? Maurice is just off to Gibraltar and wont be there but Virginia and Vita will, so you can sit with them. I'll tell you if I come up Mon or Tues.

Your E

[1] The *Dream of Gerontius*, A poem by Cardinal Newman, set to music by Edward Elgar in 1900, tells the story of the passage of a man's soul from his deathbed to judgement before God and, finally, to repose in Purgatory.

June 27th, 1934

As so often in this correspondence, there is a gap of several months, caused by letters being damaged or going missing, rather than any disagreement or change in circumstances.

Darling Elizabeth the martyrdom will be over after this week and I shall become thirsty for human intercourse. But I want you if you have time to <u>oblige me</u> by looking at a book that Germany is revelling in and that is, I think, the ravings of a lunatic. A great deal of it I simply cant understand – pseudo-philosophical stuff. But I want to know if all that about the German's "conquest of time" – i.e. [?] "relativity" means anything at all. It is called "Germany, my Country" by F. Sieburg[1].

He wrote another book greatly admiring the French called "Is God a Frenchman?" but seems to have changed his mind. And the fellow dares to speak of Goethe - !

The idea seems to be – smash up everything and from it will emerge the only person who dares look truth in the face – the German. And you come on things like this – "The man who jettisons the conception of the world which gave sense and justification to his existence will suffer a tragic loss of security, but he will liberate himself from that narrow rigidity which is an element of order, no less than tedium was an element in the Olympian system of the ancient gods." His great idea seems to be "do away with reason"…and he wants to get rid of "time and its destroying powers" (whatever that means).

But what I want to know is there any definite philosophical principle in all this stuff ? (translation admirable).

I've seen no one except adorable Lady Hartington[2] with whom I lunched one day and am waiting with trepidation the result of Martins kindly offices in my Argentina business[3] Virginia I've not seen – she's been ill off and on ever since Ireland, poor soul – and has been held up in her work and that always makes her miserable. But maybe she'll be in a mood to see me this aft. – if in.

I can't understand Germany and am agitated about it as I never was about Russia because R. always turns on her Eastern destiny – and we can more or less wash her, spiritually, off the slate. <u>But Germany</u>!! .....

1 Friedrich Sieburg (1893-1964) was well-regarded as a journalist and political commentator, in spite of his sympathy for Hitler, and (apparently) often confused and repetitive style.
2 Mary Alice Gascoyne-Cecil (1895-1988). Lady Hartington, was to become Duchess of Devonshire in 1938. Her daughter-in-law was Deborah Mitford.
3 ES had financial problems on a number of occasions. In this case, presumably relating to shares in some concern in Argentina, which, after a long period of prosperity, was suffering terribly from the 1930s crash.

June 30th, 1934

[Assorted reading, including an article: "Is Hitlerism Cracking" in Time and Tide, *30.6.1934; ES and Ottoline Morrell's concern over EMW's health; very worried about her financial affairs: "It seems to me that I will have to pay a terrible sum"; she wanted to see the Italian puppets]*

But I cannot emulate your Grandmother and am paralysed if walking in a financial mist. Ottoline lent me "The Rock"[1] which I think is going to fascinate me rather but Virginia didn't think much of it. Yet how cd she since its abt the Church? Ottoline got fever at Crete and was ill at Athens – some how I feel that it had not been quite a success. Perhaps roughish travel without a maid (I admire that in her, don't you?) is too much for her. I thought she looked rather ill and less glowing than usual – But I <u>do</u> so like her.... A horrid woman...the Mrs Tate M.P.[2] who rescued the German lady, has been here for

1½ hours – very pretty and smart with a doglike adoring gent of a husband. She is hard as nails and had a slight dig at everyone she mentioned – and is the whole time telling you how cleverly she diddled the Germans. The sort of woman I can't stand and Oh she is pleased with herself.

[On Pan and a young woman from U.C.]

On the back of the envelope among other notes.

I read "The Hour of Destiny"[3] seemed to me absolute rot.

1 *The Rock* – a pageant-play by T.S.Eliot written for performance at Sadler's Wells, 28 May-9 June, 1934 in aid of the Diocese of London.
2 Mavis Tate (1893-1947) – born Maybird Hogg - was a Conservative M.P. from 1931. She protested against the treatment of the Jews in Germany from the mid-30s, in 1940 advocated the arming of British women to resist a Nazi invasion and in 1945 travelled to Buchenwald to report on the atrocities there.
3 Perhaps Herman Frobenius (1841-1916) *Germany's Hour of Destiny*, New York, 1914.

July 14th, 1934

[Health]

I've got a really hateful job done (which I <u>settled</u> to do – <u>began</u> – and am damned if I won't <u>stick to</u> till its finished) life is a nuisance.

[Health]

I cant help being perturbed as to the outcome of my £.s.d. affair – but not too perturbed.

We are all shattered by Maggie Ponsonby's[1] death. She was one of the most original people (in the good sense) I ever knew and the most amusing. She used to call Betty (her sister) and Mary Crawshay[2] and Ella Joshua[2] and me "les veuves Brewster"!!

Your loving E

1 Magdalen Ponsonby – the daughter of ES's friend Lady Ponsonby and sister of "Fritz" Ponsonby had died on July 1st.
2 Unidentified.

July 19th, 1934

Darling Elizabeth I think it always good to know when one's being in the world gives pleasure so I enclose this. I had a delightful – no two delightful [?] with bits of my past yest. Prs. Polignac to lunch – quite delightful growing elderly with vigour and splendour and a quite unnecessary application – by day at least – of lipstick and rouge both clapped on rather vaguely, and rendered insecure by the heat - as evidently good enough for a jaunt to the country. Then Betty Montgomery, Maggie's sister, to tea – the story of her death strange and... yet an old old story. But not so strange as the death of Anna de Noailles who died simply because, being awfully deaf (at 52) and a nervous wreck, and unable to accommodate herself to the fact of the once brilliant bewilderingly gifted genius having become an ill and elderly woman she declined to go on living – not poison or anything...just said goodbye all round, dictated a few last poems, signed them in an odd shaky hand and went out in her sleep. Bravo. – I'm expecting the Worpelden clergyman about Douglas's future. Poor poor Ethel!...no cook to be had and those blasted children imminent – For me, I am trying to follow Richard Steeles[1] advice (passed on by Miss Steel of Bath) to "Prue" who was worrying as well she might about her financial situation "Let me entreat you" he writes "not to excruciate your spirit over matters you should despise and ignore"!! All very fine – but that ends in other people having to excruciate their spirits!

Yr E

[On meeting]

[1] Richard Steele (1672-1729), writer and M.P., founder of *The Tatler* and *The Spectator*, wrote a long series of letters to his second wife, Mary, known as Prue.

Enclosed is a letter from Ottoline Morrell in an extraordinarily elaborate hand that fits her personality most beautifully. The page is marked "destroy" in ES's writing.

July 16th, 1934

10 Gower St.

My dear Ethel,
I feel I must write and tell you what a <u>delightful</u> visit I had from your Elizabeth. I did enjoy it for she is really someone after my own heart...a rare thing! – I hope I shall see her sometimes. It was nice talking of you and Greece...and everything.

I feel so grateful to you for bringing her.

Would you like to come to meet T.S.Eliot?

He is back in London now – and if you would let me know when you are coming up, I would ask him. He cannot come on Wednesday.

He is coming tomorrow and you won't get this in time.

Yr aff.n
Ottoline Morrell

August 4th, 1934

Darling Elizabeth – When I think of this day 20 years ago and reflect that I wasn't in England – and that you were a child – and the uncertainty as to whether England would come in made me think – for the first time in my life seriously – of suicide à la Sappho from the S. Malo cliffs..! Incredible isn't it? And by chance I have tumbled these days on "<u>Germany, prepare for war</u>"[1] and the shameless shufflings and denials on the part of the German Govt., all of which are given in the preface to this masterly translation. I don't want to become a prey to phobia of any sort – but the European happenings and the books I have been reading lately give me the feeling that Germany is the sort of unassimilated natural power for evil that the German Romantics – people like E.T.A.Hoffmann, de la Motte Fouqué, and even Kleist[2] were so fond of handling. And that they should have escaped from all this on one plain to become the sublimest of music-builders! Isn't it inexplicable.... And frightening?

Well today I've finished a thing I intended to do before the Festival gave me a horror of musical effort and which I determined to tackle all the same – the sort of job which is akin to writing a play for the films – a job you can do now and again quite lightheartedly but which really is curiously antipathetic if you are in the wrong mood. And the absurd thing is that at present I cant afford to have the parts written out so it will probably never be played! (Its a suite on Entente Cordiale fragments and would be a god-send to provincial and municipal orchestras) and the effort – of value as discipline – seems otherwise more than futile. But what are we but beasts driven along a winding road in a mist and to ask why and whither is a still greater degree of futility. I was so glad you liked "Dulwich"[3]. I had a super funny extremely brilliant letter from Virginia – one of the kind she used to write when I was the last new toy – full of groans at having (joke I suppose) from deference to me, to read another Baring book – saying she never can submit herself to "his silvery bold fingers with any gusto" and that he is too "white waistcoated urbane and in the old Etonian style for her rough palate"! She was also furious at the bell tolling away in the Church – and at the life of Parson Venn who remarks that a frivolous lady had "mercifully swallowed a pin". I wrote her a serious letter about religion; said she must know (though she did ask Roger Fry "why" the columns of the Parthenon are so sublime) that none can tell her why a wrong word could spoil the whole balance of that final par. in "The Waves" or of that lovely thing (O how lovely) about the old woman singing in Regents Park. And that the secret of literary perfection is both a mystery and a fact, surely of the sense of religion the same is true? And I told her you and I asked ourselves whether, if she had not married a fanatical atheist, she would have been as impervious as she is now? (I think this may bring a thundering volley of abuse – one of her insulting diatribes like the "orbicular rotundity" one! But I'm in favour just now so I thought I'd risk it)

[On failing to meet Maurice Baring]

Betty, by the by, is as unappreciative of "Dulwich" as I know Virginia will be; and this surprises me in her tho' one always understands the limitations of a craftsbrother. How, she asks, can M. sit down and pour out the adventures of such an odious woman as Lita and seems to have no inkling of the [?] frenzy of interest in his guest? One of the pictures in the Academy (and you know I am rather depressed by liking some of them so very much!) is thrilling as a portrait of a deadly dull man - ? cant remember his who. No attempt at lifting his nullity into drama just his authentic likeness. But Betty is delightfully young in some things. And so amusing in her shamelessness. Boring Mary Craig – DD's daughter, foisted herself on her for 3 days – and on the second Betty went to London (I believe to get away from poor Mary) and Mary appeared here. Wd I go out for a walk with her? This I cd not do so I told her I was supervising the gardener whose methods with nettles are unconvincing and would she like to roll the lawn? Afterwards I set her to trim undergrowth but to refrain from looking at her handling of the hopper. At tea I gave her "Dulwich" and read my own book...(She ate all before her, as if she were starving) Next morning Betty came over to apologise and said how "dreadful" it was of Mary to come over. I said "I expect you told her to" – "Well, not quite," said Betty "but when she said she thought she'd go over and see the Dame after lunch I <u>did</u> say that was a magnificent idea"(!!)

[Sorting out her financial affairs; conducting the Overture *to* Entente Cordiale *and the* Fête Galante Suite; *reading matter]*

Your E

[A long PS on health and golf]

1 Ewald Banse (1883-1953) – in *Germany, Prepare for War!* , English translation published February, 1934, Banse sets out the imperative need for Germany to invade Great Britain, making use of bacteriological warfare, etc. if need be.
2 E.T.A. Hoffmann (1776-1822) - composer and author of horror and fantasy; Friederich de la Motte Fouqué (1777-1843) – German romantic novelist; Heinrich von Kleist (177-1811) German Romantic poet and novelist.
3 Maurice Baring, *The Lonely Lady of Dulwich*, 1934 – a novella.

August 9th, 1934

Southampton Station

My darling Elizabeth All yesterday in spite of mugging up, at Cromer House, my job in bed the night before and before starting to rehearse (for I had forgotten the Overture not having seen it for 5 years or so) I was thinking of you....

[On her stay at Cromer and family news. Of her niece's husband: "I hope K. is keeping an eye on him, or closing both eyes – whichever is the policy that commends itself to her as lawful spouse"; books and reading matter; her problems with nettles and income tax: "Also until that affair has matured a little I don't feel as apt to sally forth and gorge on natural beauties as usual – I never could turn on more than one tap at once." The success of her concert. More about the family, including another great niece: "..poor Ethel reminds me now of a pole sticking up in a mud landscape where it is everlasting low tide (cant go on in a train)."]

Basingstoke

I had not grasped that I had to change at this place and looking up 1½ years ago suddenly found myself at Reading!! Got a connection back here – lunched – refused to drink the beer as it was lukewarm. They said they only had ice "every other day" – and apparently I hit on the other day however I shall be back home by 3 and have 2 hours for nettle coping anyhow.

I expect you know what pain for you your news about Ellinor gives me. It recalled to me a experience of my own – in about 1893 it must have been – when Pauline Trevelyan [1] to whom I dedicated my Mass quite quietly told me she was engaged to her cousin Gilbert Heathcote. Only my pang was less justified than yours because I was far more wrapped up in P. than she in me and because tho' our musical union was very intense she never was the sort of normal complement of my life that E has been of yours. As you say love must be selfish and if it isn't it isn't love – No one else could ever occupy the place she did in yr [?] existence.....I wish I knew more – whether you know (and like) the man....

(I am now writing at Coign) Whether you think she will be happy – if it was a sudden or an old affair – when it takes place and so on. O I do wish I cd see you and learn more – I expect, the human barometer being thus constructed, that this private blow makes you feel the public situation as more than depressing (as HB declared his old billiard pal Marchese (?) always said "povero paese" when he did 2 or 3 extra bad shots running.) Myself I think all that has happened is [?] for the steadying of the balance of everything – France and Germany and the gradual evolution of some plan such as Norman Angell[2] has always advocated – <u>not</u> a European bloc in two masses....(on one side Germany and co and on the other England, France and co) but a pact that the whole of Europe will fall as one man on anyone, be it England, Italy or Germany who breaks the peace. I think I'm with you that there is no such thing as all round betterment and increase of wisdom – The world will always be like the sea, stirred up and raging in response to elemental forces none can control – and each shore has to create its own security and each fleet its own machinery for coping with death and destruction. That search for the talisman wherewith to overcome the world is life. There's no more to it than that – only I don't think one need despair at the lack of community harmony. I'm writing in haste for Betty has just come in having invented that <u>I told</u> her Brmouth was not being broadcast!!...Meanwhile O my dear...what did I find when I got home 3 hours ago...news that November 29th <u>T[homas] B.[eecham]. is doing the Prison at Manchester</u>!! Thus do they give you things when you have ceased longing too violently for them!

Your E

1 Pauline Trevelyan (d.1897) married Sir Gilbert Heathcote (1854-1937) in 1891. She was a devout Catholic and it was under her influence that ES wrote her Mass.
2 See December 23rd, 1931

August 13th, 1934

Monday night
My darling Elizabeth Of course Phyllis never told me she had been seedy and they were too adorable and too enchanted

about the Prison (I did tell you didn't I that Beecham is doing it at Manchester – the place I above all desired – on November 29th) that champagne was produced. I went off next day early in holiday-bursting trains, all of which were late – and lunched in one of them (it was Saturday closing) on a veal and ham pie purchased at the station and set to swim in a glass of beer gulped down at the counter. Yet I survive.

I feel cheered about my financial crisis and hope Mr Turner – a charmer and a megalomaniac who played the organ in his youth and wanted to be a professional musician – who also takes real interest in the case – may limit my liabilities – (I should say persuade Somerset House to limit them) to six years; but it won't be settled immediately I believe. The wheels of Gradgrinders[1] grind slowly. He says it used to be looked on as a legitimate department of sport to dodge on taxes in the days when incomes were large and taxation light. But nowadays when Governments cant make both ends meet they are sharp and pitiless. But, he said, that applies more to financial concerns that cheat on a large scale....in short I am hopeful.

About Ellinor I am glad you wont have more weddings to face – and I always understood of course that you would never be a grasping friend and that the pang of this thing is the distance. But it is a big one – I mean the pang – though better than if you had never thought such a thing might happen, as the surprise would have been such a shock – yet – I say again it's the distance that really matters –

About war....but before I go to that (for Keyserling[2] on war is interesting) I must ask whether you have read his "Problems of Personal Life". I find the book very interesting and when he goes off, from discussion of things I am accustomed to think about, using language I can follow, with a sudden plunge into metaphysical seas, I shut my eyes – as one mounting a wave that may end in making you feel seasick – and cling to the knowledge that soon I shall be once more in the homely trough I am accustomed to – Well – about war, I dont think arming brings anyone nearer to it. And I do think that all nations except Germany (who is I think in an hysterical state that only time can cure) are too horrified of the idea of its breaking out again, not to be able to sink their differences, if it came to the scratch and fall upon the aggressor which you cant do unless you arm. Before Germany can make war years must elapse during which the real danger of having such a lunatic nation in the centre of Europe will have gone home to all of us. Just as all the inhabitants of Hook Heath [3] if they knew for certain that those 3 square miles harbour a lunatic would do things, take precautions they would never dream of taking as long as it was possible to believe it was just an empty scare. I dont believe for a minute that the League of Nations is done for because of this set back. But since Maurice reminded me of that phrase in "Tasso" about life being unbearable but for "holden Leichtsinn"[4], that spirit has rather invaded me. And I don't drive it away. On the contrary.

[Health; her reading]

Another I have now finished "A lawyers notebook" Delightful I thought and Morris who is named in it tells me the writers name is Haynes[5] – a solicitor with a heart of gold, a bit of a crank and had [?] a divorce (!). I found the books charming so that I nearly wrote to ask him why he talks so much Tommy Rot about women (it doesn't go with the rest) and to tell him how much I enjoy his mind. Need I tell you that Betty tells me that Pidd had read it and said it was clear but very unpleasant! – "left a nasty taste in your mouth". He does use the word "lust" I fancy, but nothing worse than that! Really Pidd is incalculable.

O my dear don't read M.Bergeret à Paris[6]. It is too tiresome – worse than Flush because sentimental. (I couldn't read much of Flush I cant think V. wd be sentimental). She rose in the grandest style (I thought she wd!) at my remark about our wondering if she would have had any religious sense had she not married an Atheist! And then my praise of [?]was the finishing touch! She is curiously narrow in some ways. I don't mind abt M; authors often cant appreciate each other. But on religion she is childish – result of reaction from the Plymouth crew she derives from, Betty thinks.

Yr E

---

1 From Thomas Gradgrind, the headmaster in Dickens' novel *Hard Times* (1854), interested only in facts, numbers – and profit, to the exclusion of all feelings.

2 Hermann Graf von Keyserling (1880-1946), philosopher and natural scientist from the Baltic provinces of Germany, believed that the old German militarism was no-longer viable and that it was imperative to achieve an intellectual reorientation and adopt a democratic system. He wrote extensively on political and social philosophy and his *Problems of Personal Life* had appeared in English earlier in 1934.
3 The site of the Woking Golf Course, close to ES's cottage.
4 From Goethe's play *Torquato Tasso* "had not nature given us the gift of light-mindedness".
5 E.S.P.Haynes (1877-1949) was a British lawyer, who wrote on a number of legal and political subjects, notably freedom: e.g. *The Decline of Liberty in England* (1916). *The Lawyer's Notebook* was published in 1932.
6 Vol.IV of Anatole France's *L'Histoire Contemporain* published in 1901 has, among other themes, the Dreyfus Affair.

August 22nd, 1934

On the 22nd of August, Ethel wrote just as she was about to leave for Wootton and a week later wrote again from there on similar themes. Wootton Manor is a Jacobean manor house at Folkington, East Sussex, then property of the Gwynne family. One of the sisters was Violet Gordon-Woodhouse the harpsichordist, a close friend of ES. Her niece, the cookery writer Elizabeth David, was raised there.

August 29th, 1934

Darling Eliz.

[Travel plans]

I have a big job on that will take me....<u>years</u>!! But long jobs (like you and Ptolemy) suit me best.. I am so glad that you saw Elinor and that you feel she is going to be happy.. Such a consideration doesn't lessen – in fact in such moments it increases the pain of the wrench - ! Yet on the whole it is a soothing factor. But, as you say, it is time and space (that whatever yr Einstein and Kant may say, means something to us mortals) which is the devil in this case. I went over to spend 2 hours with Virginia on Sat - and she was at her most enchanting and had been taken in by my pretended find, in a book of annals at M.Mascal, of the mama of the Duke of

N...(18th cent.) who had race horses but thought it <u>vulgar to let them compete</u>!! I am so proud for tho' it took in Betty, I thought V wd smell a rat. Instead of which she says she thought "That old scoundrel Ethel who goes and digs out just the sort of thing, in someone else's library, that I should like to have found." And she added when I said I made it all up as I wrote that she always had maintained I was a "born writer"!! great success wasn't it? (I'll tell you the whole tale when we meet)

[Health]

Yr E

September 23rd, 1934

Letters in September were largely concerned with Ethel's health and the doings of Pan, until she launched into a series of impassioned diatribes against a production of *Antony and Cleopatra* at the Old Vic.

My darling Elizabeth never in the course of my life have I seen such a joyless, talentless, dead flat affair as Ant. and C. at the Vic. Fortunately Miss Baylis was ill so I was saved from a bad moment for truth loving people......The most awful of all was to my mind Cleopatra. That dreadful bourgeois little trull – that Lyons young lady[1], I had almost said, but they at least have a vision of what charm, what chic might mean, whereas that Cleopatra was more like the sort of elderly-young ladies you find behind the bar at Railway Stations! Her port, her almost bewildering lack of any sort of grip on her part.....O Elizabeth! And her death....Again I thought of the bar lady just before closing time, dozing over her last glass – sure no custom will come now – but sitting out her time....And that wild cry "There is nothing left remarkable beneath the visiting moon..!!" The whole thing was like cast iron mouldings about to be scrapped as having become too weather worn....

Cleopatra was played by Mary Newcomb (1893-1936), an American actress, in what was described as an "up-to-the-minute" modern production. The reviewer Michael Sayers writing in the New English Weekly the following month agreed with Ethel and saw the interpretation as suggesting "a prostitute past her prime".

[On other theatrical performance; health and golf]

A couple of days later, she took up the theme again and then went on to discuss work and plans to meet, adding: "By the by do find out if anything was ever done about yr Gran's debts as regards people like Cooper..."

1 Lyons Tea Rooms (1894 to 1981) at this date were popular eating places known for their interior decoration and smartly uniformed waitresses known as "Nippies".

October 11th, 1934

[Health, cures – past and present: "...the long Florentine winter of 1883-4 when, if ever anything seemed certain, it was that I should become a cripple..."; that sorrow not happiness is the natural condition of life]

I'm going forth in an hour to the rehearsal. Don Godfrey is here and says the strings are, well, non existent! And how dear Goss the permanent capellmeister could ask me to play "The Cliffs"[1] which needs above all heaps of strings I cannot conceive. I also conduct Fête Galante which will be all right – but will be what your friend Kant calls "an object of appearance", my small frisettes[2] having been forgotten, so that the wig will be on the voluminous side......

[On the possibility of EMW coming; travel plans]

The Everest Book![3] I have ordered it – if it thrills a poor wretch like you who have never (have you?) done mountain climbing, to me it will be so unbearably exciting as to keep me awake. And yet my work just now is very exciting – I mean at this moment – urged on by Betty who says my Rabelaisian view [?] specially delights her – I am trying to hint at the realities, for a woman, of being... "deflowered" (!) without risking the incarceration to which the Polish Count[4] was relegated !!

Yr E

ES was still much exercised about her finances and, on October 29th, Hilaire Belloc wrote her an extremely sensible letter of advice on the expenses of a composer and writer; see *Ethel Smyth*, Christopher St John, London, 1959, pp.280-1.

1 *On the Cliffs of Cornwall* (1908) – rearranged prelude from *The Wreckers*.
2 *Frisettes* - little bunches of false curls .
3 Hugh Rutledge (1884-1961) *Everest: the unfinished adventure*, London, 1934 - the account of the unsuccessful British expedition the previous year. One of the sherpas was Tenzing Norgay, who later accompanied Edmund Hilary in 1953.
4 In February 1932, the eccentric Count Potocki de Montalk (1903-1997), although supported by the Woolfs, was sentenced to six months in Wormwood Scrubs for trying to have 50 copies of his poems, deemed obscene, produced privately, oddly enough by the printer of the *Methodist Recorder*. In 1943, he tried to tell the truth about the massacre at Katyn in his *Katyn Manifesto*, but was again imprisoned on grounds of national security, since he tried to reveal that the massacre was ordered by Stalin, not the Nazis.

November 4th, 1934

[On meeting; Vita Sackville-West's address]

I rather expect she flies down home after the lecture as Virginia told me she (Vit) had persuaded her (Vir) to lunch with her which Vir hates and that Virg who wants to have Vit to herself (as Vita also desires) had agreed. So I suppose the ineffable Gwen[1] has to be conveyed down, back to Sissinghurst, the moment Vita has done her lecture! (O Lord!)

Your E

1 Gwen St Aubyn - see below.

November 19th, 1934

My darling Eliz I am delirious with joy that you can come to the Prison, I dared not ask you knowing your commitments but think you must be joking when you ask whether I should "like" you to come!

[Travel and hotel arrangements, for ES and her guests complicated by the Royal Wedding[1]]

Evidently you quite bowled Virginia over and she was thrilled by your astronomy. I am so exceeding glad that V. should get into touch with you as there's nothing of tht kind in her repertory so far – and I like your liking Lady R. She is one of the very best and V used to despise her (whereat I was indignant) What was yr impression of "Shireen"?[2] A little "type streets" as Lady P.[onsonby] used to say don't you think? In fact there's nothing to quite account for the infatuation. But then there never is!

[Health and more arrangements]

1 Prince George, Duke of Kent and Princess Marina of Greece, cousin of Prince Philip, Duke of Edinburgh, were married on 29.11.1934.
2 Ethel intensely disliked Vita Sackville-West's sister-in-law Gwen St Aubyn. "Shirin" was Vita's pet name for Gwen and also refers to a character in her roman à clef, *The Dark Island*, which had been published by the Hogarth Press earlier in 1934.

November 21st, 1934

Darling Elizabeth I wish you'd sent Virginia's love letter: I'd have returned it O so safely!

[On tracking down an anecdote concerning a friend of Elizabeth's mother, Irene Carisbrooke. E.F.Benson dedicated two of his "Lucia" novels to her]

November 23rd, 1934

My darling Eliz
Yes this is a letter to gratify the recipient to the core – and I really do think you can give V a good deal. So many bits of her brain or her heart seem to me waste land and she's not built on G.Moore lines – that "facts that do not fit into my lecture" shd be rejected.
I feel Maurice has been dragged into the P[rince]ss Marina train and wont turn up till the performance – if so this provokes me and I've sent him a p.c. of what may turn out to be a scale turning nature...

[What to read on the train and general arrangements]

Among various notes on the back of the envelope:

Shall love to meet Irene Carrisbrooke¹ the minute "Prison" is over. Cant you make her ask us to lunch?

1 Irene "Iris" Francis Adza Denison married Alexander Mountbatten, 1st Marquess of Carisbrooke. a grandson of Queen Victoria, in 1917.

December 11th, 1934

Darling <u>I can't</u>. Not because of deafness – I know you'd put up with that but because of the 15 piles of old letters in heaps perched in a circle round this room. You know I'm writing <u>2</u> books (!)....

[Health and bad weather]

December 15th, 1934

Scribbled out at the top "My dear Fritz am I going dotty?"

[Long account of health problems and medical treatment]

A delightful lunch at E Cunard ¹ who really is a good sort thrilled about what T.[homas] B.[eecham]said about the Prison – and about his being so keen on my doing his "portrait" in my new booklet. I think she'll support the Women's Orchestra. All Ponsonbys enchanted (so far) with my portrait of Lady P (it is good I think) but now I have to cry off that book and start the other – <u>Essays and all sorts</u>. Great fun 30 000 words – to appear in May – name <u>Salvage</u>. Then I shall go on with the big book to come out any time in the season Sep 1935 – May '36 called "<u>As Time Went On</u>..." sequel to "Impressions that Remained". I shant be able to raise my head from the table till the end of March.

[Too busy to go to Cromer; delighted by an amateur discovering a new star]

Enchanting 2 hours with Virginia on Thurs. She's in despair about Vita's literary dégringolade. "Shireen" has brought "our book" no luck (i.e. it doesn't sell) and the Hogarth Press will have to....well. You can imagine. Virginia thinks Vita will drop literature and take to slum-work à la Shireen!!! (Private!)

All luck and love to Elinor. I did give the poor creature "Imps" didn't I? or did I hesitate to contribute a last straw to her luggage (??<u>Tell me this</u>)

Yr E

(I might and will send it out to India when you have her address.)

---

1 Lady Maud Cunard (1872-1948), known as Emerald, was an American heiress and society hostess, a supporter of Wallis Simpson. She had long relationships with George Moore and, subsequently, Thomas Beecham, whose musical projects she frequently subsidized. Her daughter, Nancy, was to become well-known as a political activist, and as a figure in the avant-garde world of art and literature, particularly after she set up the Hours Press.

1935

These letters, with 1936, were loose at the bottom of the trunk, the elastic round them having perished – however they seem to have been grouped together. As usual, Ethel's are from Coign and Elizabeth's from Mount Mascal, unless otherwise mentioned.

January 1st, 1935

In 1935, there was apparently not the usual exchange of long letters between Coign and Cromer. On New Year's Day, Ethel wrote briefly about Halley's comet and social events, adding:

> I sent off the T[homas].B[eecham] article to typist yesty and now in Egypt[1] and have to stick to it. For the moment am <u>very</u> overtired....

One reason for her exhaustion was that she had been hit with a bill for back taxes that was vast in comparison to her slender means and, terrified that she might lose her home as a result, she felt obliged to take on every piece of work she could, in spite of being well into her seventies. In her uncertainty about whether her small annuity would continue after the death of Mary Dodge[2], and fear that it might be reduced, she also felt compelled to such economies as not taking a taxi – already a rarity for her - even if it were raining, cutting back on the occasional glass of wine, and so on.

1 A reference to ES's *Beecham and Pharaoh* that came out later in the year.
2 Although seriously affected by the Depression, her support for ES did in fact continue even after her death on Christmas Eve, 1934. See also September 2nd, 1931 and below, January 14th and 15th.

January 6th, 1935

[Health]

> I had a huge spate of Christmas visitors and but for the Foie Gras don't know what I shd have done. Or perhaps it would be more correct to say that without Beecham, Douglas, Nelly and Violet (in succession) to partake of the Pâté I myself shd have been done for I can't observe moderation with Foie Gras. This was the best I ever had – I wonder where it came from? It was the outside crust instead of glass or china that did it I imagine. The clever ones are riveted with Steeds[1] book No 2 "The Meaning of Hitlerism" and I've just lent them no.1 "Hitler" which I think is masterly. I cant write – too tired after a 4 mile walk and the idea of having to do the books....

[Golf with Joyce Wethered and her forthcoming book]

1 Henry Wickham Steed (1871-1956) published *Hitler* in 1934 and *The Meaning of Hitlerism* later in the same year. He was subsequently to write other works on the subject.

January 14th, 1935

Its no good darling I <u>cant</u> take my mind off this pistol at head job but don't give up sending me beautiful poems. I cant go to London – cant even write to Virginia <u>but tell me about the party</u>. The publisher is being a little tiresome about trying to bind me to write him a 50 000 word book and I had never promised more than <u>30 000</u>......Miss Dodge bless her continues an annuity from the grave but I don't know if it will [be] the same sum. I hope so. (Once I've got farther on in "Egypt" I shall be more human) Yr E

January 15th, 1935

[Thanking EMW for two poems she has sent]

I'm going on steadily and I think working awfully well. The words come easily. But both T.B. and Egypt (for I am turning all my letters to Mrs P.[ankhurst], fortunately very detailed into ordinary narrative – like Imps or Streaks or anything else) are hard work and I always have the panic I shant get done in time. And again such shocks as finding when I thought I'd written 15 000 words that it was only 12 000! I've been reading nothing but Hitler books – 2 German and 2 English. I think the Germans are a spectacle to make the Angels weep.

[On a quote from Phineas Fletcher (1633): "To cry for vengeance Sinne doth never cease"]

Did I tell you Miss D[odge]'s subsidy goes on tho' whether the same sum as before I know not yet. God bless her - E

January 23th, 1935

> 52 Tavistock Square
> Wednesday

Dear Elizabeth,

How very nice of you to enjoy that party! It was too much of a scramble and a bear garden and no chairs and not enough drinks and too many unknown people, I thought. But then my own parties always show the carpet the wrong way round. Also I felt I ought to have explained beforehand that the 'play' was only a joke hastily rigged up to give my Niece (yes, she's Angelica, Vanessa's daughter) a lark before going back to school. It was mere family jokes: not meant to ridicule anybody, certainly not the P.M., whom I think a most lovable man in many ways, but then the people were in fact, from the life, my own great grand parents, and aunts, so the jokes were mostly, I think, unintelligible. All the more thanks to you then, student of Ptolemy and the stars, for lending your eyes to these daisies, slugs and very ruinate scraps of glass, such as one picked up on the beach, thought they would always look like emeralds, even out of the sea.

I'm in such a hurry that I cannot finish a sentence.

> Yr
> VW

And do come and see me: and of course you can read the play[1]. Do you think Angelica has any dramatic gift? Her great passion is to go on stage.

1 This was Virginia Woolf's play *Freshwater*, dealing with the life of Her great-aunt, the photographer Julia Cameron, performed before friends at Vanessa's studio at 8 Fitzroy St on January 18th, 1935. Late 1934-early 1935 had been a bad time for VW, with the death of Roger Fry and Wyndham Lewis' criticism.

Thursday, January 24th, [1935]

My darling Aunt,

Yes isn't Sam Johnson superb. I don't think any book so

bowls you along as the Poets[1]. I suppose your select edition includes Savage, one of the very best to my mind. I feel his style so mirrors forth his greatness as a mind, it so shines with his goodness, crashes with his violence and turns neatly to close his arguments with his good sense. I feel taller, better looking and cleverer when I am reading him, I suppose because he heightens my vitality with his own superabundance!

[On her back problems and possible help to cope with ES's deafness]

I had a charming letter from V. quite unnecessarily answering a brief letter from me saying how amused I was by the play. She says all the jokes were family ones taken from her great grandparents.

Yr
E

---

1 Samuel Johnson (1709-1784). *Lives of the Poets* (6vols., 1779-81) was a great favourite of EMW's.

February 2nd, [1935]

Early in February, Virginia Woolf wrote to Elizabeth showing unusual concern for Ethel.

52 Tavistock Square

My dear Elizabeth,

I am so distressed to hear from Ethel that she has to pay this vast sum. I suppose nothing can be done about it? She says she absolutely refuses to take a penny or the obvious thing would be to get a subscription – as I'm sure one could. I wonder if anything occurs to you that could be worked? She was so set against sympathy, firm about being independent that I cant see any way at the moment.

But it is an awful thought – finding all that out at her own [?]: - the possibility that she may have to give up Coign.

So I send you this line - rather hopelessly. Still do let us consider something.

Yr
VW

Wednesday, February 6th, 1935

My darling Aunt,

Vesey [1] is better and quite cheery in himself. He is only allowed milk while his temperature is up and yesterday said sadly "Does nobody care that I am <u>ravenous</u>?" They say he may fluctuate a bit but so far we are daring to hope he is not going to be dangerously ill. Phyllis sends her best love and bids me say that the extra blow of not having you this week end when you could have come has almost broken her spirit!

Meanwhile Martin and I console each other in our forced absence from London by playing golf. Both our quarantines last until Monday, my test having come out mildly positive.

As to your affairs it does sound a horrible lot. Oh dear oh dear. I suppose a bank loan is your best way as money is cheap.

It is splendid your having got through your labours with time to spare. I have been thinking of you a lot although not writing much because of disturbing you.

I devoted nearly a whole day last week to tidying up my papers and letters which had begun to overflow in a tiresome way, I have now yearly bundles of letters from you from 1923 onwards amounting in all to about 360! The task of rooting in one's past always induces a mood of "Alas poor Yorick" and I hadn't the heart to read the many letters in 1925 recording Greek plans and then Greek memories! I found some very vitriolic blasphemies about Paradise Lost which made me rock with laughter. But I am still surprised that in spite of Milton's unsympathetic Weltanschauming you can get no thrill from is splendours of diction. I <u>do</u> – such a big one.

Last week I went to tea with Virginia, just her and L. and they were at their very nicest and I felt really fond of V as distinct from being excited and impressed by her. My what charm! Phew!

At last letters from Elinor are beginning. The place sounds divine and she radiant. I shall GO THERE unless prevented by some undefeatable obstruction.

[On the health and whereabouts of various members of the family]

Yr
E

1 Vesey Holt – see December 8th, 1931.

February 14th, 1935

My darling Elizabeth

[Health – hers and others']

Well as I was free after 4 on Tues, as I had no script that day and went to see Virginia who was quite quite adorable. I now begin to feel that she really does know who one is – a thing I had given up hoping for. And the old proverb or rather the old saints' wisdom has once more [proved ?] itself 'run away from God and you will find him'....

[On Shakespeare's sonnets and other poems. Her inability to read anything much except "political books like "Peace with Honor", by A.A. Milne, which had just come out and something "about The Philosophy of Hitlerism" – perhaps Emmanuel Levinas?]

Do tell me this – All my 'Egypt' – I am star mad. Were you star mad before 1913-14? I wd so love to think my star madness .....and all was connected with you. Rather that you put me on to the stars, or that my frenzy enkindled you more. Tell me. You'll like this new book of mine – specially Egypt (alas! Vernon!) I think.

On the back of the envelope.

Did you see Leonard's marmoset? I think it is the most entrancingly uncanny thing I ever saw.

(Later)

I had a piteous letter from old Marchesi[1] and am taking a ticket for and going to her concert in Regents Park on Sunday next 5.30! (Oh)

1 Presumably the singer Blanche Marchesi (1863-1940), daughter of the famous singing teacher, Mathilde Marchesi, who taught Nelly Melba, among many others. They were all friends of ES. Blanche Marchesi gave her farewell concert in 1938. At an earlier date, ES had said of her, *à propos The Wreckers*: "But if the concert seemed unlikely to cost more than £400....it was partly owing to the refusal of Blanche Marchesi, one of the largest-souled artists I have known, to accept a fee."

Friday, February 15th, 1935

My darling Aunt,

Re the stars. I barely knew they existed at the epoch you mention and only became star mad at the age of 16, viz in 1917. Then far from me inspiring you, it was you who sent me Nortons' Star Atlas[1], which I use constantly still.

I <u>deplore</u> your jaunt to the Regents Park concert. I suppose it is not out of doors!! It sounds to me crazy.

[On Milton]

I can't bear for long that you shouldn't read my King's Exequy and shall probably end by writing it out for you. Anyhow I shall bring the book when (????) I see you next. I don't suppose you realize having been so busy, the aeons of time it is since we met. Long before Christmas, and it has felt to me as if you had entered the cloister – not died but lost!

Vernon![2] R.I.P. Maurice has a "piece" about her in today's' Times which I enclose. The last time I saw her was in '22. I think when Nunky[3] and I were in Florence. We walked up the hill in blazing heat and had tea with her, and she was so dear and distinguished with the most effective "thought-out untidy" clothes – an enormous felt hat and satin tie. I shall never forget the nastiness of the meal we ate, consisting of tepid tea and biscuits apparently soaked in motor oil.

Yes I love the marmoset. It ran down the step stairs to meet me thinking I might be Leonard whom it adores evidently. V and I had quite a job to catch it, and when L came in it never left his knee or arm again.

[On reading Henry IV*]*

Don't bother to send Hitlerism as I could read it when I am next at Coign and at the moment am too poetical and metaphysical and 17th Century for it. I am in the reverse mood to "The cat is on the mat" and quite lost in the subtleties of the life of the imagination. Or rather the statement "The cat is on the mat" is invested for me with all the mystery of the world. There is nothing in the wildest flights of the fancy more extraordinary and <u>unlikely</u> than the *brute* existence of the Milky Way. And because poetry whisks one off the ground and sets things vibrating and shimmering it is more true than prose. Aristotle who I now think is ALWAYS RIGHT (on serious subjects – not on astronomy!) said that "Poetry is the most philosophical of all writing". Of course it is because it makes you feel as well as think that the world of the senses is transparent and glowing and evanescent and all that Plato thought it was.

I had better stop this and revert to Claudius Ptolomaeus – he puts one back on the mat all right!

Yr E

1 Probably the most famous star atlas for amateur use throughout the 20th c., it was first published in 1910.
2 Vernon Lee had died on the 13th February.
3 Sir Hedworth Williamson (See Introduction)

February 18th, 1935

[On her deafness and possible remedies – "I quite believe that it is curable. But music now sounds to me like two very naughty children banging about on a worn out piano."]

Virginia and Leonard motored (from Rodmell) in a snow storm to call at Lesbos Proper (Sissinghurst) last Saturday! I wonder how it went off. What I minded most about "Joan"[1] was Gwen [St Aubin] being supposed to "help" with religion!!! Fancy if Mr B wrote a life of Disraeli and his great friend Mr C "helped" with the politics!!

Your E

1 Vita Sackville West was working on a biography: *Saint Joan of Arc* (1936).

And in a further note, apparently written on the same day, Ethel adds

> We'll drain a cup to my new book...and I think I shall make you read of my star passion in Egypt unless you hate typescript! (mine's very good and I have a second copy)

And a couple of days later, uncharacteristically

> You know I am wholly unoccupied just now – on principle. Merely drifting. Did I ask you whether you'd like a ticket for Henry IV? If so I have one for you.

March 3rd 1935

Followed by a postcard, perhaps sent March 3rd.

> ...as I have no time for reading just now and have 2 rather thrilling books on the side table I wish you'd bring Lady G. Wellesley[1] "10 Years of Poetry" I wonder if they are good. They are wildly praised but up to now all she wrote had for me a slightly unpleasant twang – a certain touch of inbred sensationalism – of love of carrion. But I may have misjudged her...as I didn't like her much. E"

1 Dorothy Wellesley (1889-1956), Duchess of Wellington, was the lover of Vita Sackville West, Hilda Matheson and others. She wrote several volumes of poetry -ES presumably meant *Poems of Ten Years* (1934). Yeats considered her one of the greatest writers of the age, but his opinion is not generally shared. She was editor of the *Hogarth Living Poets* series for the Hogarth Press.

March 4th, 1935

> My darling Elizabeth I was so glad of your letter and think all agree that Robey [1] will end by being a fine Falstaff. Myself I wonder whether he has the exuberant vein that F. must have. What do you think?

I did go to the Cliffs [?] yesty because Virginia wanted me to and asked me to lunch and go with her. B played it <u>superbly</u> and did a wonderful dear kind thing I cant tell you about it now as it – the kind thing – involves a long letter to [?] (technical) V. was adorable. I couldn't hear enough to be of any use but I <u>saw</u> how finely he did it and that the public liked it awfully. V. said they yelled but that I didn't hear.

How I rejoice in your letters. More tomorrow

E

1 George Robey (1869-1954), a well-known comedian, attempted Shakespeare for the first time aged 66, as Falstaff in *Henry IV Part I*.

March 12th, 1935

Its not to be a short biography of Joan – but a big book. I had a dear letter from Vita today saying she and Gwen thought I was "so right" in all essential matters and sending me some wine (to go with Gwens oysters!). And so I said to her I thought the idea of Gwen "helping her as to the religious part" (!!) lamentable – and what's more I believed G that I cant[1] do sound work like that. I said (very gently) "If you are going to give up your life to "<u>anything</u> you can do <u>with Gwen</u>" well and good. Perhaps you're quite wise. But don't let the author of Sissinghurst and The Land[2] etc imagine that a sentimental schoolgirlish cooperation can produce anything worthy of that author. If you have lost ambition for the 1st rate, well and good, but do not deceive yourself. God is not mocked."

1 Four illegible words.
2 Poems published in 1931 and 1926 respectively.

April 9th, 1935

My darling Elizabeth I'm so fired by your words about The Waves that I am taking it to me to Wootton...a sort of holiday task!! – and going to have a 3rd go at it. But in your letter you put your finger on what is for me radical impediment to real pleasure in it, quite apart from the canary brain limitations. And oddly enough I have just been rereading vols of Heine[1] (of whose works I have a complete edition and whose analyses of the German Philosophers – and Romantics too – would interest you but alas its in German – for once a well printed edition too.) In these disquisitions of his are things that make you die of laughter – his comparisons between English, French and German ways – and all are deeply scored by me. For I was mad about Heine in my youth. But even then I couldn't stick the pessimism of his outlook, though being a Jew (this remark must be taken as gliding over people like Leonard and Moses Mendelssohn [2]) he has a far greater sense of things spiritual than Virginia. I frankly tell you I cannot care for anything that pokes you down still deeper in the slough of despond. Beauty is no help at all. Life is so cruel that, as we have to live it, we may surely be forgiven for this angle towards philosophers that increase our difficulty. We are all patients who cannot pull through if the doctor and all our friends are constantly telling us we are dying – I'm speaking of one not sick unto death, of course – Now Shakespeare never gives me this feeling of despair – not in Lear not in Hamlet – nowhere (Heine is very interesting journalising [?] over the plays) – nor does Montaigne, nor Goethe. <u>Why is that</u>? Tell me? I suppose because even the latter was under Xtian influence ....and like Napoleon felt in impossible to disbelieve in God. Anyhow my feeling is that...I allow it is weak...that one is so nearly drowning often in a sea of trouble, that one roseleaf of pessimism of the deadly Virginia spirit in such things, is enough to poke you under. And in spite of canary brain limitations HB does the reverse even to me. [In an almost illegible scrawl]The bus is nearly due I must stop. So sorry for yr mother. As you may guess by now I am a National Monument in that I can break but not

bend! I laugh now to think of my golf attempt on Wed! Do write to Wootton Manor Polegate Surrey
I may stay a week but probably home on Sunday 14th
Yr E

[On her reaction to The Waves, et al.]

1 Heinrich Heine (1797-1856) German poet, many of whose works were set to music, and radical political thinker. He also wrote on Shakespeare, particularly his heroines.
2 Moses Mendelssohn (1729-86) German Jewish philosopher, influential in the establishment of Reform Judaism.

April 17th, 1935

My darling Elizabeth I only got home yesty – motored over by beloved Miss Hudson to find Pan swept and garnished and looking so like a god that I felt touched as never before by the condescension of his welcome.

[Health, appointments, her preference for Sussex]

By the by did you see that the Hellenic Travellers (Lunn's boat) after terrific weather ran into a sandbank off Patras and while it was being got off I believe all the Lunnites including the Nicolson-Gwen lot went to Olympia. I didn't write to you from Wootton because, after the long break and the Income Tax tussling, I felt if I didn't at once tackle "As Time Went On" I never should. And while there I actually wrote 4 new chapters – not too bad I think – and wrote no letters.

I think never has a letter thrilled me more than your statement of your position and by your art you have actually made it graspable to me. It seems to me to state in learned language exactly what in my confused way (Esther Summers![1]) I feel myself.

[On Greek etymologies]

My real reason for not caring for 'The Waves' is because that world is not one that I can feel well in – and there's nothing for it to "get [?] back to one's top". This time again I gave it up after 50 pages or so...and O I had a vicious letter from Virginia saying she didn't care what I thought about her books because if I liked them at all it was through knowing her...but your appreciation of The Waves gave her real pleasure. In London yesty (she's just off to R.[odmell] for Easter) I rang her up and forgave her when I heard her delighted chuckle "I knew that would enrage you! That's why I said it!" I told her I'd replied in kind then thought she shd not have the gratification of knowing she had succeeded. "O Ethel – send me the letter!" "I tore it up" "Then write it again"! but I haven't time, nor will I pander to her. She really is, as Mary says of her neighbours dog "too wickudd: in fact a divil" ....and as I shall tell her if I have time the only reason one is fond of her is because of her writing! I think the fact is she does bitterly resent my not caring for either The Waves or....Flush!!

[On Hilaire Belloc's Milton, *which had just come out – "I cannot understand why in this particular case his style annoys you."]*

Poor poor Charles – what a painful disease! He will have to be like Vernon's father – never sit down again in this world[2]. O. I was thrilled by Belloc stating that that Arian and generally heretical tract of Miltons must really have been written in his prime but was hushed up. Do you agree. How glad I am yr back stands Cromer! And is yr mother all right? And was she able to cope with her party on the 15th ?

Yr E

1 Esther Summerson, the heroine of *Bleak House*.
2 Vernon Lee's father, Henry Ferguson Paget, had been her half-brother's tutor and married her mother after her first husband's death. The reference here is obscure.

April 23rd, 1935

[Literary discussion, but too elliptic to be easily followed in view of missing sections of the correspondence]

Tell me how your Mother is. – I dislike extremely her being "none too well" And can poor Charles now sit down or is he still like Vernon's father who (not for the same reason) used to be sent out at 8 a.m. by Mr Paget with 1 lira and never returned until midnight (having eaten in trattorie). For poor Mr Paget cd not sit down...which accounts for the brother of Vernon being unable to get up[1] (as you may remember). The main problem – how he and Vernon came into this restless world none the less has never been solved.

E

Ethel, and even more so Elizabeth, had the habit of copying out favourite poems and other passages and sending them to each other – and to friends, in this case, the "Orison of St Augustine in the Night", a great favourite of Elizabeth's. The date April 23rd - Shakespeare's death day - was of also of particular significance for her and she always marked it.

There are probably missing letters, but Ethel seems to have responded:

> Maurice read "National Velvet"[1] d'un trait!! I haven't got it yet"

[1] Vernon Lee's half-brother, Eugene Lee-Hamilton, remained prostrate as an invalid for much of his life apparently with some hysterical form of paralysis, since he periodically recovered when there was something he wanted to do, eventually marrying and producing a family after the death of his mother.
[2] *National Velvet* by Enid Bagnold, the story of a 14 year old girl who rides a horse to victory in the Grand National, came out in 1935 and was a best seller. It was later made into a film with the 12 year old Elizabeth Taylor as the heroine.

May 3rd, 1935

Darling Eliz. I'm groaning under the weight of commitments that however mean £.s.d. and take up all my time – I cant even finish W.S. sonnets and write about them – O there are so many I love best. Anyhow here's yr hank. As that's something accomplished something done.

The commitments are

1) an accpt to be written by me for Purcell's "Fairest Isle" for the Kings Concert 25 May. (no fee!)

2) A lecture, 13m. BBC on the programme of 13th June £10.10

3) Six articles of 2000 words each on music and all that. Quite easy to do. To be syndicated and me to get 50% of the

takings. They offered me a minimum fee of £15.15 per article but I am sticking out for 20gns. per article and I think I shall get it. £121

(This may swell to be a lot more but the articles **shall** be good if I can make them so)

Meanwhile am (or was) getting on with "As Time Went On"....[*medical appointments*]..and O London is Hell.

About the 1) Commitment – it's a concert of Engl. music since Tudor times and I have been set to (as it were) polish up Purcell's boots to smooth me down for not having been asked to contribute. But I think it wd be small to refuse. Only I am so off music now.

I am horror struck at Henry Wood having cut himself off from his wife and family – (who are and ever were maddening – But she adored him and has slaved for him. Damn his eyes) They went to Rome (he to conduct). She went on to Sicily to recoup – you know she had a bad taxi smash wh. made her more nervy and impossible than ever. Then one day (in Sicily) she gets a letter from bank to say she may draw no more cheques and then got another from lawyers to say all communication to be through them. Henry has joined forces with another woman and put up both houses for sale. (The lovely garden at Chorleywood was Muriel Wood's passion). Muriel has enough to live on. He has behaved like a coward and a cad pretending up to the last devotion and...funking a scene. The woman is about Muriel's age (48?) and musical. I am desperately sorry for Muriel whom I believe really adores H. and with all her tempers etc. has real depth of feeling. (I had some years ago ceased to trust H. but I did not think he'd do this.)

All this horrifies me. I'm sure she led him a hell of a life latterly and I suppose he got fed up....and suddenly determined on this very ugly way out of it. I heard it from G. Steel who knew her before her marriage. I don't even know Muriel's address....but hear she is at Hastings. I feel I must write to her, for come what may Henry has behaved shamefully. I suppose the woman (musical) took on Muriel's jobs when she was in the Nursing Home – and H's feeling was "peace perfect peace".[1]

> Yea, verily Maud's Apollo is fashioned of aloes & soap
> A lovely pill to swallow while bowels refuse to ope
> A shilling box produces a music so soft & intense
> That all the Mayfair muses hear with an inner sense
> This very privy Apollo whose lyre is the entrails of Man
> With pallid faces, & hollow they hie to the nethermost shade
> Where the baton of Thomas urges the orchestra now in Typhu
> So great is the strength of the purges that he signs to
> ~~and calls on the fiddler~~ the big bassoon
> and calls on the fiddles to squitter and demands from
> the flute B. Sharp
> He gets it & cries this is better than Apollo's golden
> harp.
> Apollo may reign in Parnassus & sit on the Grecian hill
> But we reign o'er the Stool, God praise us
> My father & I & the Pill.

George Moore's Verse on Beecham's Pills

I had a jolly little meeting with Virginia who went off last week with L – on a cross country trip to Rome and comes back June 1st. I was able to give her an adv. copy of what Maurice calls "Pharoah's Pills"[2] and hope to hear from her abt it soon. Maurice wrote divinely about it. Nina is a little shocked at parts of Egypt!! I've too much to do for life.

Bless you
Yr E

I think V. said she had had a very interesting letter from you...or am I dreaming. She'd been having headaches again.

[On meeting and matters of health]

1 In 1934, separated from his second wife who refused him a divorce, Henry Wood began a long relationship with a widowed pupil, Jessie Linton, who changed her name to "Lady Jessie Wood", so that she would appear to be his wife. See also January 2nd, 1929.
2 Beecham's Pills were a laxative invented in 1842 by the grandfather of Thomas Beecham. Their manufacture was discontinued in 1998.

May 8th, 1935

My darling Elizabeth

I've broken the record in things I've promised to do – God help me - by June 1. I cant stop to write for 2 of these commitments lie heavy on my spirit like lead – and every sort of amazing thing has happened

1) Maurice has sent me a cheque for £900! Was there ever such a man? I've told him I'll take it if he will let me pay back bits if I make extra money – from time to time.

2) Henry Wood has apparently gone mad and Muriel W. received a letter from a lawyer and one from a banker while she was in Italy (they parted at Rome after his 3 concerts – she to recoup still farther at Taormina) saying he had come together with another (musical) woman, cut himself off from her and the two girls, and put up the two houses (including the lovely farm house of which she made – and was mad about – the garden) for sale – He is 67....She worshipped him and has slaved for him all her life. She has been very "trying" specially of late – and has a violent temper. He's apparently an adoring husband! He has behaved like a coward (he is that...I know that) and as a cad unspeakable. This shakes me to the foundation and I think worse of Love than ever!

Yr E

On a separate sheet in the same envelope, very possibly from a different letter, as there is little connection.

[On her favourite sonnets]

I think Beecham and Pharoah is out now but am not sure. Maurice says my style of writing annihilates criticism. Nothing from Virginia – lazy beast – She specially asked to have an advance copy and so far not one word.

I know she'll like it so its just inertia. When I have done 2 <u>awful</u> jobs (one musical for Kings Command Concert[1]) I shall clamour to see you.

[Plans to go to the Old Vic, among other things to try out a hearing aid. And – mysteriously – perhaps connected with the Jubilee celebrations or a missing page]

St Pauls?...bad seat. Sat St Paul's Churchyard amazing – the roofs thick with people like flies on a beggars sores in Egypt

1 The first item in the King's Command Concert at the Albert Hall on May 24th 1935 was "Fairest Isle" scored by Dame Ethel Smyth sung by Miss Elsie Suddaby. See *The Musical Times* for July 1935, p.851 for details of the programme.

May 9th, 1935

Darling Elizabeth. Maurice has sent me £900! <u>I am speechless</u>.....

[Medical appointments]

...after that I am perhaps flying/rushing to Chalk Farm to talk to the Principal of Westfield College[1]... [repeat of the Henry Wood situation]...the Principal is a friend of Muriel's – a grave sound woman. Then I am going to dine at the Forum[2] (or perhaps at No. 40 and see the floodlighting. <u>I know it is worth it</u>....

[Plans to meet]

On the back of the envelope:

A nice review in Lit Sup today praising "Egypt" of which I am specially glad as I know its of my best stuff.

1 Dorothy Chapman, a classicist. It is not clear why ES so disliked her (see below).
2 Art Deco concert venue in Kentish Town opened in 1934.

May 11th, 1935

I think I have never been so ashamed of myself as for our idiotic timing yest [?]...<u>Of course</u> we ought to have gone at once/straight from <u>our</u> side (Victoria) to B. Palace where we emerged so easily yesterday and wd have seen so well.[1] And we shd have been there on the stroke on 9. Why did we assume they wd appear at 10.30? They only did that once after a banquet. I was slack and stupid or this wd not have happened thanks to a de-oxygenized brain – result of that awful woman at Westfield Coll: Lord – how I'd have liked to <u>shake</u> her! One felt all the students wd prostrate themselves before her too...O lord what a dud as human being.

Yr E

1 Celebration connected with the Silver Jubilee of King George V and Queen Mary, who occasionally came to tea with the family in the Isle of Wight.

May 16th, 1935

My darling Elizabeth I rather wonder if like me almost any book about Greece – the bits we know – has fascination for <u>you.</u> That book (Greek Salad)[1] though I rather dislike the writer did rather thrill me, utterly unappreciative tho' he was of Meteora (did you know that Megaspilion[2], unbeknownst to the monks still had masses of powder in the cellars from the time of the War of Independence – that a spark ignited it and the place blew itself up about 1930. Fancy if that wonderful treasure has been wrecked (about details of that kind he is tiresomely silent). But fancy: you know when we were marooned at Paros, well just round the corner on the island of Spetsae beyond Hydra is (or was) a Greek Eton and Harrow[3] run by an Englishman and this Matthews was assistant headmaster there for years. I believe while we were at Poros he and his wife who he says is lovely were there. And before that they had gone from Kala[m]baka over the Pindus to Jannina <u>and Dodona</u>. Being still Greece mad (I mean interested in modern Greece on which this book throws light)

I was deeply interested in it. Tho' now I come to think of it these adventures must have been later than ours as he quotes the 3 legged tour.

[On an unsuccessful attempt to use a hearing aid; again regrets at having missed the Royal Jubilee celebration]

Vita's nice friend who used to be head of the talks at the B.B.C. – Hilda Matheson – is lunching here on her way to Oxford on Sat. did I tell you the lovers are separated – Gwen away from Sissinghurst until the middle of June! I shall be curious to learn how this was brought about. I am rather overwhelmed at the thought of the dinner for the B.W. Sym-Orch [4] on Tuesday 21st. To sit through a long clatter of plates....through speeches you can't hear (Beecham and Lady Ravensdale are both speaking) and music which is torture to listen to...this I am doing for the sake of that band and I confidently look for a good place in heaven by and by. I have myself to thank 4 people in a 4 minute speech. But I've finished orchestrating that deadly "Fairest isle" for the Kings Concert and hope there is no necessity to be present (Albert Hall 25th(?) May I think)

[On going up to London and medical matters]

Yr E

[1] Kenneth Albert Matthews (1908-1994), classicist and BBC's Balkans expert, published *Greek Salad* in 1935.
[2] Mega Spileo (the Great Cave) monastery founded in 326 A.D. The last in a long series of fires, before its destruction by the Germans, seems to have been 1934.
[3] The prestigious Anargyrios and Korgialeneios School of Spetses was founded in 1927 and closed in 1983; John Fowles taught there in the 1950s.
[4] British Women's Symphony Orchestra see www.britishpathe.com for video clip from April 1934.

May 22nd, 1935

I forgot to tell you I've been knocked endways by a book called "Speak to the Earth"[1] (a woman who lived alone with tigers and elephants in the bush in Kenya). I never read a book like that and it makes me feel so ashamed of my worldliness! So cheap! E

1 Vivienne de Watteville (1900-1957) *Speak to the Earth: Wandering and Reflections among Elephants and Mountains* (1935). After her father was killed by a lion on an expedition (1923) to obtain specimens for the Berne Museum of Natural History, she continued alone and wrote an account of her experiences: *Out In the Blue* (1927).

May 26th, 1935

No I didn't think jungle life as such wd interest you (It does me of course) I'm now reading her previous book – when her adorable father aged 46 – a naturalist and a hunter – was mauled by a lion, and died in the jungle she, a huntress and skinner of beasts, and a medical student was 23 and was left alone with the 30 porters and lion-hunters and got through gorgeously. What fascinates me in the other book (don't laugh) is the philosophy – the absolute merging of oneself in nature..... So much of it reminds me of HB – its serenity – its failure to draw a line between life and death. A strange phenomenon a oneness with God in a form unknown to me hitherto (I mean I never came across her breed). E

Charming letter from Virginia!! But no response to a passionate letter to Ottoline!

May 29th, 1935

[On tracking down an article by von Harnack[1] in the London Library]

If you do go to the RA will you look in Gall[ery] I at 35 by Terrick Williams (Morning haze) I think it lovely. But all the Stanley Spencers (a scarecrow and two "builders" pictures) I think too hideous for words. At last I've written one of my 6 articles and hope to forge ahead now. This Henry Wood thing paralyses me with horror. I'll tell you about it by and by

Yr E

I am going with Kerridge to Fledermauss Matinée (1.30) and on the 3rd at 8.15 "Introduce" the BBC concert. Listen in and tell me if I am as husky as I sound to myself. Talk only 13 mins.!!

1 Adolph von Harnack (1851-1930) - German theologian and Church historian.
2 John Terrick Williams RA (1860-1936) a very popular painter specializing in land and seascapes. Perhaps *Morning Haze, Concarneau* c.1914, now in the Crawford Art Gallery, Cork.

June 2nd, 1935

[On the difficulties of meeting; medical matters, after which on Friday "....I go down to Vita for the night, Gwen being away!!"; literary debate]

Yes indeed I have all Marlowe – a very beautiful H.B. edition – and urged on by you have re-attacked Hero and Leander. But the fact is (and was...I can see this by my poverty stricken markings) I don't really care about rhapsodies of any sort – all except Lycidas. I mean long poems about the deceased (Adonaïs) or love...or anything. It is a form of literature – like everything else done with a pen – but if all dialogues (Lucan) – eclogues (Theocritus) sweep me up as the first page is opened, things like H. and L. are to me less enjoyable "How he does go on!" I say to myself. But just now am all "Christianity and Communism"...

[On Thomas Nashe's In Time of Pestilence *(1593)]*

I am under the shadow of the Wood tragedy – I have suspected Henry Wood of shiftiness, lying, and all that years ago but thought it was only in my honour – as importunate widow [?]. And as I knew how his truly bright light had, perforce, been doused by Beecham's genius I understood and pardoned (tho' I disliked meeting him and pretending all was well).[1] But he has shown a rottenness – a smug loathsome depravity I never saw equalled. And she loves him!! There's a line in Hero and L. about 'my love always my love'. All I can see is that seems to me gammon – clinging to your own blindness and stupidity instead of cutting your losses and beginning your life (and love) again.

Yr
E

1 Henry Wood and Thomas Beecham were notoriously not on good terms.

July 17th, 1935 [?]

Darling Elizabeth here are your stockings not very well washed I fear. Put it down to the heat or the gnats (evidently heathen; I never knew them rage so furiously) ----

I saw V. and Leonard yesty – both quite charming and V said my preface was "far too good' for Ralph's book[1]. But I think this viciousness was because he had been sent in by Leonard to mark time while L. had another interview[er?] and V. who was half asleep on the sofa was not glad to see him. L and I for once agreed about Wells' Autobiography[2] in every detail – good autobiog: but personally I couldn't finish the book.

If you still have it will you lend me my "Portrait of the Artist"? I want to show it to V. The point, the unutterably funny point, is that I rather expected you to say "<u>What an awful creature</u>!" Whereas you merely [?] echo Mary S. and say it is "<u>very good</u>". (!!) O my darling Elizabeth how I love you! It reminds me of when I took my best kimono (dinner dress!) in case Vita dressed for dinner (this was 3 or 4 years ago at Sissinghurst). And V. who unpacked for me (I forget why...no maid at the moment) put it <u>with my night</u>gown on the pillow as a bed jacket.

Yr
E

I wrote to Fritz[3] saying I couldn't remember his new name and as aid memory in order to fix the title in my brain he writes "It is Sysonby: a wag remarked I had exchanged a Po for a Sigh."

---

1 Ralph Brewster, *The 6000 Beards of Athos*, published by L. and Virginia Woolf, London, 1935.
2 H.G. Wells, *Experiment in Autobiography*, London, 1934.
3 Frederick Ponsonby was made 1st Baron Sysonby in the summer of 1935. and died four months later, on the 20th October. His wife, Victoria Lily - known as Ria, became Lady Sysonby. See Introduction.

> Ethel Smyth
> Coign
>   Woking
> (If found in a train or
> Elsewhere & returned,
> the finder will be rewarded)
>   2s.

THE STATUETTE

AND

THE BACKGROUND.

ES in her sister Violet's copy of *The Statuette*

August 7th, 1935

[Apologies for her silence – the heat, work on her book – and her bad writing – the paper. Plesch[1] "turned up bringing little Austrian sausages and grapes and beer – a delicate attention" but was learning English, which made communication difficult, especially given ES's deafness]

I was nearly dead with the effort of this sort of thing all the time. Decipher following sentence if you can. But I'll give you the context as a clue. We were speaking of Alba[2] whom he knows and he was saying how strange it was that his loves had always been tuberculous women (he gave me examples). Then I spoke of the Empress E[ugénie] whose letters I am reading – absolutely confirming all my feelings about her. (But her character before Destiny crushed her was even richer than I knew of.) I had been saying that her great preference in great-nephews was a worthless blackguard (to whom Jimmy [?] now tells me no one in Spain now speaks and who did enormous mischief between the King and Queen). I said that elderly people were often attracted by youthful rakes... and that the Empress and Piétri[3] both succumbed to this one. Plesch remarked: "Tell me this: why do old pice es loff filterteems?" After 3 or 4 times repeating, I, bewildered, said "say it in German" and found it meant "why do so many pious elderly people enjoy risky anecdotes?"..."Now say it again in English" I said to ascertain that "pice" meant "pious" and "filterteems" stood for "filthy themes". Followed a lesson in English....

[On the heat and its avoidance, and family visits]

Imagine I have suddenly fallen in love with Day Lewis and have been altogether in the poetical vein revelling in D H Lawrence and trying to like Edith Sitwell in the London Mercury[4] I met them at the Buck Pal. garden party (her and Osbert) and we regretted that I was not their mother – for their father persists in the legend that he was madly in love with one in the seventies! I told them he was tall and lanky and wore plusfours (then the only pair in England I should say) and orange stockings. (Catching sight of Edith S's locks I just refrained in time from adding "to match his hair".) They said he is now very good looking...Well - well – They knew all about you.

I'm slowly and absorbedly reading "The 7 Pillars of Wisdom" (weight 25 cwt) and tried to persuade Lincoln (via Kitty) to take me over to Devizes where they have taken a house and I do want to talk about Lawrence and what authority he had for persuading the Arabs that once they got to Damascus they wd. stay there. But Lincoln wont.[5]

[On children and her lack of empathy with them: "I can make them laugh (probably at me) but nothing comes of it afterwards"; plans to meet]

1 Clearly not the financier Árpád Plesch (1889-1974), but presumably a doctor, since appointments with him are frequently mentioned, also by Maurice Baring.
2 Don Jacobo Fitz-James Stuart y Falcó, 17th Duke of Alba de Tormes, nephew of the Empress Eugénie.
3 Franceschini Piétri, private secretary of first the Emperor and then the Empress.
4 A major literary journal from 1919-1939
5 T.E. Lawrence had died two months earlier and ES presumably wanted to go and talk with his younger brother and literary executor, A.W. Lawrence, who lived in Devizes.

August 8th, 1935

My darling Elizabeth what a brute I was not to thank you for the stockings.....

Strange to relate Leonard thinks my preface to Ralph Brewster's book "admirable" – this thro' the phone. I am not trying to see V who is in angelic mood as I do think she takes on too much and I would be another nail in her coffin. I want you to do a delicate thing for me and REMIND me if I forget – give the little dark housemaid who waits on me 2/- ! I quite forgot I had been there twice and I generally give her 2/- per night. Tell her straight out I forgot and asked you to make good. O!! Think of me sallying forth tonight for love of Maurice at 11.20!! but my dress is a dream and will quite hide the shoes (which I believe one can regild!!) Of course I'll send back the stockings......

Lv E

And by way of follow up, on a telegram form, Waterloo 9.8.35.

Darling Eliz "Lest I forget" here are the 2/- Maurice's party was <u>wonderful</u>!!! And I enjoyed it most frightfully - E

August 13th, 1935

Darling Elizabeth I am so awfully glad you are having such an outdoor and frivolous time. I can conceive of nothing better for your work and I did so like the <u>look</u> of you the other day – and the oxygen you bring along with you – There was a time when sorrow had taken that from you and one cannot help be happy that it has come back again. One knew it would but one likes to make sure.

No – you needn't read Lawrence[1]. One has to love reading of adventure, reading with a map and a spy glass – the whole laid out flat on a heavy table and even there I am not sure that the curtailed edition ("The Revolt in the Desert") isn't more satisfactory. Still the queerness of L's character comes out well and you come across queer wry-mouthed utterances like:

"Into the sources of my energy of will I dared not probe. The conception of antithetical mind and matter which was basic in the Arab self-surrender helped me not at all. I achieved surrender (so far as I did achieve it) by the opposite road, through my notion that mental and physical were inseparably one; that our bodies, the universe, our thoughts and tactilities were conceived in the molecular sludge of matter, the universal element through which form drifted as clots and patterns of varying density. It seemed to me unthinkable that assemblages of atoms should cogitate except in atomic terms. My perverse sense of values constrained me to assume that abstract and concrete, as badges, did not denote oppositions more serious that liberal and Conservative..." And he coins wonderful phrases...not a scrap literary but like stalactites or something...O – I see the post is going. I think Milton affects me like Bach. (<u>Lycidas</u>![2] O my God!) I must stop – shall write a p.s. later

E

1 Within weeks of his death *The Revolt in the Desert* (1926), his abridgement of *The Seven Pillars of Wisdom* (1922), was reissued; he had wanted no further editions of either book to appear in his lifetime.
2 Milton's elegy *Lycidas*, on a friend drowned in the Irish Sea in 1637.

August 18th, 1935

My darling Elizabeth,

No I'm not sure you can be let off reading "The 7 Pillars". It really is a stupendous book – arid in parts – with a sort of tribal aridity – but unlike any book in the world – things that bite into your consciousness and will never loose their hold on it. I think I shall have to acquire it. Yet now I've done it and thankful to turn the last page, what am I doing? <u>beginning it all over again</u>! And I need not buy it for even I shant read it a 3rd time at once – and on the other hand I certainly shant read anything else until the 2nd reading is over. So why lay out 30/- to have it sitting on the shelf? ------- The Authors Soc has now served a writ on my fraudulent Newspaper Syndicate Director and if he is solvent will no doubt get the money. But is he?

I'm rather worried about it but more that circumstances (putting my musical house in order and finding it as I expected an Augean Stable) have not allowed me to write more than a few thousand words at my book. And Betty is away which always makes a void. And a tiresome German composeress is coming tomorrow and I so fear I shall have a Lady Ponsonby "Let me tell you about Germany". And isn't the weather enervating? or do you like it...all muggy and devoid of outline [?]

Your E

T[urn].O[ver].

When do you come through? I so dread that when you do I shall be in Sussex. I do want a change – I know its because the idea of [?] nobody to procure it is so appalling – a sure sign it must be done.

Give me any dates you can and when it is likeliest that you might blow in?

August 20th, 1935

I think the 7 Pillars itself is Homeric. I <u>know</u> you'd see what I mean. I wonder if Maurice will. I doubt my going to Sussex till 1st week Sep. if at all. Will let you know. A German came to see me yesdy. Here are items: "A reign of terror". Her German pupils have left her because Hitler disapproves of women being intellectuals, being typists, accountants, anything professional. Mendelssohns[1] and <u>all</u> Jewish music <u>verboten</u>; if you wish to visit a foreign country you maynt take more money with you than 10 marks. If I saw her in Germany she said, she would not say one word of all this for dread of spies under the sofa. "And foreigners that come say all is so "peaceful and smiling"!" Women (as well as men) are taxed if not married. Q. "Wd. Hitler suggest their proposing to men if not proposed to?" A. "No thatd be unmaidenly." In fact you are punished for being unattractive!! I find this very funny tho' I daresay the monsters themselves don't. She says art is <u>dead</u> – that Hitler wont risk another religious war (?? I wonder) and that revolution must come.

1 Felix Mendelssohn (1809-1847), the major German composer and conductor was of a Jewish intellectual family, although his father had parted from Judaism about the time of his birth and later formally converted.

August 29th, 1935

Enchanted (Monday) you are a dear to come – Do you know why I want you to read the 7 Pillars is because I think there is something so Iliad-like (given 4000 years or so between whiles) about it. It <u>is</u> like an epic – and the mentality of the Arabs (which Laurence takes so enchantingly – as HB would have) represents the perfidy and [?] as generally of the Olympus contingent. I gloat over the book. How exquisitely Lang[1] translated Greek by the by. Don't you agree? E

1 Andrew Lang (1844-1912) translated both the *Iliad* and the *Odyssey*

September 14th, 1935

Wootton Manor,
Polegate, Sussex

With a note: "Now claim 2 golf balls of the man who pushed into the W.C.!"

Darling Elizabeth I was so glad of your address as tho' I had it in my address book I was not sure you were going back to the same place. I've done an awful lot of work here and seen various parties – E.F.Benson[1] – grown so vulgar and dreadful – so subterraneously conceited and pretentious that I didn't know how to sit out our interview. Alice Hudson drove me over and I think Rye is one of the most fascinating places I ever saw – it and Winchelsea – and the thought of Fred being mayor was very painful – I also went with A.H. to see Dr Mary Gordon[2] whose chapters I thought you were rather hard on! I think they are not at all badly written and if she prunes off a few darlings and beloveds although this certainly was the style of the Ladies the thing might appeal to some people – Virginia who with Leonard, a niece, the nieces friend, a marmoset and 2 dogs came over on Wed was quite excited about the book and told me to tell Dr.M.G. to send it along! I confess I think V's interest (tho' of course The Waves is rather on Jung lines) partly came from this. You know Alice Hudson's cousin the German ("Etta") is housekeeping for Dr Gordon and says she lives on one biscuit, locks everything up including her books – begs Etta to eat meat but is visibly upset at the amount – in fact she is very very queer. Well - I was welcomed warmly (Alice went into Etta's room while we discussed the ladies and what not) and when I went away she offered to kiss me saying with what <u>I am certain</u> was jocular intent "I know you don't mind kissing a hermaphrodite"! I said "Oh! You read that book?" (and kissed her) "Of course I did" she said. Well – Alice when I told her said "Now we know the secret of her queerness – of her going about her 5 acres in plus 4s! <u>She's a hermaphrodite!</u>" Virginia is equally convinced – is anxious to see her book and declares that as publisher she can worm out the truth! She says authors and publishers relations are like doctor and patient, that it would be quite in order for V to write "Now tell me – I think I catch a touch of abnormality – that often goes with 2nd sight and psychic powers. Are you quite like other people? This <u>interests me enormously</u>!!"I tell her and Alice its their evil minds to which V retorted "No! its you who are so full of [?] books!!" and saw only an allusion where it was a veiled confession really"! V. was very wonderful. She crossquestioned me about my sorrowful summer – all [?] and I said I couldn't discuss it – that it would bore her to death. "You <u>don't know me</u> enough" I said "you <u>care</u> too little except for the bits that [?] you to play with [?]. Well – she really made me feel that she is very fond of me – that I count in her life – that its not only the "remarkable woman" side – though she does seem to think a lot of me as writer – said she had "as she continuously does" been reading lots of "Imps"[3] and so on and so on. She said "I so often say to myself…there's one person who is <u>really</u> fond of me – who cares about my work ("Why" she said "you're <u>the only person</u> who has yet mentioned the book I'm writing")[4] I said this was perhaps because others hadn't the cheek – and she said no – it was indifference; that the thought of my being in the world – "that I can run down to old Ethel and say "produce that Veuve Cliquot" is a very great help and stay in my life when I have the blacks [?] which I often do. Well, if all this is part of the serpent of Old Nile only, one must take the risk and not withdraw (which I was beginning to do) my Virginia Investments. She tells me the new book is "very plain darling" – I said "not like the Waves?" – "<u>No</u>" she said "The Waves was a <u>bad book</u>" This is…well…very ambitious but on totally different lines." She's full of projects when she's done it (it will come out after Xmas) – a life of Roger Fry – a sequel to a Room of One's Own – Enough literary projects to last her life I should say She told me Ralph B. who I fear is a very bad hat – had asked L for more money and that they now wished that they had never touched his book[5]. As Clotilde says Ralph is like a Dostoevsky hero! Well – my darling I know all I have told you above is enough – You know how glad I am that I needn't shelve V. - to feel that she <u>is</u> humanly fond of me after all.....for what she matters? ["Otherwise" crossed out] Each of us has to grind out our fate and no one can help us except by caring how we fare in our fight through the jungle. Well – I must stop – Am longing for news of you and of Monsieur, Madame et Bébé.

Your
E

An incomprehensible postscript written round the edge of the letter apparently reads: "I'm madly happy at being a good prophet tho' not a Jung-ite at the League of Nations (go to sheet 1)", where there is in fact an obscure remark about a golf ball. September 1935 was a very important and active moment for the League of Nations, then at the height of its political significance.

1 E.F.Benson (1867-1940), known as "Fred", was author of novels, especially the *Lucia* series, biographies and ghost stories. He lived at Lamb House, once the home of Henry James, at Rye, where he was mayor from 1934. The fifth of the *Lucia* series, *Lucia's Progress*, came out in 1935.
2 Dr Mary Louisa Gordon (1861-1941) was the first woman inspector of prisons in the UK and a suffragette. She wrote *Penal Discipline* in 1922 pressing for the reform of women's treatment in prison with special reference to Holloway. Her book, *The Chase of the Wild Goose*, was published by the Woolfs at the Hogarth Press in 1936. It was at the time more admired than Radclyffe Hall's *The Well of Loneliness* (1928). The book tells of the experiences of Dr Gordon, herself a lesbian, on visiting the cottage of the famous "Ladies of Llangollen", Eleanor Butler and Sarah Ponsonby.
3 *Impressions that Remained* - one of ES's volumes of memoirs published 1919.
4 VW was working on *The Years*, which was published in 1937.
5 See August 8th. The photographs are interesting, but it is a curious book for the Woolfs to have produced.

September 25th, 1935

In the next letter, Ethel's handwriting is untypically sprawling and quite different from usual.

My darling Elizabeth I have been anxiously awaiting news- you will be amused to hear – of Dr Gordon's book – but I doubt whether V will be able to read it before she comes back (excuse chair nearly upsetting and spoiling symmetry – I'm having trouble with my new fountain pen and am having to get along with a very clumsy performer "made in Canada" till its put right) – She – V. is very much in the throws of last Will and Testament stage of her book which (did I tell you this?) is, she declares "simply a story" (?!) which he who runs may read. Which reminds me have you any idea what that phrase means? I must ask Pidd[1] with whom I have been having many a verbal scrap lately about whether "miswent"[2] is obsolete (which yr Mother says it is) – whether it is criminal in Mr Benson to have used the word "tante"[3] [?] in the old scholastic Latin sense as the equivalent of "work with" [?] And he was angry at my writing " – Piddington Esq." on the envelope and signed the protest on a p.c. with a hireogliphic (cant spell it) which looked as if the first letter was J. So I cut it out, pasted it on a p.c.....[?] Piddington and said it was his fault for never having asked me to call him Jacob "which I believe is your Xstian name". It really is John. By such pleasantries do we while away rather beautiful Autumn Days. Virginia likes the one Chap. of Part III I showed her (you know the Mass one) and today I'm going up to Longman to propose my present plan – bringing this vol. up to my departure from Frimhurst (!1904) and calling it Vol. I . I'm enjoying writing this book awfully but it's a laborious and slow job – worse than translating Ptolemy.[4]

Dr Gordon has meanwhile informed me that according to her Jung-trained perception I am, though not totally devoid of the power of feeling, a being governed by reason. (As this may not have occurred to you take note. Pidd said "May I ask do you believe these Hellenes [??] !!)

I think the woman is very cracky and so does Betty merely from what she heard of her from Con[stance] Lytton whom B adored but was a crank of cranks – vegetarian etc etc.

On Sunday a tragic-comedy – the Morrells and Julian (dau) and her dear husband, Goodman, came down and we walked on the golf course. They had a Peke – a new little idiot, the only dog that has ever loved Ottoline but which is too high bred to so far tolerate a harness – or a collar. Result it was put down and before you cd say Jack Robinson it had vanished in the high heather. It doesn't come when its called – another antisocial dog-trait – and behold the whole party quartering over different sections of the links – some calling WooWoo – and the ignorant E.S. deaf and misinformed calling Jee Jee. After ¾ of an hour (it happened on the 11th fairway) I dragged them all in to Tea Tea, and Betty came in, whereupon O so instantly disappeared followed by Philip that I thought she was taken short but after ¼ hour ("she <u>must</u> be bad" I thought. "Shall I offer first linen [?] = aids?") P came back and said O was off again on the hunt. I had meanwhile phoned the police and off we all went again... helped by Betty. I took my hunting horn not to be blown till the dog was found (just to show where <u>I</u> was) and this time, all calling correctly "Woo Woo", interrogating Sunday golfers and getting vague news of little brown dogs seen here and there, Ottoline was seen advancing from afar with the little fool. I am glad to say this means they will come again very soon ere the divine season we are having is over.

I'm lying back in an armchair hence this writing. Darling, I must stop.

Yr E

I do hope P is better

1 John Piddington. See September 26th, 1927.
2 Middle English: go astray, get lost, sin, be crooked, as in:
"If you would see a church miswent
Then you must go to Cuxton in Kent"
3 [?] the imperative "Go!"
4 EMW was engaged in translating Ptolemy's *Almagest* from the Greek at the time.
   The manuscript was completed and survives, but was never published. See January 14th, 1933.

October 10th, 1935

Now then Miss Elizabeth! read this and confess you were too hard on Dr Gordon! For this is Virginia's <u>sincere</u> opinion – (to me she wrote "in its way its quite well done")

Do you know I have come round to Darby and Joan![1] I suddenly see the story through his spectacles and think it admirable "in its way" as V wd say – tho' as I wrote to him, I shouldn't like too many potted psychology studies like that. Did I tell you my case (unless by good luck it comes on tomorrow) may come on any day next week which will too maddeningly upset my 14th to 21st visit to Lypiatt.[2] Damn. Did I tell you to read "<u>The House in Paris</u>" by Eliz Bowen[3] – recommended by Ottoline (who asked tenderly after you – go to see her) I think it <u>quite</u> remarkable. Also delicious war (nursing) book – full of natural beauty of mind and sense of fun by Monica Grenfell as was (now Lady Salmond)[4] Lady Desborough's daughter, name <u>Bright Armour</u>. Return V's letter to Dr Gordon – who she <u>will</u> call "the hermaphrodite"

Y E

1 *Darby and Joan*, a novel by Maurice Baring, London, 1935.
2 Lypiatt Manor was the home of the harpsichordist Violet Gordon-Woodhouse, a friend of ES and notorious for her eccentric private life, known as the "Woodhouse Circus". See also September 30th, 1930.
3 Elizabeth Bowen (1899-1973), an Anglo-Irish novelist who entertained many of the literary figures of the time at her house in Ireland, Bowen's Court – *The House in Paris*, was published in London, 1935.
4 Monica Salmond was the sister of the war poet Julian Grenfell and wife of the much decorated Sir John Salmond. *Bright Armour – Memories of Four Years of War* was not published until 1935, perhaps because she was not free to do so until 1933 when JS retired as Chief of Air Staff.

October 21st, 1935

Darling Eliz I am so <u>awfully</u> miserable about Fritz[1] (just came here [?]) This is only to say that I had told Virginia I wd go there at 5.15 on Thursday – but if that is a suitable day for you I wont go there – I'd rather have you. Let me know – as if you say "<u>No – I couldn't Thursd</u>" then I'll fix it up with Field and Roscoe (the solicitors)[2] and go and see Virginia as I do hold with not dropping all contact. But I'm rather seedy and not <u>mad</u> keen. E

1 Frederick (Fritz) Ponsonby died on 20.10.1935.
2 Founded 1835, at this date had offices near St Paul's. Its successor still exists today (2011) as the international firm of Field Fisher Waterhouse LLP

October 23rd, 1935

My darling Elizabeth this tiresome case is now announced to be "either tomorrow or Friday" which means that to join you at Commencio [?] seems unthinkable. For one has to be at the Court (Kings bench) at 10.30 just sit and sit as in Bleak House till your turn comes. If it got done at once all might be well – but that seems unlikely and I suppose one wd eat at a shop next door. I may hear this aft that its not till Friday (or next week even) but in any case I am throwing over Virginia. I had a very nasty turn yest.y – digestion has been rocky for some time and yesty I got horribly sick. Inward chill of the worst kind – so I went to bed supperless and feel better today but not really well at all. However you know my violent illnesses and recoveries and tomorrow I may be better. I've not been well all the time at Lypiatt and that terrific cold snap - 800ft above sea level in a house built like a lighthouse was a test. And the death of Fritz has half broken my heart because of my book. He would have adored all I say and keep on saying about his mother and what a friend he has been to us all! To me half the point of writing this book has now gone. Well that's the penalty of living a long life I suppose.

I think all the Loelia business must have worried him a lot and whether she did, in past days, or not, by now Ria will have learned of his worth and as you say be very unhappy. On my way to Wootton, I stopped (on Monday) to enquire and leave a word for her and asked the footman "How is Lady Sysonby?"and he said "Very upset" (!) I suppose its all he could say and I felt a fool for asking.

Did I tell you to read E.Waugh's "Vile Bodies", I think it's the most amusing (also horrible) book I ever read! But Lord! how funny. Its worth reading if you want to laugh. Col. Blount is quite exactly like our old relation Colonel O'Hanlon [?] How well done it is! I'll ring you up or wire you tomorrow if no news tonight.

P.S. 6.30 p.m. Wed. Eve.
No word from the lawyers so evidently my case is not coming on tomorrow... [*Complicated plans to meet*] Am putting off Virginia. Why don't you go and see her instead?

November 5th, 1935

Darling Eliz I'm lonesome for news of you but deserve nothing in the way of civility and affection for....today <u>I have finished my book!</u> you know that intensive work alone causes you to finish anything. Of course I've any amount yet to do to it, and the most difficult part of all, the Epilogue, is not yet even thought out. I cant till I've seen the thing as a whole. And I've not yet chosen the letters for the final sections: and I don't know if I have greatly exceeded Longmans word limit and what I shall do if I have. Virg. and Leonard say its bosh.....I must bluff/face it out and I daresay I shall. Still, all of it, reminds me of the Empress[1] (and Mary S!) who when you say you've "finished" a thing expect to see the thing at once put on (of music) at Cov Gard. Or (if literature) in enormous headlines in the Daily Mail. I've come to the conclusion that Virginia is right in saying that writing books puts you off writing letters.[2] I used to delight in letter writing when I was doing music – working no matter how hard – and so I shall again when I've done this long effort (I've been at it 8 ½ hours today and its only 6.30!) I don't even read but work after supper and in bed can only tackle very light (or fierce) books like E.Waugh who certainly is a remarkable writer (I'll have one here for you when you come that'll make your hair curl)[3] I <u>cant bear</u> poetry just now, Shakespeare or anyone else – am in short infatuated about the book which I thought Fritz' death would kill. What has kept off death has been the thought of writing a few words about him at the end of my Lady P.[onsonby] which is chap VI...and the last Chap. finished an hour ago (<u>and polished</u> is XVII). I saw V. and L. both delightful and she says her book will be finished after Xmas – (or out – I'm not sure which) yest. Hilda Matheson came to lunch. I'm afraid Vita has tuned herself down to the level of Gwen who really is a halfwit...in short... is the author of "Manners begin in the Cradle" and so on. Vita's talent I begin to think is a thing beautè du diable and I remember old Raikes Currie[4] saying "my dear, every boy is a poet at 20...why, <u>I</u> was" (that old boy adored poetry to the last by the by so I daresay he was) Also I think your shrewd grandmother was right when she said Vita if alone wd never wash. Hilda M.[atheson] whose psychology I don't quite trust I mean I think she's over tender hearted and sentimental – thinks Vita is unhappy...that Harold is anxious about her...that G (whether the great Love still exists or not) has dragged V. down to her level. And I think all that's true. It's a great pity but the two bore me consumedly as idea [?] because all wallowing in bogs and loss of outline is antipathetic (as we both agree) and degrading even to look in at. My case, to my fury, has not come on yet, and it is quite on the cards that I shall be called on Thursday – the one day when I have an engagement, or rather engagements, for I'm going to Ottoline after the wedding party to meet T.S. Eliot. And as I'm hating poetry now this is rather awful. I shall have to read Murder in the Cathedral again tonight I suppose and as I cant digest poetry just now....there it is. I count on seeing you on Thursday unless (that is) I am hanging about the Kings Bench like a person in Bleak House. If I cant appear at the party please explain to all and sundry why it is (I've told Hilda for one) And if the worst happens you really might come on to Ottoline's...or come here or something – pray please darling.

Yr E

1 The Empress Eugénie.
2 Which did not prevent either woman from writing thousands of them!
3 Possibly *Black Mischief* (1934)
4 Raikes Currie (1801-1881) MP and banker with considerable interests in Australia; he was a neighbour of the Smyths living at Minley Manor, not far from Farnborough.

November 14th, 1935

Darling I'm glad we are going to have more intercourse now and that my conduct abt 'Blest Pair'[1] has not done for me utterly in your eyes – My case came on today – I could hear nothing but was very much impressed by the beauty of the barristers in their most becoming wiglets all except [?] barrister who looked like Mr Vholes[2] (in a wig) – such a low down scoundrel – and the judge looked at him with aversion. He (the judge) said in other words that to defend a case when there is no defence is rather cheek – and I have judgement and costs. As the man has nothing he will be made bankrupt which is the great point. I don't think I shall get a farthing but with darling Maurice's £130 and my own Armstrong Whitworth³ I don't mind. He says Toveys⁴ concerto was <u>divine</u> and that he cried all the time. Casals⁵ (he says) <u>really</u> conducted – and Tovey just followed him in a dream! By the by in the Court <u>is</u> there a short prayer before they start? I had an idea something of the sort was going on so, to be on the safe side, furtively crossed myself. I daresay (if observed) they thought I was scratching. Divine letter from Virginia but I cant spare it yet! I went up to London by the 9.1 today and came home to vote (<u>pouring</u>) What are your plans? I've lost your letter. As yr mother is going to York shall you go to Cromer?

PS Have just found your letter and hasten to say Bishop Gore⁶ has duly arrived but have not begun him yet...for its been a hectic couple of days – yest and today – I wrote a little line to poor Phyllis – after Fritz I feel death in the guise (this comes out of going to Lincolns Inn and Bleak House) of a painted allegorical finger pointing at me from my innocent whitewashed ceiling! Not for me myself but for someone else. (But this is foolishness) – and its partly because of writing about Papa's death etc in the book!)

E

1 Presumably a reference to John Milton's *At a Solemn Musick*:
  "Blest pair of Sirens, pledges of Heav'ns joy,
  Sphear-born harmonious Sisters, Voice, and Vers...."
2 The obnoxious Chancery lawyer in Charles Dickens' *Bleak House*.
3 Armstrong Whitworth – must refer to shares owned by ES. It was a major manufacturing company, specializing in armaments, ships, locomotives, aircraft, etc. The founder (1810-1900) was convinced that the future of energy lay with renewable sources, especially hydroelectricity and solar power.
4 Probably the Cello Concerto written for Pablo Casals in 1935.
5 Pablo Casals (1876-1973) was one of the greatest cellists of the 20th century and also a conductor. This would have been the last year of his Barcelona-based orchestra: Orquesta Pau Casals; in 1936 he went into exile as a result of the Spanish Civil War.
6 Charles Gore (1853-1932), Anglican Bishop and author of numerous theological works.

November 26th, 1935

My darling Elizabeth. Its no good...I read the poem with glazed eyes and heart of dough. Tomorrow I shall (I hope) pick the last letters for the last section to send to the typist, and then...at once...begin the Last Will and Testament final chapter. I am literally lost to all else in the way of the arts. The only book I am reading – and am thrilled by it but read only about 4 pages a day is the life of Bp Gore. Someday I shall talk to you about it and the C of E for 12 hours on end – but before that moment arrives I shall have read Arch Davidsons Life[1] and think of no more enthralling conjunction of divines. O the C of E is interesting! I now now [sic] what a horse feels like galloping the last mile in the G.National – I cant look right or left – am aflame and work 8 and 9 hours per diem.[1] <u>Go on letting me know how Vesey is.</u>

1 Randall Thomas Davidson (1848-1930) served as Archbishop of Canterbury from 1903 to 1928. His biography by G.K.A.Bell had been published by Oxford U.P. earlier in the year.

Throughout the end of the year, Ethel continued to be in what she called "a tangle of commitments" with no time to read.

Poetry? Pooh! Shakespeare? Bah!

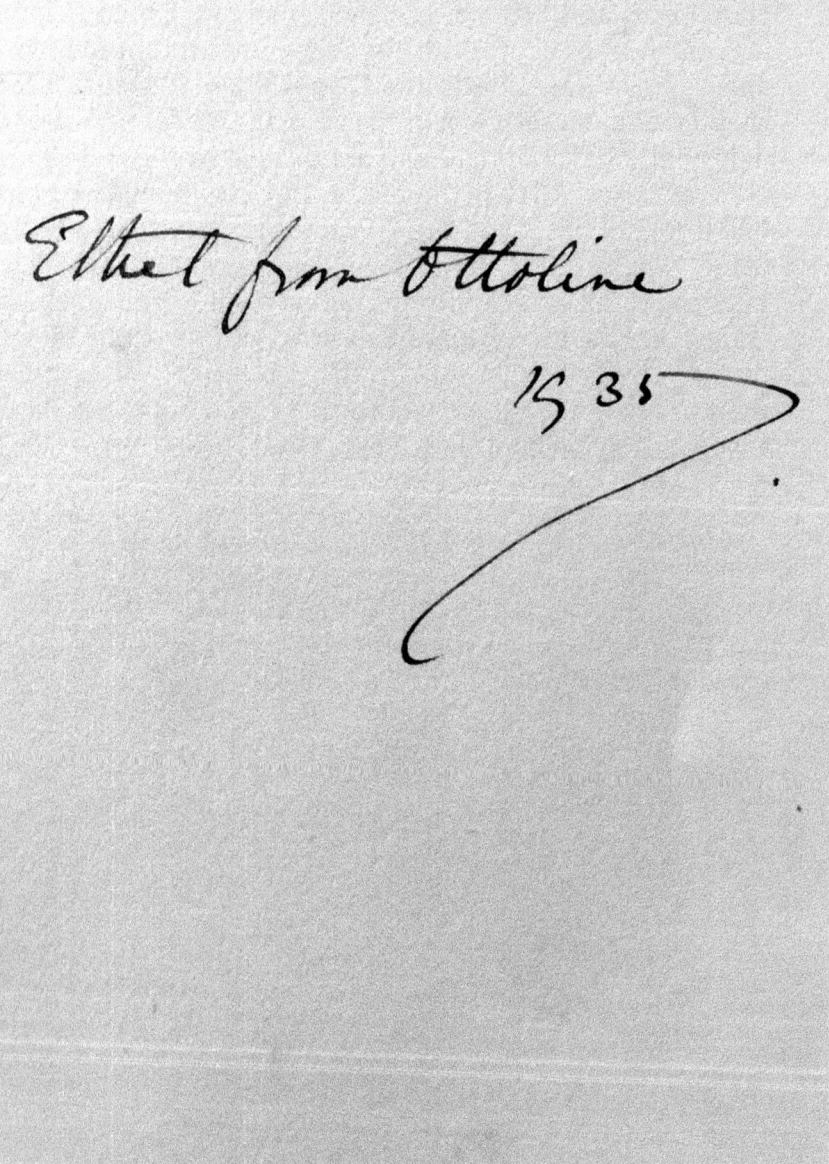

Ottoline Morrell's dedication to ES in her copy of *Murder in the Cathedral*

1936

January 1st, 1935 [*sic*], but postmarked 1936

[*Her voice, health problems – just escaped pneumonia – in some detail*]

Today Mary has like a saint gone down to Woking (its early closing day and local P.O.s are shut up) with my book. And in counting up the words – block wise – I nearly collapsed on finding that they were 25000 more than I had ever made them before!! But knowing I might count better after lunch (for appetite is quite fair!) I tried again later and found I had counted a certain block of 25000 twice over!!! Also, looking up whether it was "black as Erebus" or "<u>dark</u> as Erebus"[1] I began by forgetting in which play Jessica appears!!! Which reminds me, Plesch tells me Strauss's operas are now forbidden in Germany because his librettist von Hoffmanstal[2] [*sic*] was a Jew!! I knew and much liked V.H. (also he's a very fine poet) – apparently an ultra aristocratic Viennese, who quite believed he had, with his elegance and manners lived down the "shameful libel" that he was a Jew. But everyone knew he was ....and this is the result.

Do tell your mother that I am miserable for her at the loss of Miss Lee Warner[3]. However much people are 86 they can be adorable and irreplaceable – think of the Empress and Lady Lewis[4]. How Miss L.W. worshipped your mother. I hate to think of her having slipped her cable. I am so sorry.

You were all such dears and made me feel that in spite of disabilities you'd rather I was there than not. That is all I care for.

Yr E

1 *Merchant of Venice*, Act V, scene I
2 Hugo von Hofmannsthal (1874-1929) poet, political essayist, librettist for some of Strauss' most famous operas and founder of the Salzburg festival, was of a Sephardic family converted to Catholicism. He died of a stroke in 1929, two days after his son Franz committed suicide.
3 A relative of the author Sir William Lee-Warner (1846-1914) of the Indian Civil Service.
4 Perhaps the wife of the celebrated lawyer of Jewish extraction, Sir George Lewis (1833-1911), who was particularly well-known for prosecuting in financial cases and exposing money-lenders guilty of usury.

Sunday, 12th January, 1936

My darling Eliz do you know it's a funny thing but that bronchial thing driven in by the broadcast went very deep and not until yest did I feel able to work – As it is I really do think I have got that epilogue right, all but the last 3 pages (out of 40!) Strange how on one little tiny thing, as in cooking, depends the shape and the ease of a thing.

When its done and I'm rather well-er I shall long for you to read it and see how it strikes you....

[On her cold]

Brains have not returned yet but have read an enchanting travel book, exquisitely written ? – dear me – so all right by Mrs Lindbergh[1]. I'd like to know her...and of how many people does one say this. I got stone deaf of course with my malady but that'll soon be all right Yr E

On the back of the envelope:

I've done my index – a <u>ghastly</u> job.

1 Anne Lindbergh (1906-2001) was an American pioneering aviator and mother of the child kidnapped and killed in a sensational case in 1932. In 1935 she published her first book: *North to the Orient*, an account of her flight from New York to Nanking.

January 20th, 1936

Darling <u>don't</u> write in pencil on blue paper unless you wish me to go blind. Its <u>torture</u> to read.

[On the cold, her ill-health]

I don't like the sound of Vesey – and this weather...! How can anyone get well in it? I've lots to tell you once this d---d job is finished. Do go and see Virginia! She's immersed in <u>Hegel</u>!! and much surprised at being thrilled by it!

PS: On the back of the envelope: "Arent you miserable abt the Ring?"

And on a postcard a couple of days later.

[Her health]

> Lady Cynthia Colville[1] told me fine things about the Q[ueen]. Ill pass them on to you. I suppose you cant bring Ptolemy and stay over Sunday?? I'm in agony for Betty. Mary's 2nd operation yest.y. Ever since in pain...and sick (after 1½ hours chloroform) all night...or at least wretching [sic]. Doctors quite satisfied...But you can imagine Betty's feelings. E.

1 Helen Cynthia (née Crewe-Milnes), Lady Colville (1884-1968), Courtier and social worker; wife of Hon. George Colville; daughter of 1st Marquess of Crewe.

By the 26th, she was announcing triumphantly that her book was finished and her love of poetry had returned; by the middle of February:

> "...am literally snowed under with proofs.....no time to write today – and I have much to say – yr E

> It breaks my heart that you will be so far away when my book comes out."

February 24th, 1936

Forgive writing

[Pan's and her own ill-health with a wealth of details, especially in the case of Pan's colitis]

> One great anxiety is over. Lord Balfour[1] had a touch of bronchitis and slight fever (which at 83 is no joke) for about a week but he's up now and Betty's not too distressed at his going to London today – a very important meeting and...a big fee. I fear Mrs S's death will re-act very hard on them as all her money goes elsewhere (Why! I ask myself....unless perhaps its her husband!) and she gave a big contribution – at least I believe £250 – to the yearly expenses.

[Obscure anecdotes about various people, some of whom cannot be recovered from the initials.]

Elizabeth: Joad² has been the nail in my coffin as regards philosophy!! I know now I dont understand one single word of it...never shall and <u>dont want to</u> (anymore than I want to join the Everest expedition). Rather a comfort to know I <u>neednt try</u> – but can just trust to young and beloved philosophers...On the other hand I'm re reading – slowly – savouring it – "The Battle Ground"³. Its magnificent and has set me more than ever on rereading "L'Histoire du Peuple d'Israel" and all the old testament lives again for me in spite of the genealogies. All that old civilization Egypt, Assyria, Persia leading up to Rome and Christ always fascinated me – but I'd lost touch with it. Also Belloc is fine on the crusades. It's the most interesting book I've read for years.

I'm buried under the Index I am making...It's a terrible job... and this weather makes me sleepy and idiotic <u>all day long</u> (But I'm tackling that).

I'm going to see Maurice [Baring] on Weds at his nursing home (Empire N.H. – Vincent Square) Why don't you go and see him one day? He wd adore it so. The Mendelssohns (Balliol)⁴ are coming here to lunch tomorrow. I've not seen Dora for 40 years which, as we know, makes a difference to a girl! Mary is home and getting on....but slowly. Gwen is at Sissinghurst (!). Your loving E

And you? Are your clothes progressing? Is Martin better?

And on the back of the envelope: "My dustcover is <u>lively</u> I think".

1 Gerald Balfour had inherited the title from his more famous elder brother Arthur on the latter's death in 1930.
2 C.E.M. Joad (1891-1953) philosopher, popularizer and Brains Trust personality; his reputation was ruined when he was caught fare-dodging, something habitual with him, as he often boasted.
3 *The Battleground: Syria and Palestine, The Seed Plot of Religion*, Hilaire Belloc, 1936 must have just come out and it is remarkable that ES had had already found time to read it twice.
4 Albrecht Mendelsohn (1874-1936) was Felix Mendelssohn's grandson. Dora was his first cousin, Felix's granddaughter. An eminent constitutional lawyer, Albrecht left Hamburg with Dora when the Nazis came to power in 1933. They settled in Oxford and he was made a fellow of Balliol. Recently, one of the composer Felix Mendelsson's school notebooks, given to their landlady in Oxford in gratitude for her kindness to Jewish refugees, was sold at auction.

March 10th, 1936

My darling Eliz I'm fussed at not knowing the date of your departure. – I know not my own name, for only abt 3 days ago did I find out about the old and tiresome Index required... Well I'll spare you, but the sort of thing is a Millais picture (really a portrait of of Trelawny[1]) of the old salt meditating on the N-West Pa[ssa]ge 'It can be done and England ought to do it': So at Coign 'it can be done and Ethel ought to do it.' Well I hope to be through with it by Thursday when I'm going up to see Dolin[2] – and by next weekend – perhaps sooner – I shall practically have done all my part save reading the proofs of the Index and that's nothing once its printed. Aha my dear! wait till you begin indexing Ptolemy! And Longmans expert says 'believe me – an author always does it best'....

[Health and possible times for meeting]

Yr E

So there's good news from Biarritz? I hope to go and see poor Bob for an hour next week. Am <u>chock full</u> of thrilling gossip about the King and Mrs S!!"[3]

1 Edward Trelawny (1792-1881) adventurer, friend of the Romantic poets. *The North-West Passage* (1874) by John Everett Millais, shows Trelawney as an old man with his daughter and refers to the ongoing search for a sea-route across the Arctic. The caption in fact reads "It might be done and England should do it".
2 Anton Dolin was at this date a principal with the Vic-Wells Ballet.
2 George V died on the 20th March, 1936. Edward VIII, the new King, was openly accompanied by his mistress, Wallis Simpson, already once divorced and to be divorced again in October that year. On the 10th December, 1936 he abdicated in order to marry her.

December 18th, 1936

My darling Elizabeth Your mother has lessened my sorrow at not going to Cromer by asking me <u>not</u> to come after all.... and I do think from every point of view it is wisest. The weather is so peevish and everybody seems ill. I thought I was fairly well yesty and went up to London chiefly to ask

Hugh Allen (who is being an angel) to do what he can in the matter of the Mendelssohns and this morning I woke up with something very like sciatica in my inferior leg – I am hobbling on two sticks and cramming in Genaspirin. Such an odd sort of seizure, but I think I ricked myself in a taxi. Thus. I left Virginia and walking to Russell Sq.St. found the elastic of my knickers was not doing its duty. So I took a taxi for the ¼ mile to the Royal Coll and went through awful contortions pulling the garment up without risking being taken up for indecent behaviour in public places. Bless you, darling; get better at Cromer and make up to me for missing a visit I was very particularly bent on. (Later. 6.30)

[On Pan's health]

In the early summer of 1936, Elizabeth went out to India to visit her friend Elinor and her husband. She wrote regularly to both Ethel and her mother, describing dinners at the Viceregal Lodge in Simla, sightseeing and social life. Ethel must have replied, but her letters for this period are missing, as is the bundle for 1937.

1938

A bundle similar to the others, tied with thin string; less grubby and damaged than some other years. It begins with April and goes on into early 1939.

By the time the correspondence begins again in April 1938, the world had changed dramatically. In March, Germany had annexed Austria and was about to claim the predominantly German region of Czechoslovakia. Ethel, who had known and loved Germany, was horrified by what she had seen happening in the wake of World War I, as the country struggled with poverty and Nazism gathered strength. She had always had a lively interest in politics, but about this time she began to feel she would almost rather not know. Ethel would have been less concerned with the war in the Far East, where Japan had already invaded China and Mongolia and attempted the Soviet Union. Her outlook was, generally speaking, Europe-centred and furthermore it was still not clear to what extent that war and imminent war in Europe were to be linked.

It is interesting that Virginia Woolf now almost vanishes from Ethel's letters.

April 1st, 1938

[Mostly on philosophical terms in German]

As you know I touch these matters with a quaking heart, but I am translating (as an article) extracts from Heine's "German Religion and Philosophy". I shd like to know a term for "Nature Philosophy" (thank God it is not necessary for me to know what it means) to get it right. Now your friend F.L.[1] should be able to prompt you if you don't know yourself.

1 Feodora Leontief, economist, mother of CS, and a close friend of Elizabeth, was at the time teaching philosophy at London University.

April 29th, 1938

On April 29th, she wrote a postcard to Elizabeth on Frederick Voigt's[1] *Unto Caesar* which had just come out – on the dangers of totalitarian dictatorships, adding

He thinks Italy a negligible danger compared to Germany. (So do I, if only because the Germans are a race of warriors...)

1 Frederick Voigt's (1892-1957) – Political journalist, who from an early date tried to draw attention to the dangers of the growing Nazi party and who later worked for the B.B.C. and in the Department of Propaganda.

May 6th, 1938

Oddly, the following letter was never opened. Elizabeth had begun slitting the envelope and then for some reason stopped. There is no way the flap of the envelope could have been opened and restuck, something which in any case she never did. It is a very unusual letter - about the political situation in Europe and her reactions to it - unusual, in that while Ethel was often angry, she was rarely depressed and despairing.

Darling Eliz You told me, I think, not to send back Mussolini's Roman Empire. I am now so bewildered that with a perfect conscience I am turning my mind away from Europe! These spectacular displays make me sick and ashamed. Whatever book I read last (this Mussolini one included a leaflet which I am now going to implore some spirited agency not to send me, called "The War in Spain"![1]) I quite agree with! I feel we have not the slightest idea what is going on anywhere – nor have "they" (Germany, Italy etc.) the faintest notion what is going on here. Nor have we!! I can only perceive that N.Chamberlain[2] is pursuing A Policy – and I fell back on first principles, such as give his policy a chance, if only because nothing would delight our enemies like divided loyalties in England. I used to be pro-Franco[3]; now I know certain facts I am (if anything) for the Spanish government. What distresses me and would preoccupy me if I let myself think about it (but as I can do nothing except fire an occasional satirical remark at the Labour Exchange – which I have just done!) is the conviction that the proletariat no longer has any stomach for work and the class that organizes efforts is aware that – even such plans as might avail for defence against aircraft are waste labour, as owing to our ideas of "liberty" – and also our deep distrust of the organizing powers – nothing would come of it. In fact I am now such a pessimist that I, really and truly, have only one idea left – not to embarrass our own Government. And perhaps I shall even give up reading on that subject and go on thinking how I can make the garden look less like a concentration camp – all wire anti-dog erections round beds in which is....nothing! And the more I set my house in order the more insoluble is the problem. In fact I am settling down to the idea that Hilda – my executor – at [to] whom a Doomsday Book of Directions (for after my death) must just peacefully face dementia. I have no peace – no leisure – no work in hand (for lack of time and perpetual alarms and excursions) and am miserable. Sole bright spot – the Grandfather clock is back (repairs cost abt £30!) and at all events need not ask the real time of the phone young lady who says "just fave minutes past nane".

Yr E (miserable...but well!!)

I hope you are happy and well and will be when the NE wind is sick of blowing.

1 The Spanish Civil War – the dates of the major period of conflict are generally given as 17 July 1936 – 1 April 1939.
2 Neville Chamberlain (1869-1940) is known above all for his foreign policy of appeasement towards Nazi Germany and for signing the Munich Agreement in September 1938 in an effort to avert the threat of war. WWII began on 1st September 1939.
3 Francisco Franco Bahamonde was a Spanish general who ruled over Spain as a military dictator for 36 years from 1939 until his death. Before registering disapproval, consider the blanket acceptance of Mao by the UK left-wing or Stalin's nomination for the Nobel Peace Prize in 1948.

May 11th, 1938

My darling Elizabeth

I was awfully pleased that you liked my talk even in its truncated [?] form. Curious how they don't see that a short thing like that the entrée en matière is as important as the handles of a pair of scissors tho' of course it's the blades that do the cutting.

Yes. I agree nothing as interesting as peoples principles and you have chosen the best available, one that is enough for enabling me to call myself a Christian. I doubt very much if Christ wd have exacted more tho', once it became a school the Letter had to obtrude itself.

I'm still coping with phenomena in the shape of my effects and it takes all my time not to fling section after section of them on to a bonfire every Tuesday when "the boy" is here to do [?]. This preoccupation and the situation in the world at large, have made the spring the most NE and revolting I can remember. Really and truly my one comfort is King-Halls News Letters¹. Odd how many people are now trying to imitate them – one is now sent me weekly (and tossed into the fire unread) called "The War in Spain" edited by a man called Duff.² What people don't see is that the point lies in the Editor (S. King Hall) being so obviously a man without leanings either to the reds or the others – who simply has keen eyes, no axe to grind, almost, one might say, <u>no views</u> – only a tireless wish to find out what is going on and to tell you. One expects he is a good judge of mankind and knows how to pick, among 20 men in a café, the one whose remarks are really worth repeating; e.g. one believes him when he says he has yet to meet the average Italian who is not ashamed of all this fuss – who does not perfectly well know it is designed to buck them up after the worst let-down they have had since Caporetto[3]. He is always travelling about – is now going from Florence to the Balkans – and sees things for himself – and I cant help thinking that although no doubt he travels under a false name, Hitlers police will catch him some day and he will disappear.

On Sunday I had Winnie de P.[olignac][4] here with her niece (Mrs Chaplin?) who drove her over and who married a grandson of Lady Radnor's, but my great excitement has been meeting Baroness Blixen[5] – authoress of one of the most exquisite books I ever read "<u>Out of Africa</u>"...a queer woman, spare, about 43 I think, a big game hunter who is also a poetess, a loner, and a Dane who writes mysterious English that makes my heart thrill. It has been a sad life – for she loved (and was obviously beloved by) <u>the</u> Denys Finch Hatton[6] just a few weeks before bad years and the grasshoppers forced her to leave her farm in Kenya and the natives she had become enamoured of. I had the thought the baroness Blixen who had headed her car by mistake into the Euphrates last month was her – and for a day the sorrow stunned me. But it was her husbands 3rd wife!! A woman she was very fond of. I may see her again before she goes. She's not attractive like the last authoress whose work I fell in love with before I knew her (Virginia) but strangely arresting. Her publisher rang me up yesty to say if I was free she'd come down here....and oh! It was the one and only day I had been in London for months. I could have cried when I came home and learned of the tragedy.

I thought Phyllis looked very well and am going down to M.M. the minute the blue bells have arrived with Pan. Some day next week? O I do hope something comes of yr conjunction with the Oxf. U. Press man and that I shall see you then.

Did I tell you they are doing (in a **most** becoming spirit) The Wreckers at Saddlers Wells after Xmas! But that side of me is dead of course now. HB once said I was less capable of associating with ghosts than anyone he ever saw – and of course my music is to me a ghost. I once tried Gertrude Stein but found it didn't ring true (perhaps because mine is a cotton wool mind in which things wont ring).

Yr E

1 Commander Stephen King-Hall (1893-1966), ex-navy and much appreciated speaker on Children's Hour, produced one of several private political news letters that began to circulate in the late 1930s. *K.H. News-Letter* was an attempt to explain the situation in Germany and reached a circulation of more than 50 000. An interesting article on these news letters appeared in *Time* magazine on 31 July 1939: www.time.com/time/magazine/article/0,9171,761799-2,00.html
2 Charles Duff edited *The War in Spain: A Weekly News Letter* from January 22nd, 1938. Some issues are available on line at http://contentdm.warwick.ac.uk. It was priced 1d.
3 The Battle of Caporetto, or the Twelfth Battle of the Isonzo, was the devastating rout of the Italian army by Austro-Hungarian forces in October-November, 1917. The aftermath of Caporetto is the background to Ernest Hemingway's *Farewell to Arms*.
4 Logically, the niece would have been Daisy Fellowes whom W de P raised after her sister's death. Mrs Alvilde Chaplin was one of W de P's lovers and at this date they would have been at the beginning of their relationship.
5 The Baroness Karen von Blixen-Finecke (1885-1962). Her best known book, writing as Isak Dinesen, *Out of Africa* had been published the previous year and was an immediate success.
6 Denys Finch Hatton (1887-1931) - big game hunter and lover of Karen Blixen had died when his Gypsy Moth crashed in May 1931.

August 2nd, 1938

The Crown Hotel, Harrogate

My darling Elizabeth I was so happy reading your dear letter – except that I saw there was something very wrong at W.13 and wrote to enquire. Yesty I got a letter from yr mother and then Sylvia and Grizzy came to lunch and further explained matters. Your mothers letter made me very unhappy because as she herself confesses in it, any event that plays havoc with "the best laid plans" above all things "infuriates" her. – and I couldn't help writing to her that if (as she says) poor Charles "despises himself" in my opinion unsuccessful people are often more worth than 20 brilliantly successful ones – and I do hope she hasn't inherited her mother's "uncivilized" worship of efficiency i.e. of "success" – But of course she has, and I am miserably sorry for Charles because one feels that kind and sympathising as of course she would be (and they say is) I expect that, weak and ill as he is, he feels that spirit in the air. Also Sylvia says she's not well at all and all this is a cruel finale to her so called cure. What a tragedy it is if someone has not a single arm in her arsenal against sorrow – I can understand that to be there tore your heart and I'm half glad that, as goes without saying under the circumstances, there is no possibility of my going there on my way home – which even before all of this I could not have done anyhow, as the Womens Orchestra scheme does not look to me at all hopeful and I cease not turning over in my mind what can be done about it. To go back to yr letter Grizzy told me something I had not quite realized – that you are meditating writing a book of your own about Ptolemy, as ice-breaker across the frozen parsimony and stick in the mud mentality of our universities. I cant help wondering whether the Edinburgh university would not be more responsive. Thrice in my life – and more especially about The Prison – have I been struck by the intellectual awakeness of the Scotch compared to us.

[On problems of raising money for music and an attempt to get Royal Patronage via Lady Helen Graham; the charm of the Valley Gardens at Harrogate; her medical treatment]

But what it has been is [?] <u>absolutely</u> cleaning up my huge "Wreckers" scores on a tiny hotel-bedroom writing-table – the falling of one tool after another and rolling under the huge bed. I have lost, since here, 3 sticks, 2 umbrellas and my best fountain pen (the latter I lost twice, the last time irrecoverably) but I retrieved one lost umbrella by the good old plan of buying another (price 5/3). As for reading I read for the first time with delight and laughter "Chrome Yellow"[1] – then started "This Brave World"[2] expecting more laughter and delight; but it made me bilious with rage after 2 chapters. Too silly. But W H Smith's Library has some quite good stuff in it and I reread with immense pleasure Harold's [?] life of his father. How can such an enchanting man have begotten that odious "Gwen". Sylvia took me a marvellous drive to Bolton Abbey[3] which I had never seen – and for once in a way I loved the sight of holiday crowds, children paddling in that lovely river – and all basking in the heat (up to now it has been cold and misty). I'm writing this in the writing room and have left yr letter upstairs so will finish this a floor higher.

Upstairs

Ah! Now I have your letter. Re your depression, it reminds me again of your mother's helplessness. I don't mind your having a fit of it (kind of me isn't it?) because it's a thing every worker must have from time to time and you, thank goodness, do possess arms against these things. Aridity – insensitiveness to beauty and the Arts is one of the worst forms of failing vitality – I have had it all this year so far – mainly because "lifting the body" was such a piece of work. I was quite relieved to be so staggered at the beauty of Bolton.

[A description of Bolton Abbey]

I cannot say how profoundly I agree with all you say about politics and am conscious of leftward driftings myself (!!) Yet I am inclined to think the (relative) right thing – i.e. the thing you want to throw your own feather weight into, may be <u>left</u> and at another epoch <u>right</u>, like the state of things that made Goethe say the saying yr Gran clung to with such satisfaction (and I often wonder where she picked it up, as I don't think she was a Goethe student) "Injustice is better than disorder" (!) As for the gulf you say may open between you and your "right" friends, I don't think that follows. They too change. Also I don't think views matter much. I often reflect with amusement that HB, in the year 1900 would have shuddered a the idea of my being a suffragette – yet if he had lived it wouldn't really have made any difference <u>in the end</u> because (as regards him and me) he would have felt that the anti view was really unthinkable for people like me if you got down to the roots.

I think few things ever gave me more pleasure than your appreciation of the Baroness Blixen. There is something magical and unique about it, and the foreign turns in her phraseology here and there gave me small electric shocks. One felt while reading, that there is no note in the gamut of feeling and of instinctive knowledge. And the odd thing is that though she did not at all fascinate me – like Nadia Boulanger[4] the musician and (of course) Virginia, when you came into contact with her, that feeling that no region was unknown to her subsisted. No. I don't think I was conscious of a surfeit of imagery because you felt that a battalion of thoughts, of perceptions new and old were behind this lavishness....

[On Maurice Baring beginning Out of Africa *over again as soon as he had finished it – as she did]*

Tell me if you went on to the end in ecstasy? I think tht leaving the farm – the Danish friend – the death of the old chief....! But when I think of the old men not being allowed to dance it makes me <u>hate</u> England. I leave at cockcrow on the 10th for home

Yr E

1 *Crome Yellow* by Aldous Huxley was first published in 1921 and satirizes the world of Garsington, with which ES had little sympathy.
2 Aldous Huxley's *Brave New World*, published 1932, a futurist novel set in 2540.
3 A ruined 12th century priory in North Yorkshire, part of the estate of the Duke of Devonshire.
4 Nadia Boulanger (1887-1979) a French composer, conductor and teacher.

August 14th, 1938

A couple of weeks later, she sent a brief note to Elizabeth who was staying at Appley, giving her advice should she decide to do a cure at Harrogate.

Next time I go to Harrogate it will be to another hotel: I never really liked the Manager with his dazzling smile - but this time he was so rude, and afterwards so familiar that I got to hate the sight of him. Was interested to find Sylvia too dislikes him and feels he is always on the verge of presuming and can't understand your mother's enthusiasm! Except that as she says "Phyllis always likes being bullied by men!

August 17th, 1938

[On EMW's trip to Bath]

The Chinese Book.[1] No – I certainly don't exactly recommend your reading it. It tells you interesting things but the author repugnates you. Evidently a journalist who will have said to himself 'That's my line...!" Of course the extreme fascination of the race is such that you read on.....but the man is second-rate – not only as to intellect but all through. However he made me dig out my Laotse and Confucius and I rather feel about it all that their civilization and ours are really too divergent. It can never be "The Heritage of China" for us as "The Heritage of the Greeks" or the Romans. Exactly what I dimly felt in the Chinese Exhibition 2 years ago with which (really!) superior spirits like you and Maurice were enthralled!.....

I don't want to be narrow, but pseudo-clever and N.Y, journalese and Chinese ways don't blend sympathetically. You know he lives in America and sometimes one can't help feeling that he is consciously aiming at effect by such and such a Yankee phrase, just as Sir Thomas Lipton[2] used to drop, when in aristocratic circles, into the low [?] of his youth in Glasgow....

[Family plans]

On Sunday Henry Wood and his Lady came to lunch! Poor Muriel! What a rage she will be in if she hears about it! But I have no doubt that the common sense of the situation in accepting it as a sane solution and the only one. The only reasons that I can see for her not divorcing him are 1) she doesn't want him to give the other a legitimate wife's place 2) she knows that a lawsuit would cast an odd light on her investing 7/10 of his savings in her name 3) that in any settlement she would get less money than she has now annexed.

On the other side, tho' he may have been weak and humbugging with her, his services to music (and to women musicians) weigh down almost any scale in his favour. And there it is.

[Her Vienna fees + "Am reading Gide's memoirs ("Si le grain ne meurt") charming!"]

Yr E

1 Lin Yutang (1895-1976). The very popular Chinese writer and interpreter of Chinese culture for the west who from 1928 lived in the USA. The book in question is perhaps *The Wisdom of Confucius* which came out in 1938.
2 Thomas Lipton (1848-1931) was born into a poor family in Glasgow and left school at 13, but went on to make a large fortune providing inexpensive tea to the working classes. Both Edward VII and George V enjoyed his company. He was very active in supporting voluntary medical organizations, such as that to which ES's sister was attached in WWI, especially in the Balkans. See Helena Gleichen, *Contacts and Contrasts* (1940), Mansion Field, 2013.

August 22nd, 1938

A couple of days later, Ethel wrote again apparently to clarify some disagreement they had had on the subject of class.

> My darling Elizabeth. One rapid word (since my remark stung you to back answering it!) – no, I think you <u>would</u> be sensitive to bounder-dom. If I gave a contrary impression I spoke in haste! But I don't think you are sensitive to certain other lacks of quality and I always remember Goethe's remark that fastidious stomachs are nothing to be proud of. I think you would concentrate on some other quality of the person in question and ignore the thing, whatever it is, that might put someone else off – servility or slyness, or some such strain that (for instance) beloved Alice Davidson[1] wd not have minded. (<u>But Ethel D.[avidson] would</u>) Of course you wouldn't mind the social strata of someone's background – if their salient qualities are immaculately all right.
>
> There has been just such an instance here this afternoon – Mrs Brown, the wife of the dear man who harbours Pan for me. Ankles like bedposts, no conversation, no nothing – yet such dumb goodness in her (which comes out in her face too) that you never feel called in fact to be censorious of her social stratum and her ankles. But....When I think of people like Lady Helen Graham[2], or old Mrs Davidson, Lady de Vesci....or ...[*several other of ES's friends, unidentified*]

– all not my own class (or a peg above it) but "ladies" in the sense of the word no [one] who has not race³ <u>can</u> have, quite – (Lord Balfour is another). I know I prefer them to the class of Virginia. It is an extra touch – the weathering of a long tradition that nothing else can give. I have to fly out in the rain to clutch the last test match paper issued tonight. Madge comes tomorrow – she is anchored at the Oval all day!!

Yours E

1 ES's sister and either her niece or her sister-in-law.
2 Lady Helen Graham (1879-1945) Woman of the Bedchamber to Queen Alexandra 1937-9.
3 i.e. breeding, not ethnic affiliation.

Slipped into the packet of letters at this point is a long letter from Oxford from Elizabeth's great friend, Elinor, mostly complaining about her stepdaughter in terms which suggest that problems with teenagers do not really change much over the decades. However, it reveals nothing of the qualities which apparently charmed Elizabeth.

September 5th, 1938

On September 5th, 1938, Ethel wrote a brief note on a half sheet of paper

[On mending a chess board to give EMW + family meetings and plans]

    I've left you all my books you don't want [?] to get rid of bar a few special legacies to Virginia and such like.

September 20th, 1938

Grand Pump Room Hotel, Bath

    <u>Darling Elizabeth</u> - I am somewhat consoled by your hope that your mother will listen to reason. If only she wd except [sic] the fact that after youth is past – and indeed for some people much earlier! – life is one damned thing after another and that the only thing to do is to endure to the end – i.e.

cope as well as you can (not only in pleasant [?] form) with the tendency to lie down and die. The fact is one of the chief reasons for keeping as well as one can is that it's a bore for others when you are ill.

[Obscure family news]

I'm just playing you rather false in that about 200 books – (few of them negligible but not good for my (present) literary appetite – though no doubt these books will come again full circle and suit some tastes) are being presented by me to the Strachey Free Library[1] at 49 Marsham St Westminster to keep what she likes (when they come back to London) and fire out the rest. If you like I will ask her before she does so to range them somewhere in a row. And if there are any she doesn't want you think you'd like, I'd either take them back here and store them on my £2 worth of extra shelves, or you could carry them off to your house one day. Mind, I think it extremely unlikely that you will desire any of these derelicts – yet one never knows.

[On the problems of getting the chessboard mended]

Since yesterday I am ashamed of being English and I feel in my bones how justified is the contempt of the Dictators. Two "men of principle" – her brother [?] and Lord Cecil informed Fishers Hill that France <u>cant</u> stand up to Hitler – population too reduced. Then why mislead Benes[2]? What with Manchuria, Spain, Abyssinia and now Czechoslovakia I feel we deserve the [?] – to be the laughing stock and in 10 years or so to accept the position of being a 2nd rate power – or worse.

And the hideous thing – and yet in a way the hopeful – is that personally I feel that if in March 1935 Baldwin hadn't lied about the reports of Germanys arming (to learn the truth from <u>Hitlers</u> own lips, as delivered to Simon[3], Hoare[4] and Eden, in November '35) England would have faced the truth and played up – and by now we shd have been a real not a sham power. I remember (<u>now</u>) Baldwins remark at the time (November 35 and after), that if they had told the electors <u>the truth</u> they would have lost the general election!! Of course one assumes that he meant thereby "and where wd England have been without <u>us</u> at the helm? <u>That was, rightly, ones first</u>

1917
Catalogue of Books
Sitting room :   Little book case
Goethe Gedichte
Marcus Aurelius
Confucius
Tales of mean Streets (Morrison)
Nunc Dimittis (Micklem)
Fly Leaves C.S.C. (two copies)
Lachrymae Musarum (Watson)
Verses & Translations C.S.C.
A Modern Instance (Howells) 2 vols
The Apostolic Fathers (2 vols)
Capital & Labour — M. Benson
The Americans (H. James) 2 vols
Smith's Smaller History of Rome
    "   "   "   " Greece
Trial & Death of Socrates
Heart of Princess Osra (Hope)
The Serious Wooing (Hobbes)

An early page from Ethel Smyth's Book Catalogue

thought" But, my God, could anything in the world overstate the shame of our present situation – I cant say it keeps me awake – nothing except an air-plane attack cd do that – but it weakens one's preoccupation with one's own job.

Did I tell you that Vita came to tea with me at Moore St last week looking quite her old self – lovely, slim, redeemed from blowsiness – and apparently some application like weed-killer has been used for the moustache was hardly perceptible and she was not got up!

[On her affection for Bath]

Yr E

This presumably refers to Chamberlain's efforts for peace at the expense of abandoning Czechoslovakia to Germany. The London correspondent for the *Manchester Guardian* wrote that thousands of demonstrators marched up and down Whitehall shouting "Stand by the Czechs!" and later "It seems likely that this week we shall reach the turning-point between peace and the dreadful catastrophe of war, and as the hours pass we can only trust that it will still prove possible to preserve the peace and to preserve it with credit to ourselves", while 'Red Ellen' Wilkinson the Labour M.P. is reported as saying: "We say to Neville Chamberlain: We don't trust you. We believe that you went to Germany to fix up a sale of the liberties of Czecho-Slovakia." Mussolini had praised Chamberlain as a "flying messenger of peace" while Pravda had condemned him for betraying the Czechs.

1 The Women's Library, associated with Millicent Fawcett, the co-founder of Newnham College, Cambridge, was established in 1926 in a pub in Marsham St., under the name Library of the London Society for Women's Service. It included a reading room, a cafeteria and a small hall for lectures and events. By 1938, donations not only of books, but also of relevant archival material were being actively encouraged. It is currently part of the London Metropolitan University and, after almost ceaseless financial struggles since its foundation, the Women's Library has been hosted by LSE since 2013.
2 Edvard Benes (1884-1948), President of Czechoslovakia.
3 John Simon (1873-1954) a senior Liberal politician and Lord High Chamberlain. He was generally unpopular and by 1938 was coming to be seen as one of the "guilty men" responsible for the appeasement of the Dictators.
4 Samuel Hoare (1880-1959) a senior Conservative politician. He was made deeply unpopular by the proposed Hoare-Lovel pact, which would have granted part of Abyssinia to Mussolini. In the event, Mussolini seized the whole of Ethiopia. He was instrumental in rescuing endangered Jewish children and campaigned vigorously for prison reform and against the death penalty.

September 23rd, 1938

On a postcard:

...an amazing quotation from one of Demosthenes' speeches which <u>to a T</u> fits our case with Hitler. And Greece <u>did</u> disappear, as he foretold. And the awful thing is that like us, that democracy was too lost in sloth and self indulgence to produce a leader. Or the people <u>would</u> follow one. Myself, I believe in my bones that ½ H's gesture is bluff – but now its too late...

September 29th, 1938

Darling Elizabeth. This is the bulkiest list of my presentation to the Marsham St Library. It is a special library and it appears they only want feministic or social subjects – or things that have a direct bearing on the emancipation of women – and as the poems of G.Meredith[1] (! unfortunate as it's a very nice little edition) and relevant <u>biographies</u> and <u>novels</u> etc. [???] Nothing that youd want! If in these pages (disregard their being crossed through! That merely means "reread") there is anything you rather covet just put a blue check √ against it and <u>send the list back to me</u>, upon which I'll tell them to reserve them for you. You needn't bother about anything of Maurice's as you really <u>shall</u> have the promised goods now that my books are ready in order. Once the dining room is made gas [?] proof for Pan (his only chance!) I hope to begin work again.

I feel certain you will be, like us all, immersed in domestic problems. Myself I am not relaxing for I feel that as long as Hitler is alive anything may happen any moment – and have only limited faith in the quartet now playing at Munich[2].

I think Chamberlain is the greatest man England has ever bred – because it is done without glamour, purple patches, outbursts....nothing but character and integrity.

Yr E

I do wish I knew what of your mother? Where is she?

---

1 George Meredith, OM was an English novelist and poet of the Victorian era. He was nominated for the Nobel Prize in Literature seven times

2 On 29th September, 1938, Adolf Hitler, Neville Chamberlain, Edouard Daladier and Benito Mussolini signed the Munich Agreement which transferred the part of Czechoslovakia known as the Sudetenland to Germany.

October 6th, 1938

Darling Eliz

I too had a feeling as akin to happiness as anything can give me yet awhile at renewed contact with you. And with Donne – I think what chiefly lives with me in the domain of poetry at the moment are the two lines in a Blunt sonnet "The fair world is witness of a crime Repented every hour"[1]. Its that undying sense of guilt that is so unbearable.

I am delighted you have left the party. Myself I feel that to do it, given my general views on [the] situation, would be a case of changing horses while one crosses the stream which is, I feel, nearly always a mistake. As long as there are people on the govt. side who feel as W. Churchill, Duff Cooper, H Nicolson and others do I think that to stick to the wretched animal we are now riding is best.

I will get the verbatim report of yesterdays and todays debate and in the meantime am doing all I can by sending a larger subscription than I can afford just now (and yet it is only £2) to the Czech fund. I do like Vernon Bartlett on Benes[2] and his farewell is magnificent. I always remember one of the best obituary notices of my father said something that struck me: "He was always hopeful." And in one who is far from a fool this is a fine quality. I shall try to emulate him and Benes. Your remark, which I shall no doubt feel the justice of when I read the debate – on the absence of wanting to score on the part of the opposition is just such a cause of hopefulness as regards ones humiliated nation. Cecilia Fisher is fetching me to lunch at Hampton Court in ¼ of an hour. She is one of the few people I could bear to see – and the beauty of H.C. must (or so she says) do good to sore spirits. Like Donne. (And Elizabeth) E

1 Wilfred Blunt (1840-1922) "Two Highwaymen" – on his resentment of time and death.
2 Edvard Benes was forced to resign by the Germans on 5.10.1938 and later that month went into exile in London.

October 31st, 1938

Darling Eliz. Just to say I have found your letter – it was (<u>thank God</u>!) not on your blue paper which takes type badly nor on U.C. stationery …I hate not having told you (if I didn't) how wonderful the Wall was. The light absolutely magnificent and very [?] stormy and the fields sopping, so that when (to save your shoes) you stepped on to what you thought was firm footing you found it was a clay-clad Roman Remains and slithered into a small morass....

[The weather and her lumbago]

....Also I had the pride of introducing Bob to a most lovely spot, raved about by V – Haug[h]ton Castle[1] on the Tyne near Chollerford – a sublime place the waves dashing mountains high over the weir and I certainly wd not have ridden the ford above it under £100 (It was a relief to be informed it never was used in winter!) I never knew such a host as Bob. I really do <u>adore</u> him and have told him if he is not married within 12 months I shall propose to him myself. (<u>He has already accepted!</u>)

Do you know I – actually I – felt a poetic mood coming on! And lo! Vita's new "poem" (Solitude)[2] arrived pat! I think it wretched sham stuff, inspired by the cheaply psycho-analytical Gwen I shd say! Self conscious, pretentious skimble skamble stuff. Here and there a good line of verse of course – but the whole very poor. Tell me if you agree. (It reminds me of Maurice's anecdote of the man who pointed out to a great admirer of Rostand[3] a very feeble lyric in one of the plays and the admirer said: 'Ah ce doit être de Madame Rostand'. I feel Gwen all over the book, apart from the ridiculous dedication. Gwen – with her cultivated housemaid's mind "revealing" anyone's soul to the person in question! – Too silly! Leonard told V. (who of course hadn't read it at that time) that it was "very fine" (!). Tell me what you think of the last Auden-Isherwood[4]? I've just sent for it. Fancy your being able to cope with things like Timaeus in the midst of these <u>awful</u> days – for they are still awful. Betty sends you a message of veneration and affection. She says [illegible] is well done and O I <u>do</u> so like Edith's book. Such a relief after "Solitude" (It's called Sallys Youth)[5]

[Plans to meet]

yr E

1 Originally a 13th c. tower house not far from Hadrian's Wall, extensively rebuilt in the 19th c.
2 Published 1938.
3 Edmond Rostand (1868-1918), French poet and dramatist, best known for his play *Cyrano de Bergerac*.
4 *On the Frontier* – the third and last play written collaboratively by W.H.Auden and Christopher Isherwood. It was first produced in October 1938 at the Arts Theatre, Cambridge.
5 Edith Somerville's novel *Sarah's Youth* came out in 1938.

November 9th, 1938

A week later, Ethel wrote touchingly of her affection for Elizabeth in answer to a lost letter. Her <u>underscoring</u> on this particular occasion defies normal typography, running to six or seven lines.

> Darling Elizabeth
> In 3 days I believe I can begin on this terrific heap of material I have shaped – <u>but I darent stop</u> for if so I lose the awfully complicated thread through it all (I am nearly despairing – but not quite)
> Still I cannot help telling you how deeply, with how intense a poignancy your letter went home to me. I have it constantly by me. Thank you my darling. Strange to say metaphysics tho' it be, I <u>understand</u> !! and love the metaphysician more than ever. But...this is only to say I am lunching tomorrow with Phyllis and then seeing a person I only saw once before exactly 65 years ago <u>at the font</u>!! (my only godchild!!)
> I think Vita's Solitude very poor stuff – but in the last Lit. Sup. a lovely poem – indubitably by her. "Solitude" I think must be by Gwen!!
> "On the Frontier" is I think <u>deeply interesting</u> and somehow or other very harrowing. Do you agree?
> Yr
E

November 17th, 1938

[On Phyllis' poor health and Pan's treatment for eczema]

....I added that however little you may think of Chamberlain, by quitting the party you are subconsciously aware that you wont be asked to do things!!! (You know I think that's true; one has these subconscious promptings in defence of what to any brain worker in the prime of life is more worth than anything – peace and quiet).

I must stop. If only one could get out of this black tunnel of dismay and foreboding!

Ethel's Christmas Eve letter was, very atypically, written in green ink on grey paper and enclosed a letter from Edith Somerville, to be shown to Elizabeth's mother, Phyllis.

Monday, November 28th, 1938

Drishane House
Skibbereen
C.Cork

Written across the top by ES in green ink "'This is for your mother because of her passion for Edith" and - apparently - "Destroy"

Dearest Ethel,

I've just, with high satisfaction and gratitude, written my name in the invaluable little diary-pocket-book. Each year I'm more grateful for it, as my memory – never a good one for appointments, dates, and hateful shoppings – gets worse and worse, and I bless you more continuously [?] for saving me from shame and disaster. – As to coming to London that is absolutely uncertain. I've heard nothing definite about my play[1], only that a Producer was "immensely interested". – But as this interest is quite capable of fading in five minutes, I'm not basing any plans on it. I'll tell you, you may be sure, if anything exciting happens, but I'm preserving the calm and frigid tranquility, enjoined by Dr Johnson in similar case, and am thinking far more about the "rial Xmas surprise" that you have promised! (I hope it is the further instalment of Autobiography – but I'm afraid it is rather too soon to expect it.) I can't tell you what pleasure it has given me that you and Maurice like my poor Sally....

[On copies sent and thank you notes received]

...I heard from R.G.Longman that they're doing another little edition which is satisfactory.

On the strength of Sarah and having sold a horse in U.S.A. I'm building a long-desired bathroom in connection with my bedroom, and am deeply enjoying the superintending of its construction. The house will then have three, so the queues in summer will be shorter by one, at all events!

[Family news]

We've had one awful storm after another, and the rain has been incessant. Farming terribly interfered with, and our men will soon make it a personal matter with the Almighty and refuse to go to Mass.

In spite of the wet, however, I'm not quite such a cripple as I have been, and can walk to the farm, and similar small expeditions – (But it is maddening not to be able to get on a horse). I've got 2 nice three-year-olds now, and hope for a foal from a mare I bought Desmond. He is commanding his Regt. now and is quartered in Londonderry – in the "black north", which he and Moira hate. We can't understand de Valera's obstinacy in shoving compulsory Irish down the people's throats, and expecting Ulster to give up Partition! Moreover the school inspectors say that the average of education has gone down in a shocking way, owing to the fatuous folly of making teachers teach, in a language of which they have only a smattering, subjects to unfortunate children who know less! The fathers and mothers are frantic, but the Dublin doctrinaires are too strong for them and disregard all protests.

Well, I hope that an early use that I may make of your pocket book is a date for Coign!

Much love and many thanks.

Your loving Edith

1 Perhaps *Flurry's Wedding*, which Edith Somerville had been working on intermittently since the early '20s.

December 24th, 1938

My darling Elizabeth I'm feeling you are being rather defrauded – no golf. And walking is hellish in 4 in of snow. But thank your stars that you haven't a big dog who though mad with joy at being "mad dog" for hours on end comes home with a ¼ cwt weight of white footballs on each paw and has to have it removed by putting leg after leg in a pail of hot water – and then having them dried on new dog-towels that, not having been washed yet, absorb no moisture. And now snow has begun again and looks like going on.

[Impressed by Charles Morgan's play The Flashing Stream[1]]

Ronald S. has seen Maurice[2] and was "rather shocked" at the "deterioration" of his condition – I gather that he shakes more (before the crisis it was negligible) – but that his quickness and brilliance, and intellectual resource are as ever – and his courage absolutely so. R's impression is that all these will remain the same till the end but adds "as long as he is physically able to express himself" which looks as if that might be the dread. Last time I saw him he was so distinct that I was terrified wondering whether it was a great effort – but I noticed that his lips quivered more than before. And that was 3 months ago. I hope to go down to Wootton and get a sight of him as soon as weather mends. (I daren't risk getting ill in the winter!!) I gather…(but no <u>letters</u> arrive in this foul season, only Xmas cards. What a maddening madness!) I gather that one day he is really glad of a "nice" visitor; other days he is not up to human intercourse. Still, sometimes – on his weakest days – he will get up from his chair (he was in bed for 3 weeks) and walk upstairs by himself; just what H.B. did a week before his death – (only he did it saying "This is just to show off!") And need I say that Bollinger and Foie Gras arrived just as if Maurice were in blooming health.

Your Mother tells me you are thinking of moving to London. How I hope this is true. That coming down at night is deadly work – would be to a bargee's daughter aged 17. And you have as many houses yawning with desire to engulph you when you feel like the country...[*details*]

I've been busy with <u>correcting music</u> proofs –a hellish new system the results of which are (I must allow) brilliant and which I doubt not is very much cheaper than engraving, being so unutterably much nastier to deal with...

[Family news]

I am now able (and longing) to get to my book again. Good wishes of the best quality darling

Yr E

1 Charles Morgan (1894-1958) Today the description of weapons technology that is an important theme in *The Flashing Stream* seems curiously prescient.
2 Maurice Baring was suffering from Parkinson's Disease.

1939

January 1st, 1939

Darling Elizabeth -

[On the horrible weather, EMW's mother and her ill-health]

Edith and her terrible quotations.[1] It's a disease! Ever since I've known her I've fought it; and her cheap and unnecessary use of French words; I believe she has got it into her head that all this is part of "culture"!! I pointed out to her that in Martin Ross's day there was none of all that – that it is second rate and what not. But I think it is in her blood. Queer people the Irish are. I am quite sure for instance that Edith clings to title in a way that surprises one in such a lady! I doubt very much whether she would read as you and I do Bertie Wooster's versions of Jeeves' quotations (for I think the Code of the Woosters one of P.G.W.'s supreme masterpieces). And in a way I like her limitations!

[E. Bevan]

My love of work. But this special book is terrifically difficult. If you start to walk round the world, I expect there would be particularly baffling sections. Anyhow I have the pleasing illusion that once I am over 1899 it will be easier.

Politics About Chamberlain etc etc. If I am against Franco, it is simply because if Mussolini and Franco want him to win it is obvious that his success would be to the detriment of England (Of nothing am I more convinced that Hitler considers the disruption [?] of the B.Empire Aim No.1 – and all the other starts and surprises are subordinate to that end) It is not, I mean, that I have more sympathy with the Government (the reds, say) than the Jimmy Alba [2] lot; I know nothing about Spain, their problems, or the real truth of the whole business[3], but what I do know is that to let Germany or Italy become ruling factors in Spain is also totally [?] against our interests.

Then again about a change of government (here) – certain old adages never become non-applicable – and the one about changing horses as one crosses a stream less than any. I don't know that men of genius like Napoleon are a blessing to the countries they squeezed dry and left smaller than they were and I am quite sure Chamberlain is not a "genius" – but I have an idea he is exactly the sort of man to defeat Hitler and his anti-English aims – to oppose something by that whole spirit which they will be unable to break down. And I want him to have time and room to make mistakes [as any man may in dealing with a wholly new technique of "free" government as patented by Hitler and Co] and to be both <u>backed</u> and <u>influenced</u> by his critics – to see all that is to be seen of what he is up against. Therefore, dearly as I love an independent fighter (tho' mind I think the Duchess of A.[tholl]4 a stupid governessy woman) I was thankful she was so eagerly repudiated by the electors <u>simply because I knew that nothing would have enchanted the Germans more than her getting in</u>. They dread Chamberlain more than any figure on the chessboard – and this does not surprise me because that mentality is absolutely incomprehensible to those who long ago mastered the methods of the old diplomacy and know where they are with figures like Lord Salisbury [?]5 and even Winston – or (if they were to rise from the dead) Palmerston, Disraeli or Gladstone. I myself am frightfully interested in Chamberlain as an unknown force and I would like him to be backed for all the country is worth.

You see I don't believe there is any one way of getting there in this world [?], and I feel a grim persistence and unshowy tenacity in Chamberlain which I think is the one thing needful just now.

[On her health and other domestic matters]

Yr loving E

1 ES had written eloquently on the subject as far back as 1920: "The Quotation Fiend" in S*treaks of Life*.
2 Jacobo Fitz-James Stuart y Falcó, 17th Duke of Alba (1878-1953), was the nephew of ES's friend the Empress Eugénie and Nationalist Ambassador to Britain during the Civil War.
3 The Civil War was almost at an end. On January 26th, Barcelona fell and on February 5th the Republican Government went into exile in France. On April 1st Franco announced the end of the war. One of EMW's best friends, Persis Miller, was deeply engaged in the Civil War and was to spend her life caring for the Spanish refugees in France – see www.oasis.lib.harvard.edu . EMW would therefore surely have had strong views on the subject.

4 Katharine Stewart-Murray, Duchess of Atholl, (1874–1960). In 1938, she resigned her seat in Parliament in protest against Chamberlain's appeasement policy.
5 James Gascoyne-Cecil, Marquess of Salisbury (1861-1947) had joined Winston Churchill in protesting to Chamberlain about the slow progress of British rearmament in the face of the Nazi menace.

January 16th, 1939

Darling Eliz I have such a lot to say – but I cant write. I am gradually untangling the knot of the years (1895 to 99) and if I stop for even ½ a day (as I did today) I nearly go mad picking up the thread again with 4, no, 6 batches of letters! What I stopped for today was to rush up to London after lunch to look at Matthew Smiths[1] pictures in the Leicester Galleries – I implore you to go there and tell me what you think of them. If you admire....well! I shall never look at modern pictures again...

1 Matthew Smith (1879-1959) - English painter who, feeling himself discouraged by Tonks at the Slade, left for the Continent in 1908, where he was much influenced by Matisse and other French painters of the period.

January 23rd, 1939

My darling Eliz – The only plan is to write – to you or anyone before I have laid hands on my work! I am working rather well and fanatically and so preoccupied with it that to my horror I of late have found difficulty in getting to sleep when I go to bed whereas all these years my difficulty was to keep awake.

This is just to say that I don't really know what way your sympathies are pointing when you speak of them. To my mind there is at present only one question and nowhere have I seen it better put than in E Mowrer's article in the 21st January (past) T. and Tide[1] - to be rounded off by another on January 28th – i.e. the question how Germany can be held up in her avowed aim of destroying civilization as we know it. What you call "history quakes" have to be dealt with, step by step, by Governments and no "theorizing" about the largeness of the interests at stake transcending our wellbeing, or the wellbeing of any country cant alter the significance of Christ's remark as twisted to apply to the present state of things I mean about "How can one love God whom one has not seen if not yr brother whom ye have seen." I do very clearly see that all I care for and believe is <u>liberty</u> in the deepest sense of the word, which includes all the rest, is at stake and think the only problem at present is to do what one can to save it. <u>I cannot see further than that.</u> I wish you wd read Mowrer's book [?] and when you can (no hurry) explain to me what you are aiming at – unless it is something too vague and general to be defined.

Let me hastily say 1) I loved your little Addison poem. Tho' not as much as the Yeats (Leda) you once introduced me to! 2) I don't think any letters from Chamberlain to the Duchess of Atholl cd alter my opinion that he's the best horse to back so far as any hope of a hold-up of the <u>German Destructiveness</u>. 3) Of course the Code of the Woosters is a <u>farce</u> and meant as such. Many of them are not and insofar preferable, I agree. 4) Did you go to see the Andrew Smiths[2] at the Leicester Gall.y [? Gallery] Winnie [Singer] lunched here yest.y and says "of course the man can paint" but she cannot [?] with his vision. I said I don't care whether he can paint or not if he sees the nude the colour of raw beefsteaks. She said – "yes – that's it – <u>I</u> can't stomach such a vision" and was (like me) delighted with some of the Engelharts[3] in the next room. If its still on I do wish you'd go and see them. 5) I think my book is so far going on all right. I love doing it tho' its a worse grind than usual. I wonder how yr mother is, but who can feel well in this terrible unseasonal mushy weather 6) I'm waiting to decide whether I have [?] done – and what 7) I think Eliz Bowens "Death of the Heart" and the 2 others of hers I have read <u>House in Paris</u> and "<u>To the North</u>" wonderful tho' like "Death of the Heart" almost too sad to be borne. But she suddenly has sense of humour in her short stories, very few of which I care for. It's a queer talent in that I feel her forte is long efforts (like Beethoven)

Your lovingest E

Yes, I <u>know</u> I cant do metaphysics now (if ever!!) I am too much preoccupied with the dread lest England may no longer be able to cope with realities, which, like food and rest, really must be in ones plans.

I am sending for Penthespern [??] which Eddie Marsh[4] implores me to do; says he sure I shall like it and from the few reviews I've read I think I shall as all dwell on its lucidity.[3]

On the back of the envelope.

Winnie says the Crisis has remade France – bearing out all HB always said about the Phoenix like country" and with a different pen: "There was a scene yesdy between Pan who really is a prize playboy and the dignified Winnie who is terrified of dogs that will make me laugh till my dying day. I must tell you all abt when we meet.

1 Edgar A. Mowrer (1892-1977) an American journalist, who won the Pulitzer prize for his reporting on the rise of Nazism. *Time and Tide* was a political and literary magazine, initially with a left-wing and feminist slant.
2 An exhibition of paintings by Sir Matthew Smith (1879-1959), the Halifax artist who lived in Paris, was opened at the Leicester Galleries, London, by Jacob Epstein. He was a painter of nudes, still-life and landscape. He studied design at the Manchester School of Art and art at the Slade School of Art. Smith studied under Henri Matisse in Paris and acquired an interest in Fauvism.
3 Anton Engelhard (1872-1936).
4 Edward Marsh (1872-1953) is particularly remembered for editing five anthologies of Georgian Poetry and as Rupert Brooke's literary executor.

February 16th, 1939

Darling Elizabeth -

[On health and meeting]

Meanwhile I'm rather drunk with perpetually sipping (and dishing up) my past life. I think the bad bit I am now through with (the years 94 to 98) is good. I have just introduced – <u>very gently</u>, and in dwelling upon what she was to me in those days, the fact that had to be mentioned, that our lines deviated as time went on.[1] I shd have liked to have shown you that bit – but had to send it off today to typist and doubt it being back by Tues. Never mind! Plenty of time!

Yr E

On the back of the envelope.

I am beginning to have the <u>greatest possible</u> respect for yr enemy. Neville C[hamberlain]

1 This refers to ES's difficult relationship with her elder sister Mary Hunter, EMW's adored "Gran". The subject is discussed in various of ES's autobiographical writings and in *MH*, see Bibliography.

1940-1944

Ethel and Elizabeth continued to meet, although much less frequently than in earlier years, no doubt because of the war and Ethel's increasing infirmity. Elizabeth went to work at the Ministry of Economic Warfare; Virginia Woolf fled London.

Elizabeth spoke very little about the War. With the same courage as so many other people who stayed in Central London throughout, she had succeeded in stylizing her memories, perhaps to make them bearable, into a very characteristic series of witty and amusing anecdotes: fellow fire-fighters homely techniques for dealing with incendiary bombs – "I always let mine simmer a bit, dear"; the fact you could leave jewellery or anything else lying round but had to keep ginger biscuits in the safe; the pilot friend who loved flying and tuned his radio to jazz because it "helped him work out the manoeuvres during dog-fights" instead of listening to the Control Tower. Eventually he was shot down, but only after a brilliant career. She always said that Yeats' "I know that I shall meet my fate" might well have been written for him.

Elizabeth's correspondence with Ethel must have continued. One letter from Phyllis Williamson has survived:

September 16th, 1940

13 Cliff Avenue
Cromer

Darling Ethel,

I hope all goes well with you and that you are really throwing off your chill.

Everything that can be done, and prepared for an unknown necessity, goes on here and one is always listening, or looking, and wondering from hour to hour what one will see or hear. The sirens are infernal but nothing has been found here so far to replace them.

Naturally one's whole imagination focuses on the Battle of London and one's heart swells with pride at how people behave and endure. It is good to belong to the Race that fights instead of running away or laying down their arms.

I find it very difficult to read fiction and keep my mind on it....

[On a life of Randall Davidson and the fine portrait of the Old Queen]

...a long conversation about an old novel of Edna Lyall's "We Two"[1] caused me to hunt in my nursery bookcase for it and of course it was there.

So far I have not been overwhelmed by it but the mood may come, but the old quality of leisure-observation-timing is so good I think, and such a pleasant change from books like films and telephones.

My own work goes on just the same but it is not heroic, dramatic or dangerous but the amount to do and the time it takes increases daily and as regards the ambulance H.G. Canteen etc. it may suddenly become an Emergency Centre of real importance and then one will have to work at any moment day or night.

Elizabeth writes that she feels quite happy and safe and calm in her job and I am not to fuss or expect news or letters and I shan't. She says it is wonderful to live on such a stage in such a drama.

Saints and heroes seem to crown the scene. This will bore you I fear and tire you but I want to keep in touch and don't expect any answer.

                                    Yr devoted Phyllis
Sylvia has sublet her flat at Eswick [?] and comes back here in a few days.

1 Edna Lyall - pen name of Ada Ellen Bayly (1857-1903). Her novel *We Two* (1884) is based on the life of the social reformer Charles Bradlaugh.

September 27th, 1940

A couple of letters from Elizabeth to Ethel also survived, one on a reused half sheet of some cyclostyled message.

                              M.E.W.
                [Ministry of Economic Warfare]

My darling Ethel,

So sorry you are in bed. Please tell me how you are when you have energy to write.

I am all right re shelter at night because am not at Gl[oucester] Pl[ace] but in furnished flat which I have taken temporarily – I was moving out anyway next month as aunt Sylvia had arranged to live with Grizz for the winter. As I got back in full Blitz Krieg and Grizz was on night duty I didn't go back there as I thought it unnecessarily dangerous. (Height, no basement, no one in the house but us, etc.) Grizz is temporarily staying with a friend at her station, not too safe but anyhow surrounded by ARP appliances and at her work. She is <u>very</u> obstinate and I think idiotic, and I more or less forced her to stay away from the flat by not going back. I think it most <u>un</u>helpful to the war effort not to take rational care to stay alive!

My flat[1] is in a very solid cement block and on the ground floor which is as good as possible.

I am feeling very miserable and embittered because University College was completely gutted 2 nights ago. All the libraries gone to ashes, not to mention all our own work in the department. It is a wretched feeling after working there such years.

                                       Yr lv E

Address: 25 Malvern Court
S.W.7

1 Where I (CS) lived my first months, since my parents were sharing the flat with EMW. Oddly enough, their neighbours were the grandparents of Marina Warner, whose father and mine became acquainted at Bowes and Bowes Bookshop in Cambridge.

September [probably 21, or 28], 1940

The following seems to be the last letter to have survived from their long correspondence.
In ES's hand.
Sep 1940 (Blitz Krieg weeks)

M.E.W.
Saturday

My darling Ethel

The Blitz Krieg is not conducive to civilized correspondence, owing mostly to delays in work involving a sudden rush and so on. We have lost our front door here (Ministry) but no structural damage was done to our building though a second bomb demolished totally 2 large houses in the corner of Berkeley Square.

This is just a stop gap scrawl to send you my love and register the fact that I am all right. The nights are pretty formidable, but not as bad as one might expect. The <u>shattering</u> noise is made so much more by us than the visiting team that it is rather exhilarating. The fact that one sleeps quite well is a constant surprise to me! Also that one is not more frightened. The low [?long] whistle coming very close and then the bang is not pleasant but quite undaunting really. All around here (Bond St, Dover, Albermarle, Sackville, Bruton, etc.) has been quite badly hammered.

I came back in the middle of it all after a very nice holiday. Phyllis too, but rather beastly for her having Martin elsewhere and a great delay in all telegrams, telephone calls, etc.

I am reading the Guermantes vols again and all through the second Balbec visit. It is wonderful reading for giving a feeling of continuity in this strange month. I had to overcome an immense initial pain in reading about France but made myself do it for the wonder of the book.

Bless you darling Ethel
Yr E

November 10th, 1940

The last letter from Virginia Woolf dates from the end of 1940 and was addressed to Elizabeth at the Ministry of Economic Warfare in an envelope marked "Private' heavily underlined.

Monk's House
Rodmell
near Lewes
Sussex

My dear Elizabeth,

I was so glad to get your account of Ethel. I had some very unhappy letters from her, and though I've learned to add a grain of salt, here was something rather confused in her writing as well as the bad report she gave of her health, that made me anxious. Last week she wrote quite differently. Oh dear I hope she'll go on flourishing – she stands the test of time and the general horror so magnificently.

I'm sorry that you're in London. Yet rather envy you the experience. You see, I'm a coward: yet want to be a hero. We go up to salvage the awful mess – part ceiling part glass part natural rain water – that makes the flat like a last years nest and wander through the streets wondering how people like Elizabeth go on working in Berkeley Square. I admire them very much. We get a bomb or two most nights, but a mile or so off, and in the fields.

Do turn up here sometime and let us talk about the stars. We have your telescope in Leonard's balcony, but the stars seem to me a little inhuman at the moment. Perhaps if you would explain them, I should pluck up courage.

Forgive this scrawl – I'm in a rush and should be talking to a visitor. Thank you for writing.

Yours,
Virginia Woolf

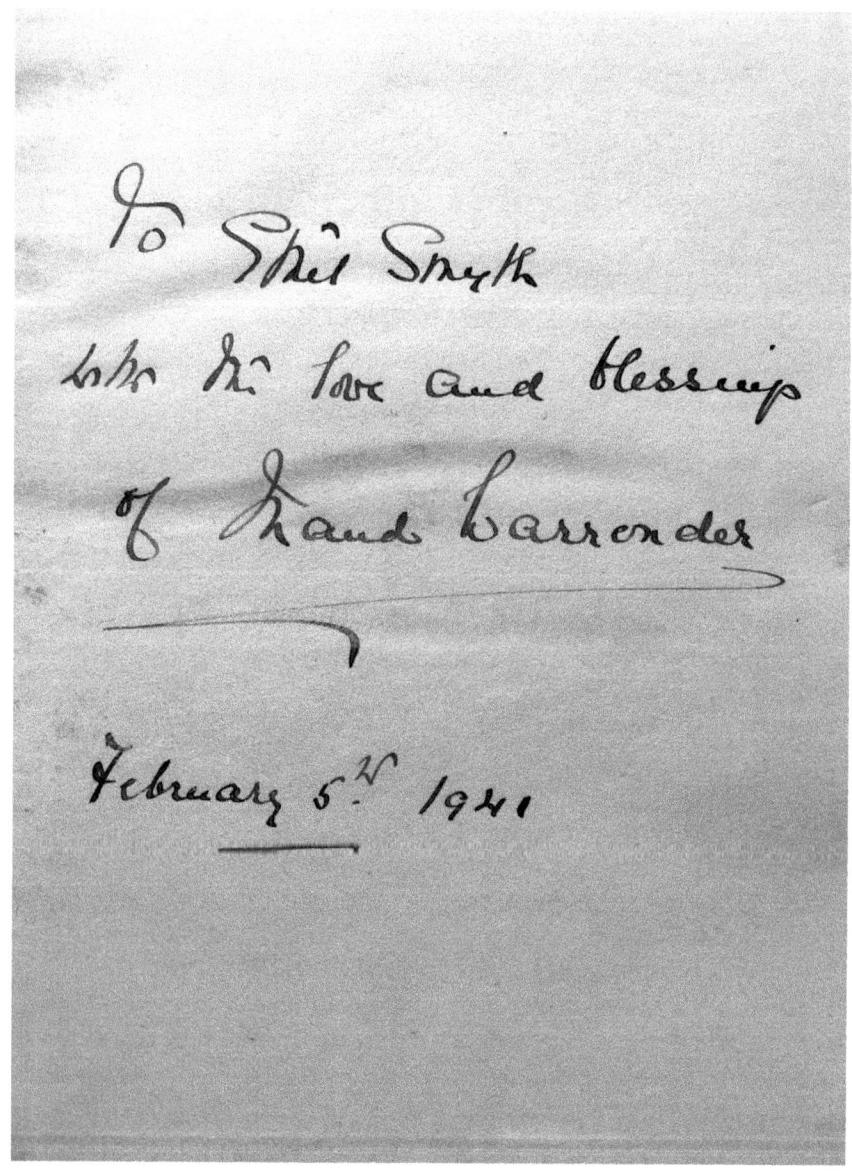

Dedication in ES's copy of *My Medley of Days* by Lady Maud Warrender

A couple of weeks later, Virginia Woolf finished *Between the Acts*. As so often after completing a piece of work, she became depressed and on 28th March, 1941 she drowned herself.

June 27th, 1941

Among Ethel and Elizabeth's letters were several sent from the Front during World War II. They were not addressed to either of them specifically, but as there are, in most cases, more than one copy, they were presumably circulated round the family. The letters were found carefully kept in an envelope marked "Important" in Ethel's hand. One, from Ethel's great nephew and Elizabeth's cousin, her aunt Sylvia's son, Peter Grant-Lawson, was sent from Syria. It has been added as representative of something that mattered very much to Ethel, who came from a military family, and as a reminder of the background events of her last years.

> Major Sir Peter Grant Lawson
> H.Q. 4th Cavalry Brigade
> M.E.F.

I was perfectly right when I told you our second expedition might not be such fun as the first. I have seldom spent two more unpleasant days than the 21st and 22nd in fact people with us who were in Dunkirk and Greece say that it was every bit as bad as there. We were being bombed and machine gunned almost incessantly through the daylight of both days. Some of the machine gun attacks were only from about 10 feet off the ground. Machine guns and cannons fired at that height from aircraft doing about 200 mph is most unpleasant, added to which we were very unlucky. Somerset de Chair[1] who took over Michael Crichton's job was wounded in five places by M.C. bullets on the first afternoon inside his car. The following morning poor Dick Schuster was killed by a bomb which landed beside his trench. I have been very lucky, I had actually shared Dick's trench in all the raids up to that particular one. Some gunners had just moved away, so as we were going to cover, I said I would use their trench to make more room in his, I was only 10 feet away from him and it absolutely smothered me with falling debris. I then had the beastly job of finding Dick's body, excavating it and burying him.

My car has also been twice hit by bomb splinters but luckily we saw the machine coming in both cases and were just far enough away to be reasonably safe.

Three days ago the Brig. had a nervous breakdown as a result of lack of sleep and the fact he has thoroughly overworked himself. This is a great blow to us and he has been sent back to rest. I wrote his wife about it all yesterday.

I can assure you that if I get the chance of a say in the matter I am not going to start out on our next expedition in a staff car, as they are far too popular targets from the air and it is hard to see out especially behind so that they are apt to catch you unawares. Even bombing in the desert is so unpleasant that the more I see of it the more I admire Grizzy. It must be hell in town.

We are very out of touch with the outside world but we hear rumours that Russia is doing quite well, and that the R.A.F. are far outdoing anything the Germans did to England. I wonder if it is true, do hope so. It should all help to speed up the end of all this beastliness.

It is really quite extraordinary how quickly one learns to live dirtily and uncomfortably, I now feel as if I had done it all my life and am very well and happy though I am the first to admit that I don't want it to last longer than is absolutely necessary.

There have been no letters since I last wrote to you and I rather doubt if there will be for some time as we are very detached from such things as Army Post Offices. Letters have to come up just when a column happens to come up and take their chance of going back for posting when anything is going back. It is a long way and I imagine may take a long time.

Dont worry about me, things are much quieter now and I am really rather enjoying the experience even though bits are very unpleasant and most frightening.....

1 Somerset de Chair (1911-1995) – a wealthy and flamboyant politician and author.
   The Independent published a lively and informative obituary of him:
   http://www.independent.co.uk/news/death-of-a-selfconfessed-heterosexual-1568079.html on January 15th, 1995.

May 8th, 1944

Ethel died on the 8th of May, 1944.

There are surprisingly few letters of condolence and, with one exception, no obituary notices or details of the funeral. As with Ethel's sister, Mary Hunter, there must have been many letters and, since more than a hundred have survived after the death of Charles Hunter in 1917, it can only be assumed that, like so many other papers, they vanished in the aftermath of the war. One came from the Duke of Alba on crested writing paper, but lacking the Alba motto; "Hombres muertos no hazen guerra" perhaps not considered tactful in 1944.

May 18th, 1944

24 Belgrave Square
London SW1

My dear Elizabeth,

Please excuse me for not having written to you before, but I did not know your address and have only just found it out now.

I want to send you my most heartfelt sympathy on the sad death of dear Ethel, one of my oldest and best friends. With her go many charming remembrances of my childhood, school days, memories of the Empress and of the old days when your aunt was fighting for the suffragette cause. I used to see her walking about the golf-course at Woking until the end of last year, but since my return from Spain I missed her there and was told she was not well.

Ethel was one of the most eminent women I have ever met and I feel very sad to think that I have lost such a dear friend.

Yours very sincerely,
Alba

Monday, May 22, 1944

The following, sent to Elizabeth's mother, was from Edith Somerville:

Drishane House
Skibbereen
Co. Cork

Dearest Phyllis,

I was so glad to have your letter of the <u>16th</u> this morning (a <u>week </u>on the road!) and I am rejoiced to know that Ethel's last days were peaceful and happy and that "The Warden" was such a success. You were very fortunate in finding her. I must tell you that I was bitterly disappointed that the few words I wrote about Ethel reached the "Times" too late for publication. I had written directly I heard, and had wired to the "Times" asking them to keep "a short space for a tribute to Dame Ethel Smyth" – But I suppose our <u>age-long</u> posts made it impossible for so long a delay, and two paragraphs had appeared almost at once. I only hope Ethel knows that I did my best. I'm sure that presently I shall be able to speak to her. I've heard from my people <u>Over There</u> of her <u>happy arrival</u>[1] – A wonderful message, and a very great consolation.

I think I will send you what I wrote (you can do what you like with it. I've kept a copy.) I couldn't say half what I wanted. The "Times" own account seems to me very good and accurate....I'm very glad Bob will take care of Pan. She was devoted to him and his predecessors.

I wish you could give a better account of yourself. I'm afraid all this long strain of the War, and the inadequate nourishment has told hard on you. Please Heaven, it won't last <u>very</u> much longer.

Much love,
Edith

You musn't call one "superior" – I'm a wretched lame cripple, scarcely worth a crutch!

---

1 Edith Somerville was a great believer in Spiritualism, especially after the death of her companion, Martin Ross.

I think I will send you what I wrote (you can do what you like with it. I've kept a copy. I could'nt say half what I wanted. The "Times" one account seems to me very good & accurate) ... I'm very glad Bob will take care of Pan. She was so devoted to him, & his predecessors.

I wish you could give a better account of yourself. I'm afraid all this long strain of the War, & the inadequate nourishment has told hard on you. Please heaven, it won't last _very_ much longer.

Much love
Edith.

You must'nt call me "Superior" — I'm a wretched lame cripple, scarcely worth a Crutch!

Edith Somerville to Phyllis Williamson, after ES's death

To the Memory of Ethel Smyth
(May 9th, 1944)

A standard-bearer has fallen. Ethel Smyth has gone, and a long and splendid life of effort and achievement has ended.

She was a Crusader to whom a Cause in difficulties never appealed in vain. A Fighter, gallant and unfailing. A Lion in the Field (fortunately, for those who loved her, not in the least like a Lamb at home!) A perfectly delightful companion, both sympathetic and argumentative, with a gift for friendship which made nothing of the differences of age, or opinion or position. Like the seeker for river-gold who shakes the water in the cradle and lets the worthless part be washed away, so was she content to harvest only the treasure.

Of her beautiful music, an unlearned observer does not presume to offer an opinion, but one remembrance of what singing can sometimes be may be told. Of how, long ago, on a soft Killarney summer night, there came to two or three rapt listeners a revelation of Music's self, and a heart-shaking voice, that had in it the enchantment that is only known when prefect quality and perfect knowledge and perfect taste are joined, and those happy listeners were taken out of themselves, and were transported to a place of beauty more wonderful than even the beauty of Killarney that lay around them.

Some are left who have not, I know, forgotten that evening. There are many to tell of Ethel's books, those remarkable and able records of a brilliant career; many who can extol her beautiful and brilliant music, or can recite the history of her many crusades, her battle for Woman-Suffrage, her unselfish activities for her less successful fellow-musicians, but this brief tribute to a beloved companion and to the memory of "a voice, divine and golden" may appeal to some of Ethel's many friends and may find an echo in some of their hearts.

E. OE. S.

To the Memory of Ethel Smyth.

A Standard-bearer has fallen. Ethel Smyth has gone, and a long & splendid life of effort and achievement has ended.

She was a Crusader to whom a Cause in difficulties never appealed in vain, A Fighter, gallant & unfailing. A Lion in the Field (fortunately, for those who loved her, not in the least like a Lamb at home!) A perfectly delightful companion, both sympathetic and argumentative, with a gift for friendship which made nothing of differences of age, or opinion, or position. Like the seeker for river gold who shakes the water in the cradle & lets the worthless part be washed away, so was she content to harvest only the treasure.

Of her beautiful music, an unlearned admirer does not presume to offer an opinion, but one remembrance of what Singing can sometimes be may be told. Of how, long ago, on a soft Killarney summer night, there came to two or three rapt listeners a revelation of Music's self, and a heart-shaking voice, that had in it the enchantment that is only known when perfect quality & perfect knowledge and perfect taste are joined, and those happy listeners taken out of themselves, and transported to a place of beauty more wonderful than even the beauty of Killarney that lay around them.

Edith Somerville, in memory of ES.

In accordance with her wishes, Ethel Smyth's ashes were scattered in the woods near Woking Golf course by her brother, Bob Smyth.

ES – Selected* Bibliography

Bell, Quentin, *Virginia Woolf: A Biography*, London, 1972
Brewster, H.B., *The Prison: A Dialogue*, with a memoir of the author by Ethel Smyth, London, 1931
___*Theories of Anarchy and Law. A Midnight Debate*, London, 1887
Brewster, Ralph, *The 6000 Beards of Athos*, published by L. and Virginia Woolf, London, 1935
Briscoe, James R., ed., *Historical Anthology of Music by Women*, Indiana U.P., 1987
Colonna, Vittoria, *Things Past*, London, 1929
Gleichen, Helena, Helena Gleichen, *Contacts and Contrasts*, London 1940, reprinted Hardinge Simpole, 2013
Harris, Amanda, "The Smyth-Brewster Correspondence: A Fresh Look at the Hidden Romantic World of Ethel Smyth", *Women and Music: A Journal of Gender and Culture,* Volume 14, 2010, pp. 72-94
Kenny, Aisling and Wollenberg, Susan, eds., *Women and the nineteenth-century Lied*, Farnham, 2015
Lovat, Laura, *Maurice Baring: a Postscript* , London, 1947
Ponsonby, Loelia, *Grace and Favour,* London, 1961
Smyth, Ethel. *Impressions that Remained.* 2 vols. 1919
___*Streaks of Life.* London, 1921
___*A Three-legged Tour of Greece,* London, 1927
___*A Final Burning of Boats.* London, 1928
___*Female Pipings in Eden.* Edinburgh, 1933
___*Beecham and Pharaoh.* London, 1935
___*As Time Went On.* London, 1936
___*Maurice Baring,* London, 1938
___*What Happened Next.* London, 1940
St John, Christopher, *Ethel Smyth*, with additional chapters by Vita Sackville-West and Kathleen Dale, London, 1959
Stone, Caroline, *M.H.*, Seville, 2002
Wethered, Joyce, *Golfing Memories and Methods*, London, 1933

* A number of other works are referred to in the text.

Index

The names of Ethel Smyth and Elizabeth Williamson appear on virtually every page and therefore have been omitted, since a detailed Index would essentially involve repeating the book. A few other names, such as Mary Hunter, Virginia Woolf and Maurice Baring also appear so frequently that these entries have been simplified. Similarly, place names appearing in addresses with no further information have been largely omitted, as have some of the passing references in the notes. In the interests of simplicity, Ethel Smyth's eccentric spelling and use of initials have been indexed under their traditional forms.

A

Abbassia Barracks 155
Adam and Eve 67, 379
A Final Burning of Boats 85, 377
After the Deluge 165, 168
Agra Bank xi
Aidin inscription 97, 99, 100, 101 n.2
Ajax fragment 98, 99, 100, 101
Alba, Don Jacobo Fitz-James Stuart y Falcó, Duke of (Jimmy) 306, 307, 356, 357, 371
Aldershot xi
Alice (see Davidson, Alice)
Allen, Sir Hugh 32, 49, 229, 232, 235, 249, 329
Allen, J.W. 95
Allingham, Margery 72, 192
Almagest xx, 222, 315
Anacreontic Ode 127
Angell, Norman 176, 177
An Incorruptible Irishman 134
Apostles (Cambridge Society) 172
Appley Hall 50, 67, 77, 112, 149, 152, 162, 198, 239, 244, 339
Aquinas, Thomas 99
Aristarchus of Samos 22
Aristotle 180, 289
Armstrong Whitworth 320
Asche, Oscar 10
Asquith, Margo 151
As Time Went On xxviii, 279, 293, 296, 377
Astronomer Royal 23
astronomy
  EMW's passion for xx, 22
  in Milton 33
  EMW lecturing on 63, 77, 83, 111, 221, 244, 278, 289
Atholl, Duchess of, (see Stewart-Murray, Katherine)
A Three-Legged Tour in Greece 29, 40, 42, 62, 301
Auden, W.H. 348, 349
Augusta, Empress 229
Avis (see Forrest, Olive) 153

B

Bach, Johann Sebastian 147, 212, 213
Bagnold, Enid 295
Baldwin, Stanley 133, 343
Balfour Family xxix, xxxv, 112, 167
Balfour, Elizabeth (Betty) née Bulwer-Lytton, Countess of xxxv, 112-4, 116-8, 137, 145, 147, 156
  ES "odious" about lending books 170
  political views 172, 174, 224, 227, 250, 260
  "delightfully young" 268-9, 271, 273
  considers ES "Rabelaisian" 275-6, 309, 314, 315, 326, 348
Balfour, Gerald, Earl of 172, 326, 342
Balkans xxxi, 64, 335

Balliol College 327
bankruptcy (of Mary Hunter) xxii, 45, 135, 139, 149
Banse, Ewald 269
Barbirolli, John 161
Baring, Maurice (MB) xxiv
  biography xxxi and xxxii
  ES leaves Brewster's letters to 6-7, 28
  his will 53, 65, 68, 73, 78
  planning to write about HB 93, 95, 117
  to tea with VW 118, 123, 125, 133
  praise for *Orlando* 138, 169, 172, 174, 177, 178, 208, 230, 249, 254, 263, 268, 269, 273, 278
  on Vernon Lee 288, 295, 297
  gives ES £900 298-9, 307, 310, 316
  gives ES £130 320
  in a nursing home 327, 339, 340, 346, 348, 351
  looking very ill 353, 377
Barnett, Norman 127, 130, 228
Baronet and the Butterfly, The xiii
Barra 240, 242, 244
Barrie, Sir James 58
Bartlett, Vernon 347
Bath 93, 94, 96, 109, 127, 128, 129, 140-5, 194, 224-5, 227, 266, 340, 342, 345
Baylis, Lilian 20, 235, 258, 275
Bayly, Ada Ellen (see Lyall, Edna)
BBC 84, 120, 123, 205, 235, 238, 248, 251, 255, 295, 301, 302
Beecham, Sir Thomas xxiv, 94, 96, 126, 152-3, 211, 232, 235, 255, 271-2, 280, 282, 297, 298, 299, 301, 303
Beecham's Pills x, 297, 298
Beerbohm, Max 196
Beggars Opera, The 9
Bell Family 119
Bell, Angelica 284
Bell, Clive 206
Bell, Gertrude 70-1
Bell, Julian 172, 174
Bell, Quentin 112, 377
Bell, Vanessa 119, 123, 143, 203, 204, 206-7, 211, 239, 284

Belloc, Hilaire xxxii, 52, 89, 92, 277, 294, 327
Belshazzar's Feast 169
Benbecula 240, 242
Benck, C. 48
Benes, Edvard 343, 345, 347 n.2, 348 n.2
Benjamin, Arthur 211
Benson Family xxviii
Benson, E.F. (Fred) xxviii, xxxi, 8, 71, 278, 311, 313, 314
Benson, Margaret xxviii
Benson, Mary xxviii
Bentinck, Lady Ottoline (see Morrell, Lady Ottoline) 213
Berlin 82, 84, 85, 96, 99
Bernhardt, Sarah 75, 77, 254
Betty (see Balfour, Elizabeth, Countess of)
Billy (see Williamson, William)
Birkenhead, Earl of (see Smith, Frederick Edwin)
birth control 114, 136-7
Bishop of Durham 89
Black Mischief 319
Blake, William 50, 51, 77, 245
Blakeney Marshes 183
Bliss, Arthur 253, 254
Blitz xxii, 365, 366
Blixen, Karen (see also Dinesen, Isak) 335, 336, 338
Bloomsbury 40, 112, 211, 212, 225, 249, 258
blue paper – ES's dislike of 78, 325, 348
Blunt, Lady Anne 155, 156
Blunt, Wilfred 347
Bob (see Smyth, General Sir Robert)
Bolton Abbey 338
Bo'sun's Mate, The x, 8, 45, 234, 235
Boulanger, Nadia 339
Boulestin's 249
Boult, Adrian 203, 205, 235, 238, 253
Bowen, Elizabeth 316
Brahms, Johannes xxvi, 95, 96, 202, 212, 213, 224, 227
Brett, Dorothy 249

Brewster, Henry B. (Harry, H.B., HB)
    biography xxiv-xxviii, 1
    Anarchy and Law 2-7, 24, 32
    EMW's appreciation of 65, 93, 115,
      family of 125-6
    publishing memoirs and letters 132-
      4, 159, 176, 186, 192, 204, 213, 248
    The Prison 260, 307, 310, 335
    views on suffragettes 338
    behaviour when dying 352, 360, 377
Brewster, Ralph 304
    ES disapproves of 312
*Bright Armour – Memories of Four Years
    of War* 316
Bristol, Earl of v, 158
British School at Athens 59
British Women's Symphony Orchestra
    84, 261, 262, 301
Brittain, Vera 247-8
Broughton, Rutland 8, 10
Browning, Robert and Elizabeth
    Barrett 253
Buchenwald 265 n.2
Bulwer-Lytton, Constance
    militant suffragette 114 n.1
Bulwer-Lytton, Elizabeth (see Balfour)
Bulwer-Lytton, Robert, Viceroy of
    India xxxv
Burne-Jones, Philip xxxiii
Bushe, Chief Justice Charles Kendal
    133, 134

C

Camargo Ballet Society 202, 210, 211
Cambridge Conversazione Society 172
Cambridge Nursing Home 89
Cameron, Julia 284
Campbell, John Lorne 174
Campbell, Roy 258 n.1
Canterbury, Archbishop of (see
    Davidson, Randall)
Caporetto, Battle of 336
Caraman-Chimay, Hélène de
    Brancovan, Princesse 230, 232
Carisbrooke (see Mountbatten)

Casals, Pablo 320
Casement, Roger 147
Castletownsend 14
Catholic Church, Catholicism xxxii, 2,
    4, 6, 11. 30, 56, 57. 89, 92, 99, 123,
    136, 174, 208, 209, 271, 324
Cecil, Lord Eustace 178, 250, 343
Chamberlain, Austen 58, 59
Chamberlain, Neville 58, 59, 333, 334,
    346, 347, 356-7, 358, 359
Chaplin, Charlie 137
Chapman, Dorothy 299
Charles (Chas – EMW's brother - see
    Williamson, Charles)
Chaucer, Geoffrey 201, 208, 209
Cheatle, Sir George 239, 249
Cheerful Weather for the Wedding 222,
    225
Chesterton, G.K. xxxii, 52, 208, 20
Chorleywood 296
Christ, Christianity 50, 73, 84, 86, 88,
    100, 101, 128, 136, 149, 168, 176,
    179, 180, 181, 182, 186, 187, 188,
    189, 191, 207, 218, 221, 258, 292,
    327, 334, 359
Chu Chin Chow 10
Churchill, Winston 73, 347, 358
Clarke, Rebecca 54
Cleopatra 73, 75, 77, 97, 275, 380
Clotilde (see Feilding, Clotilde)
Cocteau, Jean 56, 380
Coign 3, 27, 72, 91, 92, 96, 97, 105,
    113, 118, 125, 135, 157, 167, 176,
    195, 205, 208, 223, 270, 281-2, 285,
    288, 328, 351
Collected Poems 226, 252
Colonna, Vittoria Duchess of
    Sermoneta 100-2, 122, 377
Colville, Lady Cynthia 326
Compton Mackenzie, Edward
    Montague 244
Comte, Auguste 14
Confucius 340, 341
Conversation Piece xxxii
Conway, Sir Martin 64, 72
Conway, Agnes 64, 71, 72

Cooper, Lady Diana 219, 221, 256
Così fan Tutte 221
Covent Garden 154, 232
Croce, Benedetto 23
Crystal Palace 88, 89
Cunard, Lady Maud 279, 280
Cunard, Nancy 65
Currie, Raikes 319
Cyprus 63, 64
Czechoslovakia 331, 343, 345, 347

D

Daladier, Edouard 347
Darby and Joan 315, 316
Darwin, Charles 32
David, Elizabeth 274, 380
Davidson, Alice (née Smyth, ES' oldest sister) xi, 62, 136, 139, 140, 159, 207
  illness 239
  death and papers 248, 341
Davidson, Ethel 62
Davidson, Randall, Archbishop of Canterbury xxviii, 67, 90, 321, 364
Davies, Peter Llewelyn 254, 255, 380
Day Lewis, Cecil 306, 380
  deafness (of ES) xxii, 66
  treatment 68
  no better 197, 214, 247, 279, 285
  possible remedies 289, 306, 315
de Brancovan, Princess (see de Noailles, Anna)
de Brancovan, Hélène (see Caraman-Chimay)
de Chair, Somerset 369, 370 n.1, 380
de Foras, Odette (see Forrest, Olive)
de la Motte Fouqué, Friedrich 267, 269
de Montijo, Empress Eugénie xiii, xxxi, 102, 213, 306-7, 319, 357
de Noailles, Anna (Princesse Anna de Brancovan, "Toch") 130, 131, 203, 205, 230-2, death 266
de Polignac, Princesse (see Singer, Winnaretta)
Delius, Frederick 8, 96
Deluge, The 174

Derby (race) 200
Der Wald viii, ix, 63, 221
de Watteville, Vivienne 302
Dickens, Charles 137, 176, 186, 190, 192, 273, 320
Dido and Aeneas 211
Dinesen, Isak (see *also* Blixen, Kaen) 336, 379
Dodge, Mabel 249
Dodge, Mary 156, 169, 202
  illness 230, 240, 282
  annuity left to ES 283
Dodo xxxi
Dolin, Anton 220, 221, 328
Droitwich Spa 67, 68
duck shoot 183, 189
Duff Cooper, Alfred, Viscount Norwich 334, 336, 347

E

Eddington, Arthur 79, 140, 141, 381
Eden, Sir William xiii, xxxv, 235, 343, 377
Edith (see Sitwell, Edith; Somerville, Edith; Wharton, Edith)
Edith Œnone Somerville Archive xxxii
Edwardians, The 112, 118, 120
Einstein, Albert 147, 148, 197, 274
Elgar, Edward 169, 250, 251, 263
Elgin marbles, return of 79, 81, 82
Elinor (see Vaughn, Elinor)
Eliot, T.S. 14, 212, 238, 265, 267, 319
Elwes, Robert 242
Elwes, Simon 30, 36
EMW – Elizabeth Williamson
Encaenia 57, 59
Entente Cordiale 29, 32, 34, 35, 46, 48, 207, 220, 268, 269
Eothen 88
Epping 3, 18, 22, 24, 27, 28, 42
ES – Ethel Smyth
Euripedes 381

F

Fachiri, Adela 96, 256
Farnborough Hill xiii, 101
Faulkner, Mrs (Mrs F, ES' servant) 146, 147, 148, 381

Fawcett, Millicent (The Women's Library) 345
Feilding, Clotilde (née Brewster) xxviii
  ES shocked by dirt of 125
  hopeless at getting *The Prison* published 128
  "maddening" 133, 134, 241, 312
Fellowes, Daisy 336
Fénelon, François 8
Fête Galante [FG] xxiv, 29, 32, 34, 44, 48, 197, 201-2, 204, 210, 211, 219-21, 224, 269, 276
Fidelio 65
Finch Hatton, Denys 335-6
Fisher's Hill House xxxv, 118, 343
Flashing Stream, The 353
Flecker, James Elroy 8
Florence xxvi, 129, 196, 288, 335
Flurry's Wedding
Forrest, Olive (Odette de Foras) 153, 154, 156
Fort William 242, 245
Forum, The (concert venue) 253, 299
France xiii, 61, 102, 110, 143, 144, 271, 274, 343, 357, 360, 367
Franco, Generalísimo Francisco 333, 356, 357
Fraser, Simon, Lord Lovat 28
Fred (see Benson, E.F.)
Freshwater 284
Frimhurst 156, 314
Fritz (see Ponsonby, Frederick)
Frobenius, Ferdinand Georg 265
Fry, Roger 197, 268, 284, 312
Furse, Katherine 167, 203

G

Gascoyne-Cecil, Mary Alice, Lady Hartington 264
G.B.S (see Shaw, G.B.) 168
Girls' Own Paper 67, 68
Gleichen, Helena 77, 194-5, 341, 377
Gloucester Square 51, 61, 93, 105, 144
Godden, Rumer xxxi
Godfrey, Dan 10, 276
Goethe, Johann Wolfgang von 14, 18, 22, 23, 95, 263, 274, 292, 338, 341
golf *passim* including 13 n.1, 82
  VW asks about 112, 117
  showing off for VW 125, 129
  at Blakeney 286
Golfing Memories and Methods 13, 254, 377
Good Housekeeping 211
Goodman, Victor 251, 314
Gordon, Dr 96, 129
  eccentricities 311-15
Gordon-Woodhouse, Violet 130, 274, 316
Gore, Bishop Charles 320, 321
Graham, Lady Helen 337, 341, 342
Gran (see Hunter, Mary)
Grant-Lawson, Griselda (Grizzy) 42, 164, 219, 223, 256, 336, 337, 365, 369, 370
Grant-Lawson, Major Sir Peter 369
Grant-Lawson, Sylvia (née Hunter) xiii, 42, 336-9, 365, 369
Great Illusion, The 178
Greece 4, 29
  ES and EMW's trip to 32-45, 48, 58, 63, 64, 66, 78, 126, 193, 197, 199, 239-46, 267, 278, 300, 346, 369, 377
Greek language *passim* – EMW was studying Greek and it is mentioned in almost every letter
Greek Salad 301
Greek Memories 244
Greenwich 23
Grenfell, Joyce 316
Grizzy (see Grant-Lawson, Griselda)

Grosvenor, Hugh, 2ndDuke of Westminster) xxxi, 127, 198

H

Haldane, Richard Burdon (1856-1928), 1st Viscount Haldane of Cloane 25, 79, 80, 140, 141
Halévy, Fromental 149
Harrogate 336, 337
  cure 339
Haug[h]ton Castle 348
Haynes, E.S.P. 273, 274
H.B. HB (see Brewster, Henry)
Heathcote, Sir Gilbert 13, 270, 271
Hebrides 242, 250
Hegel, Georg 325
Heger, Robert 232
Heine, Heinrich 78, 332
Hellens 77, 194, 195, 249
Henderson, Arthur 156
Henry (Harry, see Brewster, Henry)
Henschel, George 109
hermaphrodite 311, 312, 316
Herodotus 29
Hess, Myra 247
Hey Nonny No 96, 127, 129
Hibbert, Major-General Hugh xxviii, 125
Hill Hall, home of Mary Hunter and childhood home of EMW – Introduction and *passim*
Hippisley, Richard (Dick) xvii, 7
Hippisley, Violet (née Smyth) xvii, 7, 156, 157
Hitler 232, 236, 254, 264, 282, 283, 310, 343, 346, 347, 356, 357
Hoare, Samuel 343, 345
Hoffmann, E.T.A. 267, 269
Hogarth Press 66, 109, 165, 193, 194, 199, 222, 278, 280, 290, 313
Hollings, Nina (née Smyth)
  ill health 75, 77, 94, 140, 194, 195, 249, 297
Holloway (Prison) xx, 257, 313
Holst, Gustav 10, 98, 382

Holt, Martin 78, 129, 173, 251, 286, 327, 366
Holt, Vesey 173, 286-7, 381-2, 325
Hook Heath 3, 134, 273
Hotel Mercédés 89
House in Paris, The 316
Hudson, Alice 293, 311-2
Hunter Family – Introduction *passim*
Hunter, Charles (EMW's grandfather) xiii
  death xv, 32, 371
Hunter, Fred 145, 146, 159, 198
Hunter, Kathleen (EMW's aunt, Kitty – née Hunter) xiii, 19, 36, 142, 151, 205, 218, 223, 307, 377
Hunter, Mary (Gran) Introduction *passim*, 20, 23-4, 27, 38
  grief at Sargent's death 41-2, 46, 62, 63, 78, 79, 85, 89, 90, 99, 135
  financial situation worsens 137-43
  bankruptcy sale 144-5, 151-61
  schemes to provide her with an income 192-4, 209
  death 222-3, 211, 214, 276, 338, 361
Hunter, Phyllis (see Williamson, Phyllis)
Hunter, Sylvia (see Grant-Lawson, Sylvia)
Hutchinson, St John K.C. 111, 112, 114
Huxley, Aldous 125, 176, 225, 339

I

Illingworth 106
Immortal Hour, The 8, 10
Imperial War Museum 64
Impressions that Remained (*Imps*) xxiv, xxvi, xxviii, 43, 95, 279, 280, 283, 312, 313, 377
India – Smyth children born there xxxv, 80 n.2, 149, 152
Inge, William, Dean of St Paul's 8, 95, 128, 129, 165
Inordinate (?) Affection ix, 50, 51, 141
Irregulariters 10

Isaacs, Rufus, Lord Reading 59
Isherwood, Christopher 349
Islington 23

J

James, Henry (H.J.) xiii, xxvi, xxxi, xxxii, 111, 156, 313
James, William xxvi, 71
Jekyll, Gertrude xxxv
　designs gardens at Tigbourne Court 13-4, 118
　death 215
Jimmy (see Alba, Duke of)
Joad, C.E.M. 327
John, Augustus 84
Johnny (see Smyth, John)
Johnson, Dr Samuel 217, 284, 285, 351
Johnston-Douglas, Walter 65, 266, 282
Jones, Bobby 13
Joyce (see Wethered, Joyce)

K

Kant, Immanuel 149, 163, 274, 276
Katyn, massacre 277
Kennedy, Richard 193, 194
Keppel, Alice 196, 255
Keynes, Geoffrey 52, 202, 235
Keynes, Maynard 52, 177, 192, 202, 211, 233
Kimpton, Gwynne 84
King-Hall, Stephen 334
　his *News Letters*, 336
Kinglake, Alexander 89
Kitty (see Hunter, Kathleen)
knickers 74, 102, 148
　ES's problems with 329
Kossevitsky, Serge 233
Kum Bak Tennis Trainer 128, 129

L

Lady Chatterley 224-5
Lady Sysonby's Cook Book xxxi
Lamb House 313, 374

Lamb, William, 2nd Viscount Melbourne 94, 96
Lang, Andrew 310
Laughton 258
Lawrence, A.W. 307 n.5
Lawrence, D.H. (DHL) 224-8, 239, 240, 249, 258
Lawrence, T.E. 64, 307
Lee, Vernon 46, 48, 57, 91, 92, 133, 226, 287, 288, 289, 294, 295, 347
Leontief, Feodora 332
Letters from the Near East xxxi
Lewes 14, 202, 367
Lewis, Wyndham 284
libraries, destroyed in the Blitz 365
Lincoln (husband of Kitty Hunter) 218, 307
Lindbergh, Anne 325, 382
Lipton, Sir Thomas 340, 341
Lisl (see von Herzogenberg, Elizabeth)
Lives of the Poets 285
Londonderry 351
London Mercury 210, 306
Longman Family xiii
Lopokova, Lydia 211, 247, 382
Lovat, Laura xxxii
　nursed Maurice Baring 28, 377
Lowes Dickinson, Goldsworthy 172, 190, 192
Lubbock, Percy 196
Lunde, Paul v, xxiv
Lutyens, Edwin xxxv, 13, 118, 156
L.W., LW (see Woolf, Leonard)
Lyall, Edna 364, 365
Lyons Tea Rooms 276
Lypiatt Manor 316
Lytton (see Strachey, Lytton)

Mac/Mc

MacCarthy, Desmond 63
Mackenzie, Sir Compton 242, 244
McLeod, Fiona 9
Macmurray, John 128, 129, 179, 182

M

Mackworth, Margaret, Viscountess Rhondda 229
Mallaig 242
Malvern Court 366
Manners, Violet, Duchess of Rutland 66
Mansfield, Katherine 141 n.1, 225
Mapp and Lucia xxviii
March of the Women, The 256
Marchesi, Blanche 287, 288
Marius the Epicurean 137, 167, 169, 170, 175, 176
Marsh, Edward 360
Martin, Violet (see Ross, Martin and Somerville, Edith) xxxii, 321, 364
Mary (MH, see Hunter, Mary née Smyth)
Masefield, John 54
Mass (in D) 19, 21, 22, 25, 73, 91, 98, 126, 235, 250, 260, 270, 271, 314, 351
Matheson, Hilda xxiv, 122, 123, 124, 194, 290, 301, 318
  ES' executor 333
Matthews, Kenneth Albert 300, 301
Maurice (MB, M.B., see Baring, Maurice)
Medical Research Council 196
Melba, Nellie 288
Melbourne, Lord (see Lamb, William)
Mendelssohn family 329
Mendelssohn, Felix 310
  school notebooks 327
Mendelssohn, Moses 292, 293
Meredith, George 346
MH xi
MH (see Hunter, Mary)
Middleton Murry, John 224, 225, 228, 249
Milne. A.A. 287
Milton, John 213, 286, 288, 294, 308, 309, 320
Ministry of Agriculture 211
Ministry of Economic Warfare (M.E.W.) 363, 365, 367
Miracle of Peille, The 174

Misses Hunter, The xiii
Monk's House 118, 129, 367
Montaigne, Michel de 144, 147, 292
Montgomery, Betty 266
Moore, George xiii, xiv, xx, 107, 111, 278, 280, 297
Morden House 52
Morgan, Charles 352, 353
Morrell, Julian 251, 314
Morrell, Lady Ottoline 213
  "pilloried" in *Women in Love* 225-6, 239, 249, 251, 254, 255, 258, 264, 266
  invites ES to meet T.S.Eliot 267, 302
  visits ES with her family 314-5, 316, 319, 322
Morrell, Philip 251, 255, 315
Morris Minor 207
Mountbatten, Alexander, Marquess of Carisbrooke 279
Mountbatten, Irene Carisbrooke, Marchioness of 278, 279
Mount Mascal Farm (MM) xxiv, 80, 105, 135, 137, 165, 173, 174, 205, 222, 224, 281, 335
Mowrer, Edgar A. 358, 359, 360
Mrs F (see Faulkner, Mrs)
Murder in the Cathedral 319, 322
Mussolini, Benito 332, 333, 345, 347, 356
My Medley of Days x, 368

N

National Portrait Gallery xxxii, xxxv
National Velvet 295
Nellie (see Smyth, Ellinor)
Nelly (the Woolfs' cook) 112
Newton, Sir Isaac
  Optics 22, 25, 27, 41, 49 n.6
New York Dramatic Mirror 30
Nicholson, Harold 6, 111, 236, 238, 293, 319, 337, 347
Nigger Heaven 62
nightingales 89, 110, 112, 113, 147, 197, 200

Nina (see Hollings, Nina)
Nippies 276
Noë 148, 149
Norton, Frederic 10
Norton's Star Atlas 288
Nunky (see Williamson, Sir Hedworth)

O

Obey, André 149
Oedipus Rex 56
Old English Sheepdogs (see Pan)
Omdurman, Battle of 227
On the Cliffs of Cornwall 277
Orientations 64
Orlando 138, 139, 254
Out of Africa (see Blixen Karen)
Outspoken Essays 8

P

Paget, Violet (see also Vernon Lee) ix, xvi, xvii, 48, 294, 295
Pan *passim* - ES' series of Old English Sheepdogs were all called Pan and one or other is mentioned in most letters
Pankhurst, Christabel 256
Pankhurst, Mrs Emmeline 53, 214, 236
  relations with her daughters Sylvia and Adela 256, 283
Pankhurst, Sylvia 256
Paradise Lost 32, 33, 66, 67, 89, 286
Paris 56, 232, 316, 359
Passfield, Lord 170
Pater, Walter 137
Pausanius 52, 126
Peace with Honor 287
Penrose, Dame Emily 58, 59 n.9
Pergamon 82, 84, 85, 232
Phyllis (see Williamson, Phyllis)
Piddington, John (Pidd) 70, 71, 273, 314, 315
Piétri, Franceschini 306, 307

Pinney, Rachel 241, 244
Pinney, Sir Reginald 241, 242
Plato 7, 163, 179, 180, 289
Plesch (unidentified) 306, 307
Ponsonby, Arthur xxxi
Ponsonby, Frederick (Fritz) xxxi, 30, 127, 198, 200, 205, 221, 265, 279, 304, death 316, 317, 318, 320
Ponsonby, Sir Henry xxxi, 229
Ponsonby, Loelia Mary (Lelia), Duchess of Westminster xxxi, 30, 127
  possible separation 194, 196, 198, 200, 317, 377
Ponsonby, Magdalen (Maggie) death 265, 266
Ponsonby, Sarah 313
Ponsonby, Victoria "Ria", Lady xxxi, 200, 220, 304, n.3, 317, 365
Potocki de Montalk, Count 277
Price, Mabel 59
Prison, The xxvi, 39, 73, 127, 132, 151, 152, 159, 167, 204, 227, 240, 337, 377
Proteus or The Future of Intelligence 48
Proust, Marcel 183, 201, 205, 208, 209, 213, 232
Ptolemy xx, 222, 274, 284, 314, 315, 326, 328, 337
Puppet Show of Memory, The xxxi
Purcell, Henry 211, 295, 296

R

Radiguet, Raymond 56
Ramsey, Frank 233
Raverat, Gwen 52
R.[oman]C.[atholic] (see Catholic Church)
R.[oyal] Coll.[ege] 33
Recollections of Three Reigns xxxi
Red Cross Voluntary Aid Detachment 167
Reith, John 123, 179, 182
Reith Lectures 182 n.2
Reminiscences of D.H.Lawrence 228

Rhondda, Viscountess 229
Robert Peckham 123
Robeson, Paul 150
Robey, George 290, 291
Rodd, James Rennell 36, 38, 74, 138
Rodmell 118, 120, 139, 166, 169, 170, 174, 206, 220, 246, 289, 294, 367
Rome 56, 93, 123, 296, 297, 298, 327
Ross, Martin (see also Edith Somerville) xxxii
  archive 30 n.1, 134 n.1, 356, 372
Rostand, Edmond 348, 349
Rottingdean 230
Russell, Bertrand 181, 193, 224
  ES' dislike of 249
Russell, Elizabeth 141
Rutledge, Hugh 277
Rye House xxxi

S

Sackville-West, Vita
  various publication 65-6, 112
  VW's views on *The Edwardians* 118, 120
  relationship with Hilda Matheson 123, 128, 174
  £10 to MH fund 200, 206, 210, 212, 214
  sails to the States 220
  ES' affection for 236
  poems 252-5, 258, 263, 277-8
  VW on Vita and Shirin 280, 289, 290, 291, 301, 303, 304, 318, 319, 345
  criticism of *Solitude* 348-9
Sadler, Sir Michael 57, 59
Sadler's Wells 7, 207, 221, 265, 335
St Andrews House 66
St Aubyn, Gwen (Shirin or Shireen) 277
  ES' intense dislike of her 278
  called "Shirin" by Vita Sackville-West 278 n.2, 289, 291, 301
  ES considered her a halfwit 318, 337, 348, 349
St Bride's House (The Press Club) 40

St Paul 4, 136, 176, 180, 187, 190, 228, 299, 316
St Teresa of Avila xxii, 174
St Thérèse of Lisieux 174, 177, 179
Salisbury, Lord 176, 178, 357, 358
Salmond, Monica 316
Sappho 24, 267
Sarah's Youth 349, 351
Sargent, Emily 58
Sargent, John Singer xiii, xxiv, xxxiv-v, 36, 37, 38
  death of 39-41, 42, 48, 51, 58-9, 89, 92, 156, 195, 205, 232, 359
Sassoon, Philip 42, 51, 52, 223
Sassoon, Siegfried 42, 51, 85
Scott, Charles Kennedy 73
Seikilos epitaph, see Aidin fragment
Seven Pillars of Wisdom, The 207-9
sex - and the Church, 186
  homosexuals 209
  ES' views 218
  D.H. Lawrence 224-8
Shaw, George Bernard 8, 179
Shelley, Percy Bysshe 33, 99
Shetland Islands 239
Shireen (see St Aubyn, Gwen)
Sibelius, Jean 228, 233
Sicily 296
Sieburg, Friedrich 263, 264
Siege of Corinth 84, 85
Siegfried 51, 85, 241
Simmonds, William 100
Simon, Sir John 57, 59 n.4, 343, 345
Singer, Winnaretta, 205 n.2, 230, 232 n.4, 255, 266, 335, 359-60
Sissinghurst 236, 254, 277, 289, 291, 301, 304, 327
Sitwell, Edith 83, 85 n.5, 306
Sitwell, Osbert 141, 169
Skibbereen 14, 59, 350, 372
Smith, Frederick Edwin, Earl of Birkenhead 73
Smith, Matthew 358
Smith, W.H.'s Library 337
Smyrna, sack of 100, 101
Smyth, Ethel (ES) *passim*

Smyth Family Introduction *passim*, 26, 30
  financial difficulties 35-39, 71, 103, 109, 145, 151, 211, 344
Smyth, General Sir Robert (Bob) 27, 30, 92
  hearing problems 128
  his letters added 135, 151, 155,
  finances 157-8, 178
  car crash 207, 218
  MH's death 222, 242, 245
  his kindness 246, 256, 328, 348
  taking care of Pan after ES' death 372
  scatters ES' ashes near Woking Golf Course 376
Smyth, Ellinor (Nelly, Nellie née Smyth) xi, 125, 157, 282
Smyth, John (Johnny) xi
Snowden, Philip, Viscount Snowden 159, 160
Sodomites, 125
Somerville, Edith
  biography, xxxii, 8, 10, 14, 24, 30, 48
  anti-matrimony 133, 134 n.1, 144, 348, 349, 350, 352, 356
  ES' death 372
  spiritualism 373, 375
Spencer, Stanley 302
Stapleton, Mary (ES' Irish maid) 157, 162
Statuette, The x, 305
Steed, Henry Wickham 282, 283
Steel, Ethel 128, 226, 227
Steele, Richard 266
Steer, Philip Wilson 111, 112
Stein, Gertrude 226
Stewart-Murray, Katherine, Duchess of Atholl 58, 59 n.10, 358, 359
Storrs, Sir Ronald 63, 64, 69, 117, 118, 210, 352
Strachey Free Library 343
Strachey, Julia 222
Strachey, Lytton xxxv, 112, 114, 186, 193
Stravinsky, Igor 56

Sudetenland 347
suffrage, suffragette xx, xxxii, 71, 102-3, 114, 229, 313, 338, 371
Suggia, Guilhermina 84
Sylvia (see Grant-Lawson, Sylvia)
Sysonby, Baron (see Ponsonby, Frederick)

T

"Teraph", The ix, 30, 31
Time and Tide 358
Taormina 11, 298
Tate xiii, 264, 265
Tavistock Square 156, 164, 165, 166, 193, 199, 284, 285
Taylor, Elizabeth 295
Temple, William, Archbishop of York, 179, 182

Theory of Anarchy and Law, the ix, 5
Thesiger, Mrs 167
Theydon Bois xiii
Theydon Mount 18
Thomas Cook (travel agency) 35, 52, 109
Through the Shadows 12
Tigbourne Court 11, 13, 91
Time and Tide 83, 118, 179, 210, 226, 229, 264, 360
To the Lighthouse 116, 154
Toch (see de Noailles, Anna)
Tonks, Henry xiii, xx, 111, 196, 358
Tovey, Sir Donald 85, 96, 320
Toye, Geoffrey 7
Trefusis, Violet 196, 255
Trelawny, Edward 328
Trevelyan, Pauline 270, 271
Trumpeters' House xxii, 135

U

University College (U.C.) 116, 150, 152, 173, 179, 251, 265, 348
University of London xx, 40, 93, 160, 191

V

V, VW (see Woolf, Virginia)
van Vechten, Carl 62
Vaughn, Elinor 85-6, 129
  engaged to be married 150, 163, 274, 280
  departure for India 286, 329, 342,
Venice 130, 230, 324
Victoria, Queen 150 n.2, 220, 279 n.1
Village in the Jungle, The 170, 171
Vile Bodies 317
Violet (see Hippisley, Violet)
Virginia (see Woolf, Virginia)
Vita (see Sackville-West, Vita)
Voigt, Frederick 332
von Arnim, Elizabeth 141
von Harnack, Adolph 302, 303
von Herzogenberg, Elizabeth (Lisl) xxvi, 212-3
von Herzogenberg, Heinrich xxvi, xxviii, 212, 213, 238
von Hofmannsthal, Hugo 324
von Keyserling, Hermann Graf 53, 274
von Stockhausen, Julia xxvi

W

Wace, Alan 59
Wach, Hugo 82, 85
Wagner, Richard 101, 232
Walter, Bruno 159, 230, 232, 237, 253
Walton, William 169
Warrender, Lady Maud x, 368
Waugh, Evelyn 317, 318
Waves, The 109, 138, 160-4, 168, 170, 174, 190, 221, 226, 238, 247, 268, 292, 293, 294, 311, 312
Weimar 14
Wellesley, Dorothy, Duchess of Wellington 123, 290
Wells, H.G. 7
Wemyss, Grace, Countess of 58, 106
West, Rebecca 253
Westminster, Duke of (see Grosvenor, Hugh)

Wethered, Joyce, Lady Heathcore-Amory xxiv, 13, 72, 91, 118, 130, 283, 377
Wharton, Edith xiii, 24, 25, 48, 196-7
Whitburn xiii
Wilde, William 14
Williams and Norgate, publishers 6, 7, 132, 302, 303
Williamson Family Introduction – *passim*, 30, 36, 51, 289
Williamson, Charles (EMW's brother) xiii, 295, 140, 141 n.3, 295
  very depressed 336-7
Williamson, Elizabeth portrait by Sargent 37 and *passim*
Williamson, Frederick (Fritz – EMW's father) xiii
Williamson, Phyllis (EMW's mother) ix, x, xiii, xiv, 20, 27-8, 72, 77, 78, 92, 107, 113, 116, 130, 142, 162, 211, 223, 251, 271, 286, 320, 335, 339, 349, 350, 363-6, 372-3
Williamson, Sir Hedworth (Nunky – EMW's uncle)
  his play *The Teraph* 30, 77, 288-9
Williamson, William (Billy – younger brother of EMW) 22, 27, 77, 86, 122, 123, 132, 140, 141 n.3, 194
Woking xx, xxxv, 3, 25, 27, 38, 73, 74, 83, 90, 118, 120, 122, 127, 134, 169, 274, 324, 371
Wolfe, Humbert 77, 78
women conductors 84, 238
Women in Love 225-8, 249
  an awful book 258
Women's Library, The 345
Women's Orchestra 238
Women's Social and Political Union (W.S.P.U.) 143
Wood, Muriel 296-9, 340
Wood, Henry 82, 84
  leaves his wife 296-9, 302-3, 340
Woodhouse, P.G. 70, 96, 129, 170, 274, 316
Woolf, Leonard 118, 120, 122
  ES "in love with" 125, 126, 133, 136 *passim* 165-76

economic theories 177, 179, 181, 190
EMW offered work at the Hogarth Press 193-4
emotional crises with VW 206-7, 226-7, 230
LW's marmoset 287-9, 292, 304, 307, 311, 318, 348, 367
Woolf, Virginia xxii, xxiv, 39, 91
  EMW's dinner with the Woolfs 109-16
  ES entertains the Woolfs at Coign 117-26, 128, 135-40, 143
  VW on MH's bankruptcy 144-5, 148
  The Waves 160
  Letters and VW's ill-health 165-74, 178, 186, 189
  Letters re EMW working at the Hogarth Press 193-9
  emotional upsets between VW and ES 202-8
  on various of VW's publications 210-14, 220
  VW on MH's death 223
  VW on D.H.Lawrence and modern art 224-8, 230, 235, 236, 238, 246, 247
  Flush 249-53
  occasional mentions 254-74, 277, 278, 280
  VW to EMW re *Freshwater* 283-4
  VW's concern re ES' finances 285, 286, 287, 289, 291, 292
  a "vicious letter" from VW 294, 297, 299, 302, 304
  various meetings between ES and VW 311-18, 320, 325, 329
  ES' passion for VW largely over 331, 335, 339, 342, 363
  Last letter from VW to EMW 367
  VW's suicide 369, 377
Wootton Manor 274, 292-3, 311, 317, 352
Wreckers, The xxvi, 69, 153, 156, 157, 159, 160, 167, 277, 288, 335

Y

Years, The 214, 313
Yeats, W.B. 290, 359, 363
Yutang, Lin 341

X

Xtian, Xtianity (see Christian)

www.ingramcontent.com/pod-product-compliance
Ingram Content Group UK Ltd.
Pitfield, Milton Keynes, MK11 3LW, UK
UKHW021045200426
11947UKWH00037B/1510